MODERN POLITICAL SCIENCE

MODERN POLITICAL SCIENCE

ANGLO-AMERICAN EXCHANGES SINCE 1880

Edited by

Robert Adcock,
Mark Bevir, and
Shannon C. Stimson

PRINCETON UNIVERSITY PRESS   PRINCETON AND OXFORD

Copyright © 2007 by Princeton University Press
Published by Princeton University Press, 41 William Street,
Princeton, New Jersey 08540
In the United Kingdom: Princeton University Press, 3 Market Place,
Woodstock, Oxfordshire OX20 1SY

Library of Congress Cataloging-in-Publication Data

Modern political science : Anglo-American exchanges since 1880 /
edited by Robert Adcock, Mark Bevir, and Shannon C. Stimson.
p.   cm.
Includes bibliographical references and index.
ISBN-13: 978-0-691-12873-3 (alk. paper)
ISBN-10: 0-691-12873-1 (alk. paper)
ISBN-13: 978-0-691-12874-0 (pbk. : alk. paper)
ISBN-10: 0-691-12874-X (pbk. : alk. paper)
1. Political science—History. 2. Political science—United States—History.
3. Political science—Great Britain—History. I. Adcock, Robert, date.
II. Bevir, Mark. III. Stimson, Shannon C.
JA81.M665 2007
320.0941—dc22   2006049336

British Library Cataloging-in-Publication Data is available

This book has been composed in Sabon.

Printed on acid-free paper. ∞

press.princeton.edu

Printed in the United States of America

10 9 8 7 6 5 4 3 2 1

Contents

Acknowledgments ────────────────

Modern Political Science derives from a conference we organized at the University of California, Berkeley, in September 2002. For their generous support of the conference, we thank the Department of Political Science, the Institute of Governmental Studies, the Institute of European Studies, and the Townsend Center for the Humanities. We also thank all those who contributed so much to our discussions at the conference: Chris Ansell, Henry Brady, David Hollinger, Martin Jay, David Robertson, and Eric Schickler. Terry Ball and Jim Kloppenberg provided detailed comments on the whole manuscript. Ian Malcolm, at Princeton University Press, provided helpful support and advice. Laura Bevir prepared the index. We are grateful to them all.

Contributors

Robert Adcock is Visiting Professor of Political Science at Stanford University, U.S.

Mark Bevir is Professor of Political Science at the University of California, Berkeley, U.S.

Sandra M. den Otter is Associate Professor of History at Queen's University, Canada.

James Farr is Professor of Political Science at the University of Minnesota, U.S.

John G. Gunnell is Distinguished Professor of Political Science at the State University of New York at Albany, U.S.

Dennis Kavanagh is Professor of Politics at the University of Liverpool, UK.

Michael Kenny is Professor of Politics at Sheffield University, UK.

R.A.W. Rhodes is Professor of Politics in the Research Schools of the Australian National University.

Dorothy Ross is Arthur O. Lovejoy Professor of History at Johns Hopkins University, U.S.

Mark C. Smith is Associate Professor of American Studies and History, University of Texas at Austin, U.S.

Shannon C. Stimson is Professor of Political Science at the University of California, Berkeley, U.S.

One

A History of Political Science: How? What? Why?

ROBERT ADCOCK, MARK BEVIR, AND
SHANNON C. STIMSON

BRITISH AND AMERICAN political scientists recently have shown an unusual degree of interest in the history of their discipline. The dawn of a
new millennium prompted leading figures in the British study of politics
to reflect on their past and to situate themselves in relation to it.[1] In
America, work on the history of political science has appeared off and on
for some time, but the last decade has witnessed a positive flourishing of
such studies. These studies include some in which luminaries in the discipline look back on their teachers and predecessors.[2] They also include a
distinct subgenre of historical studies written from within the discipline,
but by scholars outside its limelight.[3] The past of political science has
attracted further attention recently from intellectual historians outside of
the discipline in both Britain and America.[4] *Modern Political Science*

[1] Jack Hayward, Brian Barry, and Archie Brown, eds., *The British Study of Politics in
the Twentieth Century* (Oxford: Oxford University Press, 1999).

[2] For example, see Ira Katznelson, *Desolation and Enlightenment: Political Knowledge
after Total War, Totalitarianism, and the Holocaust* (New York: Columbia University
Press, 2003).

[3] James Farr and Raymond Seidelman, eds., *Discipline and History: Political Science in
the United States* (Ann Arbor: University of Michigan Press, 1993); John G. Gunnell, *The
Descent of Political Theory: The Genealogy of an American Vocation* (Chicago: University
of Chicago Press, 1993); James Farr, John S. Dryzek, and Stephen T. Leonard, eds., *Political
Science in History: Research Programs and Political Traditions* (New York: Cambridge Uni-
versity Press, 1995); Brian Schmidt, *The Political Discourse of Anarchy: A Disciplinary
History of International Relations* (Albany: State University of New York Press, 1998); Ido
Oren, *Our Enemies and US: America's Rivalries and the Making of Political Science* (Ithaca,
NY: Cornell University Press, 2003); John G. Gunnell, *Imagining the American Polity: Polit-
ical Science and the Discourse of Democracy* (University Park: Pennsylvania State University
Press, 2004).

[4] Dorothy Ross, *The Origins of American Social Science* (Cambridge: Cambridge Univer-
sity Press, 1991); Mark C. Smith, *Social Science in the Crucible: The American Debate over
Objectivity and Purpose, 1918–1941* (Durham, NC: Duke University Press, 1994); Julia
Stapleton, *Political Intellectuals and Public Identities in Britain since 1850* (Manchester:
Manchester University Press, 2001); S. M. Amadae, *Rationalizing Capitalist Democracy:
The Cold War Origins of Rational Choice Liberalism* (Chicago: University of Chicago Press,

brings together political scientists and intellectual historians from both sides of the Atlantic to pursue a comparative and transnational account of the development of political inquiry in Britain and America since the late-nineteenth century. In doing so, it not only explores "what" happened in the history of political science, it also embodies a distinctive analysis of "how" and "why" we might study this history.

The recent attention given to the history of political science is both the temporal companion to and in some tension with the avowedly historical approaches that are increasingly popular within political science itself. For several decades now, as we discuss more fully in chapter 12, various neostatists and institutionalists have presented themselves as offering a historically sensitive alternative to the formalist excesses of certain variants of behavioralism or, more recently, of rational choice theory. While *Modern Political Science* shares these scholars' concern to understand the present in light of the past that produced it, beyond this rather generic overlap parallels give way to significant differences of approach. Indeed, this volume is, in part, motivated by a worry that avowedly historical approaches in contemporary political science run the risk of naturalizing one particular conception of historical inquiry by proceeding as if their own way of distinguishing "historical" from "ahistorical" studies was obvious and uncontested. Even worse, these approaches can appear to be adopting this conception simply for their own polemical purposes, without the aid of extended reflection upon the practice and purpose of historical inquiry and its relation to social science. *Modern Political Science* attempts, then, to locate the self-described "historical institutionalism" as a contingent, recently emergent approach that is but one of multiple ways of bringing the past to bear on the study of politics. More generally, it attempts to recall the plurality and range of approaches to the past that have, at one time or another, claimed the loyalty of political scientists in Britain and America.

How to Study the History of Political Science

Modern Political Science draws on developments within the history of ideas that have transformed the ways in which we might think about disciplinary history.[5] It is indebted to a radical historicism that stands

---

2003); Nils Gilman, *Mandarins of the Future: Modernization Theory in Cold War America* (Baltimore: Johns Hopkins University Press, 2003).

[5] Of course there are not only other strands in the history of ideas very different from radical historicism, but also differences among those who belong within this one strand. We believe, however, that this broad strand best explains the shared features of the essays in this volume, which is why we invoke it here. Prominent examples of methodological writings we would include as part of radical historicism include Michel Foucault, *The Archaeology of*

in contrast to the naturalizing perspective from which political scientists commonly view their discipline and its past. The naturalizing perspective understands political science as constituted by a pregiven empirical domain—politics—and a shared intellectual agenda, to make this domain the object of a cumulative and instrumentally useful science. It thus encourages a retrospective vision that focuses, first, on the establishment of an autonomous discipline, free from the clutches of history, law, and philosophy, and, second, on charting progress made in the subsequent development of that discipline.[6]

Radical historicism, in contrast, has made intellectual historians and political theorists wary of postulating a given empirical domain or a shared intellectual agenda as the defining feature of any putative discipline. It has turned the constitution of a discipline from an assumption or a fulfillment into a problem. "Disciplines are unstable compounds," as Stefan Collini recently put it, for "what is called a 'discipline' is in fact a complex set of practices, whose unity, such as it is, is given as much by historical accident and institutional convenience as by a coherent intellectual rationale."[7] The creation of an apparently given empirical domain and shared intellectual agenda thus appears as the contingent victory of particular intellectual traditions, where these traditions legitimate themselves precisely by telling the history of the discipline as if their own assumptions were unproblematic. For radical historicists, the history of political science might unpack the contingent origins of dominant traditions, recover alternative traditions that get left out of other histories, or question the naturalizing histories by which practitioners of a discipline legitimate their own approaches as contributing to progress in the study of politics. Such radical historicist endeavors do not seek to invert naturalizing narratives of intellectual progress into despairing narratives of stagnation or decline. Rather, they typically aspire to interpret the history of

---

Knowledge (London: Tavistock, 1972); and the essays of Skinner collected in James Tully, ed., *Meaning and Context: Quentin Skinner and His Critics* (Cambridge: Polity Press, 1988). Examples of studies of the history of political science that exhibit a debt to radical historicism include Dario Castiglione and Iain Hampsher-Monk, eds., *The History of Political Thought in National Context* (Cambridge: Cambridge University Press, 2001); and Stefan Collini, Donald Winch, and John Burrow, *That Noble Science of Politics: A Study in Nineteenth-Century Intellectual History* (Cambridge: Cambridge University Press, 1983).

[6] See, for example, William H. Riker, "The Two-Party System and Duverger's Law: An Essay on the History of Political Science," *American Political Science Review* 76 (1982): 753–66; Gabriel A. Almond, "Political Science: The History of the Discipline," in *A New Handbook of Political Science*, ed. Robert E. Goodin and Hans-Dieter Klingemann (Oxford: Oxford University Press, 1995), 50–96.

[7] Stefan Collini, "Postscript: Disciplines, Canons, and Publics; The History of 'The History of Political Thought' in Comparative Perspective," in Castiglione and Hampsher-Monk, *Political Thought in National Context*, 298.

political science in ways that bypass the narrative options of progress, stagnation, or decline.

The radical historicism that informs *Modern Political Science* belongs within a tradition that has played a recurring role in the human sciences during the twentieth century. This tradition arose as a distinctive perspective following on a heightening of the concern with context and change that characterizes historicism more generally. Where the developmental form of historicism prevalent in the nineteenth century sought to bring particular contexts and changes together as parts of a larger historical whole, radical historicists worry that such synthetic efforts tame the contingency of human history: they are cautious of framing particular historical developments in relation to any overarching category, let alone of framing them in terms of an apparently natural or progressive movement. Radical historicists thus break with those grand narratives, often reminiscent of a notion of providence, by which developmental historicists seek to reconcile an attention to change and context with a desire to locate particular developments in a meaningful and progressive whole.

Radical historicism's wariness toward overarching categories and grand narratives raises the question: What sort of aggregate concepts, if any, should we use when studying the past? It draws our attention, in particular, to the dangers of an excessive focus on the idea of a discipline.[8] Disciplinary histories here risk privileging the category of the discipline as if its institutional presence—the American Political Science Association or membership of departments of Political Science—demarcates boundaries to the flow of ideas or explains the ways in which ideas have developed within such boundaries. In contrast, radical historicism encourages us to disaggregate the institutions of a discipline and thereby to portray them as the contingent products of debates that often include ideas that have come from other disciplines. It encourages us, we would suggest, to deploy traditions as our aggregate concepts, allowing that while these traditions might parallel the institutions of a discipline, they also might parallel the contours of specific subfields or cut across disciplinary and subdisciplinary boundaries. Radical historicism also casts doubt on accounts of disciplinary change that concentrate on debates about objects or topics that appear to be given outside of the context of any tradition and of which scholars can be said to be acquiring better and better knowledge. It encourages us, instead, to understand traditions as changing as

---

[8] Cf. Stefan Collini, "'Disciplinary History' and 'Intellectual History': Reflections on the Historiography of the Social Sciences in Britain and France," *Revue de synthese* 3, no. 4 (1988): 387–99.

and when their exponents respond to intersubjective dilemmas that arise within the context of those particular traditions.[9]

Modern Political Science thus employs concepts such as tradition and dilemma to demarcate its aggregate units. Radical historicists conceive of beliefs as contingent in that people reach them against the background of a particular intellectual inheritance, rather than by means of pure reason or pure experience. We thus need a concept akin to tradition in order to demarcate the background that helps to explain how people reach the beliefs they do. Of course, other related concepts can do much the same work—language, discourse, and so on. While the particular word we use is of little importance, there is, at times, a substantive issue at stake. Structuralists, and some of those influenced by them, adopt one version of the argument that people can only form beliefs and so act against the background of a social inheritance; they use concepts such as language and discourse in part to indicate that inherited modes of thought fix beliefs and actions in ways that sharply limit the possibility of human agency. It appears to us, in contrast, that such concepts rely on a false dichotomy between structures or quasi structures and the notion of an autonomous self: after all, we can reject autonomy, insisting that actors always are embedded in social contexts, and still accept agency, arguing that they can modify these contexts for reasons they form against the background of such contexts. Our preference for the word *tradition* thus represents a self-conscious attempt to allow for agency by viewing social inheritances as only ever influencing, as opposed to fixing, the beliefs and actions that individuals go on to hold and to perform. People inherit traditions that they then develop or transform before passing them on to others.

When we invoke abstract concepts such as tradition, discourse, or language, we raise the question, How should we analyze change within them? Concepts such as dilemma or problem suggest that change occurs as agents seek to respond to novel circumstances using the resources of the traditions they have inherited. A dilemma arises when a new idea stands in opposition to existing beliefs and so forces a reconsideration of them leading to at least somewhat new beliefs, and so typically inspiring at least slightly different actions and practices. While dilemmas can derive from theoretical and moral reflection, it is useful to recall that they often arise from our experiences of the world. Thus, although we cannot straightfor-

---

[9] On historiographies of problems, dilemmas, and traditions see James Farr, "From Modern Republic to Administrative State," in *Regime and Discipline: Democracy and the Development of Political Science*, ed. David Easton, John G. Gunnell, and Michael B. Stein (Ann Arbor: University of Michigan Press, 1995), 133–38; Mark Bevir, *The Logic of the History of Ideas* (Cambridge: Cambridge University Press, 1999), 174–264.

wardly associate them with social, economic, or political pressures in the "real" world, we can link intellectual history to social, economic, and political history. Ideas, beliefs, traditions, and dilemmas are profoundly impacted upon by our competing experiences of the world about us.

Because the essays in *Modern Political Science* operate at a range of levels of aggregation, pursuing differing mixes of descriptive and explanatory goals, the traditions and dilemmas they invoke vary in scope from broad characterizations of widespread patterns of thought, such as developmental historicism, to narrower depictions of networks of scholars, such as historical institutionalism. Whatever the scope of the traditions and dilemmas invoked, radical historicists should be wary of attempts to equate them with a fixed core and a penumbra that then varies over time, for doing so postulates an allegedly given content or trajectory in much the same way as do naturalizing narratives. Instead, we might think of an undifferentiated social context of crisscrossing interactions, rather than a series of discrete and identifiable traditions or dilemmas. Historians then slice a particular tradition or dilemma out of this undifferentiated background so as to explain whatever set of beliefs, actions, or practices interests them. In this view, traditions and dilemmas are aggregate concepts that are crafted by historians to suit their particular purposes; they should not be mistaken for given chunks of the past as if they were fixed in the past so that they and they alone were part of an adequate history, nor should they be mistaken for structures of thought that fix the diversity and capacities for change of the individuals located under them. The criteria for deploying the concept of a tradition, and for identifying the content of particular accounts of traditions, are thus expected to vary with the purposes of the narrative being told. When the purpose is to offer a historical explanation of specific developments in a particular context, for example, the criteria for membership will need to be grounded in the conceptual and personal links between specific individuals.

Once we have shifted attention from a reified discipline to traditions and problems that we craft for our own purposes, we then might proceed to reconsider the place of national and transnational themes in the history of political science.[10] At times, earlier historiographies have char-

---

[10] For one of the earliest and most important reconsiderations of transatlanticism see J.G.A. Pocock, "British History: A Plea for a New Subject," *Journal of Modern History* 47 (1975): 601–28. For recent discussions see David Armitage, Jane Ohlmeyer, Ned C. Landsman, Eliga H. Gould, and J.G.A. Pocock, "*AHR* Forum: The New British History in Atlantic Perspective," *American Historical Review* 104 (1999): 426–500. For recent studies of the transatlantic flow of political ideas in the nineteenth and twentieth centuries see Mark Bevir and Frank Trentmann, eds., *Critiques of Capital in Modern Britain and America: Transatlantic Exchanges, 1800 to the Present Day* (Basingstoke, UK: Palgrave Macmillan, 2002); James T. Kloppenberg, *Uncertain Victory: Social Democracy and Progressivism in European and American Thought, 1870–1920* (Oxford: Oxford University Press, 1986);

acterized political thought as cosmopolitan or universal in character, as if it comprised a set of political ideas addressed to perennial philosophical problems or to scientific empirical truths possessed of a universal validity.[11] Radical historicism queries any such characterization by emphasizing that particular beliefs are always embedded in wider webs of belief and traditions, which are themselves contingent and historical. Political thought appears, in this view, as an activity by which people make their future out of their past: political actors inherit a tradition or a set of ideas that they then can modify, perhaps through abstract and conscious reflection or perhaps through unreflective action; when they modify their inheritance so as to act in new ways, they thereby remake the world. The history of political ideas is thus, at least in part, the study of the activity by which people collectively make and remake their communities. What is more, because the nation-state has been a leading expression of community in the modern world, it can be helpful to situate much political thought within the context of loosely national traditions of inquiry. *Modern Political Science* thus focuses on the way in which particular traditions of political science have flourished and developed in two nations: Britain and America.

At other times, earlier histories of political science have had a predominantly national orientation. Naturalizing narratives can lead to a focus on the institutions that are supposed to be the telos of the emergence of an autonomous profession, and since these institutions are generally national in scope, the result can be a history of a putative "British study of politics" or "American science of politics." Likewise, widespread assumptions about the exceptionalism of Britain and America have obscured, for historians of each, the transatlantic exchanges that have informed the development of their traditions of inquiry. Radical historicism queries such purely national histories insofar as it prompts us to look skeptically upon any straightforward equation of traditions with institutional boundaries. While political thought is an activity by which people make the future out of their past, the relevant actors need not know any particular institutional or national boundary. On the contrary, political discussions take place in a variety of overlapping networks, many of which are transnational; institutions are just the contingent and changeable products of actions that embody competing views (reached through such discussions), of the

---

and Daniel T. Rogers, *Atlantic Crossings: Social Politics in a Progressive Age* (Cambridge: Harvard University Press, 1998).

[11] Compare the challenge to the universalist character of much of the history of political thought in Dario Castiglione and Iain Hampsher-Monk, "Introduction: The History of Political Thought and the National Discourses of Politics," in *Political Thought in National Context.*

ways in which we ought to maintain or to transform our communities. National influences are thus not the only ones, nor necessarily even the most important ones, upon the character of political science. By pursuing transnational exchanges, historians can query what otherwise might appear to be purely national debates and institutions. *Modern Political Science* thus combines chapters that focus on Britain or America with others that study the transnational flow of ideas between the two.

What Happened in the History of Political Science

Radical historicism leads to narratives of the history of political science that explore interacting traditions as their adherents remake and transform them, often in response to specific dilemmas or problems. The following essays provide narratives of the emergence, development, and transformation of modern political science in Britain and the United States. They do so, moreover, by locating various approaches to political science in relation both to national traditions and transnational exchanges.

In the late nineteenth century, the study of politics on both sides of the Atlantic was dominated by a developmental historicism that infused the national traditions found in each country. This developmental historicism constitutes a common point of departure against which to view the emergence and evolution of modern political science in the twentieth century. Our first three essays focus on this point of departure, highlighting its guiding concern with grand narratives centered on the nation, the state, and freedom, while also exploring differences that mark out various traditions within developmental historicism. James Farr tracks a distinctive, diverse, and evolving tradition of comparative-historical scholarship that emerged in America in the mid-nineteenth century, dominated political science there through the turn of the century, and persisted well into the early decades of the twentieth century. Sandra den Otter's chapter on Britain distinguishes the Whiggish tradition of constitutional and institutional history from the tradition of British Idealism. Dorothy Ross traces much the same distinction only in more epistemological terms as she discusses the mixture of empiricist and idealist approaches found within the late-nineteenth-century study of politics on both sides of the Atlantic.

While various empiricist and idealist strands of developmental historicism dominated the study of politics in the late nineteenth century, some proponents of an evolutionary positivism in the tradition of Comte and Spencer were also found in both Britain and America. This evolutionary positivism began, around the turn of the century, to give way to the neopositivism that would come, in time, to exert a major influence on modern political science, especially in the United States. Hence Ross argues that

American political science began to diverge from its British counterpart after World War I, when American social scientists proved peculiarly receptive to the reconfigured and tightened notion of science promulgated by neopositivists such as Karl Pearson. The later contours of this divergence between America and Britain appear in the chapters that discuss the period since the Second World War. The chapters on America offer narratives in which an empiricist political science intertwines and contends with vibrant neopositivist currents. Those on Britain, in contrast, portray a continuing stream of idealism, as well as a lively Marxist tradition, as the main counterparts to empiricism in political science.

The divergence of British and American political science in the twentieth century should not be overplayed, however. Perhaps the most central element of modern political science on both sides of the Atlantic is a common one: the rise of a distinctive modernist empiricism that sets out to atomize and compartmentalize the flux of reality and to develop new approaches to the gathering and summarizing of empirical data. This modernist empiricism took shape in the context of a series of departures from developmental historicism's reliance on grand, national narratives to situate the study of particular political events and institutions within a larger order of developmental continuity and progress. This reliance was undermined in the early decades of the twentieth century by a growing pluralist challenge to the conception of the state so central to many such grand narratives. Sandra den Otter tracks the early formulation of pluralism among British idealists, while Dennis Kavanagh and John Gunnell consider its subsequent role in the reorientations of political science that took shape on each side of the Atlantic in the interwar decades. Kavanagh looks to pluralism alongside new political dilemmas to understand both the vibrancy of interwar challenges to the older Whig tradition and the revamping of that tradition involved in the rise of accounts spelling out the components of a distinctive Westminster model of government. Gunnell explores the particular hue that pluralism took on in America, where it contributed to the crafting of a new theory of democracy and a concomitant new understanding of the character of the American polity.

Movement away from developmental historicism involved not only the formulation of new theoretical visions of British and American politics, but also the emergence of new thematic focuses and empirical techniques that looked forward to an investigation and interpretation of contemporary politics increasingly detached from grand historical narratives. Gunnell sees these developments as intertwined. He argues that the interwar rise in American political science of techniques centered on the empirical study of the present owed less to a committed rejection of historical or legal studies than it did to the ways in which a new theory of democracy inspired a new vision of what political scientists should study. Several of our authors note the early promotion of such developments by Wallas in Britain, as well as the notably warmer reception accorded to this agenda in America. James Farr tracks the early-twentieth-century emergence in America of new ordering themes of psychology and process, themes that would develop a wider appeal in the decades after the First World War. He also considers the range of ideas put into play by American pragmatism. While the more interpretive dimensions of pragmatism notably failed to influence political scientists,[12] some of its other aspects—such as its instrumentalism and faith in science as an agent of progressive social change—would be selectively drawn on as part of the interwar rise of modernist empiricism. So, Mark Smith explores the promotion of various new techniques and approaches under the aegis of an engaged reform ethos. He compares Charles Beard's advocacy of a "New History" in which historical studies would critically unmask aspects of our present self-understanding to Merriam's contention that political science's contribution to reform and progress was dependent on its adoption of new themes and empirical techniques being pioneered in psychology and other social sciences. An explicit normative thrust continued, however, to imbue Merriam's agenda, distinguishing his reform-oriented modernist empiricism from the neopositivism that was to take shape as a distinctively influential strand within American political science after World War II.

The decades after the Second World War witnessed additional shifts in the character of political science on both sides of the Atlantic, with new empirical themes and techniques gaining further ground in both countries, while a distinctly neopositivistic conception of universalizing, value-free theory also took hold among American political scientists. In his essay on British developments, Mike Kenny downplays the importance of the founding of the British Political Studies Association in 1950, attributing it to exogenous influences associated with a UNESCO initiative rather than to any groundswell among British scholars. He suggests that the dominant tradition was still the Whig one, even though this tradition underwent further shifts as modernist currents spread through British culture. Whig themes were combined ever more closely with a modernist empiricism that opened up the study of politics to new techniques emanating from America. This synthesis of Whiggism and modernist empiricism

---

[12] For more on political science's ambivalent relationship to pragmatism, and in particular its failure to pick up on the more radical, interpretive dimensions of Dewey's thought, see James Farr, "John Dewey and American Political Science," *American Journal of Political Science* 43 (April 1999): 520–41. While our own radical historicism is not directly indebted to these dimensions of American pragmatism, they have proven to be a fruitful point of reference for other contemporary radical historicists such as Richard Rorty, Richard Bernstein, and James Kloppenberg.

confronted competing traditions: the socialist tradition still thrived, Oakeshottian conservatism reshaped Whiggism in a way that can be characterized as a negative reaction to modernism, and a tradition of civic humanism that owed much to idealism also took shape.

Robert Adcock tackles the behavioral revolution in America, disaggregating prewar and postwar changes that are usually lumped together, and then tracing the varied shapes that debates took on in the postwar period. He notes the problematic relationship in the study of American politics between the growing survey research literature and historical studies, but he questions whether, on the whole, the rise of new empirical techniques led to any overall decline in the amount of concern with the past. He raises similar doubts about the impact of behavioralism on comparative politics: the explicit efforts of Gabriel Almond and others to meld new empirical techniques and new positivist forms of theory with older comparative historical perspectives suggests that behavioralists are better seen as having sought to approach the past in new ways, rather than as having rejected historical studies as such.

The essay by Adcock and Mark Bevir explores the state of political theory after the Second World War. Adcock and Bevir reject the common notion that political theory was dead or declining in this era, arguing, on the contrary, that the subfield underwent a dynamic remaking. In America, clear breaks were made with the earlier historicist tradition of institutionally grounded work on the history of ideas. Behavioralists promoted a positivist vision of empirical theory that had great influence across much of the discipline, but found little support within what became the subfield of political theory. Political theory became dominated instead by an alternative new agenda, that is, an epic tradition that was rooted in émigré critiques of the flaws of liberal modernity and of the modernist forms of social science associated with it. In Britain, older historical and institutional approaches were revamped rather than rejected. They took on the shape of a reformulated and deepened historicism that drew on recent developments in British idealism and analytic philosophy while rejecting both positivist and epic conceptions of the task of theory. This reformulated historicism acts, of course, as one of the main influences on the radical historicism that we pursue and propound in this volume.

The final three essays bring *Modern Political Science* up to the present, and illustrate more explicitly some of the contributions that the history of political science might make to contemporary debates. For Britain, Rod Rhodes and Mark Bevir counter the idea that there is any one distinctive, British way of studying politics, emphasizing instead the plurality of contemporary traditions. They suggest that a narrative of the professionalization of political science in Britain reflects the viewpoint of just one of these traditions; it embodies the self-understanding of the mainstream as it has emerged out of the intertwining of Whiggism and modernist empiricism. They indicate the partiality of this narrative by pointing to two important alternatives: an idealist tradition, embracing both civic humanist and Oakeshottian strands, and a socialist tradition, containing strands associated with both political economy and post-Marxism. Their exploration of how these traditions have developed in response to dilemmas posed by changing intellectual agendas, such as neoliberalism, and state agendas, such as the preference for relevance, echoes Kenny's chapter in its emphasis on the impact the British state has exercised on the discipline through its control of research funds.

In their essay on contemporary American developments, Adcock, Bevir, and Shannon Stimson seek to historicize the new institutionalism. They trace the expansion of new institutionalist discourse from the mid-1980s through the early 1990s, highlighting the plurality of the traditions that came to understand themselves in such terms, and the extent to which they did so in response to dilemmas posed by alternative traditions, such as behavioralism and rational choice. In doing so, they substitute a radical historicist narrative of recent political science for the naturalizing narratives that political scientists themselves are prone to offer. They seek thereby to suggest how radical historicism might destabilize those perspectives from which recent changes in political science appear as a progressive intellectual movement. Naturalizing narratives based on presentist caricatures of the past are, of course, by no means the sole property of the new institutionalism. This chapter thus suggests, more generally, one of the roles that the history of political science might play within contemporary debates.

In the final chapter, Bevir points to a further payoff of radical historicist studies of political science by exemplifying how they might shed light on developments in the state. Bevir explores the link between political science and changes in British politics by tracing connections, both personal and conceptual, between new institutionalism and some of the policy initiatives of New Labour. By illustrating how the history of political science can explain aspects of today's practices of governance, and vice versa, the essays by Bevir, Rhodes, and Kenny point to ways in which *Modern Political Science* might contribute to discussions of how changes in the concepts and techniques of social science have influenced, and been influenced by, evolving practices of governance since the late nineteenth century.

Why Historicize Political Science?

What, we might ask now, are the implications of the narratives of *Modern Political Science* for contemporary political science? To critics, radical historicism may appear to make the history of political science, and the history of political ideas more generally, almost irrelevant to current political scientists or political theorists. Some might complain that radical historicism leads to purely antiquarian or sociological studies of beliefs to the neglect of the perennial questions or big ideas that make past texts of relevance to us.[13] Others might contend that radical historicism leads to a stress on particularity and contingency that distracts us from broader questions about the progress of knowledge.[14] We want to suggest, in contrast, that radical historicism not only allows us to restate many of the benefits that others allow to histories of political science, but also to show how such histories are relevant in ways these others often overlook.[15]

To begin, then, let us restate benefits that are widely allowed to the history of political science. One such benefit is the combating of caricatures. Engaged reactions to the work of other scholars, both present and past, are fundamental to intellectual debate. One result of this dynamic is that there are surely few political scientists who cannot think of instances where their own work or that of the traditions on which they draw have been caricatured by others. It is thus not surprising that a concern to combat caricatures of the intellectual past is endorsed by diverse historians of political science, from Gabriel Almond to John Gunnell.[16] By undermining caricatures, the history of political science also can query the role that bad history often plays in legitimating dominant positions in contemporary debates. For example, Adcock's chapter challenges claims about the character of behavioralism that play prominent roles in the justificatory narratives often associated with new institutionalism.

Another widely acknowledged benefit of the history of political science is that it can lead to the recovery of lost insights. As George Stocking wrote in his classic editorial for the opening volume of the *Journal of the History of the Behavioral Sciences*, "[W]e have been limited by the lack of some of the perspectives that have not been transmitted to us."[17] Kava-

---

[13] Different versions of this complaint appear in Jorge Gracia, "The Logic of the History of Ideas or the Sociology of the History of Beliefs?" *Philosophical Books* 42 (2001): 177–86; Melissa Lane, "Why History of Ideas at All?" *History of European Ideas* 28 (2002): 33–41; Margaret Leslie, "In Defense of Anachronism," *Political Studies* 18 (1970): 433–47; Charles D. Tarlton, "Historicity, Meaning and Revisionism in the Study of Political Thought," *History and Theory* 12 (1973): 307–28.

[14] See Almond, "Political Science."

[15] For a similar attempt to show that radical historicists might accept some concepts of perennial questions see Mark Bevir, "Are There Perennial Problems in Political Theory?" *Political Studies* 42 (1994): 662–75.

[16] Gabriel A. Almond, *A Discipline Divided* (London: Sage, 1990); Gunnell, *Descent of Political Theory.*

[17] George W. Stocking, Jr., "On the Limits of 'Presentism' and 'Historicism' in the Historiography of the Behavioral Sciences," *Journal of the History of the Behavioral Sciences* 1 (1965): 216. See also Steven Seidman, "Beyond Presentism and Historicism: Understanding

nagh points to an example of such a lack of transmission when he suggests that interwar British pluralists offered insights on which the corporatist literature of the 1970s and 1980s might have drawn. Just as the history of political science might recover specific insights relevant to contemporary research, so it might recover alternative perspectives on the goals and mission of the discipline. Hence, the older goal of producing principles explored by Farr in this volume might represent a substantive alternative to the now dominant goal of producing empirical theory.

Yet another benefit widely associated with the history of political science is the chance it provides for us to learn from past mistakes. Quentin Skinner has foregrounded this benefit by suggesting that history can serve a therapeutic function: history can "enable us to uncover the points at which they [our key concepts] have become confused or misunderstood in a way that marked their subsequent history," and so perhaps "we can hope not merely to illuminate but to dissolve some of our current philosophical perplexities."[18] Historical research might help us, for example, to clarify the confusions evident in later discussions of pluralism by pursuing, as Gunnell does here, the transformation of that concept as it made its transatlantic journey.

Let us turn now to the suggestion that radical historicism also opens a vista onto neglected benefits of the history of political science. Radical historicists might argue, we believe, that the history of political science can contribute to conceptual sophistication, that it forms part of the substance of political science, and that it offers an arena in which we can evaluate rival approaches to political science. For radical historicists, concepts always need to be understood in terms of particular contexts of beliefs, purposes, and traditions. Historical studies can unpack such relations, thereby helping to provide pragmatic, contextually sensitive criteria against which to judge conceptual choices. For example, several of the essays in this volume, especially that by Ross, identify changes in conceptions of science since the nineteenth century. Such narratives might prompt a rejection of the idea that there is any one true form of science against which conceptions from different times and places can usefully be compared and ranked. Perhaps they might even encourage us to assess claims to political knowledge more closely in relation to the particular webs of belief and concerns in relation to which they arise. In this view, we might reject a neopositivist concept of empirical theory on the grounds

---

the History of Social Science," *Sociological Inquiry* 53 (1983): 79–94; and John S. Dryzek and Stephen T. Leonard, "History and Discipline in Political Science," *American Political Science Review* 82 (1988): 1245–60.

[18] Quentin Skinner, "A Reply to My Critics" in Tully, *Meaning and Context*, 287–88.

that the beliefs and hopes against which that conception once made sense no longer are convincing to us.

Radical historicism also suggests that the history of political science constitutes a part of the substance of political science. It is a commonplace that people act upon their beliefs or, let us say, their beliefs and preferences, albeit that some of the pertinent beliefs may be subconscious or unconscious. This commonplace implies that we can explain actions, and so the practices or institutions to which they give rise, only if we appeal, at least implicitly, to the relevant beliefs. Thus, political scientists who want to explain some practice or institution have to appeal to the history of political science, at least implicitly, whenever the beliefs embedded in that practice or institution are beliefs that derive from political science. Bevir suggests in his essay, for example, that to explain New Labour's Third Way, especially its attempts to promote joined-up governance, we need to invoke those new institutionalists who advocate networks as a mode of coordination that allegedly possesses notable advantages over markets and hierarchies alike. We can trace clear influences, he suggests, from political scientists through think tanks and policy advisers to recent Labour governments. A study of the history of new institutionalism thus becomes an integral part of the political science of contemporary governance.

Whenever a political practice or institution draws on tools, categories, or beliefs that arise from social science (including the techniques of media management, voting polls or interviews, and administrative planning), the history of social science becomes a crucial part of the study of politics. The developmental historicists of the late nineteenth and early twentieth centuries appear to have allowed as much insofar as they sought to tell historical stories that showed how their concepts had arisen as part of processes of reflection accompanying the evolution of political institutions. Contemporary political scientists, in contrast, are slow to recognize the integral relation between the history of their discipline and the substance of what they study.[19] They tend to marginalize questions about the holistic settings of meanings and beliefs and to treat the knowledge they produce as having a universal audience, rather than as contingent and situated in a particular tradition. Radical historicism here follows the older developmental historicism, but with a twist: its emphasis on contingency undermines assumptions of the natural, progressive, or disinterested character of the development of political science and the institutions that it informs and by which it is informed.[20]

[19] For a recent exception see Oren, *Our Enemies and US*.

[20] The critical import of radical historicism here appears most clearly in the work of Foucault and those inspired by him. See, for example, Michel Foucault, *Discipline and Punish: The Birth of the Prison* (Harmondsworth, UK: Penguin, 1977); Graham Burchell, Colin Gordon, and Peter Miller, eds., *The Foucault Effect: Studies in Governmentality* (London:

We want to suggest, finally, that the history of political science offers an arena in which to evaluate rival approaches to political science.[21] Once we allow that all our experiences are in part constructed by our prior theories, then we will likely conclude that we cannot evaluate a theory, let alone a whole approach, by reference to facts alone: after all, if the facts are infused with the theory we want to evaluate, the process of justification would look perilously circular, while if they are not, the proponents of the theory might well reject them and any evaluation that is based upon them. The evaluation of theories, narratives, and approaches must be, then, a matter of comparing them by reference to appropriate criteria and in relation to some kind of shared or overlapping subject matter.[22] Political scientists might look for such subject matter, we believe, in the history of the discipline.[23]

Because political science seeks to explain human beliefs, actions, and their consequences, including the practices and institutions to which they give rise, any approach to political science presumably will include, at least implicitly, an analysis of beliefs, actions, and the forms of explanation that are appropriate to them. Thus, because the history of political science is the history of beliefs, actions, and their consequences, any approach to political science presumably includes the claim, at least implicitly, that it might be applied successfully to the history of the discipline. That is to say, if rational choice, historical institutionalism, or any other approach purports to offer a general approach to the analysis of human life, it should be able to show that it works with respect to the part of human life that is the history of political science. Not only do alternative approaches to political science thus need to be able to generate an adequate history of political science; when they do so, they have to engage with one another in a way that generates an overlapping subject matter. So, a rational choice history of political science would have to explain the rise and content of historical institutionalism, just as a historical institutionalist history of the discipline would have to explain the rise and content of rational choice. In this way, the history of political science acts as

---

Harvester Wheatsheaf, 1991); and Andrew Barry, Thomas Osborne, and Nicholas Rose, eds., *Foucault and Political Reason* (London: UCL Press, 1996).

[21] Cf. the argument about philosophy of science in Imre Lakatos, "History of Science and Its Rational Reconstructions," in *Philosophical Writings*, vol. 1, *The Methodology of Scientific Research Programmes* (Cambridge: Cambridge University Press, 1978), 102–38.

[22] Cf. Bevir, *Logic*, 78–126.

[23] For another view of the relation of histories of political science to the evaluation of rival approaches see Dryzek and Leonard, "History and Discipline." Our position differs from theirs both in its emphasis on the need for a shared subject matter—in this case the history of political science itself—and in its avoidance of the notion of measuring approaches against some standard of "progress."

an arena within which rival approaches to political science might evaluate one another's merits without simply talking past each other.

When we recognize that the history of political science might play such a role, we begin to expose the impossibility of such a history being neutral between rival approaches to political science. Perhaps historians of political science can tell their stories without explicitly casting evaluative judgments on their subject matter. Even if they can, however, their stories always will embody, at least tacitly, analyses of beliefs, of actions and their consequences, and of the forms of explanation appropriate to these things, and these analyses could then be generalized so as to correspond to an existing or possible approach to political science. Let us be clear, then, that radical historicism implies a general approach to political science as well as to its history. While we welcome much of the diverse work that goes under the label of one or the other of the various new institutionalisms, we want to suggest that historical contingency goes all the way down, and this motion means that political scientists should pay more attention to meanings so as to denaturalize and disaggregate institutions. We believe that several emphases that currently are scattered around various parts of the literature—emphases on contingency, on meanings, on agency—these emphases can and should be brought together within a radical historicist political science. We hope that the essays in this volume will contribute not only to debates about political science's past, but also to the shape of its future.

Two

Anglo-American Political Science, 1880–1920

DOROTHY ROSS

THE PERIOD FROM roughly the 1880s to World War I—spanning the late Victorian and Edwardian era in Britain and the Gilded Age and Progressive period in the United States—is the period during which the academic discipline of political science formed in the two countries, and in many respects, it formed along similar lines. Considerable Anglo-American contact, and even more frequent reference, occurred among these scholars, and for good reasons. In both countries, liberal academic elites worked to carve out an authoritative place in the university and to salvage their political heritage in the face of new challenges posed by industrialization and mass democracy. Across several dimensions—intellectual and professional location, political purpose, and the understanding and uses of history—political science in Britain and the United States developed similar disciplinary stances. It was only after World War I that American political scientists began to veer from the common course toward a model informed by positivist science rather than historicism.

On both sides of the Atlantic, political science formed during these decades as a specialized field of study at the intersections of philosophy, history, and law.[1] Those three domains were combined in diverse ways in each country and somewhat differently weighted in each. But political science as a normative and analytical study, grounded variously in ancient

[1] For the United States, at this point and throughout the chapter, see Dorothy Ross, *The Origins of American Social Science* (Cambridge: Cambridge University Press, 1991). For Britain, see Stefan Collini, Donald Winch, John Burrow, *That Noble Science of Politics* (Cambridge: Cambridge University Press, 1983); Jack Hayward, "British Approaches to Politics: The Dawn of a Self-Deprecating Discipline," in *The British Study of Politics in the Twentieth Century*, ed. Jack Hayward, Brian Barry, and Archie Brown (Oxford: Oxford University Press, 1999); Deborah Wormell, *Sir John Seeley and the Uses of History* (Cambridge: Cambridge University Press, 1980); Hugh Tulloch, *James Bryce's "American Commonwealth"* (Woodbridge, UK: Bydell Press, 1988); Julia Stapleton, *Englishness and the Study of Politics: The Social and Political Thought of Ernest Barker* (Cambridge: Cambridge University Press, 1994). For political science in both the United States and Western Europe, see James Farr, "Political Science," in *The Modern Social Sciences*, ed. Theodore M. Porter and Dorothy Ross, vol. 7 in *The Cambridge History of Science* (Cambridge: Cambridge University Press, 2003).

philosophy, imported German idealism, and native moral philosophy, had roots in both countries. The law was a focus of political studies in both England and the United States, more in positive than jurisprudential dimensions. Most important, history provided the chief method for the study of political institutions and legal systems, and the narrative framework for political philosophy as well. Both English and American promoters of the new field debated these different approaches but tried to live with the tensions. Ernest Barker granted empirical historical and psychological study an adjunct role to normative political philosophy.[2] Graham Wallas, if trying to keep his hardheaded psychology free of idealist fantasy, recognized that it should be put to the service of a normative ideal. The scholars who organized the American Political Science Association (APSA) in 1903 were careful to include all three approaches in their delineation of the new field, as was Charles Merriam in his successive surveys.[3]

Political science emerged in both countries during this period as a specialized field of study related to, but distinct from, the disciplines from which it formed and with which it was often still affiliated in the universities. There were differences. History as a cultural genre and academic study commanded greater authority in England than in the United States and hence had greater power to keep political science in its orbit. In the rapidly expanding and modernizing American university system, the social sciences generally, and political science along with them, found relatively easy access. Professionalization along functional lines was an open route to authority. English university faculties expanded more slowly, in consultation with traditional faculty bodies and under the tighter rein of conservative private corporations. Specialization and vocational training were modified by the gentlemanly cultural standards of a close-knit political and cultural elite.[4] Still, the substantive consequences of these differences in professionalization did not clearly emerge until after the Great War.

During this formative period, political science on both sides of the Atlantic was largely the project of liberals who desired to reform, rather than overturn, their country's established, liberal political institutions. "Liberal" could cover a great range, from nationalist critics of democracy

[2] Ernest Barker, *Political Thought in England from Herbert Spencer to the Present Day* (New York: Henry Holt, 1915), 12–17.

[3] The normative dimension of Wallas's thought is emphasized in Terence H. Qualter, *Graham Wallas and the Great Society* (New York: St. Martin's Press, 1979); and of Merriam's, in John G. Gunnell, *The Descent of Political Theory* (Chicago: University of Chicago Press, 1993), chap. 4.

[4] See Sandra den Otter's chapter in this volume; Collini, Winch, and Burrow, *Noble Science of Politics*. See also Dorothy Ross, "Changing Contours of the Social Science Disciplines," in Porter and Ross, *The Modern Social Sciences*.

like J. R. Seeley and John W. Burgess to left progressives like Wallas and Charles Beard. At several points, the two political cultures nicely intersected. James Bryce—member of parliament, author of the authoritative *The American Commonwealth*, resident ambassador to the United States, and president of the American Political Science Association in 1909—could well be called an Anglo-American Mugwump. That term for the Independents who boycotted the corrupt politics of the Republican party in 1884 has come to stand for their like-minded social-cultural stratum—the American part of a transatlantic group of middle-class reformers who formed what David D. Hall described as "the Victorian connection." Nourished by the writings of John Stuart Mill and extended transatlantic journeys and emigration, the connection included E. L. Godkin and John Morley, Charles Eliot Norton, and Goldwyn Smith, Bryce's mentor at Oxford and himself president of the American Historical Association in 1904.[5] Many in the group were, like Bryce, both active politicians and political intellectuals. As secular liberals, they faced in both countries the religious domination of cultural institutions and the stirrings of mass democracy. For the British they prescribed the American model of democratic suffrage and separation of church and state, and for the Americans, "the grafting of parliamentary characteristics on to the American stem; representative and responsible government . . . a permanent disinterested civil service, . . . selfless principles overriding selfish interests"—of government, in short, rooted in democracy but carried out by the "best men." On both sides of the Atlantic, they took Britain as the model for the top half of this responsible government, America as the political democracy and social opportunity underneath.[6]

A little later, Wallas was an exemplary Anglo-American Progressive, part of a left-liberal network anchored in Toynbee Hall, the Fabian society, and the London School of Economics (LSE) on one side, and Jane Addams's Hull House, Progressive reform circles, and the social science departments of the new American universities on the other. Inspired by the social gospel, commonwealth radicalism, socialism, and often (though not in Wallas's case) T. H. Green's idealism, these Progressives joined their social ethic to a faith in science and expertise. American government was understood to lag behind Britain's in honesty, competence, and social legislation, but as the war approached, American universities seemed more open than those in Britain to new directions in social research and political science. Again, personal contact in both directions thickened this par-

    [5] David D. Hall, "The Victorian Connection," *American Quarterly* 27 (December 1975): 561–74. See also Leslie Butler, "The Mugwump Dilemma: Democracy and Cultural Authority in Victorian America" (PhD diss., Yale University, 1997).
    [6] Tulloch, *Bryce's "American Commonwealth,"* 9.

ticular stream of "Atlantic crossings." Wallas was an active participant in London reform politics and in Toynbee Hall, the model for American settlement houses. A leading Fabian and professor of political science at LSE from its founding in 1895, he made several lecture tours to America between 1896 and the First World War, and more afterward, speaking at Hull House, to civic groups, and increasingly to universities; he corresponded with Addams, converted the young Walter Lippmann at Harvard to his ideas, and sealed his American connection by joining the inner circle of writers at the *New Republic*.[7]

This common, yet differentiated, academic and political context holds as well for the role of history in political science. The understanding of history within which political science formed was, like that of nineteenth-century culture generally, nationalist. The nation-state was its central subject, understood as a unit that developed organically and was held together by common ethical as well as functional bonds. Even more profoundly, nineteenth-century culture was historicist. In response to the French Revolution and the massive changes set in motion by industrialization, as well as through the influence of romanticism, history began to be appreciated as a human process—contingent, changing, creating from every past a new future. Because time was productive of novelty, history, as the field on which humankind must work out its salvation, was both promise and problem. Many nineteenth-century thinkers worked to tame the contingency and uncertainty about the future that historicism let loose. Often using organic and evolutionary metaphors, they constructed laws and ordering principles. History became a developmental process moving along a defined and progressive path. As James Farr discusses in this volume, the new scholars of political science in the United States worked within this frame, and much the same could be said for the British students of politics as discussed by Sandra den Otter. Some worked from empiricist premises, others from idealism, and still others, especially in America, from a commonsense- or Ideal-realism that joined fact to Rational truth. If the British idealists subordinated historical truths to the rational truths of philosophy, the empiricists and Ideal-realists believed their method would produce certain knowledge of facts and principles for the guidance of current politics.[8] They drew German models of histori-

---

[7] See Daniel T. Rodgers, *Atlantic Crossings: Social Politics in a Progressive Age* (Cambridge: Harvard University Press, 1998), esp. 41–43, 53–54, 64–66, 70–73; Martin J. Wiener, *Between Two Worlds: The Political Thought of Graham Wallas* (Oxford: Clarendon Press, 1971), esp. chaps. 2, 7.

[8] See the chapters by James Farr and Sandra den Otter in this volume, as well as Rosemary Jann, *The Art and Science of Victorian History* (Columbus: Ohio State University Press, 1985). On the mixed epistemological premises of the Gilded Age practitioners of historico-politics in the United States, see Dorothy Ross, "On the Misunderstanding of

cal scholarship into native traditions opened by Walter Bagehot and
Henry Maine and in the United States also by Francis Lieber, a German
émigré trained in history who became the country's first professor of
political science.

In both England and the United States, national history was understood
in exceptionalist terms. In England, the Whig tradition had provided the
national narrative during the nineteenth century, asserting the uniqueness
of English constitutional liberty and representative institutions. English
liberty and institutions were exemplary—at the secular least, the fortu-
nate work of history—or in the evangelical terms of Edward Caird at
Balliol in 1898, English history was the story of "a *chosen people*, with
a special part to play in the great work of civilization and of Christianity,"
a part in "the great movement towards political freedom."[9] Whig historical understanding fit the political purposes of the British moderate
liberals who projected a political science—a story of continuity and gradual change, of tradition and its progressive adaptation to new conditions.
It was a species of historicism, but one meant to blur the difference between a treasured past and a novel present. Continuity was supplied
preeminently by the English constitution, its representative institutions,
its mix of local and national administration, and its common law. Equally,
this continuity was embedded in the freedom-loving character of the
English people. By the later nineteenth century, that character was itself
often grounded in Teutonic racialism, traced to Aryan or Greco-Roman
roots, or both. Change came primarily in the form of democracy and
national expansion. If continuity and change were balanced, the balance
ranged from Thomas Macaulay's more forward-looking welcome of
change to Edward Freeman's restorationist impulse to subsume novelty
in ancient forms.[10] For Whigs of all stripes, France was the counterexam-
ple, the path of centralized authority and unlimited democracy, abstract
reasoning and codified law that England had managed to escape. Such a
view of history served, as Stefan Collini notes, to reassure Britains about
the immediate future.[11]

On the American continent, that strong Whig and Reformation heritage
was refashioned in the encounter with new circumstances. The successful

Ranke and the Origins of the Historical Profession in America," in *Leopold von Ranke and
the Shaping of the Historical Discipline*, ed. Georg G. Iggers and James M. Powell (Syracuse,
NY: Syracuse University Press, 1990).

[9] On Whig history, see Jann, *Art and Science*; on Whig history as English exceptionalism,
see Collini, Winch, and Burrow, *Noble Science of Politics*, chap. 6; and Stapleton, *Englishness*, 34–41.

[10] Jann, *Art and Science*, argues that the thrust of Whig history was toward continuity
and the blurring of change, especially in the case of Freeman.

[11] Collini, Winch, and Burrow, *Noble Science of Politics*, 360.

establishment of republican institutions and the liberal opportunity guaranteed by vast stretches of uncultivated land led exceptionalists to conclude that American history was set on a millennial course, guarded by divine providence, and this faith was transmuted as secularization proceeded into a civil religion. One variant of this narrative placed American history in the historical lineage of Whig liberty, with the English past coming to final fruition in America. A complementary strategy was to stress the millennial or utopian "newness" of America, its break with all previous history, and its grounding in nature. In both cases, the American version of exceptionalism tended to take America out of history altogether, to figure America as the haven of Liberty in which history ended, in Henry Adams's powerful image, the natural ocean into which the winding river of European history flowed. American history was projected forward less as the work of history than as the unfolding of founding institutions.[12]

During the nineteenth century, currents of historicism—Scottish, English, and German—had made their way across the Atlantic without eroding the republic's invulnerability to history. But the exceptionalist ideology was severely challenged during the Gilded Age, roughly the period 1870 to 1900. The weakening of religious belief began to loose American history from divine protection and opened it to the influence of historicism. At the same time, rapid industrialization and the rise of class conflict forced Americans to face the possibility that America might change, that its own history might follow the same course that Europe's had. In that context, the Whig tradition, with its message of change tamed by continuity, was particularly welcome to the cautious Mugwump generation of political scientists. Herbert Baxter Adams, for example, found himself in deep agreement with Freeman, and posted his words and welcomed him to Johns Hopkins as authority for his own work. Adams's germ theory of American history, which traced American republican institutions back to English and Teutonic germs, and Freeman's florid Teutonism both put extreme emphasis on continuity while affirming the Whig identity of history and politics.[13]

The Whig story of continuity and progress could be joined to other nineteenth-century narratives of historical development. Some Mugwump political scientists, notably Burgess at Columbia and Seeley at Cambridge, combined their Whig history with an evolutionary, comparative framework. Burgess's Whig story of Teutonic freedom was inserted first into a Hegelian story of history as the realization of freedom in the State, and then dissected according to the evolutionary, comparative method. His *Political Science and Comparative Constitutional Law*

---

[12] See Ross, *Origins*, chap. 1.
[13] On Adams, ibid., chap. 3.

(1890) set out the formal constitutional and governmental structures of England, France, Germany, and the United States—the four that, according to Burgess, had reached the highest stage of development as democratic states—to the advantage of the United States. Seeley worked from positivist rather than idealist premises, but his *Introduction to Political Science* (1896) was also an exercise in comparative stages and categories, and likewise found Britain foremost among the few that had reached the stage of being an organic nation-state with an assembly that creates the government. If the Whig tradition blurred historical change by overlaying past and present, the broad evolutionary-comparative brush, with its universal model of progress and focus on taxonomy, worked even more forcefully against a historicist sense of contingency and context.

It is noteworthy that both Burgess and Seeley continued to write histories, which they understood more as popular works than works of political science and which illustrated history's enactment of the principles of nationalism and national expansion that they both approved. Seeley's biographer suggests that in this genre, ironically, Seeley wrote his best political science, for *The Expansion of England* (1883) made a causal analysis of the link between colonization, trade, and war, which Seeley then used as a predictive tool.[14] Most of Mugwump political science hit a dead end, at least in part because it practiced shallow forms of historical inquiry, debilitated by the infirmities of the Whig and comparative-evolutionary approaches.

Another work that in part overcame such infirmities was Bryce's *The American Commonwealth*, recognized as perhaps the only work of political science of this Gilded Age generation to analyze political practices rather than formal political institutions. His early studies in natural science and his own hands-on political experience certainly had a great deal to do with this, but the fact remains that he was also trained in and understood himself to be using historical method.[15] The empiricism and contextual analysis he claimed to practice as against Tocqueville's abstraction and deduction—typical evils of the French, of course—helped him to see how American experience shaped informal political practice. Still, as Sandra den Otter points out, Bryce assumed, rather than historically analyzed, the Whiggish development of American political institutions. Both his historical success and failure seem linked to his complex political purpose, which put him in something of a double bind. He wanted both to embed the United States in the Whig tradition so it could be used as a liberal example to the English and to disentangle democracy from its American form so it could be safely transplanted to England. He could

---

[14] Wormell, *Sir John Seeley*, 103 and chap. 3.
[15] See Tulloch, *Bryce's "American Commonwealth."*

resort to the Teutonic escape from historical context to insure continuity, but it required a finer analysis of historical and political causes to separate American evils from kindred institutional forms, a separation he effected by showing that it was informal function and particular circumstances that caused American problems, not the still vital Whig stem.

If the Whig version of exceptionalism blunted the impact of historicism in England and American exceptionalism had been even less friendly to it, this situation began to change at the end of the century. Beginning in the 1890s and accelerating through World War I, as belief in progress and continuity receded, a more contingent sense of historicism developed on both sides of the Atlantic. P.B.M. Blaas has well described this shift in historical consciousness in Britain as one that deepened the sense of difference between past and present, making visible the anachronisms in Whig historical interpretation, and shattering the teleology that tied the past to present English institutions. Very much the same can be said of historical consciousness in the United States in the same period. Just as Maitland attacked the anachronism of Whig historians who read present political meanings into medieval forms, so Charles M. Andrews countered the germ theory of his teacher Herbert Baxter Adams, declaring that the freedom of the primitive Saxon, Teuton, or Aryan, "of whatever nature it may have been, was still very different from that of the free citizen." The historical economist E.R.A. Seligman criticized the prevalent notion that Americans "are marked off from the rest of the world by certain inherent principles, relative indeed, in the sense of being peculiar to America, but eternal and immutable in their relation to ourselves."[16] Indeed, because industrialization occurred later and much more rapidly in the United States, the perception of change at the end of the century was even sharper in the United States than in England. John Dewey voiced a common American sentiment when he marveled in 1899, "One can hardly believe there has been a revolution in all history so rapid, so extensive, so complete." Wallas, who knew both countries well and shared the American perception of a rapidly emerging modernity, remarked on the greater hold that continuity continued to have on the Edwardian mind.[17]

We should note, however, that few scholars in the Progressive and Edwardian era appreciated the more radical implications of historicism explored by Wilhelm Dilthey in Germany or John Dewey in the United States; that is, few placed themselves within the hermeneutic circle. If appreciative of the different meaning of freedom to historical subjects in different periods, they did not attribute their own understanding of histor-

[16] P.B.M. Blaas, *Continuity and Anachronism* (The Hague: Martinus Nijhoff, 1978); Ross, *Origins*, 148–50, and quotations on 263, 149.

[17] Wiener, *Between Two Worlds*, 168; Ross, *Origins*, 148 and 218.

ical facts and principles to interpretation, shaped by their own contexts of purpose, values, and conceptual framework. As James Farr shows, there was little or no appreciation of Dewey's interpretive hermeneutic position among American political scientists. Even among historians, that insight was embraced only by Carl Becker and tentatively approached by Charles Beard in the 1920s, while history in England avoided epistemological reflection altogether and remained wedded to methodological empiricism and a firm factualism.[18]

Still, even if historians and political scientists retained for themselves an exterior gaze, they grounded their historical subjects more firmly in past contexts. In both countries, two additional factors were at work during these turn-of-the-century decades to accentuate the difference between present and past. Specialization and professionalism raised the standard of archival research for historians, sharpened their sense of the differentness of the past, and produced the demand that the past be studied for its own sake rather than being subordinated to present political purposes. In England, William Stubbs had already raised the bar at Oxford, and Frederic W. Maitland, when he succeeded Seeley at Cambridge as professor of History, raised it higher. After publishing his first book, *The Political Thought of Plato and Aristotle*, in 1906, for example, Barker, then a lecturer in History at Oxford, wrote, "I fear that whatever I do [in the future] will not be in the domain of history. Nobody would take me seriously if I wrote history after having given myself as a writer in political science."[19] We should notice, however, that the sharpening divide between historians and political scientists that opened up along the fissure between past history and presently viable political principle had different consequences in England and the United States. Barker remained in the School of Modern History at Oxford, and later, the School of History at Cambridge. In the United States, where professionalization along functional lines was becoming the norm, the diverging relationship of historians and political scientists to the pastness of the past precipitated a professional break between them, resulting in separate professional associations and inaugurating a trend over the next decades to separate university departments.

[18] See James T. Kloppenberg, *Uncertain Victory: Social Democracy and Progressivism in European and American Thought, 1870–1920* (New York: Oxford University Press, 1986), chap. 3; James Farr, "John Dewey and American Political Science," *American Journal of Political Science* 43 (April 1999): 520–41; Peter Novick, *That Noble Dream: The "Objectivity Question" and the American Historical Profession* (Cambridge: Cambridge University Press, 1988), chap. 9; Ian Tyrrell, *The Absent Marx: Class Analysis and Liberal History in Twentieth-Century America* (New York: Greenwood Press, 1986), chap. 1; Christopher Parker, *The English Historical Tradition since 1850* (Edinburgh: John Donald, 1990), 9–13.

[19] Stapleton, *Englishness*, 43.

Equally if not more important to the new historicism was the rise of a new liberalism. As Blaas emphasizes, the change in liberal politics was crucial in Britain. Spurred by a series of crises in democratic governance and calling on the modern need for efficiency, New Liberal reformers turned against the past, seeking to free the present from, in the words of the young legal reformer Maitland, "the accumulated rubbish of the ages."[20] In the United States, too, it was the new generation of Progressives who argued that efficiency and reform required a break with the past. No theme was more prominent among Progressive social scientists than criticism of the outmoded eighteenth-century forms in which Americans tried to deal with twentieth-century problems.

Still, the Progressive attack on the legacy of the past was necessarily selective, for liberals had also to defend their inheritance against socialism on the left; in that context, Maitland found in the medieval community the roots of a continuous English tradition of individual freedom, not a communal anticipation of socialism. As historians since Blaas have pointed out, Maitland and his generation continued to reverence English institutions and liberty and to ascribe a special, generic character to the English nation.[21] Ernest Barker, for example, had no difficulty accepting Maitland's critique of anachronism and at the same time continuing to rest an optimistic view of England's future on English national character. Much the same could be said of American historians and political scientists. They wanted to reform, rather than abrogate, America's inherited democratic institutions. Woodrow Wilson confessed that he retained a keen appreciation for "the institutions of my own day which seem to me, in an historical sense, intensely and essentially reasonable, though of course in no sense *final*."[22] And the Americans, too, continued their allegiance to the special character and significance of their own nation. Both English and American exceptionalism might be subjected more fully to the uncertainties of history, but they survived into the twentieth century.

The kinds of political science produced under this new liberal historicist regime thus continued to justify both continuity and change, but change became the operative theme. Changes in historical conditions acted as a wedge, separating political institutions, practices, and ideas that fit current conditions from those now outmoded. At the same time, the continuing assumption of historical progress added legitimacy to the newest forms brought forth by the latest conditions. The new historicism also

[20] Blaas, *Continuity and Anachronism*, 244.
[21] J. W. Burrow, *Whigs and Liberals: Continuity and Change in English Political Thought* (Oxford: Clarendon Press, 1988); Jann, *Art and Science*, epilogue and 259 n. 57; Stapleton, *Englishness*, 35; Parker, *English Historical Tradition*, introduction.
[22] Ross, *Origins*, 264.

helped to turn political studies away from the evolutionary-comparative method and in a more functionalist direction. What was important now was not constructing a chain of continuity and a taxonomy of its forms, but an account of the new forms necessitated by changing conditions. Some of the most notable works of the era, Wallas's *The Great Society* (1914), Frank Goodnow's *Politics and Administration* (1900), and Charles Beard's *An Economic Interpretation of the Constitution* (1913), all, in different ways, pursued that purpose.

We can get a good sense of the way political scientists in the early twentieth century used history by looking at two political scientists, one in England and one in the United States, both born in 1874, both centrally located, up-and-coming young authors in their Progressive and Edwardian worlds, and both trained primarily as political theorists: Charles Merriam and Ernest Barker.[23] Early in their careers, both wrote histories of the political thought of their respective countries, a genre invented in both countries primarily to satisfy the pedagogical needs of the new discipline.[24] And both books were organized around the progressive movement of history, accented by changed conditions.

Barker's *Political Thought in England from Herbert Spencer to the Present Day* (1915) began with the context of 1848 European revolutions and laissez-faire ideas and quickly moved to the 1870s, when "times were changed, and the creed was also changed with the times." The new philosophy "needed" was the idealism of Green, which showed "the vital relation between the life of the individual and the life of the community." By the end of the century, collectivism had triumphed in social, policy and in nationalism, but by 1915 "new forces" were at work again, leading to a new emphasis on the rights of groups and efforts to "discredit the state."[25] Throughout, a mix of economic, social, and political factors, as well as the attitudes they engendered, constituted the historical forces of change.

Barker secured political principle in this changing historical world by more than just the underlying assumption of progress. A graduate of Oxford "Greats" and author of a study of Plato and Aristotle, Barker limited change in part by grounding English history in ancient principle. The seeming revolution in ideas effected by Green's idealism was "only a restoration; and what is restored is simply the *Republic of Plato*." Indeed, "[t]he

---

[23] On Merriam, see Barry D. Karl, *Charles Merriam and the Study of Politics* (Chicago: University of Chicago Press, 1974); and Ross, *Origins*. On Barker, see Stapleton, *Englishness*.

[24] Although Gunnell, *Descent of Political Theory*, argues that the genre is a characteristically American invention, the evidence suggests it is equally a British one and equally a product of pedagogical need. See his 56–57, 100, 291 n. 57; and for the British case, Stapleton, *Englishness*, 62; and Stefan Collini, *Public Moralists: Political Thought and Intellectual Life in Britain, 1850–1930* (Oxford: Clarendon Press, 1991), 248–51.

[25] Barker, *Political Thought in England*, 9–10, 249.

influence of Plato and Aristotle has been peculiarly deep in England" because their texts have been central to "the curriculum of the oldest and
most important branch of studies in Oxford" and have educated generations of students who have "enforced" these truths "in the world."[26]

Equally important, Barker secured these truths by philosophy. Political
philosophy, and by implication, political science, was fundamentally a normative study. History could explain the raison d'être of institutions geneti-
cally, but like other empirical studies, such as biology, economics, or psychology, it was only an adjunct to philosophical inquiry, which alone could
provide the true moral and rational causes of human conduct.[27] Thus,
historical sequence did not entirely determine the organizational structure
of Barker's book, but was modified by the different disciplines or modes
of inquiry contributing to political theory. Green and idealism preceded
Spencer and positivism, primarily so the latter—and indeed all that followed—could be criticized by the former. "If [Green's] principles are true,
each age can progressively interpret their meaning to suit its own needs."
History and Reason vied for primacy throughout Barker's text, though at
the end, in tune with the new historical consciousness, he opted for the
endless vitality, and endless uncertainty, of historical change: political philosophy "grows on the uncertainty of human affairs; it grows on the inade-
quacy of its own successive attempts to explain them."[28]

Merriam's two histories of American political ideas inhabit more fully
the progressive historical world. Trained by Burgess and by William A.
Dunning, a historian of political theory—a less philosophical training
than at Oxford—Merriam also lacked Barker's philosophical inclination
or depth. His first book in 1903, a short history of American political
theory, showed that political ideas in America changed with a changing
history, from their Puritan roots to the English liberal individualism of
the Revolution and the more democratic forms of Jefferson and Jackson,
to the fundamentally different theory of Lieber and the Civil War nation-
alists, who abandoned the idea of the social contract and natural rights
and based the state on the organic, evolutionary character of the nation.
The tendency throughout was toward increasing democracy. The "State"
was just a systematic rendering of "the people," and the political scientists' concern for concentrated power made the government more responsible to the people. If Barker turned to an elite educated in Whig history
and classical philosophy to secure principle in changing times, for Merriam it was the democratic sentiment of the people that dictated the direc-

[26] Ibid., 11, 24.
[27] Ibid., 12, 17.
[28] Ibid., 58, 251.

tion of history. This left him in some doubt, however, when he had to admit that the rejection of natural rights was "a scientific tendency rather than a popular movement."[29]

Almost two decades later, Merriam's *American Political Ideas: Studies in the Development of American Political Thought, 1865–1917* (1920) reflected the same historical understanding, though his doubts were now much sharper. The novelty and confusion of these decades was uppermost, largely because the conflict between conservatives, liberals, and collectivists was highlighted and because changing economic, social, and political conditions were more deeply etched. Merriam had to end the period with the forces of progress still embattled. In the systematic study of politics, considerable advances had been made—he called the social-economic interpretation of history one of the most important advances of political science in this period. "The influence of class was relatively strong," however, "and the influence of modern scientific method relatively weak." Likewise, "[t]he ideals of democracy during this time were only imperfectly represented by its institutions and by their actual operation."[30] Still, democracy was preserved by the "American spirit" and national ideals. America's democratic government and her "persistent advocacy of high ideals of democracy, liberty and equality" remained her "greatest gift to humanity." Beyond that national spirit, Merriam's democracy, more than Barker's idealist community, was at the mercy of history. The book ended appropriately on a restatement of faith in national progress phrased awkwardly as a question.[31]

It is worth noting another similarity and difference. In 1915, Barker ended his text with the rise of Pluralism, a new current in English political thinking that argued for the independent sovereignty of social groups such as churches and trades unions—against what now seemed the overbearing central, national state. Merriam's 1920 text made no mention of Pluralism, though it in fact presented a vibrant picture of social-economic politics; in the American style, however, classes were labeled "groups," and it was class conflict that most challenged politics. For Merriam, a strong central state that could moderate class conflict was still the goal of politics, not the empowerment of social groups. Indeed, unlike the case in Britain, the assumption of political thinkers since Tocqueville had been that in the United States society was far stronger than the state. Thus, as John Gunnell argues, the English concept of Pluralism fit awkwardly with

---

[29] Charles E. Merriam, *A History of American Political Theories* (New York: Macmillan, 1903); quotations at 325, 332.

[30] Charles E. Merriam, *American Political Ideas: Studies in the Development of American Political Thought, 1865–1917* (New York: Macmillan, 1920), 328–31, 470.

[31] Ibid., 470–73.

American conditions, despite Harold Laski's effort to blend it with pluralistic concepts of American society.[32] Although political theorists discussed
single and plural "sovereignty," the pluralism that developed in American
political science from Bentley to the behavioralists did not so much confer
sovereignty upon social groups, as dissolve government into the interaction of social groups.

Thus far I have sketched out the commonalities and differences that
shaped Anglo-American political science along the dimensions of intellectual and professional affiliation, liberal politics, and historical consciousness. I want finally to turn to the conceptions of science at work during
this period, a theme that will tie many of these threads together and bring
this chapter to a close by anticipating the interwar and midcentury periods.
   The formation of political science was, on both sides of the Atlantic, a
project intended to wield the authority of science. At least since 1800,
"science" had denoted a learned and systematic field of study, applied to
theology or law as easily as to explorations of nature. Despite the way-
ward and fragmentary forms that political study assumed in the nineteenth century, it could claim or aspire to become, in these terms, a science. Over the course of the century, however, as the power and authority
of the natural sciences grew, they were increasingly taken as the most
fully developed and exemplary instances of the genre. The characteristics
ascribed to the natural sciences became the hallmarks of any study that
called itself a science. Theorists of positivist methods like August Comte
and John Stuart Mill urged conformance to some formulation of the natural sciences' inductive and deductive methods and forged on that basis an
invidious distinction between true sciences and other studies that did not
achieve their certainty. Many thinkers, however, continued through the
nineteenth and on into the twentieth century to define the characteristics
of natural science, and hence of the genre of science, loosely or selectively
enough to allow the inclusion of such subjects as law, politics, and history,
if not any longer theology.[33]
   Most nineteenth-century social scientists also integrated science, ethics,
and social action. They were, in Stefan Collini's fine analysis, "public
moralists."[34] The concept of progress allowed historians and evolutionists

---

[32] On English concepts of pluralism, see Burrow, *Whigs and Liberals*, chap. 6; Isaac
Kramnick and Barry Sheerman, *Harold Laski: A Life on the Left* (London: Hamish Hamilton, 1993), chap. 5; Bernard Zylstra, *From Pluralism to Collectivism: The Development
of Harold Laski's Political Thought* (Assen, The Netherlands: Koninklijke Van Gorcum,
1968).

[33] See "Introduction: Writing the History of Social Science," in Porter and Ross, *The
Modern Social Sciences*.

[34] Collini, *Public Moralists*.

to embed their values in the advance of history. Even adherents of John Stuart Mill's positivist separation of science from the art of its application in policy generally found little difficulty in crossing the line. For others, philosophical idealism, lingering conceptions of natural law, or faith in the divine underpinnings of the universe kept alive belief in, as the American sociologist Albion Small put it, the "moral economy of human affairs," making the normative and ethical tasks of social study its highest fruit.[35] In all these ways, a scientific study of "what is" was closely linked to, even if it could be analytically separated from, the tasks of normative projection of ideals and application to policies.

For Mugwump and late Victorian political scientists, science required specialization, and becoming a science was central to their formation of a distinct academic field. Equally basic was the version of objectivity held by scholars of history, politics, and law—impartiality, even-handedness in dealing with controverted subjects. To insure impartiality, Bryce did not include Britain in his comparative study of democratic governments, but most did not go that far, believing that the conscientious scholar could adopt a stance of impartiality so long as all sides were treated fairly. Science, argued the American Jesse Macy, was a method of communal discipline that banished "all liars, blunderers, and all who had a disposition to believe a false report."[36] Finally, method was an important marker of science. For the Mugwump generation, scientific method generally meant the empirical methods recommended for the moral sciences by Mill or, more specifically, the empirical method of historical science associated with Leopold von Ranke and, often intertwined with it, the evolutionary-comparative method that originated within biology and anthropology. Burgess, for example, was particularly proud that in using the comparative method, he used a method "which has been found so productive in the domain of Natural Science."[37]

Virtually unremarked by the Mugwump political scientists, however, more sophisticated versions of neopositivism were gaining authority, and the standards of scientific method were beginning to tighten. Philosophers of science and social science—most influentially for the Anglo-American world, Karl Pearson—worked to dismantle the developmental and evolutionary assumptions of nineteenth-century positivism; to pare away metaphysical and normative assumptions from scientific concepts; to make objective methods, chiefly quantification, the hallmark of scientific method;

---

[35] Quoted in Ross, *Origins*, 347.

[36] Tulloch, *Bryce's "American Commonwealth,"* chap. 3; Ross, *Origins*, 258.

[37] Collini, Winch, and Burrow, *Noble Science of Politics*, chap. 7; Ross, *Origins*, chap. 3; John W. Burgess, *Political Science and Comparative Constitutional Law* (Boston: Ginn, 1890), 1:vi.

and to make method, in turn, the hallmark of science. It is at this point, I would argue, that the differences between British and American political science began to deepen. During the Progressive and Edwardian era, American political scientists began to respond more positively to the neopositivist call for "real" scientific methods than did the British. It was just a beginning: a positivistic emphasis on methods became influential in American political science only after World War I and did not dominate the field until after World War II. Still, after 1920, when influential political scientists in the United States launched a concerted effort to adopt the new methodology, British political science remained within much the same mold as before the Great War.[38]

Why did the Americans, more frequently than the British, begin to move toward neopositivism during the Progressive era? A major factor, surely, was their greater degree of professionalization and greater reliance on professional, rather than class, authority. In American universities, unlike the case in England, philosophical supports for timeless principles in idealism or commonsense realism quickly faded after the turn of the century. Both in the universities, where political science had to compete with the other new social sciences to gain legitimacy, and in the public arena, where their prescriptions had to compete with myriad political voices, the presumed impersonality of rules of calculation was the clearest warrant of objectivity, scientific expertise, and professionalism.[39] Another important factor in the American turn to positivism lay in American exceptionalism. The English had learned to entrust their special identity to the slow workings of history. In the logic of American exceptionalism, however, it was not the workings of history, but the founding institutions that made the special character of America. The Republic was resistant to historical change; nature and natural law were its surer guarantors.

We can see these factors at work in the kind of conclusions American political scientists drew from their deepening appreciation of historical contingency after 1890. Macy in 1893 announced that if the Constitution or Magna Carta meant very different things in the past, then what was important about them was "what is believed and acted upon today." Moreover, history had been perverted by political bias. His solution was to turn history into a "genuine" science, capable of producing laws and able to forecast the future.[40] Over the next decades, however, history

[38] On the move toward scientism in the United States, see Ross, *Origins*, chaps. 8–10; Ross, "Changing Contours." On the persistence of prewar patterns in British political science, see Collini. Winch, and Burrow, *Noble Science of Politics*, epilogue; Hayward, "British Approaches to Politics."

[39] See Theodore M. Porter, *Trust in Numbers: The Pursuit of Objectivity in Science and Public Life* (Princeton, NJ: Princeton University Press, 1995).

[40] Ross, *Origins*, 286.

faded as a site for the construction of a predictive science. Historians themselves made it clear that history could not produce such laws, and if political scientists did not read the new philosophy of science, they imbibed some of its thrust from their colleagues in sociology and psychology. As James Farr emphasizes, ties with history remained strong through the 1920s, especially among the older generation who continued in the framework of historico-politics, but there is also considerable evidence of a change in direction. Having established a separate professional identity, political science was free to forge links with the other independent social sciences. The four major political science textbooks of the Progressive era declared political science to be a field within the larger domain of sociology, not of history.[41]

For a number of prominent political scientists in the United States, science now offered a road to the fixed principles history could no longer provide. Frank Goodnow looked to his sociological colleague Franklin Giddings for clues to timeless political principles and Henry Jones Ford turned to Darwinian biology to find "universal principles permanent in their applicability" instead of just "impressions received from 'accidents of development.' " The chief spokesman for a new scientific direction during the Progressive years was A. Lawrence Lowell, professor of "Existing Political Systems," president of Harvard, and president of the APSA in 1910. Trained in mathematics, Lowell believed that politics was an inexact science, but a positive science nonetheless. His comparative study of modern governments expressed the ethnocentric normative assumptions of the comparative method without its apparatus, but his most original work was a statistical study of party voting in England and the United States that was hailed by Goodnow as a "shining example." Lowell urged his colleagues to abandon the past for current function and libraries for "first-hand" observation of politics and to compile, arrange, and classify data using statistics. To become a science it was necessary to think scientifically, to uncover the causes of political phenomena. Without using the later terminology, Lowell envisioned political science as the study of separable "factors" or "variables" under different political conditions in the hope of formulating reliable causal laws. It is not surprising that Bryce, with his richer sense of historical complexity, warned the Americans not to seek a kind of scientific certainty that political science, grounded as it was in history, could not give.[42]

----

[41] Ibid., 282–300, and more generally, part 4.

[42] Ibid., quotations at 288, 291, 293. Lowell gave a number of examples of the kind of studies political scientists should pursue, such as studying the existence or nonexistence of political bosses in different locations, the extent of party voting under different suffrage conditions, and the variable lengths of actual officeholding. See A. L. Lowell, "The Physiology of Politics," *American Political Science Review* 4 (February 1910): 1–15.

Three

The Origins of a Historical Political Science in Late Victorian and Edwardian Britain

SANDRA M. DEN OTTER

"IT WERE FAR BETTER, as things now stand, to be charged with heresy, or even to be found guilty of petty larceny, than to fall under the suspicion of lacking historical-mindedness, or of questioning the universal validity of the historical method," grumbled the jurist A. V. Dicey in 1885. Paradoxically and despite his own frequently expressed disdain for what he regarded to be an antiquarian pursuit, Dicey is best remembered for his own "historical mindedness." The immense popularity of his *Law and Opinion in the Nineteenth Century* attested to at least a contemporary conviction that Dicey had captured the mind of the past century, as it swung from an age of individualism to an age of collectivism. Dicey was of course right to note the enthusiasm of his generation for things historical. Since the mid-nineteenth century, the British public had become avid consumers of history, and history vied with science as an authoritative arbitrator of a bewildering range of issues. Property rights were adjudicated in the misty distance of Teutonic village communities; scholarly controversy about matrilineal or patrilineal primitive societies became caught up in reforms of married women's property. The political economist Walter Bagehot used his podium as editor of the newly founded *Economist* to interpret contemporary problems through historical parallels. The investigations of Victorian historians into the constitutional history of England became part of political conversation, seemingly confirming Britain's unique traditions of liberty and representative government. Following in the wake of these powerful Whiggish arguments, the new discipline of political science, as it began to take on a rather amorphous identity in the 1880s, was often elided with history. For the constitutional historian E. A. Freeman, "History Is Past Politics; Politics Is Present History" (a doctrine engraved above the entrance to Historical and Political Studies at Johns Hopkins), and according to the historian J. R. Seeley's rather unhappy jingle, "[H]istory without political science has no fruit;

political science without history has no root."[1] When a chair of Political Science was finally established in Cambridge in 1926, it was given to the faculty of History and not to the faculty of Economics and Politics—for by this time at Cambridge, political science had become intricately connected to the study of history.

But this close relationship between history and politics was not uncontroversial or uncontested. Some proponents of the new discipline of politics were much less inclined to use history to illuminate their studies. For the moral and political philosopher Henry Sidgwick, who helped to carve out the new discipline, politics ought to be an analytical science that sought out first principles. Even though his lectures to Cambridge undergraduates established a historical focus to the teaching of political science at Cambridge that was to continue well into the twentieth century, his widely read and influential textbook of politics, *Elements of Politics*, was largely ahistorical. Years later, when writing Sidgwick's obituary and surveying his contribution to the study of politics, the intellectual aristocrat Leslie Stephen could regret this neglect of history: "I confess to my mind that it is impossible to discuss political questions effectively without constant reference to historical development, and that from the absence of such reference, Sidgwick's book is rather a collection of judicious remarks than a decided help in the formation of political theory."[2] A historical perspective was also absent in another important founder of the discipline: as one of the first lecturers on politics at the newly founded London School of Economics and later the first chair of Politics at the University of London, the Fabian Graham Wallas only obliquely used history as a tool to investigate politics. He elevated the classical world as a shadowy beacon throughout his writings but more as a normative argument about how modern life might best be organized; the insights of social psychology formed a much more pivotal grounding than history did for his science of politics. Neither did the philosophical study of the state and of political society advanced by the idealists incorporate a rigorously historical dimension; it was anchored in the history of political ideas rather than of the English constitution or institutions. However authoritative the new historicist turn of the late nineteenth century seems, biology, psychology, physics, evolutionary theory, and urban studies all offered alternatives (at times complementary) to history as a framework for the study of politics.

---

[1] Bryce said of Freeman's highly partisan approach to history, "Freeman was apt to go beyond his own dictum about history and politics, for he sometimes made history present politics as well as past." James Bryce, *Studies in Contemporary Biography* (New York: Macmillan, 1903), 274.

[2] Leslie Stephen, "Obituary of Henry Sidgwick," *Mind*, n.s., 11, no. 37 (1901): 1–17, 16. See Henry Sidgwick, "The Historical Method," *Mind* 11, no. 42 (1886): 203–19.

Furthermore, the boundaries between history, law, philosophy, economics, politics, and the new sociology were loose and flexible: in the
absence of strong institutional and professional bodies, this flexibility
lived on and militated against any doctrinaire definition of the discipline
of political studies. Institutional roots came later to Britain than to the
United States: although political science was taught at the London School
of Economics from its beginning in 1895, and political science had been
taught at Cambridge since the 1870s as part of the History Tripos, the
first chair of Political Science was not founded at Cambridge until 1926.
At Oxford, it was not until 1920 that Philosophy, Politics, and Economics
(PPE) was established. In contrast, history had become much more professionalized and at an earlier point. The term "discipline" gives a false coherence to the conglomerate of studies denoted by "political science" or
"political studies" at the end of the nineteenth century. Even the name
"political science" did not accurately describe the study of politics for
many, who like Bernard Bosanquet or Ernest Barker, had philosophical
objections against positivism in most of its forms. The mingling of Victorian intellectuals of various kinds in the flourishing liberal reform movement of the midcentury also facilitated a diversity of approaches to the
study of politics. As intellectuals like Goldwin Smith, Frederic Harrison,
Leslie Stephen, A. V. Dicey, James Bryce, and others collectively deliber-
ated about such common political causes as defense of the North in the
American Civil War and university and parliamentary reform, they were
collectively shaping the study of politics.

In this chapter, I briefly analyze some of the primary strands of the turn-
of-the-century debate about historical approaches to politics. I begin with
the grand narratives of the mid- to late nineteenth century: the Whig historians of Teutonic greatness and J. R. Seeley, who so vividly argued for
the merging of history and politics, and then consider how the idealists,
political theorists, historical economists, and others variously discerned
the relationship between history and politics. I trace the emergence of a
modernist empiricism at the turn of the century that challenged these
grand narratives of the previous century. While sharing common ground
with the Whig historians, the legal historians of the twentieth century
pursued a much more atomistic and empirical analysis and were much
more guarded in the contemporary uses to which they put the political
past. The study of political administration, comparative politics, and
other investigations undertaken by the Webbs and fellow scholars at the
London School of Economics and Politics are another important vein running counter (though at some times converging) with the grand narratives.
I examine the contestation between varieties of positivism in late-nineteenth-century Britain, particularly evolutionary positivism and modernist empiricism, and argue that the Whig tradition and idealist tradition,

with their heavily normative and classical orientation, had a curiously resilient hold on political studies in Britain.

Developmental Historicism and Political Knowledge

The new political science came out of the historically minded culture of the midcentury. Historical mindedness spilled beyond the confines of the universities and was reflected in reading, popular aesthetics, local societies, and travel.[3] Historians like Walter Bagehot, William Stubbs, J. R. Green, and E. A. Freeman, as well as evolutionary theorists and anthropologists, had strengthened and updated a long-standing Whig tradition that throughout the eighteenth and nineteenth centuries had appeared in numerous different disguises.[4] The term *Whig* incorporates a diverse medley of positions: initially the term denoted a political identity associated with liberal aristocratic families, and it was still used in the 1880s to describe landed liberal families who opposed Home Rule and who combined uncomfortably with Chamberlain's Liberal Unionists. But increasingly "Whig" referred less to a parliamentary bloc and more to a loosely defined tradition.[5] Three primary themes in this Whig tradition—continuity, development, and freedom—appear and reappear throughout the political histories of the late nineteenth century, and these three themes define the developmental historicism of the mid- to late nineteenth century that was so pivotal to British political science. By continuity, the Whigs meant that successive historical epochs were connected by a continuous thread, by an underlying unity of experience. As Freeman contested in his Rede Lecture of 1872: "European history, from its first glimmerings to

---

[3] See Rosemary Mitchell, *Picturing the Past: English History in Text and Image, 1830–1870* (Oxford: Oxford University Press, 2000).

[4] See Stephen Bann, *The Clothing of Clio: A Study of the Representation of History in Nineteenth Century Britain and France* (Cambridge: Cambridge University Press, 1984); John W. Burrow, *Evolution and Society: A Study in Victorian Social Theory* (Cambridge: Cambridge University Press, 1966); Rosemary Jann, *The Art and Science of Victorian History* (Columbus: Ohio State University Press, 1985); Stefan Collini, Donald Winch, and John Burrow, *That Noble Science of Politics: A Study in Nineteenth-Century Intellectual History* (Cambridge: Cambridge University Press, 1983), chaps. 6 and 7; Peter J. Bowler, *The Invention of Progress: The Victorians and the Past* (Oxford: Blackwell, 1989).

[5] P.B.M. Blaas, *Continuity and Anachronism: Parliamentary and Constitutional Development in Whig Historiography and the Anti-Whig Reaction between 1890 and 1930* (The Hague: Martinus Nijhoff, 1978); Peter Mandler, *Aristocratic Government in the Age of Reform: Whigs and Liberals, 1830–1852* (Oxford: Oxford University Press, 1990); Peter Mandler, *History and National Life* (London: Profile Books, 2002); Christopher Parker, *The English Historical Tradition since 1850* (Edinburgh: John Donald, 1990); Mark Phillips, *Society and Sentiment: Genres of Historical Writing in Britain, 1740–1820* (Princeton, NJ: Princeton University Press, 2000).

our own day, is one unbroken drama, no part of which can be rightly understood without reference to the other parts which come before it or after it."[6] This was a narrative of continuous national development, in which disparate social groups were brought together and even distant events became "bridges to the present moment."[7] Whigs interpreted historical continuity and development from the perspective of present-day dilemmas, and this presentist orientation led Whig historians to search for the origins of modern freedom and to interpret the distant past as culminating in the present. By development, Whigs most often did not refer specifically to theories of evolution propounded variously by Lamarck, Darwin, or Herbert Spencer, though the evolutionary culture of the mid-nineteenth century fostered an awareness of continuity and incremental change. Rather, Whigs posited as an article of faith that the national narrative was a story of incremental development of greater liberty and freedom. Stubbs, Freeman, and Green all wrote histories of the English constitution, and though they offer different interpretations, all accounts tell a similar story of the victory of liberty over tyranny. For these historians the victory was in some senses assured, though all dwelled on the dangerous challenges to liberty and the precariousness of progress. Stubbs ended his version of the constitutional history of England with this confident encomium: "Weak as the fourteenth century was, the fifteenth is weaker still: more futile, more bloody, more immoral; yet out of it emerges, in spite of all, the truer and brighter day, the season of more general conscious life, higher longings, more forbearing, more sympathetic, purer, riper liberty."[8] These histories described a Whiggish development of freedom: for Stubbs, the organic growth of institutions, like the shire and the hundreds, carried and preserved freedoms; Freeman imagined a cyclical pattern in history that described not so much progress as restoration or resurrection in which the past was always revived and restored: for example, modern communication and transportation networks had enabled the revival of both the federated political structure of ancient Greece, except on a much larger scale, and the Greek ideal of active citizenship.[9] Even Freeman, who tended to dwell more on the de-

---

[6] Edward A. Freeman, "The Unity of History," in *Comparative Politics* (London: Macmillan, 1873), 306.

[7] Phillips, *Society and Sentiment*, 248.

[8] William Stubbs, *The Constitutional History of England in Its Origin and Development* (Oxford: Clarendon Press, 1874–78), 2: 656.

[9] Edward A. Freeman, *Greater Greece and Greater Britain* (London: Macmillan, 1886), 15, 6; Freeman used this notion of the recurrence of Greek political structures to argue for the plausibility of imperial federation, 59–60; John W. Burrow, *A Liberal Descent: Victorian Historians and the English Past* (Cambridge: Cambridge University Press, 1981), 225, 6.

generation and decadence of specific historical epochs, did not doubt the ultimate victory of progress over degeneration.

The history of the constitution became a demonstration of the grandeur of the British nation, and the new Whig historicism was stoutly fastened to the sails of national greatness. Racial assumptions sometimes underpinned this confidence, for it was the Aryan and the Teutonic tribes who had uniquely captured and preserved the exact synthesis of economic vitality and political liberty.[10] Freeman found in the early Teutonic society and in the Aryan race and institutions the groundwork of English liberty, freedom, and representative government. Britain alone had preserved and continued these ancient Teutonic traditions, and so had refined the constitutional nation-state: "Alone among the political assemblies of the greater states of Europe, the Parliament of England can trace its unbroken descent from the Teutonic institutions of the earliest times. . . . No other nation, as a nation, can show the same unbroken continuity of political being."[11] Borrowing from von Maurer and others, the Whig historians identified the German mark community as the principal Teutonic institution that preserved political liberty.[12] The Saxons brought the mark community with them to England, and there it became the root of free and democratic government. J. R. Green eulogized: "[I]t is with reverence such as is stirred by the sight of the head-waters of some mighty river that one looks back to these tiny moots, where the men of the village met to order the village life and the village industry, as their descendents, the men of a later England, meet in Parliament at Westminster, to frame laws and do justice for the great Empire which has sprung from this little body of farmer-commonwealths in Sleswick."[13] The enthusiasm for Anglo-Saxonism in the 1870s and 1880s crossed the Atlantic; the jurist and politician James Bryce eulogized the common Anglo-Saxon legal inheritance shared by the United States and Britain, and the homogeneity of the Anglo-Saxon race was regarded as the bedrock for their democratic institutions.[14] Others like the Positivist and social democrat Frederic Harrison were more criti-

---

[10] John Richard Green, *The Making of England* (London: Macmillan, 1882); John Richard Green, *The Conquest of England* (London: Macmillan, 1883); John Richard Green, *A Short History of the English People* (London: Macmillan, 1884).

[11] Freeman, *Comparative Politics*, 30.

[12] For differing assessments of the strength of continental, especially German, influences on British historicism, see Burrow, *A Liberal Descent*, 119–25; Keith Tribe, "The Historicization of Political Economy?" in *British and German Historiography, 1750–1950*, ed. Benedikt Stuchtey and Peter Wende (Oxford: Oxford University Press, 1998), 211–28.

[13] Green cited in Burrow, *A Liberal Descent*, 125.

[14] Richard A. Cosgrove, *Our Lady the Common Law: An Anglo-American Legal Community, 1870–1930* (New York: New York University Press, 1987), 66–75.

cal of this "extravagant enthusiasm for the Saxon Englishmen and their influence on the world."[15]

While mid-Victorian historicists made grandiloquent claims about the continuity and unity of history, they nevertheless increasingly adopted positivist and empirical methods. This turn toward a more empirical method was in part influenced by the flourishing of the natural sciences in the midcentury and to German innovations in historical, ethnological, and linguistic research, specifically to the work of von Ranke and Savigny. But it also owed much to an indigenous tradition of ethical and evolutionary positivism that pared down the more elaborate positivism of Auguste Comte with its predictive powers and its religious flourishes. Mingling with a long-standing predilection for utilitarian knowledge, which was expressed so clearly in the National Association for the Promotion of Social Science, impatience with clerical politics at the ancient universities, and a turning away from schools of intuitionist thought, this evolutionary positivism shaped expectations for a rigorous, empirical historical research.[16] The grand Whig narratives were to be built on what Stubbs called the "chronologies of minutiae."[17] Regarding a political constitution as "a specimen to be studied, classified, and labelled," Freeman pursued these minutiae to an even greater degree than Stubbs, prompting the positivist Frederic Harrison to protest that the reader sank under the weight of extraneous detail, and nonetheless came no closer to a science of history.[18]

The move toward a more empirical history based on the excavation of original documents, however, did not detain the Whig historians from advancing overarching theories about liberty and development or from connecting history to present politics. History had presentist political preoccupations. Whig historians used historical precedent to animate contemporary political liberalism and to defend representative democracy against critics like H. S. Maine, who used comparative history to challenge democratic government. Freeman appealed to Greek and Roman

---

[15] Frederic Harrison, "The Historical Method of Professor Freeman," *Nineteenth Century* 44 (1898): 799.

[16] See John Stuart Mill, *Auguste Comte and Positivism* (London: Truebner, 1865); Lawrence Goldman, *Science, Reform and Politics in Victorian Britain: The Social Science Association, 1857–1886* (Cambridge: Cambridge University Press, 2002); T. R. Wright, *The Religion of Humanity: The Impact of Comtean Positivism on Victorian Britain* (Cambridge: Cambridge University Press, 1986).

[17] Stubbs to Freeman, April 13, 1858, in *The Letters of William Stubbs, Bishop of Oxford, 1825–1901*, ed. William Holden Hutton (London: Constable, 1904), 42. See also William Stubbs, "On the Purposes and Methods of Historical Study," in *Seventeen Lectures on the Study of Medieval and Modern History* (Oxford: Clarendon Press, 1886), 81.

[18] Freeman, *Comparative Politics*, 23. Harrison grumbled: "Our histories have to be constructed on the methods of a German savant hunting for microbes with a microscope." "Historical Method," 801.

history to challenge assumptions about imperial federation, which in the late 1880s and 1890s had become an urgent political issue, and to argue for Britain's duty as the inheritor of the Teutonic constitutional descent to forge links among English-speaking peoples.[19] This was consistent with a more widely held conviction that empirical history liberated judicious citizens from party spirit and enabled them to discern desirable policies.[20]

It was J. R. Seeley, Regius Professor of History at Cambridge, who most vividly and powerfully fused history and the study of politics, and who established that the political science studied at Cambridge for several successive decades was essentially historical. Sidgwick described the subject that Seeley taught in Cambridge as "political science—regarded not merely as a subject cognate to history, for which the study of history is preparation, but as a method of studying history itself."[21] Together with Sidgwick, who was much less historically minded, Seeley made an inductive science of politics an important part of the History Tripos when they were established in Cambridge in 1873. Seeley's history had scientific pretensions: he aimed at a practical science of politics that would enable leaders, administrators, and citizens to understand Britain's role in the world and would enable them to govern her affairs well. Such was his faith in an inductive science of historical facts that he believed that politicians would surely follow its findings.[22] While Freeman, Stubbs, and Green had not been enthusiastic borrowers of scientific method, science was setting the agenda for multiple strands of inquiry.[23] Collini highlights the attention to taxonomy in the historical and comparative methods, "popular assemblies and royal vetoes treated like the vertebrae and vestigial fins of comparative anatomy."[24] The impact of evolutionary science

[19] Freeman, "Imperial Federation," in *Greater Greece and Greater Britain*, 104–43.

[20] For this common motif, see Stubbs, "Inaugural Lecture," in *Medieval and Modern History*, 19.

[21] Sidgwick, "Preface," in J. R. Seeley, *Introduction to Political Science* (London: Macmillan, 1926; book first published in 1896), v. By 1909 when the History Tripos were reformed, Seeley's view of a scientific survey of political institutions was curtailed: Paper A included a comparative study of political institutions and B covered the history of political thought: Reba N. Soffer, *Discipline and Power: The University, History and the Making of an English Elite, 1870–1930* (Stanford, CA: Stanford University Press, 1994), 73, 74. On Seeley, see Deborah Wormell, *Sir John Seeley and the Uses of History* (Cambridge: Cambridge University Press, 1980); Parker, *English Historical Tradition*; Peter R. H. Slee, *Learning and Liberal Education: The Study of Modern History in the Universities of Oxford, Cambridge, and Manchester, 1800–1914* (Manchester: Machester University Press, 1986).

[22] Wormell, *Sir John Seeley*, 122.

[23] On American parallels, see Dorothy Ross, "The Development of the Social Sciences," in *Discipine and History: Political Science in the United States*, ed. James Farr and Raymond Seidelman (Ann Arbor: University of Michigan Press, 1993), 81–104.

[24] Collini, Burrow, and Winch, *Noble Science of Politics*, 359.

on late Victorian thought and culture was of course pervasive, and the continuity between biological and social evolution extensively debated. Thomas Buckle had regarded his search for the laws of civilization as a form of science, and H. S. Maine in his highly influential *Ancient Law* (1861) had adopted a scientific approach in its emphasis on evolutionary laws. By science, Maine meant "sober research into the primitive history of society and law," as opposed to deductive theories.[25] Science for Seeley was the inductive study of fact and the search for scientific laws. History was governed by laws, discernable by the study of the past; knowledge of these laws also conferred predictive powers.

Seeley grafted the rhetoric of science and technological mastery onto historical knowledge to build a new science of politics that promised sweeping powers to governing elites and to ethical citizens alike. His appeal to science was often more rhetorical than substantive: he did believe that a rigorous empirical investigation of facts was necessary, and he did believe that laws characterized human history, though he also maintained that divine intervention could determine events, and he tended to regard historical law as little more than the uniformities of human nature, true of all people in all time.[26] This is even characteristic of Frederic Harrison's understanding of historical knowledge, his positivist convictions notwithstanding. Like Seeley's, Harrison's science of history was more about the essential qualities of human nature demonstrated through the ages than any scientifically demonstrable "facts" or laws.[27] Seeley's own historical writings were scarcely the product of methodical empirical and inductive research, and he failed to articulate a science of history and politics even though he set himself this goal and even though his writings are littered with nods to the scientific orthodoxies of organicism.[28] But in regarding science as an arbitrator that was happily independent from party politics and partisan alignments, he was reflecting a more widespread concern, shared by John Morley, Leslie Stephen, James Bryce, Frederic Harrison, and others, about the impact of party on the public sensibilities.[29] Seeley counterposed this science of politics to party politics, intimating that the true interest of the nation lay in disinterested investigation, in a "purer political school."[30]

[25] Henry Maine, *Ancient Law: Its Connection with the Early History of Society, and Its Relation to Modern Ideas* (London: Murray, 1861), 3.

[26] Wormell, *Sir John Seeley*, 120–25, 151–55.

[27] Frederic Harrison, *The Meaning of History* (London: Macmillan, 1894), 14–18.

[28] Seeley described states as living organisms, for example.

[29] Julia Stapleton, *Political Intellectuals and Public Identities in Britain since 1850* (Manchester: Manchester University Press, 2001), 13.

[30] John Robert Seeley, "Ethics and Religion," in *Ethics and Religion* (London: Swan Sonnenschein, 1900), 24.

Seeley shifted attention from "the nation" of Freeman and Green to focus almost single-mindedly on "the state." The latter's attention to intellectual milieu, social relations, and so many other factors disappeared in the face of Seeley's overwhelming desire to define how Britain might continue to be a great power. Although Seeley jettisoned aspects of the Whig tradition, he retained its preoccupation with British greatness and its presentist orientation. But he was less confident than Stubbs, Freeman, and Green that Britain's grandeur was secure. Influenced by ideas of degeneration, cognizant of the realpolitik of European rivalries, and impressed by the fragility of Empire, he sought aggressively to bolster the British Empire. For Seeley, the historical and inductive study of politics provided the modern statesman with the tools to manipulate these historical forces and to defend the glorious traditions of Britain.

Seeley's confidence in the historical study of politics was shared by other of his contemporaries. W.E.H. Lecky similarly defended the utility of an inductive study of history for the political life of the nation, in guarding against rash political innovation.[31] James Bryce, the doyen of British and American political science, had long given history a central place in his own legal and political investigations and maintained in a Burkean spirit that an inductive study of politics would help minimize the divisions of party spirit or the excesses of nationalism.[32] He was closely connected to the historians Freeman, J. R. Green, and Acton and was one of the founding members of the first academic historical journal, *English Historical Review*. Elected to the House of Commons in 1880, Bryce throughout his extraordinarily long career as a parliamentarian and diplomat fused an empirical investigation of politics with an active political career. In his 1908 address as president of the American Political Science Association of America, he described the interdependence of history and political science: "Thus political science stands midway between history and politics, between the past and the present. It has drawn its materials from the one, it has to apply them to the other."[33] In a very early statement of this interdependence, in the well-known and influential collection *Essays in Reform* (1867), Bryce had used historical argument to urge the extension of the franchise: history held no forms of government to be absolutely the best, for the effectiveness of each state depended on specific historical circumstances, but history had demonstrated that democratic government best nurtured the vitality of the state and the energy of its citizens.[34] He re-

[31] William E. H. Lecky, *The Political Value of History* (London: Arnold, 1892).

[32] James Bryce, "The Relations of Political Science to History and to Practice," *American Political Science Review* 3 (1909): 15–16.

[33] Bryce, "Relations," 11.

[34] James Bryce, "The Historical Aspect of Democracy," in *Essays in Reform* (London: Macmillan, 1867), 239–78.

turned to this theme more than half a century later in his last work, *Modern Democracies* (1921), again using history to vindicate the superiority of democratic rule. History provided a sure and dependable guide because it laid bare the permanent aspects of human nature, and "[h]uman nature is that basic and ever-present element in the endless flux of social and political phenomena which enables general principles to be determined."[35] Despite these paeans to the neutrality and steadfastness of the historical record, Bryce's work was much less historical than many contemporaries wished, or than he himself claimed. *Modern Democracies* was more a conversational jaunt across numerous countries than a sustained effort to distill the principles of human nature from historical investigation. When Woodrow Wilson reviewed *American Commonwealth* in 1888, he regretted Bryce's neglect of historical argument.[36] But Bryce assumed, rather than deliberately erected, a historical framework for his study of government. He assumed a Whiggish narrative of the development of democratic institutions in an almost self-evident manner. This perspective seemed rather antiquated in the early 1920s, when he was still publishing works in this vein, for by this time modernist empiricism had become more firmly rooted, and the Whig tradition had come under attack.

By the turn of the century, history was becoming increasingly professionalized: this is not to suggest that men and women of leisure did not still write history or that local amateur historical societies did not continue to prosper—but history was being fashioned in professional societies and in the universities to meet standards of scholarship and research. The *English Historical Review* was established in 1886, and appointments to the Regius Professors of History at both Cambridge and Oxford were now made with some reference to historical credentials (this was a break with the past, as Stubbs noted of his predecessors: "I do not find that they were men to whom the study of History, either English or foreign, is in any way indebted.")[37] History enjoyed a luster and success that few other academic disciplines could boast in Britain, certainly not political science or sociology. It is not surprising, then, that the study of politics should have depended on the successes of its cognate discipline. Moreover, in the principal universities, history was conceived of as primarily political: constitutional history remained paramount, even against chal-

---

[35] James Bryce, *Modern Democracies*, 2 vols. (London: Macmillan, 1921), 1:17.

[36] Woodrow Wilson, "Bryce's *American Commonwealth*," *Political Science Quarterly* 4, no. 1 (1889): 153–69; reprinted in Robert C. Brooks, *Bryce's "American Commonwealth": 50th Anniversary* (New York: Macmillan, 1939), 169–88.

[37] Cited in Burrow, *A Liberal Descent*, 98. See Philippa Levine, *The Amateur and the Professional: Antiquarians, Historians and Archaeologists in Victorian Britain, 1838–1886* (Cambridge: Cambridge University Press, 1986); Soffer, *Discipline and Power*.

lenges from the new economic history. This overtly political focus of the study of history reflected the aim of the universities to cultivate a political and administrative elite and foster a knowledgeable and publicly minded citizenry. Constitutional history was a kind of civic education.[38]

Law and History

Counterpoised to the constitutional historians of the Whig tradition were the new analytical and empirical perspectives of the legal historians writing in the 1890s and later who articulated a modernist empiricism and even a neopositivism. F. W. Maitland, F. Pollock, and A. V. Dicey sharply divided their inquiries from the more speculative work of political and legal theorists and formulated an inductive study of law and politics that shaped the new discipline of political studies. Maitland and Pollock, in their survey *The History of English Law*, affirmed: "The philosophical analysis and definition of law belongs, in our judgement, neither to the historical nor to the dogmatic science of law, but to the theoretical part of politics."[39] What followed was a relentlessly nonspeculative account of the evolution of English law that did much to dismantle the certainties of the developmental historicists of the 1870s and 1880s, although both groups believed that the law and legal mindedness was the key to understanding the political past and present. Maitland had studied with Sidgwick; political philosophy had been his first commitment, and he turned to historical studies only by accident; so his careful separation of historical inquiry from the speculative questions of political philosophy is striking. Vinagradoff summed up this approach: "What he wanted most was to trace ideas to their embodiment in facts."[40] Maitland's discovery of historical materials at the Public Record Office had opened a new perspective on the questions of political philosophy. He described a collection of documents, "Pleas of the Crown for the County of Gloucester," thus: "a photograph of English life as it was early in the thirteenth century. . . . We have here, as it were, a section of the body politic which shows just those most vital parts, of which, because they were deep-seated, the soul politic was hardly conscious, the system of local government and police."[41] For

[38] See Soffer, *Discipline and Power*, 33–37; Stapleton, *Political Intellectuals*.

[39] Frederic William Maitland and Frederick Pollock, *The History of English Law before the Time of Edward I*, 2 vols. (Cambridge: Cambridge University Press, 1968; first published in 1895), 1:1. See also Frederick Pollock, *An Introduction to the History of the Science of Politics* (London: Macmillan, 1890), 113–14.

[40] P. Vinogradoff, "Frederic William Maitland," *English Historical Review* 22, no. 86 (1907): 282.

[41] Maitland cited in Alan Macfarlane, *The Making of the Modern World: Visions from the West and East* (London: Palgrave, 2002), 25.

the next two decades, Maitland published exacting studies of medieval law, culminating in 1895 in *The History of English Law before the Time of Edward I* (ostensibly written with Pollock, though Maitland wrote all but the first chapter).

His meticulous excavations of the past led Maitland to envision a past marked by the imprint of human law. He maintained that although law constantly changes and is constantly reworked, there is a continuity that runs between these laws and that "this continuity, this identity, is very real to us."[42] Although this language sounds Whiggish, Maitland departed from the Whig tradition by declining to depict the narrative of lawmaking as the growing liberty of the English subject. The law gained in specificity and in definiteness, but it was not the narrative of an ever-widening compass of liberty. Maitland parted company with many of his contemporaries by rejecting the idea of laws of evolution or laws of human progress. He dismissed Maine's notion that all societies move from status to contract, and instead argued that in England liberty of the individual had been enjoyed from Anglo-Saxon times onward. He contested the evolutionary orthodoxies of his day, which tended to see human civilization moving in steps or stages, from one age to the next, and argued instead that political societies are too complex to afford these easy narratives.[43] He overturned the usual interpretation of the sixteenth century as marking a radical break from the feudal world order and as introducing capitalist society and instead affirmed that the continuities with the modern world stretch far back to thirteenth-century England and beyond. Instead of finding ancient communities of family ownership, he found the contrary—that from the earliest description, individual ownership was the rule.[44]

This was a critical intervention because one of the most popular and compelling uses of political history at the end of the nineteenth century was to defend the idea of a primitive communism. The socialist land reformer Henry George made much use of the idea that private property was a recent innovation.[45] Maitland contested the image of the medieval community as a pastoral idyll that would answer the fragmentation of modern industrial existence, which had been popularized by Seebohm and others, protesting that communities were not spontaneous, self-sufficient

---

[42] Frederic William Maitland, "Old English Law," in *The Collected Papers of Frederick William Maitland*, ed. H.A.L. Fisher, 3 vols. (Cambridge: Cambridge University Press, 1911), 3:416.

[43] Frederic William Maitland, *The Domesday Book and Beyond: Three Essays in the Early History of England* (Cambridge: Cambridge University Press, 1897), 345–47.

[44] Macfarlane, *Making of the Modern*, 57; James Reese Cameron, *Frederick William Maitland and the History of English Law* (Norman: University of Oklahoma Press, 1961), 98–103.

[45] Henry George, *Progress and Poverty* (New York: Appleton, 1880), bk. 7.

bodies but subordinate members of a nation-state; they were more often the bearer of duties than rights, and the most powerful sense of "community" in medieval Britain was the "universality of the realm."[46] He contested the authenticity of medieval village communities by arguing that they lacked any legal machinery or any common legal apparatus to settle disputes or to establish agricultural practice. Maitland concluded: "This is a real difficulty, and it is apparently compelling some of us to believe that the township never was a 'free village community,' that from the first the force that kept it together, that gave it its communal character, was the power of a lord over serfs, a power which in course of time took the mitigated form of jurisdiction, but which had its origin in the relation between slave and slave-owner."[47] Similarly he dismantled the Indian village community as the prototype of a primitive communism by asserting that "[i]n the Indian village community the symbol of right is a certain share of the produce rather than any theory of soil ownership."[48] Frederick Pollock similarly did not let pass any opportunity to challenge current arguments for socialist reorganization of society and the state, employing Aristotle to contest socialist land reform.[49] This is not to suggest that Maitland saw the thirteenth century as a time of bondage and enslavement; he maintained in the *Domesday Book* that an independent freemen peopled Britain before the thirteenth century and made up a free peasant proprietorship.[50] But he did puncture the Whig narrative of the early constitutional historians by moving away from their developmental historicism, which had enabled them to make sweeping assertions about the progress of the British nation under the guise of original research, toward a modernist empiricism, which drew much more tentative political conclusions.

A second major issue Maitland and the legal historians tackled was the question of British exceptionalism: why Britain had diverged from the common trajectory it had shared with the continent up until the twelfth century. Why did England become an open society, whereas the continent suffered under political absolutism?[51] Again in contrast to Freeman, Stubbs, and Green, he did not reach for Aryan racial arguments to explain British distinctiveness, but rather read in England's island status, in its customs and traditions, and in part, historical accident, the reasons for her uniqueness. Maitland wrote: "The English common law was tough,

---

[46] Maitland and Pollock, *History of English Law*, 1:688.

[47] Frederic William Maitland, "The Surnames of English Villages" in *Collected Papers of Maitland*, 2:86–7.

[48] Maitland cited in Arthur Smith, *Frederic William Maitland: Two Lectures and a Bibliography* (New York: Burt Franklin, 1908), 15.

[49] Pollock, *History of the Science of Politics*, 22–24.

[50] Maitland, *Domesday*, 222, 339.

[51] Frederic William Maitland, *The Constitutional History of England* (Cambridge: Cambridge University Press, 1911), 512.

one of the toughest things ever made. . . . A simple, a more rational, a more elegant system would have been an apt instrument of despotic rule . . . but the clumsy cumbrous system, though it might bend, would never break. It was ever awkwardly rebounding and confounding the statecraft which had tried to control it. The strongest king, the ablest minister, the rudest Lord-Protector could make little of this 'ungodly' jumble."[52] England was saved from Roman law, which remained only in vestiges in ecclesiastical law, unlike on the continent, where Roman law retained a much more central place.

The attention paid to national institutions by legal historians became a major area of political studies in the twentieth century. Maitland's attack on whiggism was echoed by other writers: Barbara and J. L. Hammond, for example, in a succession of books dismembered the Whig myth of the ineluctable progress of an industrial nation: in *The Village Labourer* (1911), *The Town Labourer* (1917), and *The Skilled Labourer* (1919).[53] Beatrice and Sidney Webb began in 1906 an ambitious project to trace the history of local government, which eventually culminated in a six-volume study. They wished to put the current dilemmas in local government reform in a historical perspective, explaining: "in the course of our journeyings up and down the country we found even the present Local Government so firmly rooted in the past and the past so complicated and obscure that it became indispensable to us to make a special study of the period immediately preceding the reforms of 1832–35."[54] Several decades later, this project was eventually completed. John Neville Figgis and Ernest Barker both wrote ecclesiastical histories that explored alternatives to state structures, and Laski in 1926 could point to administrative political science as an area of primary significance to the discipline. The new administrative political science had its roots in the empiricist methodologies of the legal historians who rejected for the most part grand narratives and turned their gaze instead to meticulous, atomized studies. Their modernist empiricism militated against the grandiose confidence in imperial greatness and Britain's manifest destiny ritually intoned by the constitutional historians of the previous generation. Law was becoming a discipline tied to the training of legal practitioners, and the opaqueness of the boundaries between history, law, and politics began to close.

[52] Maitland cited in Macfarlane, *Making of the Modern*, 76.

[53] J. L. Hammond and Barbara Hammond, *The Village Labourer, 1760–1832* (London: Longmans Green, 1911); J. L. Hammond and Barbara Hammond, *The Town Labourer, 1872–1949* (London: Longmans Green, 1917); J. L. Hammond and Barbara Hammond, *The Skilled Labourer, 1760–1832* (London: Longmans Green, 1919).

[54] Sidney Webb and Beatrice Webb *English Local Government from the Revolution to the Municipal Corporations Act: The Parish and the County* (London: Longman, Green and Co., 1906), vi.

The Historical Study of Political Thought: The Idealists and Philosophical Theories of the State

The idealist school also contributed to the flourishing of a historical study of politics in Britain, though here the focus was on the history of political thought and was largely resistant to the modernist empiricist ambitions that had begun to animate constitutional and legal historians. Important conjunctions as well as disjunctions with the Whig tradition characterized British idealism. Advanced first by T. H. Green, F. H. Bradley, and Edward Caird in the 1870s, idealism rapidly became one of the primary traditions of thought in Britain and for several decades thereafter dominated philosophical debate. Much of its authority lay outside the university. As R. G. Collingwood recalled: "The School of Green sent out into public life a stream of ex-pupils who carried with them the conviction that philosophy and in particular the philosophy they had learnt at Oxford was an important thing and their vocation was to put this into practice."[55] Practicing politicians and idealist philosophers inhabited a shared world and remained in some cases in close contact. While the idealists worked on moral philosophy, logic, and aesthetics, they also wrote extensively on political philosophy, and this corpus was to have an enormous impact on the formation of political studies at the turn of the century. In their inaugural addresses, the new chairs of Political Science at Cambridge and the London School of Economics both paid tribute to the idealists in laying the foundations for the discipline.[56]

First, the idealists made the state, freedom, and the problem of political obligation central to the study of politics, and to this degree shared the same focus as the Whig historians. But the idealists' view of the state was much more ambivalent. On one hand, they depicted the state as possessing modest powers. Reflecting a Kantian influence, they regarded the state as unable to command the will of the citizen; it could not command citizens to feel certain duties, motivations, or dispositions. Yet on the other hand, Green fundamentally enlarged the powers of the state by affirming that the state had a moral responsibility to provide the conditions by which citizens would feel a duty to behave in a certain manner. Although the state could not force a citizen to feel a duty toward the common good, for example, the state had a responsibility to facilitate and encourage a disposition toward the common good. Moreover, as in the Whig constitutional histories, the idealist state was to a very significant

---

[55] R. G. Collingwood, *An Autobiography* (Oxford: Oxford University Press, 1939), 16.

[56] Laski and Barker in Preston King, ed., *The Study of Politics: A Collection of Inaugural Lectures* (London: Cass, 1977).

degree the arbitrator of the freedom of the individual. The idealists further refined the preoccupation with freedom in human history that had been so central to the Whiggish historians of Teutonic democracy in the 1860s and 1870s, and tended to view human history in Whiggish terms as the narrative of freedom.

A foremost text was Bosanquet's *The Philosophical Theory of the State* (1899). To Bosanquet, the critical question was how freedom could be reconciled with political obligation, and why this "freedom—the non obstruction of capacities—is to be found in a system which lays burdens on the untamed self and 'forces us to be free.' " He attempted to reconcile these polarities by distinguishing between an actual and a real will; by identifying the real will with the general will; and by identifying the general will with the state. By the outbreak of the First World War, *The Philosophical Theory of the State* had become the center of a controversy that continued to influence political theorists for decades. A. D. Lindsay recalled that when he began to lecture on political theory in 1917, dissatisfaction with *The Philosophical Theory of the State* influenced him "more than anything else."[57] In the intense climate of opinion created by the Great War, Bosanquet's notion of sovereignty was interpreted as embodying all that was destructive in the Prussian state.[58]

Although the idealists made the state so pivotal to political studies, idealism also fostered the growth of pluralist thought, which conversely challenged claims for the centrality of the state. The idealists devoted much attention to social institutions—the family, the church, society, charity organizations—because they were interested in the panoply of institutions and groups that made up civil society and could be viewed in Hegelian terms as expressions of an ethical spirit. The desire to cultivate those points of connection that recovered the collective was a characteristic idea of fin de siècle political culture, prompting Sidney Webb to observe: "In short, the opening of the twentieth century finds us all to the dismay of the old fashioned individualist, 'thinking in communities.' "[59] The starting point for idealist discussions of community was, in common with most late-nineteenth-century theorists, a form of social organicism. This was reminiscent of the Whigs' emphasis on a continuous connection

[57] A. D. Lindsay, "Symposium: Bosanquet's Theory of the General Will," *Proceedings of the Aristotelian Society*, suppl. vol., 8 (1928): 31.

[58] See C. Deslisle Burns, B. Russell, and G.D.H. Cole, "Symposium: The Nature of the State in View of Its External Relations," *Proceedings of the Aristotelian Society* 16 (1915–16): 293, 311, 312, 317, 323; Louise Creighton, W. R. Sorley, J. S. Mackenzie, A. D. Lindsay, H. Rashdall, and Hilda D. Oakeley, *The International Crisis: The Theory of the State* (London: Oxford University Press, 1916), 2, 38, 100.

[59] Sidney Webb, "Twentieth Century Politics," in *The Basis and Policy of Socialism* (London: Fifield, 1908), 78.

between people of different historical epochs. Reacting against the atomism of Bentham, Mill, and Spencer, the idealists looked back to Plato and, even more authoritatively, to Aristotle and to the Hegelian discussion of *sittlichkeit*. Idealists like Green, Caird, Bosanquet, Wallace, and others who produced commentaries on and translations of Greek and German philosophers were instrumental in transmitting the communitarian accounts of these authors to a wide audience particularly concerned to uncover such themes. According to idealist variants of social organicism, society itself conferred meaning on the individual. As Green argued, "[W]ithout society, no persons." Any political theory that imagined the individual was unencumbered and autonomous failed to recognize that the individual "implies in every fiber relations of community."[60] As John Gunnell shows in his chapter, the pluralists after the war developed this perspective much more fully, shaking off the idealist inclination to see the state as the supreme expression of a communitarian ethos. The continuity between idealism and pluralism, however, is often obscured by the virulent pluralist attacks on the idealists around the outbreak of the First World War.[61] The rise of pluralism in Britain dethroned the state, and political "scientists" became increasingly concerned to trace the history not just of the central state and of obligation to the central state, but of a host of other institutions that make up corporate life: trade unions, local government, and the church.

While history played an insignificant role in idealist political studies in comparison to the political science of Freeman, Seeley, and others, the history of political thought was essential to idealist political studies. Their initial task was historical exegesis; they analyzed past political philosophies and, on the basis of this historical work, built up an alternative account. Green spent the bulk of the first part of *Lectures on the Principles of Political Obligation* interpreting Spinoza, Hobbes, Locke, and Rous-

---

[60] F. H. Bradley, *Ethical Studies* (Oxford: Clarendon Press 1876), 155, . Thomas Hill Green, *Prolegomena to Ethics* (Oxford: Clarendon Press, 1883), sec. 288.

[61] See Paul Q. Hirst, ed., *The Pluralist Theory of the State: Selected Writings of G.D.H. Cole, J. N. Figgis and H. J. Laski* (London: Routledge, 1989); David Nicholls, *The Pluralist State: The Political Ideas of J. N. Figgis and His Contemporaries* (Basingstoke, UK: Macmillan, 1975). Bosanquet's principal pluralist critics were Harold J. Laski (1893–1950), whose early works advanced a pluralist theory of society; *Studies in the Problem of Sovereignty* (1917); *Authority in the Modern State* (1919); *A Grammar of Politics* (1925); Ernest Barker, "The Discredited State," *Political Quarterly* 2 (February 1915): 101–21; and G.D.H. Cole, *Guild Socialism Re-stated* (London: Parsons, 1920); *Social Theory* (London: Methuen, 1920). See Michael Freeden, *Liberalism Divided: A Study in British Political Thought, 1914–1939* (Oxford: Oxford University Press, 1986), 27–41, 66–77 for an analysis of the decline of the idea of the state under both New Liberal and pluralist criticisms; and Cécile Laborde, *Pluralist Thought and the State in Britain and France, 1900–1925* (New York: St. Martin's Press, 2000).

seau (and a range of minor noncanonical thinkers) and only then turned to construct his own account of political obligation. He entered into a historical conversation, his interlocutors in the past leading him to define with greater clarity his own alternative position. He was not particularly concerned with historical personalities or the historical circumstances that gave rise to the ideas he examined, though he often made prescient observations about this linkage. Such an approach tended "to spread the notion that philosophy is a matter about which there has been much guessing by great intellects, but no definite truth to be attained." Green then defined his own approach to the history of philosophy: "It is otherwise with those who see in philosophy a progressive effort towards a fully-articulated conception of the world as rational. To them its past history is of interest as representing steps in this progress which have already been taken for us, and which, if we will make them our own, carry us so far on our way towards the freedom of perfect understanding."[62] These are powerful echoes of the twin themes of the Whig tradition—development and freedom. Through the study of the development of thought, the political theorist was carried closer to a true understanding, though a full and perfect understanding remained illusory. The idealists tended not to intone the triumphalism of the Whig constitutional historians.

The British idealists were to some extent indebted to Hegelian ideas of history, though this influence mingled with other potent influences on their thought. For Green, Hegel had illuminated the idea that freedom was realized in the state: the state represented "objective freedom"—it established laws and institutions and customs that secured the common good of its members, enabling them to become the best they can be.[63] Through laws, customs, and institutions, the individual became conscious of an ideal to be realized in life and the need to contribute to a good that would lead to the perfection of them and of humanity. True freedom was achieved by that individual who desired this permanent good, instead of fleeting desires guided by those rational ends that would satisfy the yearning for self-perfection. Green turned from the Hegelian idea of freedom worked out in historical progress to emphasize instead the liberty of the individual, as he or she individually was guided by ideals of human perfection. The freedom of the individual through the cultivation of character was for Green more compelling than any grand movement of human

---

[62] Thomas Hill Green, "Introduction to Hume's Treatise on Human Nature," in *Works of Thomas Hill Green*, ed. R. L. Nettleship, 3 vols. (London: Longmans, Green, and Co., 1893–1906), 1:4–5. Green examined past systems of thought to identify inconsistencies and difficulties, for these failures were not anachronisms but "have brought out a new truth and compelled a step forward in the progress of thought," 5.

[63] Thomas Hill Green, "On the Different Senses of Freedom" in *Works*, 2:312–13.

history.[64] This distinctively idealist emphasis on each individual's moral development undercut to some degree the grand sweep and triumphalism of contemporary constitutional historians.

There is no monolithic idealist understanding of a historical politics. While most idealists subscribed to some form of an evolutionary account of historical change (most often as a succession of stages; each stage had distinctive ideas and perspectives), there was more divergence about the public utility of historical knowledge. Some, like Green, had very modest expectations of historical knowledge and maintained that the historian could only ever partially understand the past. Green accordingly described philosophers as "the mouthpiece of a certain system of thought determined for him by the stage at which he found the dialectic movement that constitutes the progress of history."[65] For him, history was an internal reflective activity removed from the world of public affairs and practical ends. Bradley stated this position more strongly yet. He argued in an influential essay first published in 1874 that grand laws of social evolution were illusory; nor was there any power to predict future events. Historical knowledge could not be anything other than partial, incomplete, and confined to the individual.[66] This broke down the close identification between history and the practice of politics upon which Seeley had been so insistent and that had underwritten the developmental historicism of the mid- to late nineteenth century. The history of political thought provided instruction about how to conceive of the state, political obligation, civil society, individual rights and duties, but history could not provide unambiguous guidance on practical politics. Its knowledge was too relative and too contingent. This was an early and very tentative version of the radical historicism that came into prominence in the twentieth century, for like these later radical historicists, Bradley and Green regarded historical contingency as an obstacle to drawing any overarching conclusions based on discrete historical events. But this radical historicism was simultaneously undercut by the essentialism of the idealist conviction that metaphysical, though not historical, investigations could reveal truths about the right ordering of political society.

Other idealists advanced a much more utilitarian and politically charged view of history. While the idealists helped to diffuse a Hegelian

---

[64] L. T. Hobhouse, *The Metaphysical Theory of the State* (London: Allen and Unwin 1918), 17.

[65] Green cited in David Boucher, "The Creation of the Past: British Idealism and Michael Oakeshott's Philosophy of History," *History and Theory* 23, no. 2 (1984): 199–200.

[66] F. H. Bradley, "The Pre-suppositions of a Critical History," in *Collected Essays*, 2 vols. (Oxford: Clarendon Press, 1935), 1:1–70. Michael Oakeshott expanded on this suggestive essay (one of the few extended idealist writings on history) to make historical knowledge a more central element in a reconstituted idealism.

view of history as the unfolding of human freedom, they tempered the determinist undertones of this Hegelian influence with a strong tradition of individual liberty. Hegelian influences mingled with a stronger attachment to Kantian thought, to a Kantian insistence upon the active, conscious, deliberate, and free-willed character of moral action. History or social evolution could never simply be the manifestation of an immanent spirit but was produced by deliberate acts of will.[67] Idealists like D. G. Ritchie recast the Hegelian notion of a rational history moving toward the realization of a final end or ideal to emphasize the role of political and social reformers who could shape each step of the progress of society through aggressively interventionist state policies.[68] Convinced that evolution was at least in part guided by human reflection or "consciousness," he maintained that the most significant factors in social evolution were not biological but "social" factors, notably traditions, customs, and institutions that could be manipulated by political leaders. Ritchie therefore explained the origin of what he called "the social factor" in utilitarian terms by suggesting that societies deliberately formed ideals, customs, and institutions that facilitate social well-being and thereby ensure progress.[69] This supplied a clear rationale for extensive intervention in the evolution of history, and it is not surprising that Fabians found Ritchie's account to be so suggestive, for it buttressed their own view of an elite management of political and economic reform. The expectation that intellectuals had a duty to provide guidance on contemporary issues was widespread in Britain at the turn of the century: both Bryce and Dicey were consulted on Home Rule for Ireland,[70] and a generation of political reformers (Arnold Toynbee, Alfred Milner, Asquith, Haldane, Sidney Ball, the Barnetts), who had imbibed idealism at Oxford, had little hesitation in applying idealist political theory to such contemporary political problems as poor relief, determining the extent of state intervention, progressive taxation, or the Boer War. Later political theorists who had been educated in the crucible of idealism emphasized to an even greater degree the role of polit-

---

[67] This duality was also reflected by L. T. Hobhouse, who at one hand maintained that there was "an objective order" to human history, but that human progress at the same time was the product of deliberate acts of willing: L. T. Hobhouse, *Social Evolution and Political Theory* (New York: Columbia University Press, 1911), 6.

[68] Sandra den Otter, *The British Idealists and Social Explanation* (Oxford: Oxford University Press, 1996), 108.

[69] David George Ritchie, *Darwin and Hegel, with other Philosophical Studies* (London: Sonnenschein, 1893); David George Ritchie, *Darwinism and Politics*, 3rd ed. (London: Sonnenschein, 1895), 97–101; David George Ritchie, "Social Evolution," *International Journal of Ethics* 6 (1896): 165–81.

[70] Stefan Collini, *Public Moralists: Political Thought and Intellectual Life in Britain, 1850–1930* (Oxford: Clarendon Press, 1991), 230–36.

ical leaders and moral citizens to advance the good society. As Ernest Barker insisted: "Things only move when we make them move, by the work of our thoughts and the effort of our will."[71] Although idealism continued to have a strong influence throughout the twentieth century, this perspective was also increasingly under attack by the time hostilities broke out in 1914.[72] Graham Wallas had little but scorn for the intellectualism and optimism of idealist political thought, even though he retained an admiration for the Aristotelian study of politics.[73] The history of political thought, however, which was central to the idealist study of politics, remained a strong strand in British political studies.[74]

The Moral Science of History and Politics

A moral outlook adumbrated the study of the political at the turn of the century. This was by no means uncontested: there were social scientists who argued for positivist, impartial, value-neutral investigations. T. H. Huxley, for example, lampooned those "who prefer to prophesy from the sublime cloudland of the a priori so that, busied with deductions from their ideal of what 'ought to be,' they overlooked the 'what has been', the 'what is' and 'what can be.' "[75] But a heavily normative overtone was remarkably resilient in Britain. When Ernest Barker gave his inaugural address as the first chair of political science in Cambridge in 1926, he rejected the sobriquet "political science" (with its pretensions to an exact objective science) in favor of the rather more unwieldy "a form of inquiry concerned with the moral phenomena of human behaviour in political studies."[76] This thoroughgoing ethical perspective should be distinguished from those who used historical parallels or examples to justify the rationality of certain positions. That use of history was widespread but not necessarily normative, ethical, or moral. Henry Sumner Maine, for example, used his investigation of the evolution of human law to make prescrip-

---

[71] Ernest Barker, *Greek Political Theory: Plato and His Predecessors* (London: Methuen, 1925), 243.

[72] See Alison Falby, "Gerald Heard (1889–1971) and British Intellectual Culture between the Wars" (DPhil thesis, Oxford University, 2000).

[73] Graham Wallas, *Human Nature in Politics* (London: Constable, 1908), 123–27, 195–96.

[74] J. N. Figgis, *The Divine Right of Kings* (Cambridge: Cambridge University Press, 1896; 2nd ed. 1914). See also Ernest Barker, *Political Thought in England from Herbert Spencer to the Present Day* (New York: Henry Holt, 1915).

[75] T. H. Huxley, "Natural Rights and Political Rights," in *Collected Essays*, 9 vols. (London: Macmillan, 1894), 1:312.

[76] Ernest Barker, "The Study of Political Science" in *Church, State, and Study: Essays*, (London: Methuen), 18.

tive arguments about appropriate political systems for advanced societies. In the polemic against popular government he wrote in his bad-humored old age, he used the weight of his historical and comparative research to argue against contractarian models of government and to inveigle against extension of democratic government; though forceful, this polemic was not a normative argument.

The primacy of philosophical idealism, which overshadowed British intellectual life for several decades, powerfully entrenched a moral perspective. Indeed, many idealists argued that the historical method was limited precisely because it could not authoritatively define the ideal ends of the state: this task fell to philosophy. T. H. Green, Bernard Bosanquet, and others did not argue so much about the difficulty of value neutrality, but rather that value neutrality was undesirable. A meaningful political or social theory could not avoid making moral and prescriptive conclusions, and it was indeed their task to do so. This normative perspective was partly dictated by idealist metaphysics that posited the presence of an ultimate spiritual reality (an Absolute): any explanation of the state and political society must be made in reference to this ideal. Bernard Bosanquet argued that political and social theorists must attempt to answer "when and how and how far by social aid, the human soul attains the most and best that it has in it to become."[77] But the normative and prescriptive urgency of idealist political studies also sprang from a much vaguer, humanist belief in an underlying spiritual ideal or perfection, and this belief was by no means specific to idealism. Political studies was also rendered normative by a pervasive moral organicism that defined the state and political society as the means for individual realization and the common good as the political expression of self-realization. Idealists defined the state as an ethical entity that "makes it possible for men to realize themselves, which they can only do by attaining a good that is a common good."[78]

There were other strands of political study that rejected idealist metaphysics and nonetheless advanced a normative political science. The ethical movement of the late nineteenth century attracted Victorian intellectuals of many hues: positivists like J. H. Bridges, Frederic Harrison, Beesly; Fabians, notably the Webbs, G. B. Shaw, and Graham Wallas; the idealists, H. Sidgwick, J. A. Hobson, and many others. The movement sought to reintroduce "the moral factor in all personal, social, political and national and international relations," and also to find some alternative to

---

[77] Bernard Bosanquet, *Philosophical Theory of the State* (London: Macmillan, 1899), 17.

[78] David George Ritchie, *Principles of State Interference: Four Essays on the Political Philosophy of Mr. Herbert Spencer, J. S. Mill, and T. H. Green* (London: Sonnenschein, 1896), 141.

the orthodox Christian doctrine of regeneration that could bolster ethical living.[79] The latter-day utilitarian Henry Sidgwick constantly affirmed the need for doctrines and disciplines "establishing the moral order of the world."[80] Barker's retrospective look at the 1880s is useful: "In the *Elements of Politics* and the *Principles of Political Obligation* the method of Henry Sidgwick and T. H. Green is fundamentally similar. Whatever the difference of their views, both of these thinkers postulated a conception of the human good, and both of them attempted to determine, on the basis and by the criterion of that conception, the system of relations which ought to be established in a political community. In its essentials the problem of political theory is a constant. It has to determine the end, or ultimate value, which governs and determines the life of political society."[81] Building on an indigenous utilitarian tradition, the later utilitarian New Liberal J.G.A. Hobson set up social utility as a standard against which to measure political life and deliberately parted company from those who strove for a "purely inductive treatment of explicit facts."[82] Hobson based the demand for a normative social and political philosophy on such notions as "social utility," "social satisfaction," and common good.[83] Social science became an essentially normative inquiry set within a moral framework of modified utilitarianism. Neither Sidgwick nor Hobson regarded this moral perspective as antithetical to an objective and impartial science of politics—in this they differed from the idealists. Hobson described social utility as "an objective standard of reference."[84] Similarly, Sidney Webb's socialism infused his approach to the study of politics with an ethical and normative fervor.[85]

The potent influence of classical Greek thought further embedded a moral orientation to political science. This generation of political thinkers and historians had been steeped in the classical world: classical meta-

---

[79] British Humanist League, London. West London Ethical Society, Minutes of General Meetings, December 4, 1902. The history of the ethical movement in Britain has been closely studied in Ian Duncan Mackillop, *The British Ethical Societies* (Cambridge: Cambridge University Press, 1986). See also Susan Budd, *Varieties of Unbelief: Atheists and Agnostics in English Society, 1850–1960* (London: Heinemann Education Books, 1978), chaps. 9 and 10.

[80] Sidgwick to Ward, March 1898. Quoted from Arthur Sidgwick, *Henry Sidgwick: A Memoir* (London: Macmillan, 1906), 560.

[81] Barker, Inaugural Lecture, 31.

[82] J. A. Hobson, *The Social Problem* (London: Nisbet, 1901), 63.

[83] Ibid., chaps. 6 and 7; J. A. Hobson, *Work and Wealth* (London: Macmillan, 1914), chap. 22; and Michael Freeden, "J. A. Hobson as a New Liberal Theorist," *Journal of History of Ideas* 34, no. 3 (1973): 421–43.

[84] Hobson, *Social Problem*, 63.

[85] See Mark Bevir, "Sidney Webb: Utilitarianism, Positivism and Social Democracy," *Journal of Modern History* 74 (2002): 217–52.

phors, languages, and history resonated throughout their writings.[86] The revival of Aristotelian and Platonic studies in the midcentury had revolutionized the study of politics. Until the reformer and pedagogue Benjamin Jowett had begun to teach Aristotle's *Politics* and to make available the Platonic Dialogues, only a few Aristotelian texts—*Rhetoric, Categories, Prior Analytics,* and parts of the *Poetics* and *Nicomachean Ethics*—were recognized. Jowett pointed to Greek political thought as a necessary corrective "to recover a sense of the ethical dimension of politics contrary to the mechanistic view of the last century's philosophers."[87] Aristotle, however, was also the patron saint of more empiricist strands of political science. Pollock found Aristotle's "patient analysis and unbiased research which are the proper marks and virtues of scientific inquiry" much more persuasive than the Platonic "exercise of philosophical imagination" (which was not political science at all).[88] Yet even Pollock, despite his scorn for Platonic morality and his admiration for Aristotle's putative division of ethics from politics, attributed to the modern state the responsibility of "encouraging the completeness of life in their citizens."[89] Late Victorians did not regard this moral or ethical tone found in classical thought to be antithetical to a scientific treatment of politics: indeed, Aristotle was such a popular figure because his analytical and scientific method resonated in a scientific age, as much as Plato's more metaphysical reflections. Nonetheless, this moral passion that lived on far into the twentieth century militated against any less ambivalent turn toward a neopositivist science of politics.

"The Fact Is the Sure Thing"

If political studies at the turn of the century remained vigorously ethical, more empirical and less speculative branches of political inquiry flourished and came to define more and more the new discipline of political studies.

[86] See José Harris, "Platonism, Positivism, and Progressivism: Aspects of British Sociological Thought in the Early Twentieth Century," in *Citizenship and Community: Liberals, Radicals, and Collective Identities in the British Isles, 1865–1931,* ed. Eugenio F. Biagini (Cambridge: Cambridge University Press, 1996), 343–60; Frank M. Turner, *Contesting Cultural Authority: Essays in Victorian Intellectual Life* (Cambridge: Cambridge University Press, 1993), chaps. 9–12; Frank M. Turner, *The Greek Heritage in Victorian Britain* (New Haven, CT: Yale University Press, 1981); Richard Jenkyns, *The Victorians and Ancient Greece* (Oxford: Blackwell, 1980).

[87] Benjamin Jowett, trans., *"The Politics" of Aristotle* (Oxford: Clarendon Press, 1885), xii, xiiii, cxxi.

[88] Pollock, *History of the Science of Politics,* 2, 14.

[89] Ibid., 30.

Whether or not this increased emphasis on empirical investigation was a response to the incommensurability of such notions as social utility, the good life, or the moral state (an exception was Graham Wallas) is debatable.[90] Certainly contemporary politics was the arena for sharp controversy over poor law reform, free trade, progressive taxation, suffrage, reform of the House of Lords, and numerous other issues, and this controversy could be regarded as proof sufficient of how incommensurable ideas of the social good were. The formation of an Independent Labour Party, the lively presence of the Fabian Society counterpoised by the Charity Organisation Society, and a revived Edwardian conservatism demonstrated the broad range of opinion about how the political affairs of the nation ought to be organized. Intellectuals—historians, political scientists, and sociologists—were at times actively involved in these debates, for universities, social reform organizations, and politics overlapped at the turn of the century. Divisive debate about current political dilemmas led some to repudiate this normative approach. The vigorous apologist for an objective, empirical political science James Bryce, had little patience for deliberations over moral theories of the state: "So again let the philosophers imitate Plato and Aristotle and many after them in considering what is the best form a state can take, and what the organs through which it must work. But if their enquiries are to be fruitful, their state and its organs will have to be tangible things, such as belong to the field of experience, not chimeras buzzing in emptiness. . . . The Fact is the sure thing."[91] Facts demonstrated persistent and certain patterns; facts permitted inductive conclusions, even modest predictions. Bryce claimed the authority of science for the discipline of political studies: the impartiality of science conferred greater authority and buttressed claims for the expertise of the political scientist. Others, like Harold Laski, praised the virtues of inductive, systematic investigations without endorsing claims to scientific objectivity and impartiality.[92]

The attractions of modernist empiricism and neopositivism were expressed in the organization of political studies at the London School of Economics. Empirical investigations of institutions and political practice took the large place that traditionally had been given to the history of political thought. The Webbs were critical figures in articulating an empirical and neopositivist approach to the study of politics, as were Edwin Canaan and Graham Wallas, who both lectured at the LSE.[93] Early LSE

[90] Wallas, *Human Nature in Politics*, 117–18.

[91] Bryce, "Relations," 10.

[92] Laski, "On the Study of Politics" in King, *The Study of Politics*, 9.

[93] Mark Bevir, "Sidney Webb"; D. O'Brien, "Edwin Cannan: Economic Theory and the History of Economic Thought," *Research in the History of Economic Thought and Methodology* 17 (1999): 1–21; Ralf Dahrendorf, *A History of the London School of Economics and Political Science, 1895–1995* (New York: Oxford University Press, 1995).

calendars clearly indicate the empiricist rather than speculative orientation of political studies: lectures on comparative politics, political economy, and administrative history were the staples of the program, though constitutional history remained a bulwark of the discipline.[94] A series of books published under the auspices of the LSE and edited by one of its founders, W.A.S. Hewins, entitled *Studies in Economics and Political Science*, defined political science as an empirical, positivist inquiry with utility for current public policy, and included lectures on German Social Democracy (offered by Bertrand Russell in 1896), the referendum in Switzerland, Frederick Galton's collection of documents on the history of trade unionism, and Cannan's history of local rates in England.

Political Economy, History, and the Study of Politics

Another important though ultimately unsuccessful avenue for a historical approach to political studies in the late nineteenth century was the school of historical economics. The historical economists (H. S. Foxwell, William Cunningham, W. J. Ashley, W.A.S. Hewins, and L. L. Price) collectively sought to rehabilitate the declining discipline of political economy, undermined by the rise of marginalism and the professionalisation of the new economics. Marshall's Marginal Revolution had broken the close association between economics and political and public policy that had characterised the classical economists (despite Marshall's interest in social and political issues), and economics became increasingly a professional discipline more remote from contemporary political issues.[95] Much influenced by Maine's historical and comparative study of law, the Irish economist Cliffe Leslie attempted to restore the close identification of economics and politics that had characterized the classical economists but with a historical approach: "every branch of the philosophy of society, morals and political economy not excepted, needs investigation and development by historical induction."[96] Arnold Toynbee, in his influential lectures on the Industrial Revolution delivered in Oxford in the early 1880s, also

[94] See, for example, Calendar of the London School of Economics and Politics. 1902: List of Subjects, Political History.

[95] See Tribe, "The Historicization of Political Economy?"; John Maloney, *Marshall, Orthodoxy and the Professionalisation of Economics* (Cambridge: Cambridge University Press 1985); Alon Kadish and Keith Tribe, *The Market for Political Economy: The Advent of Economics in British University Culture, 1850–1905* (London: Routledge, 1993); Gerard M. Koot, *English Historical Economics, 1870–1926: The Rise of Economic History and Neomercantilism* (Cambridge: Cambridge University Press, 1987).

[96] T. E. Cliffe Leslie, *Essays in Political and Moral Philosophy* (Dublin: Hodges Figgis, 1879), v.

made a powerful defense of the necessary interdependence of political economy and history. Defining the role of the state depended upon a proper understanding of the history of that society and its stage of civilization: it was impossible to define abstract theories about the proper extent of state intervention.[97] Despite their patchy and sometimes simplistic conclusions, Toynbee's lectures had a lasting impact on political studies, and on a Christian socialist collectivism and progressive liberalism. Historical contingency and relativism were the critical components of the new historical economics.[98] The Oxford economist Walter Cunningham also used these ideas to elucidate the place of the state in the economic life of the nation. He was particularly influenced by both German and British idealism and tended to attribute great authority and centrality to the nation-state and Empire, and accordingly insisted that the discipline of economics would be meaningful only by reference to actual states and polities. The historical economists became actively involved in the politics of tariff reform at the turn of the century, in opposition to Alfred Marshall, A. C. Pigou, and most other orthodox economists who supported free trade. W.A.S. Hewins resigned from his directorship of the London School of Economics to work for Joseph Chamberlain's tariff reform campaign; he also advised the Tory prime minister A. J. Balfour.[99] These economists became vital allies in an attempt to convince the public of the credibility of tariff reform, for, as Andrew Bonar Law wrote to W. J. Ashley, "there is nothing which tells more against us than the idea that scientific authority is against us."[100] Their politics were increasingly conservative and neo-mercantalist, in contrast to the vague socialism of the earlier historical economists. The historical economists continued to have an influence into the twentieth century at Oxford, the LSE, and Birmingham, though at Cambridge, Marshall succeeded in entrenching economic theory, and very little economic history, in the curriculum. The dominance of marginalist economics and the authority of Marshall led to the relegation of a historical political economy to the discipline of history; the strength of the discipline of orthodox economics may have contributed to the slow growth of a professional political science in Britain. Nonetheless, the increasingly radical historicism of the historical economists contributed to the slow dismantling of the certainties of the early Whig tradition.

[97] Arnold Toynbee, *Lectures on the Industrial Revolution in England*, edited by Benjamin Jowett (London: Rivingtons, 1884), 11.

[98] W. J. Ashley, "On the Study of Economic History," in *Surveys, Historic and Economic* (New York: Longmans Green, 1900), 3.

[99] E.H.H. Green, *The Crisis of Conservatism: The Politics, Ideology and Economics of the British Conservative Party, 1880–1914* (London: Routledge, 1995), 162–67.

[100] Cited ibid., 177.

Epilogue

The professionalization of economics, history, politics, sociology, and philosophy in the new century undermined the triumphalism of the mid-nineteenth-century historical study of politics. So too did the dilemmas associated with studies of poverty and war, initially the South African War and then the global conflict of the Great War. As the idealist Bosanquet observed in 1920, "The War has taught us two things, that the art of living together is our deepest need, and that in this art, as yet, we are not very far advanced."[101] The moral certainty of the grand narratives—whether the Whig histories or philosophical idealism—had been punctured. The state, which had been so central to the constitutional historians and political theorists of the previous generation, came under attack. Bertrand Russell's *Principles of Social Reconstruction* (1916) expressed a prevalent suspicion of the strong central state.[102] Every prominent idealist delivered public lectures or wrote popular essays during the First World War that attempted to adjudicate the place of the state in relation to other institutions and to ask whether the state was ethical. These were not questions posed by the Whig political historians of the previous century, who saw the state as the protector rather than the enemy of uniquely British freedoms. The potency of evolutionary accounts, which were common to the grand narratives, was also challenged by the assault on social evolutionary ideas. The self-development of individuals had not translated into a harmonious ethical social order; neither had the market economy meant rough equality. In place of the confidence of evolutionary accounts of British and American exceptionalism, increasingly radical historicist ideas, toward which idealists like F. H. Bradley had much earlier pointed, became more pronounced. Nonetheless, elements of the previous century's grand narratives had a curious resilience in Britain in the postwar period, even though the self-assured confidence of a nation pursuing its manifest destiny had evaporated.

[101] Bernard Bosanquet, Letter to the Editor, *Times*, September 20, 1920.
[102] Bertrand Russell, *Principles of Social Reconstruction* (London: Allen and Unwin, 1916).

Four

The Historical Science(s) of Politics: The Principles, Association, and Fate of an American Discipline

JAMES FARR

> Political science must be studied historically and
> history must be studied politically in order to
> [achieve] a correct comprehension of either.
> —John W. Burgess

POLITICAL SCIENTISTS AT the turn of the last century conceived their science as continuous with history, so much so that it deserves remembrance as *the historical science of politics*. Its object of inquiry was the state; its method was comparative, as well as historical; and its principles were offered as scientific bona fides. As an American science, it presented the United States as a modern state, in its history, in comparison to other states, and set upon distinct principles. Therein lay a sense of identity and unity for self-identified political scientists, but also an invitation to debate what was meant in any specificity by the state, the historical method, or the principles in question. The diversity of opinion that emerged in debate made it appear that political scientists were somehow, at the same time, to explain, interpret, inspire, regulate, guide, edify, and educate the state. Further diversity of opinion emerged in interlocking debates upon which the identity of a nascent discipline turned: whether principles were themselves historical; whether America owed its history to some Teutonic heritage; whether political scientists ought to organize themselves into a separate professional organization or make judgments about superior races or states. All told, the debates suggested an underlying plurality as *the historical sciences of politics*.[1]

---

[1] My account owes much to Dorothy Ross, *The Origins of American Social Science* (New York: Cambridge University Press, 1991); Jens Bartelson, *The Critique of the State* (Cambridge: Cambridge University Press, 2001); and Robert Adcock, "The Emergence of Political Science as a Discipline: History and the Study of Politics in America, 1875–1910," *History of Political Thought* 24 (2003): 481–508. Yet, I find less doctrinal coherence, more methodological debate, longer life, and fewer things changed by the creation of the APSA in what they call "historico-politics" than in what I am calling "the historical science(s) of politics."

The preceding paragraph has presented a crib of the argument and re-constructed narrative of this chapter. In what follows, the chapter arrays the debated opinions of the most prominent historical political scientists in America. It reveals three temporal moments in which the debates un-folded. And it provides early instances of (or resistances to) the different programs that "historicized the political" during the last century, for ex-ample, developmental historicism, evolutionary positivism, and modern-ist empiricism (as identified in the introduction to this volume). The de-bates in question trace to Francis Lieber, who was America's first professor of History and Political Science in 1858, at Columbia, and whose writings upon the twin subjects went back another quarter century. Lieber's popularizer at Yale, Theodore Dwight Woolsey, entered the de-bates before and after the Civil War, especially when his lectures were published as *Political Science, or The State Theoretically and Practically Considered*.[2] Lieber and Woolsey, as well as nonacademic political scien-tists like John Fiske and Elisha Mulford, populate the first of three mo-ments in the historical science(s) of politics, spanning the late antebellum period through Reconstruction.

The second and most defining moment occurs in the 1880s and 1890s. The crucial figures here include John W. Burgess, who succeeded Lieber at Columbia and established its School of Political Science; Herbert Baxter Adams, who created the "seminary" in History and Political Science at Johns Hopkins; and Alfred Bushnell Hart, who united the twin studies at Harvard. Fiske was most active as a political writer and propagandist for Teutonism during this time; a Lieber revival was under way; and Wood-row Wilson wrote his comparative historical treatises, *Congressional Government* and *The State*.[3] Others who deserve counting during this defining period followed Lieber in assuming the mantle of professor of History and Political Science, like Jesse Macy at Iowa, William M. Sloane at Princeton, and Bernard Moses at California, Berkeley. The Scottish historian and political scientist (not to mention British ambassador to the United States) James Bryce figures here, too, because of his prominence in the American Historical Association (AHA) and the American Political Science Association (APSA).

The debates would continue well into the twentieth century. The first two decades roughly demarcate a third moment in the temporal arc of

[2] Theodore D. Woolsey, *Political Science, or The State, Theoretically and Practically Con-sidered*, 2 vols. (New York: Scribner, 1878).

[3] Paul D. Carrington, "William Gardiner Hammond and the Lieber Revival," *Cardozo Law Review* 16 (1995): 2135–52; Woodrow Wilson, *Congressional Government* (Boston: Houghton Mifflin, 1885); Woodrow Wilson, *The State: Elements of Historical and Practical Politics* (Boston: D. C. Heath, 1889).

the historical science(s) of politics. (The roughness of the demarcation allows, indeed requires, drawing upon figures across all three moments, depending upon the issue, sometimes to note change, as often to confirm continuity). Many of the political scientists noted above shaped and survived this period, as did some relatively younger scholars like W. W. Willoughby (at Johns Hopkins), William A. Dunning and Frank J. Goodnow (both at Columbia). They and students, like James W. Garner and Charles E. Merriam, were to carry forward the debates well after the APSA emerged out of the AHA in 1903. The creation of the APSA proved decisive for the professionalization of a discipline, but not the fate of its substantive debates. However, the years between the formation of the APSA and World War I witnessed some thematic trends (in terms of *psychology*, *process*, and *pragmatic inquiry*) that prophesied a much less historical political science later in the century. World War I, more importantly, completely transformed the terms of debate over the state, German affinities, and Teutonic heritage. The war thus dates the conclusion of this chapter and serves as a temporal benchmark against which later developments and debates can be measured.

The State of the Historical Method

Throughout the nineteenth century and after, scholars who championed a science of politics in America thought historically. Even when they demarcated a subset of abstract or theoretical sciences of politics—as did Lieber in 1832 and 1853, Woolsey in 1878, Wilson in 1889, Willoughby in 1896, or Garner in 1910—they more strongly emphasized "historical or practical" sciences that dealt with "actual politics," past or present.[4] (Even then, however, they used the vehicle of the history of political thought to deal with the abstract and theoretical sciences of politics). Recognizing "that vast region of Politics—the main staple of what is called History,"[5] they ritually recited the motto of Edward A. Freeman, the great Oxbridge scholar, once it was coined: "History is past politics; and poli-

---

[4] Francis Lieber, ed., *Encyclopedia Americana* (Philadelphia: Blanchard and Lea, 1857; first published in 1829–32), s.v. "Politics"; Francis Lieber, *Civil Liberty and Self-Government*, ed. Theodore D. Woolsey, 4th ed., 2 vols. (Philadelphia: Lippincott, 1901; first published in 1853); Woolsey, *Political Science*; Wilson, *The State*; Westel W. Willoughby, *The Nature of the State* (New York: Macmillan, 1896); James W. Garner, *Introduction to Political Science: A Treatise on the Origin, Nature, Functions, and Organization of the State* (New York: American Book, 1910).

[5] Francis Lieber, *Miscellaneous Writings*, 2 vols. (Philadelphia: J. B. Lippincott, 1881), 1:293

tics is present history."[6] Politics concerned the public matters of government, administration, diplomacy, and law, as well as police, policies, and ideas. Moreover, *behind* or *above* these public matters of politics loomed the state. "[T]he idea of *politics* depends on that of the *state*," Lieber announced with an eye to its plural consequences, "and a definition of the latter will easily mark out the whole province of the political sciences."[7] The state, like Freeman's politics, had a mutually constitutive relationship with history.[8] "Whoever will understand the political situation of any State must study its past history" just as "the essential matter of history [is] the conduct of the state."[9] Indeed, "the national State is the consummation of political history."[10] Thus, the American scientists of politics professed themselves historians of the state, and they surveyed history from the vantage of the state.

A sense of identity was forged by this mantra that political science was historical in orientation and fixed upon the state, especially the American state. Its earliest expression may be dated at least to Lieber in the 1830s, given full expression by his major works in 1838 and 1853, and rendered symbolic by his professorship in 1858. Lieber's historical sensibilities were already honed by the time of his arrival in the United States in 1827, due largely to his teacher and benefactor Barthold George Niebuhr. And they were pressed into duty when Lieber confronted and overhauled the moral philosophy curriculum of his day. Rights and duties were the primary concerns of moral philosophy, but in its curriculum the principles of "the science of politics," history, and the state were also treated. Lieber further elevated the state, deepened the historical sensibilities of moral philosophy, and propagated the critical and institutional methods of Niebuhr in practice and pronouncement.

Disciplinary identity based upon history and the state would last into the twentieth century. However, it reached high tide in the 1880s and 1890s in the works of Burgess, Adams, Wilson, and the all-but-American Bryce. They presented in grand narrative and great detail what Woolsey

---

[6] Freeman's "chance proverb," as he called it, was the "chosen motto" for the *Johns Hopkins University Studies in Historical and Political Science*. It also hung on the wall of the Historical Seminary that contained the manuscripts of Lieber and Johann K. Bluntschli, Herbert Baxter Adams's teacher and Lieber's friend. See Herbert B. Adams, "Is History Past Politics?" *Johns Hopkins University Studies in Historical and Political Science* 13 (1895): 67–68.

[7] Lieber, *Encyclopedia* 9:232.

[8] Bartelson, *Critique*, 35–63.

[9] Adams, "Is History Past Politics?" 78; William M. Sloane, "History and Democracy," *American Historical Review* 1 (1895): 9.

[10] John W. Burgess, *The Foundations of Political Science* (New York: Columbia University Press, 1933), 247.

had called "the course of politics in the historical way."[11] "Historical political science" was Willoughby's summary phrase for it.[12] The sense of disciplinary identity was reinforced or restated in newer methodological terms
that conveyed—through liberal use of definite articles—unity of purpose.
Political science followed "*the historical method.*" It also followed, according to Moses, Adams, Sloane, Garner, and others, "*the comparative
method.*"[13] The basic injunction of *the* (one or other) method was to compare the origins, development, or contemporary conditions of forms of
the state, in one or more nations, ancient or modern. Wilson thought
the two versions were indistinguishable and so brought them together as
"*the historical, comparative method.*" "Certainly," he declared, "it does
not now have to be argued that the only method of study in politics is the
comparative and historical."[14] Professing *the* method under one name or
another, political scientists proved themselves mainly to be "developmental historicists"; they poured out their substantive works narrating
and comparing actual systems of representative government (Wilson),
constitutional law (Burgess), bureaucratic administration (Goodnow),
party organization (Macy), and other forms of the American state in comparison to other states.

Political science, in its allegiance with history, was by no means unique
or narrow in its appeals to *the* method. The established and emergent
disciplines, in varying degrees, heralded their rigor and epistemic authority in terms of historical comparison, notably philology, law, theology,
anthropology, political economy, and sociology. The disciplines rested
their factual claims on original sources, the older the better, and they situated their theoretical aspirations in the larger intellectual frameworks of
evolution and organicism, broadly understood. Not just time and change,
but progress was everywhere afoot. States, races, and languages, no less
than species and organisms, admitted of germs and germination, seeds
and growth.

"The historical method is many-sided," noted Frederick Pollock in *An
Introduction to the History of the Science of Politics.*[15] Aware of the

[11] Woolsey, *Political Science* 1:vii.

[12] Willoughby, *Nature*, 4.

[13] Bernard Moses, "Outline of Lectures on the Constitutional History of England and
Scandinavia," *Daily Evening Tribune* (Oakland, CA, 1878); Herbert B. Adams, "Special
Methods of Historical Study," in *Methods of Teaching History*, ed. G. Stanley Hall (Boston:
D. C. Heath, 1883); William M. Sloane, "The Science of History in the Nineteenth Cen-
tury," in *Congress of Arts and Sciences, Universal Exposition, St. Louis, 1904*, 2 vols, ed.
Howard J. Rogers (Boston: Houghton Mifflin, 1906); Garner, *Introduction to Political
Science*.

[14] Wilson, *The State*, xxxv.

[15] Frederick Pollock, *An Introduction to the History of the Science of Politics* (London:
Macmillan, 1890), 118–19.

broader intellectual frameworks of the age, he saw the many sides in lots of places. He saw it in the "scientific doctrine of evolution," the historical school of law, especially Savigny, as well as in the writings of Burke, Coleridge, Freeman, Cornewall Lewis, and Sir Henry Maine. No "school" could contain such multitude; at most there were aphorisms like "institutions are not made, but grow" and "whatever is becoming is best." Garner quoted Pollock to this effect in his own *Introduction to Political Science: A Treatise on the Origin, Nature, Functions, and Organization of the State*,[16] dedicated to Dunning. He dared a rather expansive definition, well beyond its basic injunction about the comparison of states: "the historical method . . . brings in review the great political movements of the past, traces the organic development of the national life, inquires into the growth of political ideas from their inception to their realization in objective institutions, discovers the moral idea as revealed in history and thereby points out the way of progress." While a testimony to its many (more) sides, even this definition did not fully capture the wealth and variety of the authorities that he went on to add to Pollock's list, including Bluntschli, Seeley, Bryce, Jellinek, Laboulaye, Deslandres, and Sidgwick, with glances back to Montesquieu and Tocqueville. In the course of his huge textbook, Garner also mentioned many Americans in matters of state, most notably Burgess. Burgess boasted of his own methodological "peculiarity" regarding historical comparison. He did allow, however, that "German publicists," including his teacher and friend Gustav Droysen as well as "Boutmy, Bryce, Dicey, Moses, and Wilson have already broken the ground."[17]

The many-sidedness of *the* method revealed the kind of disciplinary identity that existed among American political scientists, given their numerous European authorities. There was neither monolithic theory nor

---

[16] Garner, *Introduction to Political Science*, 29.

[17] John W. Burgess, *Political Science and Comparative Constitutional Law*, 2 vols. (Boston: Ginn, 1890), 1:vi. The many-sidedness of *the* method may be seen not only when looking "out" upon so many authorities, but looking "in" upon the ways that one of them, for example Burgess himself, characterized the methodological status of his corpus. In 1883, he advocated "a critical comparison of the sequence of facts in the history of different states or peoples at a like period in the development of their civilization." In 1890, he proclaimed that his was "an attempt to apply the method, which has been found so productive in the domain of Natural Science." In 1897, he boasted that "the most important element in political science" was "philosophical speculation which is the forerunner of history." One could wonder, as some critics did, whether this was not too much to expect from one method or one man. John W. Burgess, "On Methods of Historical Study and Research in Columbia University," in *Methods of Teaching History*, ed. G. Stanley Hall (Boston: D. C. Heath, 1883), 220; Burgess, *Political Science*, 1:vi; John W. Burgess, "Political Science and History," *Annual Report of the American Historical Association for 1896* (Washington, DC: Government Printing Office, 1897), 210.

hegemonic doctrine nor detailed blueprint of inquiry. Rather, disciplinary identity was consistent with—nay, it consisted in—diversity of opinion and debate. Identity was forensic and problematic; it was debated in terms of problems. The method of historical comparison was itself a problem that invited debate over the nature of its principles. Like any noteworthy problem, it was specified and respecified, over and again, in practice and proclamation. The range of specifications, especially concerning principles, disclosed a parallel range of aspirations and anxieties about political science, organized professionally, *as* science, *in* the public world.

The Problems with Principles

To judge by their ubiquity, *principles* dominated the methodological discourse of the historical scientists of politics. While seldom defined or treated to philosophical analysis,[18] they were repeatedly invoked, and much more often than "laws," "theories," or "models" (which were beginning to be discussed and would in the later twentieth century replace "principles" in most fields of political science). Science, philosophy, law, history, human nature, indeed most everything, had principles as foundations or consequences. Principles of politics and science connected political science to the venerable history of political thought more generally. As Moses recounted, "[T]he record of political thought is synonymous with the history of the science of politics."[19] In celebrated thinkers like Bacon, Hume, Montesquieu, and the great German philosophers, as well as American moral philosophers and statesmen, "principles" were the governing generalities for understanding politics, especially when conceived as "first," "fundamental," or "universal" principles. The historical scientists of politics later in the nineteenth century thus carried forward an earlier discourse. They did so, of course, under conditions dramatically changed by Civil War, Reconstruction, expanded suffrage, foreign immigration, industrial agitation, and imperial expansion, as well as their own disciplinary professionalization. In confronting these political and professional problems, political scientists also dealt with the recurring methodological problems surrounding the function, scope, and substance of principles. They did so with a deeper "historical consciousness" than obtained

---

[18] Woolsey discussed book 3 of *Spirit of the Laws*, where Montesquieu distinguished between the *nature* of government and the *principle* "by which it acts." He considered the changed context that modified Montesquieu's four major principles—that is, fear, honor, moderation, and virtue, but "principles" remained. Woolsey, *Political Science*, 2:519–20.

[19] Bernard Moses, "A Brief Survey of the Field of Political Inquiry," *Berkeleyan*, September 15, 1884, 28.

earlier, with their minds on seeds, germs, and growth.[20] Consider a short but representative list that confirms the many-sidedness of the historical method and indicates what the historical scientists were doing in using "principles" so diversely.

> Lieber in 1832, to Leopold von Ranke: "It is important for the historian to live in a politically active country. . . . And for the present time, of which the key is the democratic principle . . . the United States and France seem to me to be the high-schools of history."[21]

> Mulford in 1870, while identifying "the presentation of the nation" as "the aim of political science": "There is the unfolding of principles which are deeper than a formal order and a formal organization."[22]

Hart in 1883, to "lay down certain fundamental principles" of American history:[23]

1. *No* nation has a *history disconnected* from that of the rest of the world: the United States is closely related, in point of time, with previous ages; in point of space, with other civilized countries.
2. *Institutions* are a *growth*, and not a creation: the Constitution of the United States itself is constantly changing with the changes in public opinion.
3. Our institutions are *Teutonic in origin*: they have come to us through English institutions.
4. The growth of our institutions has been *from local to central*: the general government can, therefore, be understood only in the light of the early history of the country.
5. The *principle of union* is of slow growth in America: the Constitution was formed from necessity, and not from preference.
6. Under a *federal form of government* there must inevitably be a perpetual contest of authority between the States and the general government: hence two opposing doctrines of States-rights and nationality.
7. *National political parties* naturally appeal to the federal principle when in power, and to the local principle when out of power.
8. When parties become distinctly sectional, a *trial of strength* between a part of the States and the general government must come sooner or later.

[20] Dorothy Ross, "Historical Consciousness in Nineteenth-Century America," *American Historical Review* 89 (1984): 909–28.

[21] Quoted from Frank Freidel, *Francis Lieber: Nineteenth Century Liberal* (Baton Rouge: Louisiana State University Press, 1947), 88.

[22] Elisha Mulford, *The Nation: Foundations of Civil Order and Political Life in the United States* (New York: Hurd and Houghton, 1870), 383.

[23] Albert B. Hart, "Methods of Teaching American History," in *Methods of Teaching History*, ed. G. Stanley Hall (Boston: Ginn, Heath and Co, 1883), 3, emphasis in original.

Burgess in 1890, by drawing "the all important hermeneutical conclusion" that the Constitution was to be explained by "political history and political science," not juristic methods: "From this review of the history of the original formation of our present constitution, I contend that the procedure cannot be scientifically comprehended except upon the principle that the convention of 1787 assumed constituent powers, that is, assumed to be the representative organization of the American state, the sovereign in the whole system."[24]

Sloane in 1895, when providing the reason why the seat of sovereign power in the state is never the same in different stages of society: "Truth, justice, honor, the great principles of human association, have not changed, but man's apprehension of them has steadily grown clearer as his determination to live up to them has grown stronger, and as the individual has become ever more conscious of his powers."[25]

Burgess in 1896, to admirers and critics in the AHA: "Thrown into the form of propositions, ideals become *principles of political science*, then articles of political creeds, and at last laws and institutions. . . . National popular sovereignty, the basis both of government and of liberty, is the most fundamental principle of modern political science. Now, the development of this principle, and its objective realization in constitutional law, is the most complex and comprehensive of all the movements of history."[26]

Ford in 1905, when arraying its purpose in foreign states: "Political science must supply general principles for the guidance of statecraft."[27]

Bryce in 1909, to the political scientists gathered for his presidential address to the APSA: "Your science may be defined as the data of political history reclassified and explained as the result of certain general principles."[28]

Principles clearly carried weight and were made to do much work in the historical science(s) of politics. But, evident from this short list alone, they varied considerably in function and scope, as well as inspired contests over which among them deserved the grandest superlative. Principles were conceptualized as functioning in different ways: as *normative ideals*, *practical guides*, *regulative maxims*, and *explanatory generalities*. These four were conceptually distinct but not exclusive in actual use; one often blurred into another. In use, they also intertwined analytic and narrative

---

[24] Burgess, *Political Science* 1:107–8.

[25] Sloane, "History and Democracy," 5.

[26] Burgess, "Political Science and History," 207.

[27] Henry Jones Ford, "The Scope of Political Science," *Proceedings of the APSA, 1905* (1906): 205.

[28] James Bryce, "The Relations of Political Science to History and to Practice," *American Political Science Review* 3 (1909): 3.

approaches to the state or political topics more generally, thereby resisting or occluding the later twentieth century's tendency to distinguish these increasingly antithetical approaches. Furthermore, principles were *historicized* in three senses: there were principles *in history*, *of history*, and *unfolding in history*. Political scientists, thus, were historical not only when thinking of history as past politics or politics as present history, that is, in terms of Freeman's motto, but when their principles cast light on particular historical contexts, developments over time, or the grand sweep of evolutionary history.

First, as normative ideals, principles embodied deeply held or long revered values or virtues that were realized (or realizable) in the state. Truth, justice, and honor—on Sloane's tally of 1895—were prime examples of such normative ideals. So, too, were liberty, equality, and community, among a much longer (and debatable) list. Burgess offered an interesting variant of this view when he opined in 1896 before the AHA that ideals "when thrown into propositions" became "principles of political science"—the most fundamental of which was national sovereignty. These, in turn, via creeds, made laws and institutions possible. For him, it may be said, laws and institutions were *ideals made actual* by *the interposition of principles* promulgated as popular creeds.[29] As practical guides, second, principles directed political practice, often in light of the normative principles they too could embody. Burgess's was a particularly grand statement of this view, as of the other, since principles guided the most important practice of statesmen, namely, legislating as an act of sovereignty. This was the function that Ford had in mind a decade later when he spoke of "the guidance of statecraft." He thought such guidance particularly urgent for would-be democracies like China and Russia, "states whose activities are the chief centers of disturbance in world politics."[30] For such disruptive revolutionary states, Lieber's earlier bon mot to Ranke was

[29] "Actual" went beyond the merely factual for Burgess and his contemporaries. In his influential textbook *Actual Government*—remembered today, if at all, by title alone—Hart "attempt[ed] to describe the government as one might undertake to describe a great railroad." However, the "descriptive part" of this attempt was at one with the "historical part;" it began with "fundamental ideals"; and "description of realities sometimes becomes a criticism." Description, in short, implicated history, ideals, and criticism. Albert B. Hart, *Actual Government, as Applied under American Conditions* (New York: Longmans, Green, 1903), vii, viii, xix. In any case, "the actual" was widespread: see, for example, James Bryce, *The American Commonwealth*, 2 vols. (New York: Macmillan, 1893; first published in 1888), 1:4; Wilson, *The State*, 3; Jesse Macy, "The Relation of History to Politics," *Annual Report of the American Historical Association for 1893* (Washington, DC: Government Printing Office, 1895), 185; Willoughby, *Nature*, viii; Henry Jones Ford, *The Rise and Growth of American Politics: A Sketch of Constitutional Development* (New York: Macmillan, 1898), v; and Frank J. Goodnow, *Politics and Administration* (New York: Macmillan, 1900), 3.

[30] Ford, "Scope of Political Science," 200.

perhaps still apt: the two great postrevolutionary states, America and France, were "the high schools of history" capable of instructing other states in the proper understanding of "the democratic principle." The metaphor of schools underscored how principles, in this function as practical guides, were to edify, instruct, and educate. Not only did statesmen need education; so did ordinary citizens. Principles were the vehicles of civic pedagogy when Willoughby taught *The Rights and Duties of American Citizenship*.[31]

Principles served a third and fourth function for political inquiry, as regulative maxims and explanatory generalities. Both were displayed in Hart's striking list of 1883, as elsewhere. The list codified eight "fundamental principles" as an answer to the question, how shall American history be studied? The first two on the list functioned as maxims regulating how a student or a political scientist should undertake historical inquiry at all. They were reminiscent of the way Lieber, in his 1839 *Legal and Political Hermeneutics*, had articulated "principles of interpretation" for understanding or constructing texts or speech.[32] For Hart, then, the historical connectedness of nations (principle 1) and the organic growth of institutions (principle 2) were guides to inquiry. They made discoveries and explanations possible. They essentially restated central tenets of the historical, comparative method. Other principles on Hart's list functioned as explanatory generalities. In this role, they came closest in function to general laws or empirical generalizations, as was uppermost in Bryce's mind when he identified political science in terms of the explanatory function of "certain general principles" regarding "the data of political history." For example, farther down Hart's list, the Teutonic origin of American institutions via England (principle 3) and the increasing centralization of the American state (principle 4) were putative explanations of how or why the United States in fact evolved the way it had as a modern nation. Things might have turned out otherwise in America, as they did elsewhere in the world, had there not been a Teutonic diaspora or a successful policy of centralization in the face of sectional resistance unto civil war. Whereas the one sort of principle regulated inquiry, this sort explained what was found as a result of inquiry. These functions could be blurred, however, as could normative ideals and practical guides. For example, where the main clause of Hart's fourth principle explained institutional centralization in America, its subclause concerning the prior necessity of understanding "the early history of the country" clearly regulated inquiry. (No

---

[31] Westel W. Willoughby, *The Rights and Duties of American Citizenship* (New York: American Book, 1898).

[32] See James Farr, "Francis Lieber and the Interpretation of American Political Science," *Journal of Politics* 52 (1990): 1027–49.

historical scientist of politics would have repaired to anything other than early national history.) Similarly, while Teutonic origins (allegedly) explained the English provenance of American institutions of state, political scientists often presumed Teutonic origins and then proceeded to find them nearly everywhere they looked. This blurring of function did not erase the conceptual distinction between explanatory and regulative principles, and was defensible in light of the way that, for example, Newton's principles were used in natural science. However, it led critics to accuse political scientists (as the historian H. Morse Stephens did of Burgess at the 1896 AHA meeting) of finding what they were looking for. Alternatively, principles conveyed, via their blurred functionality, the multiple tasks that political scientists saw themselves performing, namely, explaining, interpreting, regulating, guiding, edifying, and educating at the same time.

Apart from their functional differentiation, principles were also *historicized*, in at least three different senses. Each casts a different light on what it was that made political science(s) historical. First, there were principles *in history*. Principles, that is, were historicized in that they claimed (normative, practical, regulative, or explanatory) relevance only for a particular context or a specific set of conditions or events. Historically specific claims to eras or epochs—even to some grandiose temporality like "modernity"—were standard fare. They were certainly of special relevance to the self-consciously *modern* political scientist when understanding the state after the eighteenth century. A variation of such principles—for example, the democratic principle that Lieber clocked for Ranke "at the present time"—presumed the particular contexts or conditions of particular states, like France or the United States. Even more historically specific (indeed, hermeneutical) claims could be a matter of principle, as in Burgess's 1890 allegation about the assumption of constituent powers by the Constitutional Convention in the year 1787. He could have dated it even more precisely, had he wished, or called the sovereignty of the American state the principle of 1787.[33]

Second, some key principles were understood as *unfolding in history*. The principle that Mulford had in mind when using this very phrase in 1870 was that of the nation. The principle of the nation unfolded over time in the experiences of particular people in particular lands. The national principle in the United States was, after the conclusion of the Civil War, near its maturity. It had by that time, to use synonyms of the day,

---

[33] When comparing the French and American declarations of rights, the Teutonist legal theorist Georg Jellinek declared: "The principles of 1789 are in reality the principles of 1776." Georg Jellinek, *The Declaration of the Rights of Man and of Citizen*, trans. Max Farrand (New York: Henry Holt, 1901), 89.

unfolded, emerged, developed, matured, grown, or progressed. Burgess, in 1896, hailed the "development" and "objective realization" of the related principle of national sovereignty as "the most complex and comprehensive of all the movements of history." The same was said of representation, federalism, and individualism among such principles. Sloane in 1895 offered in effect a quasi-psychological variant of this view. While "the great principles of human association" like truth, justice, and honor were in some ideal sense changeless, "man's apprehension" of them grew with his determination and consciousness over time.

Third, there were alleged principles *of history*. Evolution, broadly understood, figured as a paradigm for such principles. The principle was good for history as a whole, though its mechanism could be stated without reference to particular historical contexts. Some popular political scientists, like Fiske, and some academic ones, like Moses, endorsed a version of the evolutionary positivism associated with Spencer.[34] (In this regard and in terms of this volume, they went beyond the developmental historicism that was more often behind or on display in the work of their contemporaries.) For them, the language of laws came as readily as that of principles in connection with historical explanation on such a grand scale. Fiske, for example, equated "the laws of history . . . to which social changes conform" with "trustworthy primordial principles," noting how difficult it was to discover them amid "the mass of details" of history.[35] Other political scientists, like Willoughby, were critical of the biological basis of evolutionary doctrines;[36] however, they held no brief against the methodological vision that certain principles could be good for history as a whole. No political scientist, however, dedicated much energy to specifying with any exactitude a political mechanism analogous to natural selection or even the cruder "struggle for existence." Gestures to conquest or to organic development sufficed. Sometimes conquest and organic development vaguely went together, as when Fiske invoked "the law of organic development" to explain divergent courses of the history of "the Germanic tribes" who conquered the Roman Empire in the fifth century.[37] Later, Fiske would explicitly trace the tribe to America, via England, and allege that this coincided with "the Doctrine of Evolution."[38] Here was his version of "the Teutonic principle" that appeared on Hart's list of 1883.

[34] John Fiske, "The Laws of History," *North American Review* 109 (1869): 197–230; John Fiske, *American Political Ideas, Viewed from the Standpoint of Universal History* (New York: Harper and Brothers, 1885); Bernard Moses, "Social Science and Its Method," *Berkeley Journal of Social Science* 1 (1880): 1–14.

[35] Fiske, "Laws," 197–98.

[36] Willoughby, *Nature*.

[37] Fiske, "Laws," 216.

[38] Fiske, *American Political Ideas*, 109.

The Teutonic Principle

The Teutonic principle exerted an especially powerful hold on the imagination of most of the historical scientists of politics.[39] There were methodological reasons for this, as well as political and ideological ones. Known more simply as *Teutonism*,[40] the principle admitted of variations. The core notion was straightforward enough. American ideals and institutions of state were adaptations of earlier English ones that, in turn, found their lineage in Anglo-Saxon Britain and thereby in the history of the Teutonic tribes of Northern Europe. The germs and seeds of American ideals and institutions first sprouted, so to speak, in the ancient soil of the German forest. (Indeed, this rolling back could continue even further by placing the Teutons within the historical family of Aryan peoples, rendering Teutonism a northern variant of Aryanism.) The list of American ideals and institutions of state allegedly explained by the Teutonic principle proved impressive. Representation, federalism, deliberation, democracy, self-government, individualism, and nationalism were among the ideals. These ideals ("when thrown into propositions," as Burgess put the larger point) were some of the most important principles of political science, making the Teutonic principle a higher-order principle. Institutions, which actualized these ideals and principles, included municipal governments, town meetings, cooperative husbandry, parliamentary procedures, independent judiciaries, written charters, and public elections. All of these, and more, were traced to the fierce independence, the public meetings (*moots*), and federal arrangements (*marks*) of the village communities of the Teutonic north, running back to before the fifth century.

The Teutonic principle thus satisfied the highest standards demanded by the historical, comparative method and realized the highest ambitions

[39] For the Teutonic "germ" principle in America, see Peter Novick, *That Noble Dream: The "Objectivity Question" and the American Historical Profession* (New York: Cambridge University Press, 1988), 76–89; Ross, *Origins*, 262–74; and Adcock, "Emergence." For Britain, see, in addition to den Otter's chapter in this volume, Reginald Horsman, "Origins of Racial Anglo-Saxonism in Great Britain before 1850," *Journal of the History of Ideas* 27 (1976): 387–410; Stefan Collini, Donald Winch, and John Burrow, *That Noble Science of Politics: A Study in Nineteenth-Century Intellectual History* (Cambridge: Cambridge University Press, 1983), chap. 7 on Freeman and Maine; Richard A. Cosgrove, *Our Lady the Common Law: The Anglo-American Legal Community, 1870–1930* (New York: New York University Press, 1987), chap. 3

[40] Lieber, *Civil Liberty*, 620; John Fiske, *The Beginnings of New England* (Boston: Houghton Mifflin, 1889), 29; William A. Dunning, "Review of Hannis Taylor, *The Origin and Growth of the English Constitution*," *Political Science Quarterly* 5 (1890): 188; John W. Burgess, "Chief Questions of Present American Politics," *Political Science Quarterly* 23 (1908): 391

of developmental historicism. But its appeal for the Americans was also political and ideological. It suggested that the principles of union binding the American nation existed long before the Constitution or the Declaration of Independence. In this way, the principle reached back beyond the breach of the Civil War and Reconstruction to ideals and institutions of state prior to any founding document that could still inspire sectional discontent or the spirit of disunity. The most important and binding principles of union, that is, were centuries old and unwritten. They could encompass and recover the post-Reconstruction South by extending everyone's memory deeper into time. The American Revolution was thereby rendered less memorable in the course of forging improved relations with England. Where England had a problem dealing with non-Teutonic peoples in its colonies, America had problems with such peoples domestically, as well as in its incipient imperial advance. Any grounds for reparations for slavery or indigenous dislocations, much less those for expanded suffrage or unfettered immigration, could not be traced to the Teutonic heritage of American ideals and institutions. Indeed that heritage counseled against enfranchisement and immigration of non-Teutonic peoples while it encouraged a mission of empire to bring the state and civilization to such peoples. In this way, the Teutonic principle served the purposes of racial exclusion and what surely must count as academic racism.[41] America was, would remain, and should promote that which was English, Anglo-Saxon, Teutonic, and Aryan.

The Teutonic principle proved popular, as well as powerful. "By the 1880s," it was "generally accepted within the historical profession" and "for several years dominated American historical thought."[42] It was also accepted in political science since the thinkers in question—like Adams, Wilson, Burgess, and Hart—composed the same academic population. The principle thus coincided with the second moment and therefore high tide of the historical science(s) of politics. However, the historical scientists often gave credit to earlier figures, the most celebrated of whom was Montesquieu, who had stated that in reading "the admirable work of

---

[41] Indeed, racialist theory and academic racism found expression beyond the Teutonic principle. Dunning, for example, criticized Teutonist historiography, but believed that African descendants were inferior to whites. They were without "pride of race," he proclaimed, and unfit for suffrage during Reconstruction (cited in Novick, *That Noble Dream*, 75). Bryce admonished Americans: "you must not . . . legislate in the teeth of facts. The great bulk of negroes were not fit for the suffrage." James Bryce, *The Relations of the Advanced and Backward Races* (Oxford: Clarendon Press, 1903), 39. When Teutonism ended after World War I, other racial and racist doctrines came in train with eugenics and mental testing, of which Merriam approved. Charles E. Merriam, *New Aspects of Politics* (Chicago: University of Chicago Press, 1970; first published in 1925), chap 6.

[42] Novick, *That Noble Dream*, 87–88.

Tacitus, *On the Mores of the Germans*, one will see that the English have taken their idea of political government from the Germans. This fine system was found in the forests."[43] (Adams made this, in French, an epigraph for his 1882 essay, "On the Germanic Origin of New England Towns," alongside the saying of Freeman, "If you wish to see Old England, you must go to New England.")[44] Earlier nineteenth-century scholars were more immediate authorities for the Teutonic principle, including John Kemble, Francis Palgrave, William Stubbs, Maine, and especially Freeman (whose lectures in the United States in 1880 and 1881 did much to further popularize Teutonism). If true that "by the early 1890s many were disenchanted" with the principle,[45] many others would stay enchanted, at least until World War I. Garner in 1910, for example, stated as matter of fact, in reference to Montesquieu and Freeman, that "the beginnings of the modern representative system are found in the folkmoots of the early Teutons of Germany."[46] It may be that Teutonism owed its popularity and relative long life to "its imprecise expression and the changing nature of its codewords."[47] Or, it might be that its codewords stayed the same amid different attempts at more precise expression. Either way, the Teutonic principle admitted of variations and did not go utterly unchallenged. The unity it provided for the historical science(s) of politics was thus forensic and problem oriented, like the discipline itself in its articulation of *the* method of historical comparison.

The main variations turned upon the matter and meaning of race. The core notion of the Teutonic principle could be stated in nonracial terms, as above, or in Hart's list of 1883, or in Garner's compact expression of 1910. Many variations that invoked the terminology of "race" could have been and at times were expressed in terms of "culture," "institutions," or just "history." However, over time, the Teutonic principle was increasingly racialized, with noted exceptions. The process began early. Indeed, in what must be one of its earliest expressions in America, Lieber in 1838 used the codewords of Teutonism to explain the origins of "hamacracy," that is, those states that brought independent parts into an organic whole, as representative and federal systems did. "The true germs of hamacratic polity must be sought for in the conquests of the Teutonic races, and the consequent feudal system." The conquests brought to post-Roman

---

[43] Charles Louis Montesquieu, *The Spirit of the Laws*, ed. Anne Cohler, Basia Miler, and Harold Stone (Cambridge: Cambridge University Press, 1989; first published in 1748), 165–66.

[44] Herbert B. Adams, "The Germanic Origins of New England Towns," *Johns Hopkins University Studies in Historical and Political Science* 2 (1882): 5–38.

[45] Novick, *That Noble Dream*, 88.

[46] Garner, *Introduction to Political Science*, 475.

[47] Cosgrove, *Our Lady*, 109.

Europe a "national singleness of heart," as well as the rule of "the northern man, calmer, more phlegmatic, duller, [who] weighs things more individually, learns to consider the state in relation to himself, and is led more easily to reflect on individual interests—on rights."[48] These were "race" characteristics of a minimal sort that could be unpacked into elementary psychology, national character, or institutional history. When Lieber returned to the topic in 1853, at a time when it was still relatively novel, he allowed that northern Europeans formed a "Cis-Caucasian race" whose highest claim was "the Teutonic spirit of individual independence." However, the Teutonic nations had by then gone their separate ways. Germany had lost its liberty by copying "Gallican" (that is, French) centralization. Only England and America held the last and most important race vestige, "Anglican liberty."[49] By 1871, Lieber went further still. He allowed the existence of a "Teutonic race" only to deny a "Latin race," much less a "Southern race" as some Confederate "rebels" had claimed. Moreover, "races are very often invented from ignorance, or for evil purposes." Indeed, "the word race has probably been abused in modern times more than any other" and "all the noblest things" like truth, science, and civil liberty, "are not restricted to races."[50]

By the 1880s, the discourse of race in connection with the Teutonic principle was more pronounced and emphatic. It nonetheless kept in the foreground the institutional heritage of northern Europe, as developed subsequently in England and the United States. (The Teutonic race gave the world good government, not good genes, as it were, though this came as no consolation to the races that needed good government imposed upon them.) In a series of essays, Adams developed a case that "the germs of our state and national life" were to be found in the townships of New England that embodied "the great principle of self-government." These germs and this principle could be traced to Old England and eventually to "a band of Saxon pirates." The Pilgrim fathers, like their piratical forebears, "were merely one branch of the great Teutonic race, a single offshoot from the tree of liberty" still "budding, spreading, and propagating" in America.[51] This racial-cum-institutional argument, decked out in organic metaphor, found expression in other sources, including "The Germs of National Sovereignty" by Fiske, who also drew upon the organic imagery of "blood" to convey the sanguinary power of Teutonism,

---

[48] Francis Lieber, *Manual of Political Ethics*, ed. Thedore D. Woolsey, 2 vols. (Philadelphia: J. B. Lippincott, 1911; first published in 1838) 1:356, 374–75.
[49] Lieber, *Civil Liberty*, 47–48, n. 53.
[50] Lieber, *Miscellaneous Writings* 2:308–9.
[51] Adams, "Germanic Origins," 5, 6, 23.

if not the mechanism of its transmission.[52] This deeper racialization of the Teutonic principle was neither fully developed nor conceptually stable, but it was telling nonetheless. In *The Beginnings of New England,* for example, Fiske lauded "the Teutonic method," especially for explaining the origin of "the principle of representation." This principle was "the common property of Teutonic tribes," especially England, "the most Teutonic of all European countries" despite the fact that it was "only half-Teutonic in blood." In America, the bloodlines were much murkier, though the Teutonic principle had been "worked out even more completely." While Americans were working it out, Fiske added, "Indians were simply thrust aside, along with the wolves and buffaloes."[53] This, notoriously, was the larger message of Fiske's most famous essay, "Manifest Destiny." The conceptual conundrums of Teutonic racial identity were similarly on display in *The State,* where Wilson spoke warmly of "Saxon blood" and the "Aryan race," fearfully cognizant that the United States "possess[ed] so large an admixture of foreign blood." But it was "Aryan practice we principally wish to know" in a comparative and historical account of the modern state. The Teutonic Aryans had uniquely discovered and implemented "the principle of individualism" and "the principle of representation" in assemblies under trusted individuals speaking for the nation. This was "the peculiar fruit of Teutonic political organization" that had become "thoroughly Anglo-American" after historical transmission by conquest and colonization. Moreover, conscious and progressive adaptation of the "fierce democratic temper" of those "primitive Teutonic institutions" was now historically possible in America, despite its admixture of bloods.[54]

Burgess was the veritable dean of Teutonism among the historical scientists of politics. In his lectures, speeches, and writings, over half a century, he made the Teutonic principle the grand explanation for the development of the modern state, usually in the most explicitly racialized form. Indeed, at times, he essentialized race as a fixed, ethnic, blood property that determined political life: "The Teuton really dominates the world by his superior political genius."[55] "Only the race-proud Teutons" had "preserved the Aryan genius for political civilization" because they "suffered but in small measure the mixture of other Aryan blood" and "resisted amalgamation with non-Aryan branches."[56] At other times, Burgess conceived the

[52] John Fiske, "The Germs of National Sovereignty in the United States," *Atlantic Monthly* 58 (1886): 648–66.

[53] Fiske, *Beginnings of New England,* 20, 23, 26.

[54] Wilson, *The State,* 2, 26, 367, 499, 580.

[55] Burgess, *Political Science* 1:4.

[56] John W. Burgess, "The Ideal of the American Commonwealth," *Political Science Quarterly* 10 (1895): 406.

Teutonic heritage in less racialized and much less essentialized terms. Indeed, for him, in general, the state was the political organization of a nation that was in turn identified in terms of a people inhabiting a fixed territory. The people need not *necessarily* be identified in terms of "sameness of race" as opposed to the commonalities of language, literature, and tradition. It was precisely this that allowed nations to emerge from the confluence of different races and eventually to create a state for themselves—or have one provided for them. This made it possible for "Teutonic nations . . . to carry the political civilization of the modern world into those parts of the world inhabited by unpolitical and barbaric races." From them, "the propaganda must go out." This justified "a colonial policy" of advanced states, while underscoring the power of "education" for races at various stages of civilization. Even then, however, Burgess's racialization of Teutonism—and the specter of germination—limited the power of education or the propaganda of civilization. "Education," he admitted, "can only develop what already exists in seed and germ; no amount of Roman discipline could have evolved the national idea unless this idea had been an original principle of Teutonic political genius." In America, moreover, education and racial amalgamation may go forward, at least for different Aryans, but "the Negroes . . . seem destined to maintain a separate race existence."[57] Immigration from Africa, as well as Asia and southern Europe, should thus be limited, if not halted. Besides racializing Teutonism, Burgess also adjusted its historical and Anglophilic character. The Teutonic state was an emergent property of history, over the long haul, but the conquests of Rome and Britain in the fifth century did not figure strongly in Burgess's historiography; the primitive forms of the Teutonic state were far less important than later developments, when the German empire stirred itself. Indeed, "the German empire is the great political representative of the continental Teutons and the moving power in the spread of Teutonism to other parts of Europe."[58] This provided Burgess with the historical comparative grounds for identifying German as well as English precedents for American institutional developments, not to mention securing the allegiances of America with Germany as well as England, if not Germany over England in the event of contest.

Not every historical scientist of politics embraced the Teutonic principle,[59] whether in weaker institutional or stronger racial form. Their objec-

---

[57] Burgess, *Political Science* 1:2, 45, 37, 29.

[58] Burgess, "Chief Questions of Present American Politics," 391.

[59] Objections came from others, too, like Marx: "Germanomaniacs . . . seek our history of freedom beyond our history in the primeval Teutonic forests. But what difference is there between the history of our freedom and the history of the boar's freedom, if it can be found only in the forests? Let us leave the ancient Teutonic forests in peace!" Karl Marx, "Introduction to Contribution to the Critique of Hegel's *Philosophy of Law*," in *Marx-Engels Collected Works* (New York: International, 1975), 3:177, 180.

tions were significant in their respective contexts. Well before the high tide of Teutonism, for example, Mulford rejected "a certain school" that explained the development of the state and the more laudable bits of history as a result of "the power and supremacy of *a* race," where race was based upon "a physical foundation." Worse, their "dream of a vast federation of the Anglo-Saxon race" was "an illusion" and a sign of "the decay of national spirit." The nation was its own force of history, not a front for a race of Teutonic Aryans.[60] For Dunning, race was less an issue than were claims about primitive origins and institutional developments that he found in admirers of Freeman, like Fiske and Hannis Taylor. In 1890, he spoke scathingly of the unfulfilled "promise of ultra-Teutonism" in the case of Taylor, a Southern Teutonist and historical comparativist who became minister to Spain. Alleging "the historical method," Taylor and his ilk never "hesitated to proclaim that practically the whole fabric of modern civilization rests upon the simple fact that some half-savage villagers in Sleswick and Friesland used to send some of their number now and then to wrangle over neighborhood matters with their kinsmen from other villages."[61] Dunning virtually said of Taylor what he later said of Fiske: "It is quite typical of his mental attitude that his *Beginnings of New England* starts with the year 476, the assumed year of the mythical fall of a hypothetical empire."[62] Speaking to this issue in *Actual Government*, Hart continued to endorse English precedents of American institutions, while debunking the bogus historiography of other Teutonists. "We have no positive evidence that German institutions were conveyed over into England by the Saxons in the fifth century. We know very little of the Saxon governments previous to the Norman Conquest."[63] But the problem went far beyond corroborated knowledge of dates, places, and primitive forms. The Normans as much or more than the Saxons and Teutons had influenced institutions of state in England and thereby America. Modern federalism in the United States was in any case a novel development designed to balance the centralization that a modern state required; it was not the lingering result of primitive arrangements. Furthermore, counterfactually, "the much-lauded Teutonic principle of local self-government, left to itself, would have maintained or further subdivided the Heptarchy."[64] There would have been seven or more petty kingdoms, not a modern state.

[60] Mulford, *The Nation*, 360–61.

[61] Dunning, "Review of Hannis Taylor," 188–90.

[62] William A. Dunning, *Truth in History and Other Essays*, ed. J. G. de Roulhac Hamilton (New York: Columbia University Press, 1937), 158.

[63] Hart, *Actual Government*, 39, 41.

[64] Dunning, "Review of Hannis Taylor," 190.

Hart and Dunning chose not to criticize Burgess by name, although he was as much "an ardent worshipper of Teutonism triumphant" as Taylor or anyone else.[65] Willoughby was more direct in criticizing what Burgess called "the practical conclusions" of the Teutonic principle in matters of empire. In *Social Justice*, he sought to place conditions under which a "superior race" was justified in imposing state and civilization upon an inferior, including disinterestedness, attentiveness to the "peculiar needs and circumstances" of the people in question, demonstrated surety of their improvement, and consideration of consequences that such imperial action might form a pretext for future "criminal aggression." Yet, with these qualifications in mind, Willoughby endorsed and quoted at length Burgess's editorial about the "mission" of world organization having fallen to "Teutonic nations."[66] When he subsequently returned to consider Burgess's views of political science, he proved much less indulgent of the latter's "historical theory," "racial psychology," and "absolutist reasoning." Quoting the very same page as before, Willoughby let Burgess's words about "Providence" and "'manifest mission'" damn themselves. He found Burgess's reasoning "unwarrantable" in thinking so highly and divinely of the modern state in Europe and America. It had defects, would change, and had no chance of achieving the "ethnically homogeneous citizen body" that Burgess desired. He looked forward to a time in the not-distant future when "men will . . . rise superior to the ordinary prejudices of race, history and tradition" and form a more moral union. He ended, in effect, by withdrawing his earlier endorsement of Burgess and denying to Teutonic states any superiority, providential mission, or use of force against other peoples until they were "prepared to adopt" modern forms of political life.[67]

World War I would have a more decisive effect on the fate of the Teutonic principle. However, the criticisms were a sign of trends in the early twentieth century, that is, during a third moment in the temporal arc of the historical sciences of politics. In the run-up to war, other trends emerged as harbingers of a later political science. But before political scientists embraced a new identity, they would go on debating principles, comparing states, teaching citizens, guiding statesmen, and thinking of their science in historical terms long after associating into a professional disciplinary body.

[65] Ibid., 188.

[66] Westel W. Willoughby, *Social Justice: A Critical Essay* (New York: Macmillan, 1900), 266–67.

[67] Westel W. Willoughby, "The Political Theories of Professor John W. Burgess," *Yale Review* 17 (1908): 68, 71–72.

The Association of Historical Political Scientists

The American Political Science Association was founded on December 30, 1903, at Tulane University in New Orleans. Its setting was the American Historical Association's nineteenth annual meeting and its first in the Old South. The American Economic Association (AEA) met with the AHA and the new APSA. It was an important occasion in itself. It certainly marked, as the founders knew, a moment of further professionalization of political science as a discipline. It established more formally a community of inquirers—many academics, many more from outside the academy—as well as the means of communication between them, mainly through annual face-to-face meetings and journals that published scholarly articles and professional news. It symbolized a distinction and a nominal break from the parental association, as well as other associations. And in retrospect it created what was to become (by now) a century-old institutional body that exerted enormous influence over the shape of the discipline. Beyond these professional milestones, caution is in order about what to make of the founding of the APSA, at least to judge by the founders' intentions as recorded in their documents. It did not create a group of experts cut apart from or elevated above society, whatever snobbishness attended the turn-of-the-century professorate. It did not lend any greater authority to professionals than their academic institutions or individual efforts secured. It did not deflect or redefine the inherited duties to engage practical life, especially in terms of civic education. It did not amount to a reform institution by the standards of the Progressive Era, let alone progressive politics. And it did not mark the end of the historical method or filial relations with the discipline of history. The historical scientists of politics would create the APSA, and they would live comfortably under its auspices for many years. They would also tolerate or accommodate newer (modernist empiricist) interests and methods that bore upon the future identity of political science, notably psychology, pragmatic inquiry, and the idea of process.

The founding of the APSA was preceded by some noteworthy developments in the AHA. A new generation of professional historians was emerging to propound a deeper historicism of contextual understanding as a challenge to the developmental principles and political orientation of the historical scientists of politics like Burgess and Adams. History was to be studied "for its own sake," pronounced Stephens in his clash at the AHA meeting of 1896 with Burgess over the words of our epigraph. "We should study history," Stephens insisted, "with the endeavor to find out the truth, not with the endeavor of understanding how free this or that or the other country is; not for the purpose of explaining how superior the government of our own country is to any other country, and still less for the purpose of justifying any particular theory of government."[68] While Dunning joined the fray as "a man rather interested in political science quite as much as in history," it was apparent that many historians needed political science far less than political science needed history.[69] There was no immediate institutional consequence from this encounter. But it was clear that the AHA need not be the *only* professional association to serve the institutional needs of historically minded political scientists, any more than it need do so for historically minded economists who had already formed their own association (in 1885) or historically minded sociologists who were on the path to forming theirs (in 1905). Indeed, there was a longer history of associations in which the historical scientists of politics had taken part before or alongside the AHA, including the Historical and Political Science Association (at Johns Hopkins), the Political Science Association (at Michigan), the Academy of Political and Social Science (in New York), the Political Science Association of the Central States, and especially the American Social Science Association.[70]

The AHA helped the momentum toward an institutionally distinctive APSA through an ad hoc committee at the 1902 annual meeting. The committee set about to consider creating an American Society of Comparative Legislation. The focus of this never-to-be society sounded tailor-made for, among others, Burgess and Frank J. Goodnow (who, like Dunning, was Burgess's former student and current colleague at Columbia). Burgess and Goodnow joined the committee, along with eleven others, including Jeremiah W. Jenks of Cornell. The committee as a whole soon discovered far broader interests than legislation across the country, in and out of the academy. The focus shifted to "political science" as a whole. The committee itself morphed, keeping seven original members, including Jenks as chair, and adding eight more, among them Willoughby, Simeon Baldwin, Henry Pratt Judson, and Paul S. Reinsch.[71] Burgess declined to participate, and Goodnow had competing commitments. Goodnow

[68] H. Morse Stephens, "Remarks upon Professor Burgess's Paper," *Annual Report of the American Historical Association for 1896* (Washington, DC: Government Printing Office, 1897), 211–15.

[69] William A. Dunning, "Remarks," *Annual Report of the American Historical Association for 1896* (Washington, DC: Government Printing Office, 1897), 219.

[70] Haskell dates "the deathblow to the American Social Science Association" to "the organization of the APSA in 1903." Thomas L. Haskell, *The Emergence of Professional Social Science* (Urbana: University of Illinois Press, 1977), 230.

[71] The composition of these committees has been pieced together from William Anderson, "Political Science Enters the Twentieth Century," in *Political Science in American Colleges and Universities, 1636–1900*, ed. Anna Haddow (New York: D. Appleton-Century, 1939), 262; and from Westel W. Willoughby, "The American Political Science Association," *Political Science Quarterly* 19, no. 1 (1904): 110n.

would return shortly in high fashion while Burgess (allegedly, colorfully) "receded into the midnight of neglect."[72]

At the 1903 meeting, the new association began by operating like any proper ministate: it wrote a constitution, named departments, and elected officers. In the American way, the constitution was lean and brief, as if pretending to avoid future hermeneutical disputes. The first article named the association; the seventh and last article made provision for amendments. The object of encouraging "the scientific study of Politics, Public Law, Administration, and Diplomacy" was stated without specifying what "scientific study" actually entailed. There was not a word about reform or Teutonism, and the only reference to practical politics was hedged by express denials of partisanship, establishing a precedent for similar disclaimers to follow. Goodnow, whose scholarly credentials were based upon the historical comparative study of administration and law, was elected president. He defined the topics of his well-received 1900 book, *Politics and Administration*, in terms of the state: politics was about legislation and administration, "the will of the state." Critical of those who revered the unadorned words of constitutional texts, Goodnow quoted Burgess at length regarding the separation of state and government in terms of sovereignty; and he used a phrase of Burgess's to characterize his methodological intent, namely, "to get back of the formal governmental organization and examine the real political life of the people."[73] The administration of Goodnow's own presidency of the APSA mainly included historical comparativists or theorists of the state. Wilson (who declined to serve), Reinsch, and Baldwin were elected vice presidents, with Willoughby as secretary and treasurer. An Executive Council included, among others, Moses, Macy, Judson, William A. Schaper of Minnesota (later martyr to academic freedom during World War I), and Andrew Dickson White, then ambassador to Germany and formerly head instructor of the "course of history and political science" at Cornell. Present to endorse these professional first steps were, besides the officers, Hart, Dunning, and Merriam, then known for work in the history of political thought, especially on sovereignty.

The new association issued forth into the academic world with notices by two of its officers, Reinsch in the *Iowa Journal of History and Politics*

---

[72] Albert Somit and Joseph Tanenhaus, *The Development of Political Science: From Burgess to Behavioralism* (Boston: Allyn and Bacon, 1967), 52n.

[73] Goodnow, *Politics and Administration*, 1, 3–4. Goodnow draws here on Burgess's oft-quoted line: "[G]overnment is not the sovereign organization of the state. Back of the government lies the constitution; and back of the constitution the original sovereign state." Burgess, *Political Science* 1:57. Merriam also approved. See Charles E. Merriam, *History of the Theory of Sovereignty since Rousseau* (New York: Columbia University Press, 1900), 180.

and Willoughby in the *Political Science Quarterly*, the house organ of the Columbia School of Political Science, still under Burgess's wing. Each underscored the association's intent to avoid political controversy by taking no sides. "Practical politics" were still of interest, nonetheless, and the broader purpose of political science to "promote the better understanding of the obligations resting upon our citizenship" was announced as in keeping with partisan neutrality. Despite the professional breach with the AHA, history was still taken to be "an allied subject," and the seven departments clearly entailed historical work in areas like comparative legislation, constitutional law, and political theory. One department—Comparative and Historical Jurisprudence—used the very language of the historical science(s) of politics.[74] In his sketch, Willoughby identified the similarity of interests between the two disciplines of history and political science. He looked beyond formal departments to name three broad fields of political science that the search committee had originally identified, namely, political theory, public law, and the general study of government. "All these topics," he stated, "lend themselves to theoretical, descriptive, comparative or historical treatment" and "involve or at least lead up to the discussion of practical problems of government."[75]

No sooner had the APSA taken flight than nearly every effort was made to keep in close organizational contact with the AHA and in intellectual proximity to history as a field of political learning. Most members in the new association kept their membership in the old one. The annual meetings of the two associations were frequently held jointly: Chicago, 1904; Baltimore, 1905; Providence, 1906; Madison, 1907; Richmond, 1908; New York, 1909; Buffalo, 1911; Boston, 1912; Washington, 1915; Cincinnati, 1916; Philadelphia, 1917; Cleveland, 1918; Washington, 1920; and Columbus, 1923. The joint meeting in Washington in 1927—when William B. Munro unleashed his presidential address "Physics and Politics"—finally saw the end of the tradition. The presidential addresses of the respective associations were usually presented in joint session, as well. The pairings of APSA and AHA presidents during those sessions usually confirmed complementarity of disciplinary orientation. In any case, the pairings included Albert Shaw with Baldwin in 1906; Judson with J. Franklin Jameson in 1907; Bryce with George B. Adams in 1908; Lowell with Hart in 1909; Baldwin with Sloane in 1911; Ernst Freund with Stephens in 1915; Macy with George Burr in 1916; and Reinsch with Edward Channing in 1920. Five historical political scientists were presidents of both the APSA and AHA, respectively: Wilson in 1910 and 1924;

---

[74] Paul S. Reinsch, "The American Political Science Association," *Iowa Journal of History and Politics* 2 (1904): 157, 160.
[75] Willoughby, "American Political Science Association," 108.

Baldwin in 1911 and 1906; Hart in 1912 and 1909; Dunning in 1922 and 1913; and Charles Beard in 1926 and 1933.[76] The filial relations between history and political science were routinely announced in the texts or during the sessions of the presidential addresses. Those of Goodnow, Bryce, Wilson, Baldwin, and Hart stand out in this regard. During one prominent session, Dunning raised a toast that echoed the point of Freeman and Burgess, as well as the rhetoric of Daniel Webster: "History and Political Science, now and forever, two and inseparable."[77]

Outside of professional associations, pronouncements of intellectual affinity continued apace, as did soldiering on the fields of historical comparison of state forms. Political scientists often came off, without apology, simply *as* historians of the contemporary state or comparative states, armed with political theory, concerned to provide principles, and obligated to discharge practical duties like civic education. There was plenty of debate and diversity of opinion about all this (as amply discussed above). But here was the discipline still, in its third moment, forensically united around the problems of the historical method. The Congress of Arts and Science at the Universal Exposition at St. Louis, a few months after the founding of the APSA, provided a celebrated stage for the major figures to continue the work of the historical science(s) of politics. Wilson, Sloane, Baldwin, Dunning, Willoughby, Bryce, Moses, Reinsch, Shaw, and Burgess all delivered addresses. (So did Max Weber, and Merriam officiated a session.) When surveying the scene in 1907, Dunning found "the historical method" to be dominant in the United States. The large books canvassing the American discipline, notably those by Garner and Gettell, both in 1910, prominently advertised their comparative and historical method when analyzing the state. (Garner would do so again in 1928, as would Gettell in 1933, when issuing revised tomes.) Burgess actively pursued publication of the programmatic chapters of *Political Science and Comparative Constitutional Law* in 1917; they would eventually be published, posthumously, as *The Foundations of Political Science* in 1933. As president of Johns Hopkins, Goodnow gave lectures in China in 1913 and then published them in 1916 as *Principles of Constitutional Government* in Harper's Citizen's Series (the same series in which Hart's *Actual Government* had appeared). Not only was the terminology

---

[76] Information compiled from *Annual Reports of the American Historical Association and American Political Science Review* (overlooking minor inconsistencies).

[77] In his introduction to a collection of Dunning's essays, J. G. de Roulhac Hamilton quotes Dunning's toast (at "the Cincinnati meeting," presumably 1916) as "his gratification that the political scientists had come home." Dunning, *Truth in History*, xv. Alas, the previous annual meeting had in fact been held jointly. Ironically, Dunning gave both of his presidential addresses at meetings that were not held jointly.

of "principles" prominently displayed; so was *the* method of historical comparison and the will to edify foreign statesmen and American citizens. On the eve of World War I, the members of the APSA who were academics found their homes in various departments. Among them were thirty-eight departments of "political science" compared to eighty-nine of "history and political science."[78]

The Process, Psychology, and Pragmatic Inquiry of a Future Political Science

There was never to be a remarkable moment or dramatic rupture when the historical science(s) of politics came to an end in the United States. There were certainly never any formal declarations of independence by political scientists from the discipline of history or from historical inquiry as such. Slower processes eventually did the work of separation in some fields, but not for the discipline as a whole. By 1923, a select group of scholars felt confident to announce the arrival of a "new science of politics" in a national conference with this title. Two more conferences followed in successive years. In 1925, Merriam—the leader of a new "Chicago School"—wrote a manifesto, *New Aspects of Politics*. The new science was to "get behind" legal "formalities" to the "actual" world of politics. In short, familiarly and ironically, it was heralded in the very way that the historical scientists announced their work on the state, four or more decades earlier. Prior to World War I, though, there were certain trends that foretold a future political science less oriented to principles, history, and the comparison of states. Three seem particularly noteworthy.

From the vantage of 1925, Merriam looked back on the first of these trends as "the beginnings of the psychological treatment of politics." This was a natural extension of tendencies toward observation and measurement that began in 1900 with the later generation of historical comparativists and statists. Merriam found it worth quoting Bryce that "politics has its roots in psychology, the study (in their actuality) of the mental habits of mankind." Graham Wallas pursued this line in *Human Nature in Politics*, an antirationalist treatise that proved influential on Wallas's American student (and John Dewey's antagonist) Walter Lippmann in *Public Opinion* and *The Phantom Public*.[79] The "borderland between psychol-

---

[78] Anderson, "Political Science," 263.

[79] Graham Wallas, *Human Nature in Politics* (London: Constable, 1908); Walter Lippmann, *Public Opinion* (New York: Macmillan, 1922); Walter Lippmann, *The Phantom Public* (New York: Harcourt Brace, 1925).

ogy and politics" that Merriam espied in Bryce, Wallas, and Lippmann had undergone even further exploration by the teens and twenties. On one side, there was the individual, especially his or her attitudes and opinions, being researched by "statistical inquiries and actual surveys." *Actual surveys*—the phrase echoing the boasts and ghosts of the recent past—proved crucial. They *constructed new facts*, quite literally, that the historical method could not provide. On the other side of the border, there was the state—"in the army, in the court, in the administration, in the custodial institution, in the schools"—deploying the new psychology *as* education, mental testing, or propaganda.[80] Political scientists were clearly not over "the state," in theory or practice. Rather, they were fascinated with new forms of popular control that psychology made possible in states, whether democratic or nondemocratic.

A second trend advanced the (competing or complementary) belief that politics or government was a process consisting in the dynamic play and pressure of groups organized around the interests of their members. Political science, in short, was to be the systematic study of interest group process. A sociological imagination was at work here; process language was already to be found in the sociological treatises of Albion Small and Franklin Giddings, peers and colleagues of the historical scientists of the state, as well as in the pragmatist philosophies of William James and John Dewey. Arthur Bentley made the most sustained case for this belief among political scientists, in his 1908 *The Process of Government*. In the pragmatist spirit, Bentley's epigraph announced that "This Book Is an Attempt to Fashion a Tool" for inquiry. Bentley implemented his case in accusatory and spirited vocabulary. Political scientists needed to abandon "the piteous, threadbare joke" of sovereignty, the "soul stuff" of German statists, and the fantasies of "mystic philosophers of history." More constructively, they needed to disaggregate "the state" into states, then states into governments, and then (once again, though in different direction) to "go back behind the governments" to the "actual development process" of interest groups "pressing one another." Group process was not the end of the state, or of history. It was "the backbone of history" and the way a "theoretical political science" could meaningfully speak of the state, if it must. In this way, Bentley's process theory of politics deserves to be remembered for criticizing "history of the older style" in order to reorient—not overthrow—the historical and comparative method. Consider:

> When we succeed in isolating an interest group the only way to find out what it is going to do, indeed the only way to be sure we have isolated an interest group, is to watch its progress. When we have made sure of one such interest,

[80] Merriam, *New Aspects*, 132, 148, 155, 161, 173.

or group, we shall become more skillful and can make sure of another similar one with less painstaking. When we have compared many sets of groups we shall know better what to expect. But we shall always hold fast to the practical activity.[81]

As would most political scientists until the 1940s and 1950s, Merriam neglected Bentley when he hailed the study of "actual processes of government." Instead, he referred to Bryce (again) while alluding to a new "logic" of inquiry by "the pragmatists, best represented by Dewey."[82]

Mention of Dewey's logic suggests the third trend portending a political science beyond the historical comparison of states, namely, pragmatic inquiry. Pragmatic inquiry was experimental, instrumental, and oriented to specifying and solving problems. It elevated to the status of science the ordinary methods of trial and error. It emphasized evolutionary process and possibilities, informed by Darwinian theory while underscoring human agency. It directed methodological attention to the future—to consequences rather than precedents or antecedent causes. It eschewed guarantees of certainty, as vainly promised by the search for principles. It gave prominence to the contextual interpretation of meaning as revealed and expanded in social relationships. It also encouraged or underwrote civic engagement, social reform, democratic politics, and a pluralist conception of the state. Pragmatic inquiry understood this way provided Dewey a platform for criticizing "the abuse of the comparative method" since "facts are torn loose from their context" and "meaningless detail[s]" remain without "interpretation" or "coherent scheme."[83] Spencer was the principal target, but in other works Dewey implicated Burgess, Wilson, and Maine, among others. (By 1927–at a time when Merriam thought *the* method still in its "ascendancy"[84]—Dewey judged "the attempt to

---

[81] Arthur Bentley, *The Process of Government: A Study of Social Pressures* (Chicago: University of Chicago Press, 1908), 214, 263n, 269, 319, 481.

[82] Merriam, *New Aspects*, 123, 126.

[83] John Dewey, "Interpretation of the Savage Mind," *Psychological Review* 9 (1902): 217–30, 217.

[84] Merriam, *New Aspects*, 142. The status of *the* method in Merriam's view of political science, even in the forward-looking *New Aspects of Politics*, was ambiguous. Its very ambiguity suggests the persistence of the historical science(s) of politics well into the twentieth century. Merriam confessed to having "trained in the historical and comparative method, 'sitting at the feet of Gamaliel' in Columbia University." It is not clear whether Merriam's analogy to the teacher of St. Paul was to his teacher Dunning or to his (and Dunning's) teacher, Burgess. Merriam dated "the historical and comparative method" between 1850 and 1900 as the second of a four-stage calendar. But *the* method was neither a relic nor finished by 1900, since he admitted "the historical and comparative studies remained the dominant type for many years, and may be said to be in the ascendancy at the present time." *New Aspects of Politics*, 57, 142.

find by the 'comparative method' structures which are common to antique and modern, to occidental and oriental states . . . a great waste of industry.")[85] Pragmatic inquiry also backed Dewey's castigations of racism and nationalism, as well as Teutonism (that James dismissed as "sniveling cant").[86] The trend toward pragmatic inquiry (with its criticisms of Teutonism, principles, and the historical comparison of states), as exemplified in Dewey's writings, did not take hold in political science for some time. Indeed, Dewey's writings themselves attracted scarcely any attention by political scientists well into the twentieth century[87]—save for the decidedly hostile and uncomprehending account found in W. Y. Elliott's *The Pragmatic Revolt in Politics*.[88] Merriam's notice of "the pragmatists best represented by Dewey" in *New Aspects of Politics* was an exception; even then, this phrase exhausted his discussion of Dewey or pragmatism's logic of inquiry. In the interwar period, however, pragmatic inquiry of one sort or another found adherents, many of them from Merriam's "Chicago School" who were engaged in political activity or civil service. By midcentury, the trend toward pragmatic inquiry was more pronounced, especially in the study of public policy, though positivism was even more pronounced. Dewey was at last hailed as having "done so much to affect the climate of the social sciences, at least in America."[89] By then, Dewey had teamed up with Bentley to forge further pragmatic tools, in *Knowing and the Known*.[90]

Evident by 1914, the trends toward psychology, process, and pragmatic inquiry—as well as pluralism (see Gunnell in this volume)[91]—pointed to-

[85] John Dewey, *The Public and Its Problems* (New York: Henry Holt, 1927), 47.

[86] Quoted in Novick, *That Noble Dream*, 81.

[87] See James Farr, "John Dewey and American Political Science," *American Journal of Political Science* 43 (April 1999): 520–41. Dewey's emphasis on interpretation and meaning in pragmatic inquiry waited an even longer time for notice. See James T. Kloppenberg, *Uncertain Victory: Social Democracy and Progressivism in European and American Thought, 1870–1920* (New York: Oxford University Press, 1986), 100–107; Timothy V. Kaufman-Osborn, *Politics/Sense/Experience: A Pragmatic Inquiry into the Promise of Democracy* (Ithaca, NY: Cornell University Press, 1991), 239–43; Farr, "John Dewey." This provides support for the view (in this volume's introduction and chapter 12) about the interpretive road not taken in American political science.

[88] William Yandell Elliott, *The Pragmatic Revolt in Politics: Syndicalism, Fascism, and the Constitutional State* (New York: Macmillan, 1928).

[89] David Braybrooke and Charles E. Lindblom, *A Strategy of Decision: Policy Evaluation as a Social Process* (New York: Free Press, 1963), 18–19.

[90] John Dewey and Arthur Bentley, *Knowing and the Known* (Boston: Beacon Press, 1949).

[91] See also John G. Gunnell, "The Declination of the 'State' and the Origins of American Pluralism," in *Political Science in History: Research Programs and Political Traditions*, ed. James Farr, John S. Dryzek, and Stephen T. Leonard (Cambridge: Cambridge University Press, 1995); John G. Gunnell, *Imagining the American Polity: Political Science and the Discourse of Democracy* (University Park: Pennsylvania State University Press, 2004).

ward a reconfiguration of the historical science(s) if not a new science of politics sometime in the future. But it was World War I that exacted more immediate and demonstrable effects, especially after Woodrow Wilson, theorist of the state elected president of the United States, committed forces against Germany in April 1917. The war breached the affinity and affection that many American scholars felt for German ideas and ideals that resonated with their own science of the state. It certainly ended the American embrace of the Teutonic principle in almost all forms; positive references to Teutonism or things Teutonic fell from use nearly for good. Tellingly, though, Burgess was an exception, as was Schaper. Their sympathies for the German cause cost the latter his job at Minnesota and earned the former the charge of being "an American perverted by too close contact with Germany and German ideas," not to mention a "doddering old idiot."[92] In 1917, Dunning assailed "the Anglo-Saxon militant, the Teuton rampant, and the Aryan eternally triumphant."[93] For their war work, Willoughby battled Prussian political philosophy and Garner judged guilty the German war code.[94] In creating the Committee on Public Information (CPI), the Wilson administration offered employment to writers of pamphlets like "Lieber and Schurz: Two Loyal Americans of German Birth." More significantly, the CPI brought historians and political scientists into direct service of the American state as propagandists, including Garner, Lippmann, Munroe Smith, and Merriam (as CPI field head in Rome). Hart served in similar capacity for the National Security League. Thus did the historical scientists of politics in America go to war; and thus did propaganda come to occupy a central place in their conceptions of civic education and public opinion. Their erstwhile identities having been challenged and changed, political scientists emerged from the Great War ready to rethink, without abandoning, history, the state, and the principles of their science.

---

[92] Hart as quoted in Carol S. Gruber, *Mars and Minerva: World War I and the Uses of the Higher Learning in America* (Baton Rouge: Louisiana State University Press, 1975), 49n.

[93] Dunning, *Truth in History*, 157.

[94] Westel W. Willoughby, *Prussian Political Philosophy* (New York: Appleton, 1918); James W. Garner, *The German War Code* (Urbana: University of Illinois Press under the direction of the War Committee, 1918).

Five

The Emergence of an Embryonic Discipline: British Politics without Political Scientists

DENNIS KAVANAGH

THE INTERWAR YEARS are a key stage in the development of the academic study of politics in Britain. The main figures or Founding Fathers—Cole, Barker, Laski, Jennings, Muir, Wallas, and Finer—were drawn, narrowly, from Oxford, Cambridge, and the London School of Economics. From the 1950s, as the study of politics in Britain acquired the marks of a discipline, in the form of a professional association and a journal, the writings of the above fell into neglect. Yet the Fathers have commanded interest for their lives as well as their work; five of the seven have been the subject of lengthy biographies and in the cases of Laski and Wallas more than one. (One wonders how many of the more professionalized leaders of today will be the subject of a biography.) They also formed some of the ideas of British political scientists in the 1950s and 1960s (see Kenny chapter in this volume). The Founding Fathers are a bridge to the present and have helped to shape much that is distinctive about the discipline in Britain, notably a skepticism about model building and grand theory and a preference for empirical historical approaches.[1]

Few of the writers in the interwar period would have regarded themselves as political scientists. They clearly looked back to their late-nineteenth-century precursors who wrote about politics, principles of government, and the relations between the state and citizen. But for methods they drew on other disciplines and, indeed, most would have shuddered at the idea that the subject should seek to emulate the natural sciences. Politics was a small subject operating in the small world of British higher education. Before 1914, and for some time later, as a subject let alone as a discipline, it lacked a distinct identity; it was studied alongside economics, philosophy, law, and history, all of which were more securely established as

I am grateful for comments on an earlier draft from Hugh Berrington, Jack Hayward, and Julia Stapleton.

[1] See Jack Hayward, "British Approaches to Politics," in *The British Study of Politics in the 20th Century*, ed. Jack Hayward, Brian Barry, and Archie Brown (Oxford: Oxford University Press, 1999).

separate subjects and even departments in universities. For the most part politics operated under the shadow of more dominant subjects, and few entertained the idea that politics was a self-contained university subject. These values remained important after 1945 and can still be found today.

The scholars were children of the later Victorian or early Edwardian period. Wallas (b. 1852), Muir (b. 1872), Barker (b. 1874), Cole (b. 1889), Laski (b. 1893), Finer (b. 1898), and Jennings (b. 1903) grew up in a Britain that was an industrial powerhouse, the center of a great empire, and in which a largely hereditary House of Lords enjoyed nearly coequal powers with a House of Commons, popularly elected but on a restricted suffrage. Although they were strongly influenced by nineteenth-century ideas, they also looked forward, writing about themes and issues that still resonate today, and pointed toward the emergence of a discipline in the 1960s. In 2002, when the British Political Studies Association, as part of its fiftieth anniversary, paid tribute to a handful of so-called Founding Fathers of the discipline in the United Kingdom, its Hall of Fame included, among others, Laski, Cole, Barker, and Muir.

This chapter analyzes three different traditions or narratives of British politics among scholars in the interwar period. The dominant view for much of the nineteenth century was shaped by the Whig interpretation of British history. By the end of the century it was being transmuted into the *Westminster model* of the British constitution. The main features of the model are well known: strong cabinet government; parliamentary sovereignty; majority party control of the government; accountability to the electorate through regular competitive elections; institutionalized and legitimate opposition; and evolutionary change or progress. It was also judged to be superior to anything else on offer. Many of its proponents, however, admitted that it faced pressures, notably from the emergence of a mass electorate, an increasingly interventionist state, and disciplined party government.

In the interwar period this view was challenged but never replaced by two other interpretations that, for shorthand purposes, are termed *pluralist* and *collectivist*. The first looked beyond the elected House of Commons as the highest form of representation available and attacked the ideas of state sovereignty and an omnicompetent Parliament. The second justified a more active role for the state and public authorities, even at the cost of sacrificing some individual liberty, in the interest of promoting a common good. It accepted not only a collective representation of interests through political parties and pressure groups, but also the case for the government's regular intervention in social and economic affairs. Both views were a response to perceived inadequacies of a Whig view fashioned when the electorate was very small and the role of government limited. There was also a more dramatic break with each of the above from the burgeoning Marxist ideas whose main spokesman was Harold Laski—at different times he is an important spokesman for each of the above. The key point, however, is that it is in these years that different approaches are emerging.

The chapter first examines the British context in which the Founding Fathers operated, analyzes the intellectual inheritance from pre-1914, discusses the main themes of their writings, and, finally, assesses the legacy of that work.

Context

A number of features are important in understanding the status of British political science in the interwar period. The first is its small scale. Between 1900 and 1939 the number of British university students more than doubled, but the numbers were small, increasing only from twenty thousand to fifty thousand.[2] The main centers for the study of politics were Oxford, the London School of Economics, and Cambridge, in that order of magnitude. At Oxford, courses in politics were taken in the History School until the establishment of "Modern Greats," or Politics, Philosophy and Economics, which enrolled its first undergraduates in 1920. The "Politics" papers covered political history from 1760, the British constitution, and moral and political philosophy, all taught with a strong historical bias. At Cambridge, two papers, both largely historical, were offered as part of the history course.[3] At the LSE, the politics syllabus included public administration and political history, with some constitutional law and history of political thought.

This concentration in a few educational institutions and in subject matter (political theory, British government, and the institutions of a few other major states) lent a sense of coherence to the subject. This was achieved without a professional association, journal, or grant-awarding body, badges that only emerged from the 1950s (see Kenny, below). By 1939 there were no more than fifty or sixty teachers of the subject, a third in Oxford. The main figures knew each other and their work well, moved easily between political theory and institutions, and had no idea of fashioning a particular approach or school. The small size also meant that

[2] Peter Scott, *The Crisis of the University* (London: Croom Helm, 1984).
[3] Stefan Collini, Donald Winch, and John Burrow, *That Noble Science of Politics: A Study in Nineteenth-Century Intellectual History* (Cambridge: Cambridge University Press, 1983).

there was no specialist audience of a reasonable size, the academics were generalists, and there was a "pervasive amateurishness."[4]

A second feature is the relative lack of specialist politics teachers and writers. Few of those who taught politics as a university subject had a first degree in it. Most had taken a first degree in the humanities, usually history, philosophy, or the classics. There were no postgraduate centers offering training in the subject. As late as 1966 nearly 40 percent of university teachers of the subject in Britain had still taken history as a first degree.[5] Of the major interwar figures, Harold Laski and Ramsay Muir had been trained as historians, W. Ivor Jennings as a lawyer, Ernest Barker and Graham Wallas as classicists; G.D.H. Cole was promoted to a chair in political and social theory at Oxford from a readership in economics. Muir and Jennings held chairs in their original disciplines. Inevitably, what the early political scientists brought with them affected their definition of, and approach to, the subject.

Some idea of the qualities sought in would-be leaders of the profession may be indicated in the early appointments to the Gladstone Chair of Political Theory and Institutions at Oxford. The first incumbent, W.G.S. Adams (1912–33), was better known as a man of public affairs (he was a member of Lloyd George's secretariat in 10 Downing Street after 1916) and wrote little. The same could be said of his successor, Arthur Salter, appointed in 1933. From 1937 he also served as a member of Parliament, and for four years took leave from his academic post to serve in Churchill's War Cabinet. Both presumably brought with them the insights of practical men, derived from their personal experience of government. During the years 1940–44, R.C.K. Ensor, the Oxford historian, temporarily filled Salter's chair.

For the most part, as one don recalls: "Students were tutored by teachers who taught themselves or remained essentially philosophers or historians."[6] He added: "A well-accepted teacher of politics could get by through reading a dozen standard works and taking an interest in contemporary affairs."[7] Another history-cum-politics don, R. S. McCallum, complained in 1932: "The subject is taught by a very few specialists and a large number of philosophers and historians who approach it with vary-

---

[4] Brian Barry, "The Study of Politics as a Vocation," in Hayward, Barry, and Brown, *British Study of Politics*, 431.

[5] Bernard Crick, "The Tendencies in Political Studies," *New Society*, November 3, 1966, 683.

[6] Norman Chester, *Economics, Politics, and Social Studies in Oxford, 1900–1985* (Basingstoke, UK: Macmillan, 1986).

[7] Norman Chester, "Political Studies in Britain: Recollections and Comments," *Political Studies* 23, nos. 2–3 (1975): 151–64.

ing degrees of enthusiasm or disgust."[8] W.J.M. Mackenzie, builder of the famous Manchester Department of Government in the 1950s, grew bored teaching classics at Magdalen College, Oxford, and in 1936 switched to the politics post at the same college. He effectively taught himself the subject and was one of the very few British academics to follow developments in the United States, to the point of taking out a subscription to the *American Political Science Review*.[9]

Another feature of note is the lack of a distinctive methodology, or at least one separate from philosophy or history. The Founding Fathers were less concerned to define political science as a discipline separate from history or philosophy or law than to stress the interconnections between them. There is no doubt about the importance to this generation of history, including ancient history, as a source of methods, knowledge, and values. The writers are historical insofar as they systematically describe and analyze phenomena that have occurred in the past and explain contemporary political phenomena with reference to the past. As preprofessionals they did not regard political studies as novel but continuous with activities dating back to Aristotle.[10] The emphasis was on explanation and understanding, not on formulating laws.

Although these academics were also charged with founding a new or relatively new university subject, their methodology drew on philosophy or history. This is confirmed by a reading of some inaugural lectures—which provided an opportunity for the new professor to define the subject and his own approach to it.[11] Ernest Barker, for example, was unhappy at his title at Cambridge of professor of Political Science.[12] Interestingly, a committee of historians and political philosophers appointed Barker to his post, and the subject was based in the History faculty. In his inaugural, "The Study of Political Science," he attacked the scientific model and advocated a more humanistic approach, one based on moral philosophy. He admitted: "I am not altogether happy about the term 'Science.' It has been vindicated so largely, and almost exclusively, for the exact and experimental study of natural phenomena, that its application to politics may convey suggestions, and excite anticipations, which cannot be justified." He

---

[8] Chester, *Economics*, 48.

[9] W.J.M. Mackenzie, *Explorations in Government: Collected Papers, 1951–1968* (London: Macmillan, 1975).

[10] Richard Rose, "Institutionalizing Professional Political Science in Europe: A Dynamic Model," *European Journal of Political Research* 18 (1990): 581–604.

[11] Preston King, *The Study of Politics: A Collection of Inaugural Addresses* (London: Cass, 1977).

[12] Julia Stapleton, *Englishness and the Study of Politics: The Social and Political Thought of Ernest Barker* (Cambridge: Cambridge University Press, 1994), 128–29.

stated his preference for the study of "moral phenomena of human behaviour in political studies" and wished it to be called "Political Theory."

Harold Laski's 1926 inaugural, "On the Study of Politics," expressed his indebtedness to history and asserted that a historical approach is the only possible way to study politics: "for the study of politics in terms of history . . . to have value, the study of politics must be an effort to codify the results of experience in the history of states" and "[t]he true politics, in other words, is above all a philosophy of history."[13] For Laski this meant that one had to study how traditions and institutions had evolved from the past. When he mentioned important but neglected topics, he referred to the lack of a history of the cabinet, or local government, or the civil service.

The complaint of later critics about the Founding Fathers' failure to develop a core or distinctive set of techniques and a sense of boundary was here being celebrated as a borrowing from and an incursion into other disciplines. After all, the Founding Fathers "were historically inclined philosophers and theoretically disposed historians."[14]

A final feature is the comparative lack of U.S. influence. Perhaps such political institutions as federalism, the separation of powers, and a written constitution encouraged the view that the United States was irrelevant to the British experience. In the United States the Progressive concern to root out corruption and promote good government encouraged academic studies of grassroots politics and pressure groups, a stimulus lacking in Britain. But, in spite of the standing of Lord Bryce and the regular visiting academic appointments of Laski and Wallas to the United States before and after the First World War, one is impressed by the general lack of British interest in contemporary developments in American political science in the interwar years.

Indeed, the balance of interest and approval was in the other direction. Many American (and European) scholars had been schooled in the Whig view of British history, accepted Bagehot's dictum that Britain was "a first-rate nation," and believed that the British political system and its history was a success story. Starting with Professor Woodrow Wilson, would-be reformers of the U.S. parties and the civil service, as well as critics of the Madisonian model of the U.S. system, also looked to Britain for lessons in promoting strong and responsible party government.[15] Jack Hayward, in his overview of British approaches to the study of politics,

[13] King, *Study of Politics*, 3.

[14] Malcolm Vout, *Oxford and the Emergence of Political Science in England, 1945–1960* (Strathclyde, UK: Centre for the Study of Public Policy, 1990), 17.

[15] Dennis Kavanagh, "The American Science of British Politics," *Political Studies* 22, no. 3 (1974): 251–70.

notes that at the time a similar admiration for the British system was widespread among Continental political scientists.[16]

This background is important in understanding the factors that have shaped the academic study of politics in Britain, namely: the influence of history and philosophy; the relatively late (compared to the United States) development of many of the marks of professionalism; and the preference for an inductive, reflective, and largely atheoretical approach, rather than a quest for general theories and deductive models.[17]

The Inheritance

A recognizable British approach to political science had already emerged in the late nineteenth and early twentieth centuries.[18] The subject, as reflected in the teaching and writing on the subject at Oxbridge, was part of a humane tradition, deeply rooted in the classics, literature, and history, one that provided a liberal elite education. Studying the relationship between, on the one hand, political ideas and, on the other, the events and the actions of politicians in the past would, it was claimed, provide practical knowledge and wisdom for future political leaders. Because of this practical orientation, the Westminster (née Whig) model "therefore tended to be prescriptive and make judgements, proclaiming its values and priorities openly."[19] It was a means of inducting would-be rulers into a political tradition and an appreciation of the wisdom embedded in British political institutions and culture. Only the London School of Economics and Political Science, founded by the Webbs in 1895, provided a different approach; it was wedded to empirical research and developing a social science that would be useful for politicians and administrators. But there was little methodological self-consciousness or concern with building "grand" theories of politics.

Perhaps it could have been different. Collini and his colleagues have shown how, in late-nineteenth-century Cambridge, Benthamite proponents of a deductive approach, which would lead to a science of legislation, lost out to advocates of an inductive approach, based on history.[20] Rather than working from hypotheses to universal generalizations, historians claimed that their inductive approach would furnish the knowledge

---

[16] Hayward, "British Approaches," 28.

[17] Andrew Gamble, "Theories of British Politics," *Political Studies* 38, no. 3 (1990): 404–20.

[18] Hayward, "British Approaches."

[19] Gamble, "Theories of British Politics," 408.

[20] Collini, Winch, and Burrow, *Noble Science of Politics*.

for a so-called noble science of politics. Ironically, as Hayward claims, the victory of "the Whig protagonists of the exemplary excellence of the British Constitution was to leave an enduring antiscientistic mark upon the study of politics in Britain."[21]

It also induced a strong complacency. Macaulay, the most celebrated spokesman for this national approach—and its "obvious" superiority over the Continental (usually French)—boasted: "Our national distaste for whatever is abstract amounts undoubtedly to a fault. Yet it is, perhaps, a fault on the right side."[22] France, because of its history of regime instability, excess of rationalism in politics, and bitter divisions between ideologies of left and right, was a negative model. Before 1914, Sydney Low in his *Governance of England* claimed that a strength of the British system was that it had grown over time in contrast with the creation of systems elsewhere: "Its development has been biological rather than mechanical."[23]

The lawyers dominated constitutional history and above all in the doctrine of parliamentary sovereignty. It is remarkable that, pre-1914, the key figures of Maine, Bryce, Pollock, and Dicey all held chairs in Law.[24] In an autobiographical essay W.J.M. Mackenzie recalls that it was these knights of the textbooks (his phrase) who dominated student reading at interwar Oxford. Yet, this strand, apart from the work of Jennings and, to a lesser extent, K. C. Wheare and William Robson, virtually disappeared from British political science in the interwar years.

For some years now political scientists in Britain have claimed to uncover a number of weaknesses of the Westminster model. However, both Low and A. L. Lowell were analyzing the decline of Parliament in the late nineteenth century and the related rise of disciplined parties and dominance of the executive.[25] Indeed, Lowell was an early number cruncher, proving his case about the rise of party and of party discipline in Britain by analyzing House of Commons vote divisions to chart the steady decline in the number of defeats of government bills and of amendments to its bills.

An alternative path, reflected in Graham Wallas's *Human Nature and Politics*,[26] found no followers in Britain, but did so eventually in the United States. He urged that psychology should figure more prominently in political analysis, not least to achieve a more realistic perspective.

[21] Hayward, "British Approaches," 3.

[22] Collini, Winch, and Burrow, *Noble Science of Politics*, 4.

[23] Sidney Low, *The Governance of England* (London: Fisher Unwin, 1904), 6.

[24] Collini, Winch, and Burrow, *Noble Science of Politics*, 359.

[25] Low, *Governance of England*; A. L. Lowell, *The Government of England* (New York: Macmillan, 1908).

[26] Graham Wallas, *Human Nature in Politics* (London: Constable, 1908).

His warnings against the "rationalist fallacy" or exaggeration of the intellectuality of public opinion, discussion of the voters' use of the party image, and advocacy of more quantitative techniques sketch out a behavioral approach to politics, one that was in Britain largely stillborn. Wallas was in truth more of a moral reformer, largely interested in creating the Great Society.[27] His successor as professor at the LSE, Harold Laski (who brought with him an Oxford tradition) and Ernest Barker at Cambridge emphatically rejected the psychology route. Interestingly, over forty years ago Richard Rose in the introduction to the first edition of his *Politics in England* invoked the social and psychological insights of Wallas and Bagehot. He regarded them as well as Low, Lowell, and Ostrogorski as pioneering students of the relationship between English politics and English society. When Rose followed this approach, it was regarded as distinctive.

Themes

Understandably, some of the pre-1914 themes persist into the interwar years and beyond. But they were being increasingly challenged by political events. Belief in progress and the rule of reason could no longer be taken for granted after the experience and aftermath of the 1914–18 war, the rise of totalitarian regimes in Europe, and the instability of some of the states created in 1919. In spite of the post-1918 continuity of virtually all the main British political institutions, the system changed in many respects. The extensions of the suffrage in 1918 and 1928 confirmed the era of mass politics. A new party system, with Labour as one of the two main parties, increased the scope for a more class-based collectivist politics, one that raised questions about redistribution between the haves and have-nots and the more active role of government, particularly in welfare provision and economic management. The system and the political elites struggled to cope with the new forces. Some of the collectivists regarded the 1926 General Strike, the 1931 political and economic crisis that led to the collapse of the minority Labour government, and enduring mass unemployment as signs that the much-vaunted political system had failed.

In these years the *Westminster model* remains the orthodoxy. The narrative of constitutional history encompasses the successful adaptation of political institutions, gradual spread of liberty and political rights to the adult population, rule of law, and the executive's accountability to Parliament. From the constitutional settlement of 1689, England had achieved a balance of effective and accountable government. It was established that

[27] Mark Bevir, "Graham Wallas Today," *Political Quarterly* 68 (1997): 284–92.

the consent of Parliament, as the highest authority in the land, was required for raising taxes or making laws. Ancient institutions like the monarchy and the House of Lords survived because they had adapted, however unwillingly, to democratic pressures. The cabinet depended on Parliament, and Parliament in turn depended on public opinion. Dicey, in his *Law of the Constitution*, asserted that the sovereignty of Parliament was the central feature of the constitution. But, he continued, behind Parliament was the electorate and the essence of representative government was that the legislature represented "the will of the political sovereign, i.e. of the electorate." There emerged therefore a balanced constitution, one that blended effective government with checks on the exercise of power, in the forms of a legitimate opposition and respect for civil liberties.[28]

This view of British political development acknowledged the good sense and self-restraint of the rulers and the tolerance and trust of the public. Other key features of this narrative included the limited role of government and the vigor of civil society. Britain, in contrast to France or Prussia, developed as a "low profile" state. The thesis (often implicit) of British exceptionalism was reinforced by Britain's physical separation from the Continent, the unwritten constitution, the "club" culture among the political elite, and later perhaps by the failure of Westminster type institutions to survive in most of the British colonies when they were granted independence after 1945.

In the interwar years nobody better expressed these views than Ernest Barker. His biographer, Julia Stapleton, notes that in its blend of pluralism, Whiggism, and Idealism, much of his work was essentially a rearguard defense of the prewar political order.[29] Barker had been a student of T. H. Green at Oxford, when it was the center of Whig historiography. Like the Idealists, Barker believed that it was in the community that individuals expressed their true selves. He was steeped in Greek political thought and this remained "the cardinal reference-point for his understanding of political science."[30] He wrote a book on Plato and Aristotle in 1906 and was still publishing articles on Aristotle nearly fifty years later. He was committed to what he called the "parliamentary system of government" and its importance in upholding English liberties. His optimism derived from his view that the flexibility and genius of the British constitution had enabled it to adapt to new challenges since 1689.

---

[28] Albert Venn Dicey, *Introduction to the Study of the Law of the Constitution* (London: Macmillan, 1889).

[29] Stapleton, *Englishness*, 4.

[30] Ibid., 22.

These values emerge strongly in two of the chapters in *Essays in Government*: "The Parliamentary System of Government" and "British Statesmen." For Barker the essence of civilized politics, and a feature of the British system, was the role of discussion, rather than the will of a majority, as a means of reconciling differences. In his *Reflections on Government* he argues that the British political system facilitated discussion in four stages—the debates within and between political parties, the choices voters make between political parties at general elections, the debates in Parliament, and, finally, the deliberations of the cabinet. Not surprisingly, one of Barker's later interests was "the character of England," the title of his book in 1946 and an early attempt to sketch something approximating English political culture.[31]

The public lawyer W. I. Jennings, writing from a center-left political viewpoint, was also comfortable with the British system and impressed by the role of discussion and the effectiveness of its political checks and balances. (But he was also a collectivist; see below.) British government was "government by opinion," as Parliament and the institutionalized opposition in the House of Commons provided the opportunity for the views of the public to be expressed. In his eleven years at the LSE (1929–40) he produced eleven substantial books on British and other political institutions. His *Law and the Constitution* (1933), *Cabinet Government* (1936), and *Parliament* (1939) were heavily descriptive, using history to point to precedents.[32] Martin Loughlin notes that the work is "empirical and historical," based on statutes, legal cases, and available nineteenth-century political memoirs and biographies.[33] Unfortunately, Jennings jumbled together precedents from different periods, treating them all as equivalent and equally binding.

Also interesting, if now largely neglected, was the academic historian and Liberal politician Ramsay Muir. His *How Britain Is Governed* was perhaps the first recognized textbook on the British system and anticipated many of the criticisms and recommendations made by reformers some fifty years later.[34] The book's subtitle, revealingly, was *A Critical Analysis of Modern Developments in the British System of Government.*

[31] Ernest Barker, *Essays on Government* (Oxford: Oxford University Press, 1945); Ernest Barker, *Reflections on Government* (Oxford: Oxford University Press, 1942); Ernest Barker, *The Character of England* (Oxford: Clarendon Press, 1947).

[32] Ivor Jennings, *Law and the Constitution* (London: University of London Press, 1933); Ivor Jennings, *Cabinet Government* (Cambridge: Cambridge University Press, 1936); Ivor Jennings, *Parliament* (Cambridge: Cambridge University Press, 1939).

[33] Martin Loughlin, *Public Law and Political Theory* (Oxford: Oxford University Press, 1992), 168.

[34] Ramsay Muir, *How Britain Is Governed: A Critical Analysis of Modern Developments in the British System of Government* (London: Constable, 1930).

He was concerned by the electoral decline of the Liberal Party and what he regarded as the threats to the Westminster constitution. He complained about the cabinet's "dictatorship" over Parliament, stifling effects of party discipline, rise of interest groups, and power of "the Permanent Civil Service" (about which, he noted, historians and textbooks had been "strangely silent"), all of which had resulted in the bypassing of Parliament. He proposed what has become a litany of familiar reforms: specialist departmental committees in the Commons, elections by proportional representation to the two Houses of Parliament and devolution to Scotland, Wales, and the English regions. In contrast to the collectivists, his purpose was to reinvigorate the Westminster model, rather than to replace it.

Muir had little immediate influence on decision makers, and as a scholar he paid a price for spending so much energy on journalism, pamphleteering, and speeches on behalf of the declining Liberal Party. An obituarist (Barker) observed that the effect of all this activity was that his work "occupied the unsatisfactory middle ground between political thought and party proselytising."[35]

Pluralism in the early twentieth century was, variously, a reaction: against earlier individualist notions; against the Whig emphasis on the superiority of territorial representation in an elected Parliament; and against the legal doctrine of state sovereignty. Pluralists favored the dispersal of power between many groups and sought to limit the increasing powers of the state. Another version of pluralism in the United States in the 1960s was a counter to elitist theories of power. Gabriel Almond correctly objected that the recent (1970s and 1980s) "discovery" of pluralism (in the form of corporatist institutions developed as a response to economic problems in Western states) betrayed a failure of "professional memory."[36] It was actually a revival of an important theme of the first two decades of the twentieth century, particularly in Britain and France, as well as of the pressure group literature in the 1950s and 1960s.

The young Harold Laski and G.D.H. Cole, as well as Ernest Barker, no doubt influenced by their student reading of Maitland, Gierke, and Figgis, were all sympathetic to pluralism. They valued liberty highly and thought that it was best gained and preserved by the spread of power among different institutions. Dismissing the idea that society was either a collection of individuals or an organic whole, they asserted that it consisted of self-governing units and voluntary groups that had rights that were prior to and independent of the state. They also rejected claims that

---

[35] Michael Freeden, *Liberalism Divided. A Study of British Political Thought, 1914–1939* (Oxford: Oxford University Press, 1986), 129.

[36] Gabriel A. Almond, *A Discipline Divided* (London: Sage, 1990).

the centralized sovereign state could be realized in practice or, even if it could, was normatively desirable. Laski argues the case in his *Problems of Sovereignty, Authority in the Modern State*, and *The Foundations of Sovereignty*.[37] In this early work he advanced a liberal case for pluralism, praising a "federal" society of different groups and the checks and balances that follow from the interplay of separate political institutions wielding separate powers. According to Laski: "That is why the secret of liberty is the division of power. But that political system in which a division of power is most securely maintained is a federal system."[38] By the time of his 1925 *A Grammar of Politics*, however, his support for pluralism is waning and the active collectivist state is held up for admiration (see below).[39]

Cole advocated a more thoroughgoing pluralism. Where J. N. Figgis supported self-government for a wide range of bodies, notably churches, Cole was more interested in self-government by workers in their industries. In his 1920 *Social Theory* he argued that representation should be based on a person's function in society; because work was something directly experienced and better understood, it was more meaningful than one based on residence.[40] His advocacy of creating a series of functional representative bodies challenged prevailing ideas about representation and the role of the state. Samuel Beer defends this view on the grounds that members of such groups "have special skills, experience, and expertise which government must have at hand if it is to understand and control the complex and interdependent social whole."[41] Guild Socialists like Cole wanted control of industries to be vested in industrial guilds that would consist of representatives of the workforce. In the event, such demands went unheeded when the 1945 Labour government at last had the opportunity to implement its plans for the public ownership of industry. Cole's dislike of bureaucracy, which distinguished him from the Fabians, and hostility to the sovereign state made him an uncomfortable ally for most Socialists. He feared that the centralized state would provide a haven for the official and limit the scope for community, liberty, and democracy.[42]

[37] Harold J. Laski, *Studies in the Problem of Sovereignty* (New Haven, CT: Yale University Press, 1917); Harold J. Laski, *Authority in the Modern State* (New Haven, CT: Yale University Press, 1919); Harold J. Laski, *The Foundations of Sovereignty and Other Essay* (London: Allen and Unwin, 1921).

[38] Laski, *Foundations*, 87.

[39] Harold J. Laski, *A Grammar of Politics* (London: Allen and Unwin, 1925).

[40] G.D.H. Cole, *Social Theory* (London: Methuen, 1920).

[41] Samuel H. Beer, *Modern British Politics: A Study of Parties and Pressure Groups* (London: Faber, 1965), 73.

[42] A. W. Wright, *G.D.H. Cole and Socialist Democracy* (Oxford: Oxford University, 1979).

A second challenge to the Westminster approach came from supporters of *collectivism*. In his *Law and Public Opinion*, Dicey had argued that in the last third of the nineteenth century collectivist ideas overtook individualism, or laissez-faire, as a principle guiding public policy and the role of government.[43] The belief grew that the actions or intervention of the state, rather than the market, would deliver greater benefits. Writers of a center-left persuasion, including the Webbs, were confident that the tide was gradually but inevitably turning in their direction. Socialists could use parliamentary sovereignty and the unitary state to implement their program and realize the will of the electorate. Within striking distance of achieving power, they had no interest in promoting more checks and balances for the benefit of their opponents. Administration by the state promised to be more efficient than that by private agencies, particularly in providing better and uniform health and education services, improving standards of employment for women and children, and supplying a range of other public goods. This attitude easily lent itself to a "top down" view of government, with policies being decided at the center and applied uniformly across the country.

Collectivists were unsympathetic to the idea of checks and balances on the elected government, and particularly an active one. Laski, in his *Grammar*, had dismissed such devices as the referendum, devolution, proportional representation, and MPs electing their own select committees in the House of Commons because they could be restraints on the majority party and therefore on the electorate. He restated this view in his posthumous *Reflections on the Constitution*.[44]

It was during these years that collectivists and the Labour Party developed their suspicion of constitutional reform. Both Laski and Jennings were alarmed by the rulings of the U.S. Supreme Court striking down "progressive" measures of the New Deal. A British Bill of Rights would, they warned, give more power to judges who were drawn from the upper class and traditionally more sympathetic to the rights, for example, of private property and of the authorities than, say, of organized labor. They feared that any increase in the powers of the Commons vis-à-vis the executive could be used by opponents of a radical Labour government. Calls by Muir and Hewart, for example, for greater parliamentary oversight of delegated legislation that gave more discretion to officials and allowed more private consultation with interests, were dismissed by Laski and Fabians like Jennings as inappropriate to the needs of modern interven-

---

[43] Albert Venn Dicey, *Lectures on the Relation between Law and Public Opinion in England during the Nineteenth Century* (London: Macmillan, 1905).

[44] Harold J. Laski, *Reflections on the Constitution* (Manchester: Manchester University Press, 1951).

tionist government. According to Jennings, collectivist pressure "has changed the constitutional organisation, the practice of government, and the principles of political action," and the evolving and enabling British constitution allowed for "the progressive intervention of the state" in response to the wider suffrage and changing economic circumstances.[45]

In moving to his neo-Marxist phase, Laski was profoundly affected by the 1926 General Strike and the political and economic crisis that resulted in the collapse of the minority Labour government in 1931. He now argued that the Westminster system's legitimacy had to date relied on economic growth and a general agreement about political ends and means. In *Democracy in Crisis* he expressed fears that the coming economic crisis and sharper social class divisions, reflected in the Labour and Conservative Parties, would tempt the ruling class to abandon the traditional rules of the game.[46] He doubted that there could be a peaceful path to the social and economic transformation promised by a radical Labour government. Parliamentary democracy might not survive the strains of sharp social and economic inequalities. To overcome "unconstitutional" resistance from the holders of capital, normal parliamentary procedures might have to be suspended and emergency rule introduced. This is a rejection of the Whig beliefs in the state's neutrality and optimism about progress and was restated in *Parliamentary Government in England*.[47] The pluralist and the liberal Socialist Laski had been displaced by the supporter of strong government, one that uses its electoral mandate and the battering ram of its parliamentary majority to implement its program. In an anticipatory celebration of the idea of the elective dictatorship, there is no praise for checks and balances or independence of the courts and local government.

Laski was more explicit than the other writers in relating politics to socioeconomic factors. He used elite and social class analyses to demonstrate the fragility and outdatedness of the Westminster model when capitalism is in crisis and doubted that political democracy could coexist with great social and economic inequality. The Marxist approach raised questions about who the winners and losers are under the political arrangements, the alternative of violence rather than peaceful accommodation as the path to change, and the scope for sharp discontinuity rather than gradual change. The Webbs had already abandoned their confidence both in the ability of a Labour government to deliver a socialist program and

[45] Jennings, *Law and the Constitution*, xvii.

[46] Harold J. Laski, *Democracy in Crisis* (London: Allen and Unwin, 1933).

[47] Harold J. Laski, *Parliamentary Government in England* (London: Allen and Unwin, 1938).

in their belief that history was moving in the direction of socialism and a stronger state. After 1931 they turned to the Soviet Union and its system of centralized economic planning as the preferred means of advancing these ends.

The critique of democracy under capitalism did not go unanswered. Richard Bassett, Laski's colleague at the LSE, argued that political parties, particularly when in government, had to practice some self-restraint.[48] Attempts to introduce drastic or irreversible (sic) social and economic transformation would only goad political opponents into resistance. A Socialist government, contra Laski but in accord with the British tradition, would have to accept a large part of the status quo. The rules of the political game had to be above politics.

Assessment

Critics have complained that much of this interwar work was often complacent, insular, and atheoretical. The first two charges are unfair. In the spirit of the nineteenth-century comparative historians, these writers were cosmopolitans, well informed about European history and politics. For example, Jennings (*Law and the Constitution*) often refers to the different legal traditions and scholars in France and Germany, and he wrote a textbook called the *Constitutional Laws of the British Empire* and, prophetically, *A Federation for Western Europe*.[49] Laski wrote on American politics and French syndicalism as well as the history of European Liberalism, and Barker, on the history of the West European public services and on the emerging totalitarian regimes in Europe.

Above all, there was Herman Finer's remarkable *Theory and Practice of Modern Government*.[50] This was a systematic comparative study of the political differences and similarities across Britain, the United States, France, and Germany, conducted topic by topic and institution by institution, rather than country by country, the traditional approach as in Bryce and Lowell. Topics were presented "not only in their legal form but also in their operation."[51] Finer was the son of Romanian immigrants, deeply versed in European history and languages, and eventually left the LSE to settle in Chicago in 1942. In his work the comparison came

---

[48] R. Bassett, *The Essentials of Parliamentary Democracy* (London: Macmillan, 1935).

[49] Ivor Jennings, *Constitutional Laws of the British Empire* (Oxford: Clarendon Press, 1938); Ivor Jennings, *A Federation for Western Europe* (Cambridge: Cambridge University Press, 1940).

[50] Herman Finer, *Theory and Practice of Modern Government* (London: Methuen, 1932).

[51] Ibid., viii.

from the juxtaposition of material on constitutions, parliaments, executives, and so on. But the analysis was confined to the great states. It was left to his younger brother, Sammy Finer, in his *Comparative Government* to explore the patterns of political regularities and uniformities across all states.[52]

Although the works are legal-institutional, it is certainly too simple to say that they are *only* legal-institutional. A student of the literature would be aware of the activity of pressure groups, influence of officials, effects of party discipline on the alleged decline of the independence of MPs and power of the House of Commons, rise of the Cabinet, and how such features undermined the balanced constitution. However, with the exception of Laski, there is a failure to relate the politics to social and economic forces. There were certainly challenges to uncritical views of the British constitution. Witness, for example, Laski's doubts about the possibility of democratic parliamentary government under capitalism or Lord Hewart's *The New Despotism*, which claimed that the sovereignty of Parliament and the rule of law were being destroyed by the growth of government and increase in delegated legislation.[53] Both authors, however, were wearing their polemical hats at the time, and Laski wrote as a critic of parliamentary democracy under capitalism rather than of Britain per se. The behavioralist ideas of Wallas and the critical thrust of the neo-Marxist Laski connect with themes in British political science from the late 1960s onward. Later calls in the United States for "the state to be brought back" to political analysis had no echo in Britain. In spite of the relative weakness of the pre-1939 British state, the writers never discounted it. Indeed, some of the pluralists like the young Cole and young Laski feared that its power was becoming so far-reaching as to threaten liberty and wished to constrain it. And, as noted, the ideas of corporatism, so important to political scientists, economists, and sociologists in the 1960s and 1970s, were anticipated in the work of Laski and Cole.

This was also a generation that did not shy away from political engagement, both as activity and commentary. They assumed that their approach to the subject, with its study of the interconnections between theory and practice, gave them an authority to pronounce on the issues of the day. Laski was chairman of Labour's National Executive Committee in 1945 and a member of numerous Labour Party and government committees and working parties. Jennings was consulted by ministers on constitutional issues and after 1945 helped to draw up written constitutions for newly independent Commonwealth states. Muir was a Liberal MP (briefly), president of the party and coauthor of the famous Liberal pro-

[52] S. E. Finer, *Comparative Government* (London: Penguin, 1970).
[53] Gordon Hewart, *The New Despotism* (New York: Cosmopolitan, 1929).

gram, *Britain's Industrial Future.*[54] Wallas taught many civil servants at the LSE and was active in London local government, and both Adams and Salter were prominent in national government. Many were also active social reformers and believed that the study of politics could provide the knowledge to reform society.

They were also public intellectuals, expressing views on issues of the day in newspapers, magazines, public lectures, and on radio, serving on party or government committees, and, in the cases of Laski, Cole and Muir, actively writing party programs. Laski wrote literally hundreds of articles for the *New Statesman* in Britain and the *Nation* and *New Republic* in the United States. They were consciously writing for an audience outside academe partly because the latter provided only a small audience. But Trevor Smith observes that their idea of the informed commentator also involved not just conventional political activity "but also the sense of engaging themselves professionally with the public issues of the day by writing, teaching and public oratory," and they accepted "the linkage between thought and action for, to them, political science was part of the public domain."[55]

According to Stapleton, Barker consciously sought to straddle the worlds of journalism and scholarship. The role of "citizen-scholar," he claimed in his autobiography, was integral to his "Greats" birthright.[56] He and, in his later writings, Wallas (*The Great Society*, 1914; *Our Social Heritage*, 1921),[57] no doubt influenced by their earlier studies in moral philosophy, sought to provide a moral underpinning in their analyses; making better citizens should be a crucial justification for studying politics. For Wallas: "The political scientist was to be not a philosopher but a social engineer."[58] All would have rejected the idea of a value-free social science.

But there was a downside. There was too much engagement with contemporary events, occasional moralizing, and, in much of Laski's work in the 1930s in particular, ideological special pleading. The quality of Cole's work suffered as "[t]he perennial search for relevance implied a shifting focus, a constant willingness to respond to the pressures of the time."[59]

[54] Liberal Industrial Inquiry, *Britian's Industrial Future* (London: Benn, 1928).

[55] Trevor Smith, "Political Science and Modern British Society," *Government and Opposition* 21, no. 4 (1986): 423.

[56] Ernest Barker, *Age and Youth* (Oxford: Oxford University Press, 1955), 183, 223–24.

[57] Graham Wallas, *The Great Society* (London: Macmillan, 1914); Graham Wallas, *Our Social Heritage* (London: Allen and Unwin, 1921).

[58] Martin J. Weiner, *Between Two Worlds: The Political Thought of Graham Wallas* (Oxford: Clarendon Press, 1971), 67.

[59] Wright, *G.D.H. Cole*, 7.

Legacy

The efforts of the interwar generation did much to define the character and development of political science in Britain for the first two decades of the post-1945 period, although not much beyond that. The choice in 1950 of the title Political Studies, rather than Political Science, for the professional body is telling. Many of the original members still regarded politics as a subject that properly borrowed from history and philosophy; a more practical consideration was that the new body had to accommodate the historians, constitutional lawyers, and philosophers who formed a majority of those teaching politics. Most of them explicitly rejected the ideas of a political science and of competing or emulating the American model. Michael Oakeshott, Laski's successor at the LSE, dismissed such talk and held that politics had to be studied historically because of the need to understand political activity as a tradition. Cole, in the 1950 UNESCO symposium *Contemporary Political Science* forcefully repudiated the claim that that the study of politics could be a science, on the grounds that, in contrast to economics, it had no core.[60] Bernard Crick took a different line in his attack on American political science, claiming that behavioralism was culture bound and, rather than being value free, was actually shot through with liberal American values.[61] He wanted to restore an older tradition, going back to Aristotle, which he did in his later *In Defense of Politics*.[62] It is therefore not surprising that the major institutions like the LSE and Oxford did not offer anything comparable to the American graduate schools like Berkeley, Johns Hopkins, Columbia, and Michigan, which provided training and a disciplinary identity. It follows that the behavioral revolution was slow to have an effect.

In the immediate postwar years students had no general textbook on British politics, and the works of the past masters still clung heavily. A typical reading list still included Bagehot's *English Constitution*, Jennings's *Cabinet Government*, and Mill's *Representative Government*. In the late 1960s there came the first generation of textbooks on British politics to meet the demands of the growing number of students. Unsurprisingly, the literature still operated within the old paradigm, reflecting a confident view of the British system and culture (often encouraged by empirical U.S. studies as well as by success in the 1939–45 war), and the themes of stability, strong government, consensus, social homogeneity,

---

[60] See chapter by G.D.H. Cole in *Contemporary Political Science* (Paris: UNESCO, 1950).

[61] Bernard Crick, *The American Science of Politics: Its Origins and Conditions* (London: Routledge, 1959).

[62] Bernard Crick, *In Defense of Politics* (Chicago: University of Chicago Press, 1962).

and pride in the political system were still prominent. Even Ralph Miliband, echoing Harold Laski at the LSE, explained the Labour Party's failure to effect a Socialist transformation largely in terms of the strength of the Whig tradition and the party's deference to the political consensus and the parliamentary culture.[63] Richard Rose began his *Politics in England* with a claim that few would have contested, namely, that England "is important as a deviant case, deviant because of its success in coping with the many problems of the modern world."[64]

Change began in the late 1960s under the twin impacts of expansion and Americanization. The new departments of politics at Essex and Strathclyde provided a home for developments in American political science. A pioneering and widely read study was Jean Blondel's *Voters, Parties, and Leaders*, an examination of the social fabric of British politics.[65] It had chapters on voters, party members, interest groups, bureaucracy, and the Establishment. Richard Rose was alone in writing within a theoretical framework, using the structural-functional categories of Talcott Parsons and Gabriel Almond. His *Politics in England* has no chapters on Parliament, cabinet, or civil service, but it does have chapters on political socialization, political culture, and communications. The overall picture of British political science, however, remained one of "tolerant eclecticism" (Crick) and "atheoretical empiricism" (Hayward), features that would gratify the Founding Fathers.

What might they make of British political science today? Most would probably be impressed at the continuity of the main political institutions (monarchy, House of Lords, electoral system, unwritten constitution, Labour-Conservative duopoly of the party system, first-past-the-post system for electing the House of Commons, and the permanent civil service) amid the large changes in society and economy and to Britain's position in the world. The persistence of the former would confirm their belief in the continuing strength of political tradition in Britain. They would be surprised, however, at how the internationalization (read Americanization) of contemporary political science is eroding a distinctive British approach to the subject. Although the influence of approaches rooted in history and philosophy remain, the United States is influencing the main scholarly techniques and areas of inquiry.

One suspects that they would be unprepared for the widespread critique of the British political system among academics over the past three

[63] Ralph Miliband, *Parliamentary Socialism: A Study in the Politics of Labour* (London: Allen and Unwin, 1961).

[64] Richard Rose, *Politics in England* (Boston: Little, Brown, 1964), 1.

[65] Jean Blondel, *Voters, Parties, and Leaders: The Social Fabric of British Politics* (Harmondsworth, UK: Penguin, 1963).

decades. The Westminster political system of government is now widely regarded by reformers as a frail defense against the elective dictatorship of the executive. The much-vaunted continuity of the institutions and links with the past are more likely to be seen as a burden and a barrier to adaptation, and the incremental approach to reform and flexible constitution as a defensive conservatism. For some years, the once-praised elite political culture has been more often criticized as amateurish and antientrepreneurial, and comparisons with the United States and the Continent are more frequently made to Britain's disadvantage. Contemporary political science, like a number of other social sciences, has taken onboard the debate about British "decline."[66]

Another difference from today is the extent to which the small group of Founding Fathers sat at the same table, to borrow Terence Rattigan's metaphor. This was a consequence partly of the small London and Oxbridge axis but also of their shared educational background and interest in both political institutions and political theory. The pre-1914 interest in history and philosophy was still strong, as was the suspicion of positivism and scientism. They were generalists, and in their hands the subject had a coherence that it has steadily shed in the postwar development of new specialisms and various approaches—although less so in Britain than in the United States.

There were significant developments in British political science in the interwar years. By 1939, however, the study of politics still lacked a separate identity, and outside a couple of universities, it was insecure as a subject. These breakthroughs would be achieved under a later generation of scholars.

[66] Richard English and Michael Kenny, "Public Intellectuals and the Question of British Decline," *British Journal of Politics and International Relations* 3 (2001): 259–83.

Six

A Tale of Two Charlies: Political Science, History, and Civic Reform, 1890–1940

MARK C. SMITH

As THE PERIOD of developmental historicism and evolutionary positivism faded in the late nineteenth century, political scientists began to develop an alternative approach, one based on rigorous accumulation of facts coupled with the modernist view of science and reality as parts of a probabilistic world and of various new ways of ascertaining this reality. For the purpose of this volume, I am referring to this approach as modernist empiricism. Yet just as Dorothy Ross demonstrates in her chapter of this volume that historicists and evolutionary positivists differed strongly on such key issues as the germ theory of democracy and exceptionalism, so did empirical modernists disagree, especially on the meaning of science, the place of ethical values in social science, and especially the role, if any, of history in the study of politics.[1] Complete disciplinary paradigms in the strict Kuhnian model simply did not conform to reality in early-twentieth-century political science. The two dominant figures in American political science during the first third of the twentieth century, both graduates of John Burgess's Columbia and both incongruously nicknamed "Charlie," reflect not only the differences within the discipline but, especially at the end of their careers, their similarities compared to the newer group of neopositivists.

In 1925 the first of these, Charles Merriam, chairman of the dominant University of Chicago department of political science and cofounder of the American Political Science Association (APSA), the Social Science Research Council (SSRC), and Chicago's Local Community Research Council, published his most important work and one of the most important in the history of American political science: *New Aspects of Politics*. Assigned the task of assessing ongoing American political research in 1921 by APSA president William Dunning, Merriam noted such work in a series of essays eventually collected in *New Aspects*. Unlike such principal figures as Wesley Mitchell in economics, Franz Boas in anthropology, and

---

[1] See also Dorothy Ross, *The Origins of American Social Science* (Cambridge: Cambridge University Press, 1991).

Robert Park in sociology, Merriam broadened rather than deepened the study of his subject, suggesting new and relatively untried ways of examining politics. As far as the use of history for the study of politics, he argued that the study of politics had gone through four methodological periods: (1) from classical times to about 1850 one used a priori and deductive reasoning; (2) the period from around 1850 until 1900 was dominated by the historical and comparative methods; (3) beginning in 1900 and continuing until the present new and important methods included observation, survey, and measurement; and (4) finally, starting around 1920 and existing simultaneously with observation, survey, and measurement were the psychological approach and a strict reliance upon the scientific method.[2] Both of the last two would be classified as modernist empiricism. While Merriam spoke boldly of the fourth approach and mentored and later hired such pioneers and former students as Harold Gosnell and Harold Lasswell to pursue such approaches, he himself remained solidly wedded to the third approach. The following three vignettes symbolize three changing views toward the use of history in the study of politics during the period of this chapter.

The first involves one of the mantras of academic history and political science around the year 1900. English historian Edward Freeman's blunt declaration "History is past politics, and politics present history" graced seminar rooms from Oxford to Baltimore and provided a central focus for how the disciplines conceived their mutual tasks. Historians believing in pure documentation and objectivity concentrated on research on institutions like the state and the military that preserved conventional documents. They likewise ignored areas like social and cultural history that lacked such material. In the words of the French historians Charles Langlois and Charles Seignobos, "Pas de documents, pas d'historie."[3] Likewise, as James Farr has noted in this volume, American political scientists, reflecting their national consciousness and fearing the abstractions of philosophy, and starting from the specific and near sacred text of the Constitution, latched onto concrete historical facts to study the state from either a comparative or evolutionary perspective. Not until 1903 did the specialists on government break away from the American Historical Association to found the American Political Science Association. When Merriam headed for graduate school in 1896, he chose Columbia over the more

[2] Charles E. Merriam, *New Aspects of Politics* (Chicago: University of Chicago Press, 1970; first published in 1925), 132.

[3] Charles Victor Langlois and Charles Seignobos, *Introduction aux études historiques* (Paris: Hachette, 1898), 316, quoted in Peter Novick, *That Noble Dream: The "Objectivity Question" and the American Historical Profession* (Cambridge: Cambridge University Press, 1988), 39.

prestigious Johns Hopkins in part because Hopkins's professor of government and history, Herbert Baxter Adams, was one who literally posted "History is past politics, and politics present history" on his seminar walls. Not only Adams but also individuals like Columbia's John Burgess, who called themselves professors of government, studied and knew far more history than government. As Farr notes for the previous generation, the representative toast was that of Columbia's William Dunning, "History and Political Science, now and forever, two and inseparable."

The second example involved a key event of 1929. On December 16 and 17, a group of prominent social scientists came to dedicate a new building at the University of Chicago conceived by Merriam and paid for by the Rockefeller Foundation. Called Eleven Twenty-six for its address on East Fifty-ninth Street, this new social science building reflected the growing neopositivism of the social sciences. The building's design reflected the positivistic orientation of sociologist William Fielding Ogburn, who had begun as a social reformer and supporter of psychoanalysis but had over the years come to model his work on the physical sciences and demand statistical verification for all conclusions. Ogburn had been brought in from Columbia to provide a more scientific methodology to Chicago sociology, and the floor plan reflected his thinking in minimizing lecture rooms and space for books. Ogburn covered the outside with scientific symbols such as a graph, an adding machine, a sphere enclosed in a cube, and the sign of the Greek *psephos*. Under a bay window he had chiseled, ironically in Gothic script, his favorite paraphrase from Lord Kelvin: "when you cannot measure . . . your knowledge is . . . meager . . . and unsatisfactory."[4]

Yet, the dominance of scientism was not as clear as Ogburn's choices seemed to indicate. Merriam had been absent during Ogburn's work and upon his return opposed his choices and threatened, only half-humorously, to take him for a ride Chicago-style. Representatives of the theoretical Chicago school of economics, who were also moving into Eleven Twenty-six, sniped at the Kelvin quotation. Frank Knight sneered "And if you cannot measure it, measure it anyhow," while his colleague Jacob Viner philosophically added, "And if you can measure . . . your knowledge will still be meager and unsatisfactory."[5] They joined the anthropolo-

[4] Robert C. Bannister, *Sociology and Scientism: The American Quest for Objectivity, 1880–1940* (Chapel Hill: University of North Carolina Press, 1987); Leonard D. White, "The Local Community Research Committee and the Social Science Research Building," in *Chicago: An Experiment in Social Science Research*, ed. Leonard D. White (Chicago: University of Chicago Press, 1929), 26–27; Fred H. Matthews, *Quest for an American Sociology: Robert E. Park and the Chicago School* (Montreal: McGill-Queen's University Press, 1977), 109.

[5] Barry D. Karl, *Charles E. Merriam and the Study of Politics* (Chicago: University of Chicago, Press, 1974), 155; Charles E. Merriam, "Dedication of the Social Science Building

gists, political scientists, sociologists, and about half of the historians in Eleven Twenty-six. Yet, clearly most of the economists and historians and the sociologists and anthropologists specializing in ethnography and life histories opposed Ogburn's insistence upon only statistical research and did so at the supposed physical heart of the neopositivist movement.

The third example came during World War II and involved the specialist on public administration and lobbying groups E. Pendleton Herring. A longtime Harvard professor and future head of the SSRC and the Woodrow Wilson Foundation, Herring during World War II served as a consultant to the armed services. In 1945 in response to Truman's desire to create a unified armed service, Secretary of War James Forrestal called Herring to Washington and put him to work with his chief aide, Ferdinand Eberstadt. Eberstadt immediately asked for help applying "the lessons of history" to the problem. Herring's words forty-three years later remembering that episode remain quite revealing: "That was rather a stopper, since I'd never quite thought of history in that fashion." One could hear the disbelief in his voice over all the years. In approximately forty years the situation had gone from a situation where almost every political scientist knew and believed in the uses of history to a time where almost no one—not even the future head of the interdisciplinary SSRC—did.[6]

The two men who dominated political science in very different ways during these interwar years were Merriam and Charles Beard. I am hardly the first person to notice and contrast them, nor, indeed, is this the first time I have done so. Richard Jensen, Raymond Seidelman and Edward Harpham, Barry Karl, Dorothy Ross, and even the venerable Bernard Crick have discussed the differences between these superficially similar individuals. By concentrating on their approach to history in the interwar years, this essay points out how two political scientists sharing a common background, a commitment to activism, and a methodology of modernist empiricism could still develop entirely different approaches to political science. Their biggest difference lay in their approach to history.[7]

at the University of Chicago," December 17, 1929, Charles E. Merriam Papers, University of Chicago Library (hereafter cited as Merriam Papers); Frederick C. Mills, chair, "Quantification—the Quest for Precision—a Round Table Discussion," in *Eleven Twenty-Six: A Decade of Social Science Research*, ed. Louis Wirth (Chicago: University of Chicago Press, 1940), 169, 177.

[6] Michael A. Baer, Malcolm E. Jewell, and Lee Sigelman, eds., *Political Science in America: Oral Histories of a Discipline* (Lexington: University of Kentucky Press, 1991), 29.

[7] Richard Jensen, "History and the Political Scientist," in *Politics and the Social Sciences*, ed. Seymour Martin Lipset (New York: Doubleday, 1969), 1–28; Raymond Seidelman, with the assistance of Edward J. Harpham, *Disenchanted Realists: Political Science and the American Crisis, 1884–1984* (Albany: State University of New York Press, 1984); Karl, *Merriam*; Ross, *Origins*, 449–67; Bernard Crick, *The American Science of Politics: Its Origins and Conditions* (Berkeley and Los Angeles: University of California Press, 1959).

The two had very similar backgrounds. They were the same age, came from rural midwestern towns and had fathers who were small-town Republican speculators and businessmen. They attended small local denominational colleges. Both did their graduate work at Columbia—Merriam beginning in 1896 and Beard in 1902. Each had a short but impressive political career. Merriam was a Chicago alderman and the Republican candidate for mayor in 1911; Beard impressed Ramsay MacDonald so much that he was offered a cabinet post in the shadow Labour government thought to be on the verge of power.[8] They also were two of the few members of their generation who continued to insist upon civic education as a significant goal for the study of politics. Merriam edited a series of studies on civic education in different nations of the world, wrote two different works on American civic education, and encouraged political scientists to provide citizens with information useful for their tasks as citizens.[9] Like Merriam, Beard was actively involved in the American History Commission on the Social Studies in the Schools during the 1930s. He also pioneered in the fields of adult and worker education beginning with the cofounding of Ruskin Hall in Oxford in 1899 and served as a consultant to the New York Bureau of Municipal Research. While Merriam's pedagogic experience centered on the training of graduate students to research civic topics and teach citizenship to their eventual undergraduate students, Beard was personally involved in citizenship training for individual citizens. John Burgess had hired Beard to design and teach an undergraduate curriculum in political science in 1907 after he completed his degree in history. In 1913 the APSA chose it and his text, *American Government and Politics*, as the models for introductory American government classes.[10] A brilliant and dynamic teacher, Beard lectured to huge classes and until his resignation over an issue of free speech in 1917, students considered him as practically the entire undergraduate program.

The two had similar personality characteristics as well. Avuncular and outwardly jolly, the two were often called "Charlie" by those around them. While Beard welcomed the name and even delighted in "Uncle Charlie," Merriam preferred "Chief" or "Carlo." Still, Merriam treated his graduate students as a cherished uncle as well, attending their wed-

---

[8] Ellen Nore, *Charles A. Beard: An Intellectual Biography* (Carbondale: Southern Illinois University Press, 1983).

[9] Charles E. Merriam, *Civic Education in the United States* (New York: Charles Scribner's Sons, 1934); Charles E. Merriam, *The Making of Citizens: A Comparative Study of Methods of Civic Training* (Chicago: University of Chicago Press, 1931); Merriam, *New Aspects*, 286–89.

[10] Clyde W. Barrow, *More Than a Historian: The Political and Economic Thought of Charles A. Beard* (New Brunswick, NJ: Transaction Publishers, 2000).

dings, introducing himself to their parents, and even inviting his favorites for a drink in his office at special occasions.[11]

In their infrequent short notes to each other, Merriam and Beard jocularly referred to each other as "Charlie." Privately, the two distrusted each other and eyed each other cautiously. Beard coveted Merriam's access to research funds and talented graduate students. Merriam envied Beard's public popularity and, until 1917, his Columbia position. Still, they presented an outwardly cordial front. Merriam would invite Beard to come to Chicago and stay at the exclusive City Club, a prospect that must have thrilled the populist Beard almost as much as the urbane Merriam's reaction to his invitation to the Beards' Connecticut dairy farm. Merriam dismissed one of Beard's researchers as "essentially a propagandist" and expressed anger at Beard's unfavorable, even snide, reviews of Merriam's books. Beard, in turn, would show his contempt for Merriam by frequently turning off his hearing aid in committee meetings whenever Merriam spoke.[12]

Yet, for all their differences, both Merriam and Beard retained the Progressive faith in the power of knowledge, the intellectuals' control of that knowledge, and, at least initially, the people's recognition of those truths. Both were heavily involved in municipal reform. Merriam emphasized the need for efficient urban administration, researching German cities as models for public ownership of municipal utilities and a competent civil service. He argued that the chief goal of political science was the "elimination of waste in political action." Still, he did not become fully active in the field until the 1930s, saying it was only then "he entered the school of Public Administration." He helped professionalize such occupations as city managers, city secretaries, municipal finance officers, and police chiefs by providing them with official organizations, office space for them at the University of Chicago, and means of communicating with one another. Merriam especially found the city managers attractive for their reliance upon technical expertise alone and alleged complete objectivity. Municipal reform of this nature reflected that part of progressivism which saw the true and, indeed, only component of reform as technical efficiency.[13]

[11] Baer, Jewell, and Sigelman, *Political Science in America*, 124.

[12] Merriam to Beard, November 3, 1925, Merriam Papers; George S. Counts, "Charles Beard, the Public Man," in *Charles A. Beard: An Appraisal*, ed. Howard K. Beale (Lexington: University of Kentucky Press, 1954), 219.

[13] Charles E. Merriam, "The Education of Charles Merriam," in *The Future of Government in the United States*, ed. Leonard D. White (Chicago: University of Chicago Press, 1942), 15; Merriam, *New Aspects*, 51. Robert H. Wiebe, *The Search for Order, 1877–1920* (New York: Hill and Wang, 1967); Samuel P. Hays, *Conservation and the Gospel of Efficiency: The Progressive Conservation Movement, 1890–1920* (Cambridge: Harvard University Press, 1959); Samuel Haber, *Efficiency and Uplift: Scientific Management in the Progressive Era* (Chicago: University of Chicago Press, 1964).

Beard began working with the New York Bureau of Municipal Research, an organization that similarly emphasized efficient, businesslike government in 1907. By 1912 he had become one of the three directors of its new Training School for Social Service and in 1918, its director. In 1922 Beard traveled to Tokyo at the request of its mayor to recommend administrative and governmental changes. A year later, he was one of the first outside consultants called to advise the government after Tokyo's devastating earthquake. Like his and Merriam's original public administration teacher at Columbia, Frank Goodnow, Beard also believed in the efficacy of a strictly empirical approach. That is, technical efficiency was an important and necessary component of progressive reform. But it was not enough by itself. Despite his and other superb technical plans for Tokyo, powerful imperial and business interests had blocked any meaningful change and had retained the previous convoluted public streets and lack of public space. In 1926, he stood before the National Government Association to argue that public planners had failed the American public by concentrating on "merely material and numerical ends" and overlooked ethical issues. Beard thus represented both technical efficiency and the part of progressivism relying on America's moralistic tradition.[14]

This element of progressivism with its explicit ties to moralism and social reform reflected the origins of American social science. The American social sciences had begun in the American Social Science Association, whose executive secretary, Franklin Sanborn, proclaimed, "To learn patiently what is—to promote diligently what should be—that is the double duty of all the social sciences." A widely used 1915 college textbook asserted, "The purpose of sociology . . . is to formulate a scientific program of scientific betterment."[15] Many of the professional social science associations included specifically activist aims in their original constitutions, with the APSA calling for the devising of active and efficient local and state governments. The turn away from a declared reformist perspective to a more technical, scientific approach came later, largely from threats to academic freedom and necessary research funds.[16]

[14] Charles A. Beard, "Government Research: Past, Present, and Future," address to annual meeting of the Governmental Research Conference, Rochester, New York, November 23, 1926, Charles and Mary Beard Collection, DePauw University, p. 8; Robert M. Crunden, *Ministers of Reform: The Progressives' Achievement in American Civilization* (New York: Basic Books, 1982).

[15] Franklin B. Sanborn, "The Social Sciences: Their Growth and Future," *Journal of Social Science* 21 (September 1886): 6; Frank W. Blackmar and John Lewis Gillin, *Outlines of Sociology* (New York: Macmillan, 1915), 36.

[16] Thomas L. Haskell, *The Emergence of Professional Social Science: The American Social Science Association and the Crisis of Authority* (Urbana: University of Illinois Press, 1977); Mark C. Smith, *Social Science in the Crucible: The American Debate over Objectivity and Purpose, 1918–1941* (Durham, NC: Duke University Press, 1994), 17–23.

Merriam and Beard's differing views on the approach to public admin-istration reflect their differing perspectives on the utility of history for the political scientist—Merriam's that it was the bastion of the status quo and Beard's that it provided the data and alternatives to transcend established institutions. Yet both viewpoints arose out of their commitment to re-form. As Terrence Ball has explained in an apt metaphor, political scien-tists have always had to steer between the Scylla of disinterested science and the Charybdis of committed pedagogy. Beard and even Merriam for all his emphasis upon scientific methodology always steered closer to Charybydis. Despite their earlier hopes, the 1940s left both seriously disil-lusioned and rudderless.[17]

Of the two, Merriam studied more history at Columbia. Merriam had chosen Columbia over Johns Hopkins in part because of the dominating presence of history at the latter. Still, at Columbia Merriam took three courses with the pedantic colonial historian Herbert Levi Osgood as well as history of political thought with his mentor William Dunning, history of constitutional law with departmental founder John Burgess, and the history of philosophy with newly inaugurated Columbia president Nicho-las Murray Butler. Dunning provided the model for Merriam's later his-torical work; Dunning wrote well-regarded histories of political thought and became the central figure in the dominant school of Southern history. Dunning's work was allegedly purely empirical, trying to create a science of history through Baconian induction. Still, he frequently lamented the difficulty of writing objective history, especially after Merriam remarked that he and others could identify Dunning's prejudices. In 1913, Dunning directed his AHA presidential address against his Columbia colleagues James Harvey Robinson and Beard for their New History and its admitted biases and prejudices.

Merriam was never a political theorist but rather a historical theorist, one who examines theory from a historical perspective. Merriam's best work such as the 1903 *A History of American Political Theories* and *American Political Ideas: Studies in the Development of American Politi-cal Thought, 1865–1917*, of 1920 followed the Dunning model, sensitive reconstructions of thinking about politics in the context of their times. Merriam protested that these "theories" were nothing more than rational-izations of particular interest groups; over time he changed his titles from political "theories" to "thought" to "thinking." Still, most of his own teaching was on these subjects, even if one of his 1930s students, David

[17] Terence Ball, "An Ambivalent Alliance: Political Science and American Democracy," in James Farr, John S. Dryzek, and Stephen T. Leonard, eds., *Political Science in History* (New York: Cambridge University Press, 1995), 43.

Truman, complained that the lectures were simply notes from Dunning, who himself copied them from an untranslated French work.[18]

Merriam was not content with such work. While he saw developmental historicism as key to the raising of general intelligence and the core of political science in the early twentieth century, in the chaos following World War I he came to search for certainties, infallible truths to provide solutions in desperate times. This was especially true now that the public had demonstrated through their rejection of Merriam's mayoral bid and the election of business-oriented Republicans like Harding and Coolidge their inability to follow the advice of progressive experts. History only reflected the biases and prejudices of the age. Modernist empiricism, on the other hand, had the potential to deliver answers to real problems. Perhaps historians could continue to write political history, but they had no place among those who would write the history of institutions or the history of science and certainly not among the technical experts who would run the country. "The historian could distinguish genuine writing from the bogus, could scour the world with immense enthusiasm and industry to uncover hidden manuscripts or archives hitherto unknown. In his critical analysis, however, he waited on the activities of other social studies. At their methods and results he was not infrequently prone to cavil and complain."[19]

Beginning in 1921, Merriam made a series of moves that revolutionized political science. In an address before that year's APSA convention, he criticized the historical and comparative approaches and emphasized the use of statistics and psychological and sociological points of view. This would lead to the Committee on Political Research and for three summers the National Conference on the Science of Politics. In early 1925 a summary of his writings and thoughts appeared as *New Aspects of Politics*, and in December of that year he further clarified his position in his APSA presidential address, "Progress in Political Research."

All of Merriam's work as well as the conferences reflected two themes. First of all, science and the scientific method were worshiped, although, in fact, he was referring to the scientific method alone. Merriam insisted that its use, especially with adequate physical and intellectual apparatus, would solve all the problems of social research. Merriam became such a monomaniac on the subject that several contemporaries remember heading for the exits at its very mention.[20] Yet, his definitions were less than

---

[18] Charles E. Merriam, "William Archibald Dunning," in *American Masters of Social Science*, ed. Howard W. Odum (New York: Henry Holt, 1927), 45; Baer, Jewell, and Sigelman. *Political Science in America*, 137–38.

[19] Merriam, *New Aspects*, 57–58, 114–15.

[20] Crick, *American Science*.

clear; at one time he defined science as "intelligence in human affairs." Secondly, he insisted that science and reform were inextricably linked but never stated how. He even maintained that scientific studies of issues like the Ku Klux Klan and Prohibition would automatically solve these problems. Such certainty was absolutely necessary since "least of all can there be anarchy in the social sciences or chaos in the theory of political order." Unlike the historical method, which noted the differences between ideas according to circumstances, Merriam demanded eternal truths, because, after all, "who will deny that the perfection of social science is indispensable to the very preservation of this . . . civilization."[21]

Merriam, like many social scientists of the time, could be so cavalier in his definitions because he believed that pragmatism, especially an instrumental version of John Dewey, provided him with ample philosophical justification. Certainly, the social sciences at Chicago were a hotbed of this position. Dewey had taught there from 1894 until 1904, while Merriam had arrived in 1900. Chicago's department of sociology contained many strong, pragmatic adherents such as Robert Park, W. I. Thomas, and, above all, the social psychologist George Herbert Mead, who profoundly impacted all of the Chicago social sciences with the exception of economics. Merriam even had a good word to say for Dewey in *New Aspects*.[22]

Dewey certainly shared with Merriam an attachment to the scientific method. It represented to him the highest development of human intelligence and the only plausible way to test hypotheses. As a philosophy graduate student, Dewey had embraced those philosophic systems that claimed to provide definitive answers to the constant debates of philosophy. Yet, at the same time, as the historian Louis Hartz has noted, "American pragmatism has always been deceptive because, glacierlike it has rested on miles of submerged conviction."[23] Dewey consistently displayed a paramount need for normative values to direct human activity toward positive ends. To the extent that the scientific method did this, it was a pragmatic good. Without preconceived normative values, it was useless, even dangerous. By the 1920s, he was already blasting the Ogburns and, implicitly, the Merriams of social science. "Observing, collecting and filling tomes of social phenomena" without values led to an acceptance of "what is" for "what should be." For Dewey, this resulted in the abandonment of the goals of the social sciences articulated by such founders as

[21] Charles E. Merriam, *Systematic Politics* (Chicago: University of Chicago Press, 1945), 328; and Merriam *New Aspects*, 83.

[22] Merriam, *Systematic Politics*, 123.

[23] Louis Hartz, *The Liberal Tradition in America: An Interpretation of American Political Thought since the Revolution* (New York: Harcourt, Brace and World, 1955), 59.

Franklin Sanborn. "Anything that obscures the fundamentally moral nature of the problem is harmful, no matter whether it proceeds from the side of physical or psychological theory." In 1929, Dewey and Beard's respective invited lectures at a University of Virginia symposium showed a remarkable similarity with regard to this point.[24]

More disturbing to adherents of developmental historicism was Merriam's advocacy of interdisciplinarity. As he stated boldly in New Aspects, "[P]olitics must follow its problem wherever the problem leads." Merriam believed that the more scientific the study, the more suited it was for political research. Meanwhile, juristic and historical methods were "antiquated modes of study." Leonard White in his introduction to a collection of essays honoring Merriam noted his subject's "bold and persistent effort to marry political science with biology, anthropology, psychology, sociology, economics, and medicine." History was noticeably absent in this long and inclusive list.[25]

Still, things were not as straightforward as they might seem. During the 1930s, Merriam became a trusted, perhaps the most trusted, academic adviser to Franklin Roosevelt. Yet even when factual evidence was available as during his service on the National Planning Board and the Committee on Administrative Management, opposing groups produced equally scientific facts and blocked implementation of Merriam's preferred reform.[26] Perhaps science did not provide the infallible answer to all questions, or perhaps Merriam's progressive faith in the people and the power of facts was misguided. His original passion sometimes resurfaced as when after the end of World War II he called for political scientists to copy atomic scientists as the most scientific of all disciplinary groups. But for the most part he puzzled over what he termed "examination of the relations between values and scientific conclusions." Mathematical precision without the dominance of values meant nothing, yet in the elimination of such studies as philosophy and history he had removed exactly those types of disciplines that would have helped him.[27] Charles Beard understood this point but overlooked equally important others.

[24] John Dewey, "Social Science and Social Control," New Republic 76, July 29, 1931, 276–77; John Dewey, Liberalism and Social Action (New York: Capricorn Books, 1963; first published in 1935), 47–48; John Dewey, "Philosophy," in Research in the Social Sciences: Its Fundamental Methods and Objectives, ed. Wilson Gee (New York: Macmillan, 1929).

[25] Merriam, New Aspects, 57, 228–30; Leonard D. White, "Introduction," in The Future of Government in the United States: Essays in Honor of Charles E. Merriam, edited by Leonard D. White (Chicago: University of Chicago Press, 1942), iii.

[26] Barry D. Karl, Executive Reorganization and Reform in the New Deal: Genesis of Administrative Management (Cambridge: Harvard University Press, 1963).

[27] Charles E. Merriam, "Physics and Politics," American Political Science Review 40, no. 3 (1946): 445–57; Charles E. Merriam, "What Would You Do If You Were a Professor of

Charles Beard had studied mostly English history as an undergraduate at DePauw University and after graduation studied medieval history at Oxford with Frederick York Powell, a crusty medieval historian who listed Americans as the first of his active dislikes yet praised Beard as "the nicest American I have ever met."[28] From Powell Beard learned history's purpose was not to praise institutions or theories but to understand them; history was a science, rather than theology or ethics. In 1902 he entered Columbia's Graduate School of Political Science and graduated in 1905 specializing in history. Beard impressed his instructors so much that Burgess appointed him lecturer in History in 1905 and in 1907 transferred him to an adjunct position in Politics and Government. While most individuals think of Beard as a historian, early in his career he was primarily a political scientist. One critic has asserted that twenty-eight of Beard's forty-nine books were on conventional political science topics; they included American government, municipal government, public administration, public policy, political theory, political economy, comparative politics, and foreign policy. Only the works on foreign policy and the American government texts used history to any degree. The department placed him in charge of undergraduate education, and he developed an introductory course chosen by the APSA as its model for introductory courses nationwide.[29] The text written for this course, *American Government and Politics*, became the standard college text and remained in print for close to fifty years. Both it and the course moved away from moral philosophy to conflicts based on social and economic disputes. Beard soon came to head the New York Bureau of Municipal Research and the National Reform League and was a leading adviser to municipal and international governments. The American Political Science Association rewarded him with its presidency in 1926, but the American Historical Association did not do so until 1934.

Beard was consistently critical of the move of political science away from history and ethical standards. In his first university lecture as a professor of political science in 1908, he proclaimed: "The real student of government knows that there is no hope for knowledge except in descriptions of the bewildering types of society gathered from the past and the four corners of the earth." Two years later he entitled the first section of his government text "Historical Foundations" and insisted that a real understanding of the American political system required knowledge of

Poetry, Philosophy, and Politics," unpublished lecture in honor of T. V. Smith, November 10, 1948, Merriam Papers.

[28] Burleigh Taylor Wilkins, "Frederick York Powell and Charles A. Beard: A Study in Anglo-American Historiography," *American Quarterly* 11, no. 1 (1959): 36.

[29] Barrow, *More than a Historian*, 1, 10.

history.[30] History was useful not just for its information, but because its narrative provided insight into how events interconnected and evolved. The emphasis was upon comprehension and understanding.

One of the best ways to recognize the differences between Merriam and Beard over the role of political science is an examination of their successive APSA presidential addresses. Merriam's 1925 address, "Progress in Political Research," had begun with a review of the last twenty years of research in political science. While acknowledging the significant progress, Merriam argued for increasingly scientific work and especially the use of quantitative methods. This, however, remained within the limits of an empirical modernism that emphasized data accumulation without completely abandoning abstract speculation. Still, Merriam was convinced that political participants and scientists would come to appreciate political scientists only after movement in the direction of quantitative empiricism.[31]

By this time Beard had already left academics and had few connections within the APSA. Nevertheless, he was convinced to take the position to publicize his particular viewpoint. In his 1926 presidential address, "Time, Technology, and the Creative Spirit in Political Science," he noted the deficiencies of Merriam's scientific study of politics. While he never mentioned Merriam by name, he came close to literally quoting from Merriam's widely known and published presentation of the year before. Without taking history into account, the social scientist could see only the short term. Reliance upon mathematical methods and specialization led to donor support but also work that was "myopic," "barren," and destructive of the creative imagination and the moral vision. The scientific approach sacrificed "the man of hunches," who searched for answers to the central problems of culture, for the technician. At the end, he called for "the daring to be wrong in something important rather than right in some meticulous banality."[32]

Two years later, Beard would present a more developed presentation on the nature of political science at a University of Virginia symposium entitled Research in the Social Sciences. Featuring such figures as Park in sociology, Dewey in philosophy, Arthur Schlesinger in history, Clark Wissler in anthropology, and Roscoe Pound in jurisprudence, the symposium

[30] Charles A. Beard, "Politics," in *Columbia University Lectures on Science, Philosophy and Arts, 1907–1908* (New York: Columbia University Press, 1908), 8; Charles A. Beard, *American Government and Politics* (New York: Macmillan, 1910), 3.

[31] Charles E. Merriam, "Progress in Political Research," *American Political Science Review* 20, no. 1 (1926): 1–13.

[32] Charles A. Beard, "Time, Technology and the Creative Spirit in Political Science," *American Political Science Review* 21, no. 1 (1927): 1–11.

directors chose Beard rather than Merriam or one of his followers to present an overview of political science. Beard agreed that the scientific method was essential for many of the questions of the discipline; however, politics also contained "emotional and intellectual imponderables" for which statistical and logical methods were useless. Recent political research had concentrated upon minutiae and avoided the great issues and debates of the time. Moreover, emphasis upon such small-scale studies could not provide the data for the grand scale narratives necessary for an understanding of society. While detractors argued that such issues could not be examined objectively, Beard saw this as exactly the point. If the question were between objectivity and examination of central political and economic concerns, Beard would always choose the latter in large part because of his passion for social justice. His interest in the development of the social sciences lay in his commitment to reform and ethics and how well this research fit the needs of meaningful social change.[33] Yet, at the same time, he never denied the importance of factual and even statistical research for the study of politics.

Beard was commonly recognized as the individual who represented best this ethical orientation to the study of politics. Merriam in his introduction to the second edition of *New Aspects of Politics* referred to Beard as someone who worried that concentration upon scientific methods would leave the humanistic aspects unexamined. Yet, in a characteristically Merriam remark, he dismissed such concerns as a "caveat."[34] Certainly Merriam's approach was more popular especially at the major universities and research institutes where imaginative research required extensive funding. Merriam, above anyone else, had convinced foundation officials, especially of the Laura Spelman Rockefeller Foundation, that scientific and mathematical studies were by definition objective, unbiased, and yet practical. While Beard's approach was more popular among historians, educational theorists such as George Counts, and public intellectuals like Max Lerner, he did have followers within political science such as his old Columbia colleague and future chief Brains Truster Raymond Moley, public administration specialists Ordway Tead and Marshall Dimock, national planners Lewis Lorwin and H. R. Hinricks, and, if inadvertently, historian of political theory George Sabine.

Developmental history was essential for Beard's perspective on political science. First of all, history was *the* one truly integrative discipline. Again, its narrative form emphasized overall comprehension by integrating as many perspectives as possible. Moreover, since the only things that we are

---

[33] Charles A. Beard, "Political Science," in *Research in the Social Sciences: Its Fundamental Methods and Objectives*, ed. Wilson Gee (New York: Macmillan, 1929), 269–91.

[34] Merriam, *New Aspects*, 40.

close to being certain about have occurred in the past, then history is the best guide to public policy. Finally, if one seeks ethics and values by which to judge public behavior, such values are found in the past. Indeed, as Beard grew older, many of his historical works like *The Republic* found universal human values through an examination of an exceptional American past.[35]

The clear corollary of historical activism and relevance became the central aspect of the New History by Beard and his former mentor, James Harvey Robinson. Their approach sought to overcome the conservative nature of developmental historicism by emphasizing three main points: (1) a subordination of the past to the present by selecting facts useful for present needs; (2) a widening of the scope of history beyond political, institutional, and heroic history; and (3) an alliance with the social sciences. The New History was openly reformist and activist. Robinson proclaimed "The present has hitherto been the willing victim of the past; the time has now come when it should turn on the past and exploit it in the interests of advance." Both Robinson and Beard championed relatively recent history. In a private letter of 1913, Beard admitted that he favored this even if it were not scholarly. "The important thing is that college students should not go out without some understanding of the new economic forces which are transforming the very world under our eyes."[36]

No one used the method to greater recognition than Beard. In 1938 the *New Republic* hosted a symposium, "Books That Changed Our Mind." Beard's *An Economic Interpretation of the Constitution of the United States* of 1913 came in second only to Thorstein Veblen's *The Theory of the Leisure Class*, beating out such central figures for the decade as Marx, Freud, and John Dewey.[37] He and his wife Mary's two-volume survey, *The Rise of American Civilization*, was not only the most widely read history book of its time but arguably the most widely read and influential American history text ever. It, like all of his works, reflected his consistent progressive reformism.

Beard and Robinson's approach had at least one methodological dilemma. On what basis does one make this selection of facts? Was history relativistic? At least one of their allies, Carl Becker of Cornell, did seem to approach this in his 1931 AHA presidential address, "Everyman His Own Historian." Becker appeared at times to argue that history ulti-

[35] Charles A. Beard and Alfred Vagts, "Currents of Thought in Historiography," *American Historical Review* 42, no. 3 (1937): 460–83; Charles A. Beard, *The Republic* (New York: Viking Press, 1944).

[36] James Harvey Robinson, *The New History: Essays Illustrating the Modern Historical Outlook* (New York: Macmillan, 1912), 24; and Beard to Lewis Meyers, January 21, 1913, Charles and Mary Beard Collection, DePauw University.

[37] Malcolm Cowley and Bernard Smith, *Books That Changed Our Mind* (New York: Kelmscott Editions, 1939).

mately depended upon the observer and thus that all history and reality was relativistic and dependent upon personal whims. Robinson and especially Beard never accepted this. While objectivity and absolute truth were ultimately unachievable, they must be pursued. In his 1933 American Historical Association presidential address Beard compared writing history to an act of faith, obtaining as much data as possible and then deriving the best conclusion possible.[38] Just as William James perceived his personal acceptance of Christianity as equal parts accumulated data and leap of faith, so too did Beard regard the decision-making process of writing history. Empiricism and the scientific method of empirical modernism were still essential, but the modern condition denied by definition absolute certainty. It's not that one should not be objective, it's that one can't be completely objective. As Beard noted in a 1939 interview, "I don't say that you ought to write history on the basis of your assumptions—but I say that you do."[39]

Their opponents simply refused to grant this. They claimed to be completely objective, all evidence to the contrary, and insisted that only the so-called relativists were biased. They argued, like Merriam, that social phenomena could be explained and, in certain cases, even controlled through scientific methodology. They argued that the relativists were too lazy and bent on directing conclusions toward their own preconceived social ends. Their actions, on the other hand, were by definition ethical through their own self-proclaimed lack of bias and prejudice.

The best way of noting the two Charlies' differences as to the proper nature of political science comes out though their common participation in the American Historical Association Commission on the Social Studies. In 1924 the AHA, following a long lead of previous social science organizations, established a commission to study and make recommendations on civic education in the secondary schools. The commission began with four historians, three professors of education, an economist, and Merriam and several years later added a geographer, a sociologist, two more professors of education, an educational administrator, a foundation representative, and Beard as member and temporary research director. From the beginning the committee noted its goal of designing social studies courses to create better citizens and the establishment of social objectives to ensure this development. Unlike its predecessors, it went on record as denying the claims of the American Legion, Chambers of Commerce, and other right-wing groups.

---

[38] Charles A. Beard, "Written History as an Act of Faith," *American Historical Review* 39, no. 2 (1934): 219–31.

[39] Hubert Herring, "Charles A. Beard: Freelance among the Historians," *Harper's* 178, March 1939, 651.

Beard and Merriam had both been interested in this issue for some time. As early as 1915 Beard had pronounced the lack of citizenship training in the public schools as a disgrace.[40] In his writings of secondary as well as college textbooks, his championing of adult education in the United Kingdom and America, and his continuous lectures to public school teachers, Beard reflected the centrality of the issue for himself. Merriam too spoke constantly on the issue. He had been an active politician, served on innumerable national social science and planning committees, and during the time of the AHA Commission directed a roughly comparative series on international civic education.

In 1931, Beard's good friend, protégé, and fellow relativist, the historian of education George Counts became director of research. While Counts and Merriam were also quite close, it was the Beard-Counts alliance that dominated the publications of the commission. The commission came to publish sixteen volumes, but most were technical works on issues such as testing. Five of them, however, dealt with the key questions of the commission—the determination and determiners of objectives for the social sciences. Beard wrote two of these, Counts another, Merriam one, and Beard and Counts coauthored the conclusions. In the first volume, *A Charter for the Social Sciences*, Beard set the tone by insisting upon the need for the development of decision-making tools for all citizens. Teachers of social science must emphasize the significance of choice and the use of ethics in that process. Just as historical relativism permitted the historian to make informed judgments in part upon his moral role, Beard's plan for civic education placed decision-making responsibilities in the hands of the ethical teachers and not those of the materialistic school boards, chambers of commerce, or other civic organizations.[41]

Merriam's perspective on political science was, ironically, both more and less democratic. In its reliance on expensive equipment and elaborate technique, only well-trained technicians could do social science. Yet, as a former politician, Merriam insisted that popularly elected individuals, not educators, make the determination of social objectives. In the 1920s, Merriam had gone so far as to defend the state of Tennessee's right to outlaw the teaching of evolution in its public schools. While he wished for control by the technicians, he could find no way to bypass the actual politicians. Technical control would be indoctrination and, although some control was good, a clear—if undefined by Merriam—line existed.[42] Interestingly,

[40] Charles A. Beard, "Methods of Training for Public Service," *School and Society* 2 (December 25, 1915), 909.

[41] Charles A. Beard, *A Charter for the Social Sciences in the Schools* (New York: Scribner's Sons, 1932), vii.

[42] Merriam to John Merriam, July 10, 1925, Merriam Papers, University of Chicago; Merriam, *Civic Education*, 177–80.

it was a line that individuals like Ogburn and Merriam students like Lasswell and White were willing to step over.

Beard and Counts's *Conclusions and Recommendations of the Commission* did not fairly summarize the previous volumes. It disparaged technical developments and methods of which they disapproved. Ethical values, not methods, were the key to education, and educators obtained ethics through reliance upon a personal frame of reference. The responsibility for directing students lay with their teachers, unencumbered by political and economic control of communities. Teachers alone were "servants of the community as a whole . . . and trained to think in terms of more abiding interests of mankind." Again, one sees Beard's emphasis upon ethics over technical skill or elected officials. Certain groups automatically possessed more credibility than others; yet these groups were neither Merriam's elected officials nor his technicians.[43]

Not surprisingly, Merriam strenuously opposed the *Conclusions*. He initially promised to swing ten of the seventeen members of the commission with him. He had no difficulty with selection of objectives for social science and its practitioners. While he did find fault with the historical emphasis of Beard and Counts in the conclusions, his primary objection lay with the teachers as the source of these decisions. They were mere technicians and must answer to the political and, although he never said it specifically, economic elite. Originally, Merriam swayed a number of the members but gradually most fell away. In the end only the foundation official, the superintendent of the Washington, D.C., public schools, and an expert on testing refused to sign the conclusions. Like Merriam, they either gloried in technical expertise or served the political and economic elite who traditionally controlled such decisions. A conservative congressman later accused Frank Ballou, the Washington school superintendent, of communist sympathies for his committee membership despite his opposition and resignation.[44]

Beard and Merriam were not nearly as opposed to one another as it seemed. Merriam's position in *Civic Education in the United States* was very close to that of the *Conclusions*. Beard often feared that his allies had become too radical. At one point he scolded Counts half-humorously, "You put on a red coat, jump up on the ramparts and say to the American Legion, the D.A.R., and every school board in America: 'Here I am a good Red, shoot me!' " Especially as the 1930s progressed and many of the old progressives joined the socialists and communists on the one hand or the Liberty League on the other, the two quietly began to praise each other's

[43] American Historical Commission on the Social Studies, *Conclusions and Recommendations of the Commission* (New York: Scribner's Sons, 1934), 125.

[44] Smith, *Social Science in the Crucible*, 200–202.

work. Beard, in particular, recognized Merriam's rationale for attempting to copy the natural and physical sciences to achieve certainty. Merriam, on the other hand, recognized Beard's determination not to abandon values and seemed stunned at his own students' positivistic dismissal of ethical issues. As the two looked around at the new generation of political scientists, they seemed to come to recognize their basic similarities forged in an earlier and simpler time.[45]

This became especially true as the two found themselves increasingly isolated by changing circumstances. An initial supporter of Franklin Roosevelt, Beard began to see him as a villain, accusing him of using international affairs to take attention away from a weakening economy. When the United States entered the war, he began a quasi-conspiratorial overlook of Roosevelt's role in precipitating the war. Lifelong friends shunned him; old enemies gloried in his downfall; in retrospect all of his work was summarily dismissed. While Beard used extensive documentation especially in *President Roosevelt and the Coming of the War, 1941*, he was refused access to the official archives, home to the "real" scientific facts. In September 1948, Beard, completely deaf and totally frustrated by the obstinate direction of the world, died. Like his old adversary Merriam, who would die virtually unknown five years later, Beard had outlived his time. In the final analysis, neither the banishment of history from political science nor the near replacement of political science with history met the activist needs of the two Progressive reformers. More importantly, neither brand of empirical modernism satisfied the needs of Merriam's students or their peers. Political science would subsequently pass closer and closer to the Scylla of disinterested quantification as time passed on.[46]

---

[45] Beard to George Counts, August 5, 1934, George S. Counts Collection, University of Southern Illinois.

[46] Charles A. Beard, "Peace for America: Solving Domestic Crises by War," *New Republic* 86, March 11, 1936, 127–29; Charles A. Beard, "Who's to Write the History of the War?" *Saturday Evening Post* 220, October 4, 1947, 172; Charles A. Beard, *President Roosevelt and the Coming of the War, 1941: A Study in Appearances and Realities* (New Haven, CT: Yale University Press, 1948).

Seven

Making Democracy Safe for the World: Political Science between the Wars

JOHN G. GUNNELL

> [W]e have forgotten that we are anything
> but citizens.
> —Ernest Barker, 1915

DESPITE THE NOW quite extensive literature devoted to the study of the development of American political science, there is still an inadequate grasp of certain important periods in the history of the discipline and of how they are related to the contemporary character of the field. One such period is that between the two World Wars, and particularly the 1920s, when much of the basic contemporary structure of the discipline, as well its dominant and most persistent visions of both democracy and science, took form. The so-called behavioral revolution at midcentury was more a reaffirmation of this transformation than a fundamental theoretical innovation.[1] The difficulty in interpreting this period is the consequence of neither insufficient accounts of the work of prominent individuals, such as Charles Merriam, nor any special complexity that attends their arguments, nor lack of knowledge about the broad political and intellectual situation in which they were located. The problem derives, instead, from a failure to recover the internal discursive context and the evolutionary path of the conversations in which they were engaged and the original meaning of the concepts around which these conversations revolved. In the study of disciplinary history, we are still burdened with various forms of "presentism" that, although more sophisticated than some of the earlier crude versions of Whig and anti-Whig narratives, continue to inhibit interpretation.[2]

---

[1] For an elaboration of this point, see John G. Gunnell, "The Real Revolution in Political Science," *PS* 37, no. 1 (2004): 47–50.

[2] For a discussion of these issues and a critical examination of the historiography of American political science, see the introduction and appendix in John G. Gunnell, *Imagining the American Polity: Political Science and the Discourse of Democracy* (University Park: Pennsylvania State University Press, 2004).

Both political scientists and students of the history of the discipline, drawing on images such as Morton White's account of the "revolt against formalism,"[3] have tended to interpret this period as a protobehavioral era and to accept the image of a widespread rejection of historical and institutional studies that ushered in the beginnings of scientism in American political science and significantly distinguished it from the study of politics in Great Britain. The motives and claims that are often ascribed to this literature, however, really belong to a later generation and to individuals such as Robert Dahl, who did present themselves as rebelling against "conventional political science" and the "historical, philosophical, and the descriptive-institutional approaches."[4] It is, indeed, possible to describe what happened in American political science between the wars in this manner or to say that it amounted to something that could be labeled as a turn away from a historical and institutional approach to a naturalistic scientific vision, but all of this does not bring us very close to an adequate understanding of this period. This is not to say that there were not some significant differences between the British and American contexts as well as between the respective traditions of political inquiry, nor is it to say that an important change in the theory and practice of political science did not take place. This revolution in political science was, however, closely tied to a crisis in democratic theory, and there was in many respects a parallel and similar transformation in the British study of politics as well as instances of an important dimension of interaction between these two realms of discourse. At this point, however, it is as necessary to emphasize what did not happen as what did happen.

No significant portion of the discourse of political science during the interwar years involved either any general or widespread conflict between what was understood as scientific and historical approaches or any such conflict between the professions of history and political science. For example, it had been at a joint meeting of the American Historical Association and the American Economics Association that political scientists had declared their professional independence, but it was their separation from the American Social Science Association and the establishment of their autonomy alongside the American Economics Association and the AHA that was crucial, rather than an attempt to divorce themselves from the methods and subjects of economics and history. The British historian James Bryce's account of American democracy and the American political system had been one of the major impetuses for a more empirical study

[3] Morton G. White, *Social Thought in America: The Revolt against Formalism* (New York: Viking, 1949).

[4] Robert A. Dahl, "The Behavioral Approach in Political Science: Epitaph to a Monument to a Successful Protest," *American Political Science Review* 55, no. 4 (1961): 763–72.

of politics in the late nineteenth century, and he was elected president of the American Political Science Association in 1907, as was the historian Charles Beard in 1927. In 1920, the third volume of William Archibald Dunning's seminal *A History of Political Theories* was published. Dunning had been Merriam's dissertation director as well as one of the principals in the foundation of the political science curriculum at Columbia, but he had also been one of the charter members and founders of the American Historical Association and a principal historian of the Reconstruction period as well as both a president of the AHA and, when he died in 1922, president-elect of the APSA. Maybe the most significant indication of the continued affinity between history and political science is the fact that the study of the history of political theory continued to flourish as the core subfield of the discipline and function, as Adcock and Bevir suggest in their chapter, both as providing an account of the past of American ideas and institutions and as an account of the pedigree of political science. The genre continued to develop and reached its culmination in the paradigmatic work of George H. Sabine in 1937.[5]

W. W. Willoughby, for example, a principal practitioner of both the history of political thought and the juristic and historical approach to the study of the state, emphasized, in a manner not unlike that of a wide range of individuals from Merriam to David Easton, how the principal goal of political theory was the development of analytical concepts for the purpose of empirical analysis. This was also the general thrust of one of the most significant calls for the application of the methods of science—Stuart Rice's *Methods in Social Science: A Case Book* (1931), which viewed history as producing much of the factual "raw material" of an inductive social science. And G.E.G. Catlin, arguably the most outspoken advocate of scientism, did not so much wish to reject historical studies as incorporate them as a source of data for a generalizing science that would, in the end, be directed toward a solution of practical issues. As Smith suggests, the "new history" propagated by James Harvey Robinson was in tune with changing emphases in social science, and in the pivotal case of Merriam there was, once again, despite his embrace of the methods and theory of psychology, no rejection of historical studies, which Merriam viewed as an important, and by no means obsolete, stage in the evolution of social science.[6] It is important to recognize

---

[5] For a fuller discussion of the development of political science and political theory, see John G. Gunnell, *The Descent of Political Theory: The Genealogy of an American Vocation* (Chicago: University of Chicago Press, 1993).

[6] See John G. Gunnell, "Continuity and Innovation in the History of Political Science: The Case of Charles Merriam," *Journal of the History of the Behavioral Sciences* 28 (April 1992): 133–42.

that the scientific enthusiasm of the 1920s predated any coherent philosophy of science such as logical positivism and involved a somewhat amorphous set of commitments to pragmatism, statistical and quantitative
analysis, conceptual rigor, and interdisciplinary approaches. The term
positivism surfaced occasionally, but whether used critically or approv-
ingly, it usually referred to Comte or to some general commitment to the
scientific attitude.

Dispelling the idea that we can interpret the evolution of the discipline
during this period as generated by a sharp conflict between historical and
scientific orientations does not, however, entail the assumption that there
were not important transformations and changes in distribution of emphasis regarding both the substance and method of historical approaches.
Subsequent to World War I, there was a marked Americanization of
American political science. This was in part a consequence of the embrace
of the indigenous philosophy of pragmatism that provided a new theoretical foundation for political thought and dominated the intellectual ambi-
ence of institutions such as Harvard,[7] but it also involved a pointed rejection of German philosophy, which was widely perceived as associated
with authoritarian ideas. While the image of progress continued to dominate, it was understood as less inevitable than from the perspective of
nineteenth-century Hegelian philosophy, and this provided an even
greater commitment to the pursuit of science, which was never detached
from the goal of social amelioration and political reform. Significantly
new accounts of American history, and particularly the founding period,
had emerged in the work of individuals such as Herbert Croly, Beard, and
J. Allen Smith as the study of history became a more critical than celebra-
tory endeavor. Finally, and most important, changes in historical reflection were closely tied to some fundamental transformations in democratic
theory. During the nineteenth century, the mode of historical analysis and
the content of the interpretation of history had reflected the concept of
democracy embodied in the theory of the state. The decay of that theory
was accompanied by a vision of history that served to provide the new
democratic theory with a provenance, and it, in turn, reflected the values
of that theory, which, by the 1930s, would be called liberalism.[8]

The theory of the state that had structured political science from its
inception with Francis Lieber and that was developed most fully by Burgess and persisted well into the twentieth century carried with it a historical and descriptive account of the United States as a democracy. As Farr

[7] See Louis Menand, *The Metaphysical Club* (New York: Farrar, Strauss, and Giroux,
2001).

[8] John G. Gunnell, "The Archaeology of American Liberalism," *Journal of Political Ideologies* 6, no. 2 (2001): 125–45.

suggests in his chapter, the American regime was presented as the apotheosis of the evolution of the subjective and objective manifestations of the idea of the state as it passed from its Teutonic origins to English institutions and finally reached its culmination in the thought and practice of American democracy. This theory of the state involved a rejection of contract theory and was predicated upon the claim that there was an American people, a historically emergent sovereign community, that was represented in the Revolution, suppressed in an act of usurpation by the Articles of Confederation, and reestablished by the counterrebellion of the Convention, which gave rise to the Constitution, which in turn both authorized and limited the offices and officers of government. It was the slow declination of this theory and its philosophical and historical backing that created a crisis in democratic theory, which was resolved, in a period from the early 1920s to the early 1930s, by the articulation of a theory of pluralist democracy, which would continue to capture the imagination of mainstream political science for the next two generations.[9] Although the pluralist tradition would be pointedly rearticulated after World War II, individuals such as David Truman and Dahl would introduce very little in the way of conceptual and theoretical innovation. The attack on the traditional idea of sovereignty that accompanied the emergence of pluralism was significant less because it entailed a rejection of legalism and formalism than because it contributed to undercutting the idea of popular sovereignty, what came to be called the "democratic dogma," represented in the theory of the state.[10] This idea had been a key to the nineteenth-century conservative demand for limited government, but it was equally essential, in various ways, to the theory of the next generation and to the ideology of Progressive politics. Merriam did much to transform the direction of political science, but his conception of democracy owed more, as in the case of John Dewey, to the old paradigm than to the new. For individuals such as Croly, Beard, Smith, Mary Parker Follett, and Dewey, pluralism was accepted, as it had been by Lieber, as an essential characteristic of democracy, but they could not let go of the assumption that a democracy required an organic community. Merriam may have lost faith in the Progressive dream of finding and awakening a democratic people, but he believed that science, as a basis of social control, might contribute to creating a democratic and unified society that would make it possible to speak in substantive terms about a public interest.

[9] See Gunnell, *Imagining the American Polity.*

[10] See, for example, John Dickinson, "Democratic Realities and the Democratic Dogma," *American Political Science Review* 24, no. 2 (1930): 283–309; Walter J. Shepard, "Democracy in Transition," *American Political Science Review* 29, no. 1 (1935): 1–20.

There was a distinct belief that the theory of pluralist democracy that emerged in the 1920s and early 1930s would make democracy safe for the world, just as Woodrow Wilson had wished to make the world safe for democracy. Not only was monism perceived as a bad form of philosophy, but in the guise of the concept of sovereignty, as a dangerous form of political organization. Despite the British contribution to pluralist thought, the theory of pluralism that developed in the United States was, in the end, a distinctly American theory, and the methodological changes in the discipline were to a large extent less a product of some abstract commitment to science than an adaptation to a new vision of social, and democratic, reality. This entailed a certain depreciation of historical studies, since society as a whole was no longer conceived as a community with a distinct pattern of development, and the elements of society, conceived as groups, were less historical entities than fungible aggregations of individual interest that were cognitively accessible by methods such as those employed in statistics and psychology. Although there was no general rejection of historical approaches, the nineteenth-century equation of history and science was dissolved as scientism became defined in distinctly new ways by individuals such as Merriam.

The end of World War I ushered in a period of Americanization in the field of political science as the discipline turned away from its roots in German philosophy, but there were some significant new Atlantic crossings. The evolution of the new theory of democracy involved an important engagement with British political theory, which had also been significantly touched by German idealist philosophy, as den Otter noted in her chapter. Despite the absence in Britain of the kind of institutionalized discipline of political science that existed in the United States, some quite similar theoretical, methodological, and ideological transformations in the study of politics were taking place. What corresponded to, and interacted with, the American conversation was the work, and person, of individuals such as Bryce, Catlin, Harold Laski, Graham Wallas, G.D.H. Cole, Ernest Barker, and A. D. Lindsay. They were all educated at Oxford, and the continuities between that education and their subsequent careers as well as their academic and ideological innovations are as striking in many ways as the generational differences that characterized Columbia University in the United States as Beard, Merriam, Frank Goodnow, Theodore Roosevelt, and the like emerged as the progeny of Burgess.

Although, after Bryce, maybe the most determinative liaison was Laski's relatively brief presence at Harvard, Wallas and Barker were also visitors to the Massachusetts campus, and the university awarded Barker an honorary doctorate. William Yandell Elliott, who was a major participant in the debates of the period and the severest and most consistent critic of scientism and pluralism, was one of the dominant figures at Harvard. He had received his Doctor of Philosophy degree at Oxford, where he had studied with Lindsay, to whom he dedicated his *Pragmatic Revolt in Politics* (1928), and Catlin, who most directly confronted Elliott, had been an undergraduate at Oxford. Walter Lippmann studied with Wallas at Harvard, and Wallas subsequently wrote with Lippmann in mind. Wallas's and Lippmann's images of political science and its possibilities significantly influenced Merriam's program and his rhetoric of inquiry. It is impossible to understand fully what transpired during the 1920s and early 1930s without a grasp of these connections, which were crucial in reconstituting the theory of democracy, the uses and images of history, the methods of political study, and the perceptions of the relationship between political science and politics. Despite the common assumption that the commitment to science involved a retreat from practical concerns and even from the idea of democracy,[11] the new image of science in the United States was intimately related to the issue of the relationship between public and academic discourse and to the problem of creating a more democratic society, and, despite the great difference in the relationship between these realms in Britain, the practical concerns were equally prominent.

Subsequent to Bryce, the work that had most immediately made the greatest impact on the conversation of American political science was that of Wallas. As in the case of many American social scientists, both before and after the turn of the century, his socialism, scientism, and political zeal were rooted in deep Christian commitments. Although there was little focused theoretical depth to Wallas's work, which consisted largely of anecdotal explorations of politics coupled with pleas for realism, the rejection of abstract images of politics, and the application of modern psychology, it fitted well with the American agenda advanced by individuals such as Merriam and Lippmann. He, in turn, by his own interpretation, had been inspired by the work of Jane Addams as well as the Chicago school of social science and, later, the New School for Social Research. In his first book, written shortly before assuming his chair in Political Science at the London School of Economics (of which he was initially urged by the Webbs to be the director), Wallas claimed that although representative democracy was increasingly accepted in theory and practice, there was wide dissatisfaction with how it performed and, following the lead of William James, that this could be remedied by the kind of "political invention" that studying "men" and human nature, rather than institutions, would yield. Wallas advocated a "change in the conditions of political

[11] See, for example, Bernard Crick, *The American Science of Politics: Its Origins and Conditions* (Berkeley and Los Angeles: University of California Press, 1959); David Ricci, *The Tragedy of Political Science: Politics, Scholarship, and Democracy* (New Haven, CT: Yale University Press, 1984).

science" at universities such as Oxford, where, he claimed, it was assumed that "intellectuality" determined things in politics and, instead, called for a focus on instinct, emotions, habit, and nonrational inference. In order to deal with such factors, it was necessary, he argued, to employ experts and focus on "relevant and measurable facts" and quantitative and descriptive methods that could be the basis of an effective political science and better political reasoning. This, he claimed, could "transform the science of politics" and create a "new political force" by harmonizing "thought and passion" and establishing realistic "ideals of political conduct" that could inform the "structure of our political institutions."[12]

Wallas's second book, *The Great Society*, was an elaboration of the material that he presented in a course on government at Harvard in 1910, and it was directed in part to Lippmann, who had taken his course and who was much influenced by the argument when the latter wrote both *Preface to Politics* (1913) and *Drift and Mastery* (1914). The dilemma, he claimed, much as Dewey would in 1927 (*The Public and Its Problems*), was that while technology had created the "great society" and an environment that was no longer natural, our "state of consciousness" lagged behind. Social psychology, however, could be deployed to understand the complex "dispositions" associated with "Instincts" and "Intelligence," and through the use of techniques of social control such as eugenics, it would be possible to unblock our dispositions, change our habits, and make it possible to move forward toward the good life and happiness both domestically and internationally. Strategies such as individualism, socialism, and syndicalism were too partial for the "State" as a whole, and while it was important to seek the "mean," the "extreme" could be a source of ideals. Wallas continued to pursue these themes after the war and argued that "our social heritage" had outpaced our biology and that it was urgent that we gain control of it and direct it. Although this required cooperation within groups, "national cooperation" was essential and demanded mental unity and contentment grounded in social and economic equality and a vision of positive liberty.[13] Wallas was not, any more than Merriam, a normative pluralist. He recognized the fact of pluralism and that diversity was part of modern democratic society, but he also viewed it as a problem to be overcome in establishing a national democracy.[14]

[12] Graham Wallas, *Human Nature in Politics* (London: Constable, 1908), 18–19, 169, 198.

[13] Graham Wallas, *The Great Society: A Psychological Analysis* (New York: Macmillan, 1914); Graham Wallas, *Our Social Heritage* (London: George Allen and Unwin, 1921).

[14] For a full discussion of Wallas, see Terence H. Qualter, *Graham Wallas and the Great Society* (London: Macmillan, 1980).

Just prior to the war, Barker and Lindsay had both confronted the problem of the theoretical status of the state and the issue of the place of groups in the polity, which were at the heart of the emerging American conversation. They each embraced important elements of British idealism, such as that represented in the work of T. H. Green, but they were less than happy with the established Oxford study of politics in terms of the "Greats" and with the assumption that this scheme of study was politically relevant as a foundation of public policy and as training for political leadership. Although in 1896 Beatrice Webb had given up attempting to find a lecturer in political science that would fit her hope of creating something on the order of the École libre des sciences politiques and had concluded that it was "a trifle difficult to teach a science that does not yet exist,"[15] it would be a mistake to assume that the old Whig historical/comparative method of Seeley and Sidgwick was accepted by the new generation.[16] Lindsay began his campaign for a reformation of the curriculum when he came to Oxford in 1906. He finally succeeded in instituting the "new greats" program (PPE) in 1920, and the emphasis on political thought was more radical than it might seem from a later perspective. Cole, the first Chichele Professor of Social and Political Theory at Oxford, was a dedicated socialist with a deep practical involvement, and he was a friend and associate of Lindsay. Lindsay and Cole were also intensively involved in public affairs, and although Barker, a liberal and Whig, was less so inclined, which may have cost him the appointment to the Gladstone Chair of Political Thought in 1912 (for which Wallas had applied and was rejected), he continually urged greater practical relevance for the study of politics.[17]

Although much has been made of Barker's less than positive comments, as in the case of his inaugural address, about the study of politics as a science, he was among the first in England to identify himself professionally as a political scientist and political theorist. Although he never rejected philosophical and historical analysis, he divorced himself from the

[15] Quoted by Jack Hayward, "Cultural and Contextual Constraints upon the Development of Political Science in England," in *The Development of Political Science: A Comparative Survey*, ed. David Easton, John G. Gunnell, and Luigi Graziano (London: Routledge, 1991). See also Jack Hayward and Philip Norton, eds., *The Political Science of British Politics* (Brighton, UK: Wheatsheaf, 1986).

[16] See Stefan Collini, Donald Winch, and John Burrow, *That Noble Science of Politics* (Cambridge: Cambridge University Press, 1983).

[17] See Robert Wokler, "The Professoriate of Political Thought in England since 1914: A Tale of Three Chairs," in *The History of Political Thought in National Context*, ed. Dario Castiglione and Iain Hampsher-Monk (Cambridge: Cambridge University Press, 2001); Julia Stapleton, *Englishness and the Study of Politics: The Social and Political Thought of Ernest Barker* (Cambridge: Cambridge University Press, 1994).

emphasis of British historians on constitutional history, which depreci-
ated contemporary political and economic issues and practical concerns,
and, beginning with his position on the Modern History Faculty at Oxford in 1897, he pursued a more innovative approach to the "greats,"
which stressed the connection between law and political science that he
would continue to advocate when he went to King's College in London
and when he accepted the chair in Political Science at Cambridge in 1927
(for which Lindsay was one of the electors). This chair, as well as that
occupied by Wallas at the London School of Economics, was funded by
the Laura Spelman Rockefeller Memorial, which had underwritten much
of the new social science at the University of Chicago and was devoted
to propagating abroad the emerging conception of American empirical
political science. Barker lamented what he took to be the persistent divorce between law and politics in British political theory and the manner
in which it had drifted off in an excessively philosophical and moralistic
direction. "The English system of political science, so far as we can speak
of such a thing," had, he claimed, taken on an abstract and "normative
character," focusing on "moral norms and standards." Barker complained that "our English political science has hitherto had no great
method" and that a greater emphasis on law would contribute to making
"political science a genuine discipline" and return it to its foundation in
public matters. Although he noted that "the word 'science' seems to make
a large claim for any study of human beings," he stressed that it was
necessary to go beyond an abstract discussion of political forms to a consideration of how things actually worked. Even though it was important
for political science to take on the role of "moralist" and consider matters
of "purposes and ends," including "ultimate ends," which were at the
heart of the concept of natural law, a greater emphasis on actual events
and processes was necessary. Although he did not mention Wallas by
name, he indicated his sympathy with a psychological and biological approach to the study of "'human nature' in politics."[18]

Lindsay described the later half of the nineteenth century as marked,
in both theory and practice, by a transition from "individualism to collectivism" and to the idea of the state as a corporate personality and as an
"organic unity." In Lindsay's view, this transformation in theory was not
only the product of idealist philosophy but somewhat of a "reflex" response to increased practices of state "interference," but by 1914, he
perceived, in both spheres, the beginning of "notes of discontent" and
evidence that "the state itself is on trial." Whether it was by socialists, syndicalists, pacificists and internationalists, or pluralists, all of the

[18] Otto Gierke, *Natural Law and the Theory of Society, 1500–1800*, trans. Ernest Barker
(Cambridge: Cambridge University Press, 1934), 1:xix–xx, xv, xxx.

elder claims justifying the unity and supremacy of the state had been called into question, and Lindsay found it safe to say that "the theory of the sovereign state has broken down" as associations and organizations such as unions, the church, and political parties became an integral part of society. Lindsay maintained that once the state had been accepted as a corporate personality, it was impossible to deny such status to other associations. Despite his democratic collectivist propensities, his answer to the dilemma was to insist that neither individualism nor collectivism were theoretically adequate to account for the facts of modern life. The state was neither an aggregate of individuals nor a "higher personality" into which individuals were absorbed. While he found it necessary to relinquish all the traditional theories of state priority, he did find some truth in the general idea that the state was, in the end, the "organization of organizations" and that it was "special" in that it represented "men's sense of obligation to one another" and constituted a general ethical system of rights and duties grounded in common culture and traditions. The extent to which the state, through the agency of government, should interfere, however, was, he claimed, a situational matter with respect to which no a priori principles were available, but, in his view, such action was clearly more necessary in contemporary society with its complexity and high degree of economic development.[19] In the same year, Barker offered a very similar assessment.

Barker had advocated a juristic theory of the state as a legal personality and as a way of establishing the "rule of law" and the responsibility of government in opposition to the authority of the "mysterious" inviolable and invisible Crown. Although he still tended to equate the state with a sovereign public and to view government as its agent, he argued that "the state had been generally discredited in England" as far as constituting anything possessing a transcendent will and personality. Although, he claimed, this disposition to deflate the status of the state was originally rooted in religious Nonconformity and the elevation of voluntary associations, a tradition with which he was generally sympathetic, the basic attitude had spread to classic political economy and was more recently represented in Marxism and the work of pluralists such as J. N. Figgis and Frederic Maitland. Barker maintained that it was important to resist a metaphysical image of the state and, instead, to see it, as well as all other associations, as consisting of individuals related by a common organizing idea and interest. The problem was that of the relationship between the state and other associations. Barker rejected both Hegelian and Austinian theories of state authority and sovereignty and, instead, argued that peo-

---

[19] A. D. Lindsay, "The State in Recent Political Theory," *Political Quarterly* 1 (May 1914): 128–30, 136, 140.

ple who live in a "community must have an ultimate source of adjustment of their relations" and that this was the function of the state and the basis of its special status. England, he claimed, was marked by "polyarchism" and an "unstable equilibrium" between associations, and it was the task of the state, with its instrument of law, to mediate as needed. He suggested that, paradoxically, the state was often discredited when it was doing well (and appeared not to be needed) and credited when it was doing badly (and appeared to be needed). In a footnote, Barker remarked that his assessment had been written in May of 1914 but that by the time it was published, in January of 1915, the facts had changed. Suddenly the state was "having its high midsummer of credit."[20]

Barker, like a number of Americans such as Dewey and Willoughby, went on to condemn the German philosophy of the state and the "worship of power" in the work of writers such as Nietzsche and Treitschke, but he also criticized Austin's theory of sovereignty as never having fitted the reality of the "heterogeneous unity" of English society. Like Americans such as Sabine and Francis Coker, Barker was a cautious pluralist who, while recognizing and validating the diversity of society, did not let go of the idea of an underlying social unity that the government represented. His concern about excessive unity was expressed early on in his worries about Plato's Republic and his praise of Aristotle for reconciling unity and diversity as well as in later criticisms of Rousseau. He rejected contract theory but, like Willoughby, held to a notion of natural rights and law as rooted in society and history.

For Barker and Lindsay, the concept of the state hovered between government and a comprehensive association, and their arguments were very similar to the position developed by Willoughby—who also indicated his indebtedness to T. H. Green and Kant. For Willoughby, the state was both a juristic entity and an ethical association, but he rejected the transcendental aura that had been accorded to it by individuals such as Burgess as well as any status as a primordial community that preceded government. For all of these individuals, society was the fundamental entity, and that entity was ultimately a plurality. By the end of the 1920s, the state, in American political science, through the work of individuals such as Willoughby, had largely become a synonym for government. In Laski's early work, however, the state, despite his depreciation of it, was still an association and a "whole."

Although some of the early literature of the twentieth century, such as the eventually paradigmatic book of Arthur Bentley, adumbrated and would be incorporated in the pluralist tradition, it was largely through

---

[20] Ernest Barker, "The 'Rule of Law,' " *Political Quarterly* 1 (May 1914): 117–27; Ernest Barker, "The Discredited State," *Political Quarterly* 2 (February 1915): 101, 118, 120–21.

Laski's work, and the controversy that surrounded it, that the term *pluralism* was first introduced into America. Both his concept and the arguments of his most vocal and persistent opponent, Elliott, were, however, rooted in the British intellectual context. When Laski, a socialist with practical aspirations, returned to England, he was the anointed successor to Wallas at the LSE. Although Laski's image of pluralism and the initial American debate over pluralism and monism had, in the end, a somewhat attenuated relationship to the theory that, by the 1930s, became sedimented in the discourse of political science, they were crucial elements in the dialogue.

Laski's principal concern was what he took to be the centralization of power and authority in Parliament and the common law, and he undertook a constant attack on idealism, the monistic theory of the state, and the idea of state sovereignty.[21] He ridiculed the "exaltation of unity," which he perceived as having evolved in political theory from Dante to Hegel and which was now represented in politics by Bismarck and Treitschke, but initially Laski did not so much reject the underlying ontological assumptions on which the theory of the state had been predicated as displace them to other associations. According to Laski, each church, town, university, and labor union had its own distinct reality and "group-life" and "will." Laski suggested that William James's image of the pluralistic universe supported the political idea of a federated republic and "pluralistic theory of the state." What constituted the entity that he now conceived as plural was less than clear, but he argued that, as a philosophical principle, the whole is not known before its parts and has no moral superiority. Consequently, he claimed, the "State is but one of the variety of associations and groups to which the individual belongs" and to which allegiance is paid. The source of law was, in fact, not a command of a sovereign, as Austin had claimed, but something sociologically generated from the "opinion" of individuals and instances of their consent or "fused good-will." Laski also sought support for his arguments in Aristotle's idea of mixed government and suggested that this conception of the polity amounted to "a pragmatist theory of the state" in which progress came not from uniformity but from variation and conflict.[22] These ideas were explicitly formulated in the context of Laski's associa-

---

[21] Harold J. Laski, *Studies in the Problem of Sovereignty* (New Haven, CT: Yale University Press, 1917); Harold J. Laski, *Authority in the Modern State* (New Haven, CT: Yale University Press, 1919); Leon Duguit, *Law in the Modern State*, trans. Frida Laski and Harold Laski (New York: R. W. Huebsch, 1919). For recent biographies of Laski, see Isaac Kramnick and Barry Sheerman, *Harold J. Laski: A Life on the Left* (London: Hamish Hamilton, 1993); Michael Newman, *Harold Laski: A Political Biography* (London: Macmillan, 1993).

[22] Laski, *Studies in the Problem of Sovereignty*, 1–25.

tions in the United States with Roscoe Pound, Felix Frankfurter, and Herbert Croly, but he more explicitly drew on the work of Maitland, Figgis, and Gierke and their accounts of pluralism in medieval society.[23] He also attempted, through his studies of the Reformation and other instances of religious dissent, as well as by reference to more modern examples such as syndicalism in France, guild socialism, and Cole's notion of functional group representation, to give historical and rhetorical depth to his concept of pluralism. While the modern state had sought its independence from religion, it attempted, he claimed, to appropriate for itself that same kind of universality.

Laski initially found in the United States, in both theory and practice, what he believed was in many respects an exemplification of his claim about the "moral insufficiency" of the idea of the unitary state. He argued that the very fact of the American Revolution, as well as the nature of the government of the United States manifest in the principles of federalism and the separation of powers, demonstrated the "absurdity" and the practical abolition of Austin's theory of sovereignty and Dicey's image of a unitarian and omnipotent state. Laski's image of the founding of the United States was considerably different from that of Burgess and other nineteenth-century American theorists. He argued that the founders had taken the individual states as a "foundation to be built upon" and did not attempt "to create a complete system of government" at the national level. And this, he argued, was still sociologically apparent in the "fundamental diversity of circumstance" in the country, "in the variety of its group life, and in the wide distribution of sovereign power" that promised the "guarantee of its perennial youth" and the "preservation of liberty." The eminent, imminent, and immanent danger, however, was, as in all modern countries, that of "centralization" and the loss of local autonomy.[24] In his successive essays, Laski moved more and more toward the thesis, and logical conclusion already so evident in the work of Willoughby, that "what we term state-action is, in actual fact, action by government." And, in his view, this, in turn, amounted to little more than what was functionally accepted by groups in society and made operative.[25] But while his primary target was the idea of centralized authority and the myths that sustained it, his work also served to undercut the elder notions of popular sovereignty and democracy. With the publication of his second major book, Laski began to claim that the state, or what in his formulation now seemed to be government, really was always, and had

---

[23] For a representative selection of some of this literature, see Paul Q. Hirst, ed., *The Pluralist Theory of the State* (London: Routledge, 1989).

[24] Ibid., 268–82.

[25] Laski, *Authority in the Modern State*, 30.

always been, controlled by a segment of society and a dominant economic interest. But historically it had also been subject to all sorts of limitations including the conscience of the individual, institutional checks, group diversity, and popular resistance and revolution. The fact that governments were always forced to gain support "leads to a pluralistic theory of society." This account of the political process, he claimed, was "realism," while the notion that the state can be identified with some general community was idealism.[26]

Laski pursued the same themes in yet a third volume, but the concepts of the monistic state and the pluralistic state no longer represented simply different theoretical accounts. The monistic state was now presented as the characteristic structure of contemporary political power, and pluralism was offered as an alternative normative program in opposition to the "unified sovereignty of the present social organization." Pluralism would involve the substitution of "coordination" for "hierarchical structure" and entail the "partition" of sovereignty. He continued to stress the manner in which government was controlled by dominant economic forces and how liberty was incompatible with power in the hands of "a small group of property owners."[27] Laski still sought his exemplars in the Conciliar Movement of the Middle Ages, Edmund Burke, and early American federalism. He argued that in the Middle Ages, where unity was achieved "through a system of groups," sovereignty was "unthinkable," despite the universalistic claims of the Roman church to which the modern unified state was the successor.[28] Laski went to great lengths, like Gierke, to demonstrate that corporations and similar entities were not just fictions and functions of the state but rather were "real" and had distinct "personalities" and "wills" of their own that made them self-governing. This, he claimed, demonstrated that the state was not in reality sovereign and that it was not possible to "doubt this polyarchism."[29] Laski was finally explicit that even the idea of popular sovereignty was a myth that tended, as in the work of Rousseau, to depreciate the value and necessity of representative government while abetting the idea of state supremacy. The notion of the state as an organic people acting as one was, he claimed, at least in modern times, an impossible fiction that obscured the fact that society was composed of "different wills."[30]

By the time that Laski wrote his most famous and "more positive" work, *The Grammar of Politics* (1925), and announced, echoing Tocque-

[26] Laski, *Authority in the Modern State*, 65–69.
[27] Harold J. Laski, *Foundations of Sovereignty and Other Essays* (New York: Harcourt, Brace, 1921), v, 209.
[28] Ibid., 1.
[29] Ibid., 169.
[30] Ibid., 230.

ville, that "a new political philosophy is necessary to a new world," the focus on pluralism had all but disappeared. Elliott believed that he perceived a "new" Laski in this work. The book was a rejection of Benthamite and Hegelian attempts to find some unitary principle of politics and an attempt to account for the way things worked, and should work, under the complex conditions of modern society. Laski continued to attack traditional theories of sovereignty that implied "unlimited and irresponsible" power was located in some "organ." "In the theoretic sense . . . the United States has no sovereign organ," since power is shared among the branches and levels of government. But, to the surprise of some of his erstwhile critics, Laski now claimed that "the State is the keystone of the social arch." He was, however, basically talking about government. Although he still spoke about the (capitalized) "State" as some kind of a whole and a "fellowship of men" and an "association," this was largely the conventional use of the term for distinguishing territorial, social, and legal units. He stressed the "difference between State and Society," because he wished to demonstrate that the state was an instrument of society and responsible to the individuals and groups that composed it. In effect, "the will of the State is the will of government," and "a theory of the State . . . is essentially a theory of the governmental act."

Lindsay once again noted that the issue of sovereignty had become "a storm center of political theory" and although it might seem that it admitted of "no answer," he argued that some confusion was involved in the controversy. He maintained, first of all, that Austin's concept of law was an obsolete absolutist model and an abstraction from past political forms that was not applicable to "modern constitutional government" such as that of the United States or England. And attempts to locate sovereignty in the state, the people, or some other abstract entity also failed. Lindsay's alternative was to advance a "theory of the sovereignty of the Constitution" that he claimed was particularly applicable to the United States. He claimed that what was behind law was a consensus among citizens about the basic "interests" and "principles" regarding methods for the "legal or constitutional settlement of differences" and about the government as representing the paramount "purposes" that must be safeguarded. In the case of the United States, this was what was involved in the creation of the Constitution as well as in the Civil War. Second, Lindsay focused his criticisms on arguments such as that of Bernard Bosanquet (*The Philosophical Theory of the State*, 1899) and his Hegelian resurrection of the idea of a general will. Although Lindsay agreed that law is based on social solidarity, he rejected the notion that there should, or could, "be in the minds of the citizens of a state some general conception of the whole multifarious life of the society" that stood behind the law and the constitution. For Lindsay the unity of society was simply the functional "adherence of the great mass of the people to a definite principle for settling differences."[31]

Laski's British successor as a visitor to America was Catlin. He had studied at Oxford, under Barker among others, before and after the war, but he considered Wallas his mentor, and even though he was offered a scholarship to continue at Oxford, he took the opportunity to escape what he referred to as an "academic cloister" and move to the United States and pursue the "Scienza nuova" or a "systematic political science." He had asked if he might be allowed to teach "political philosophy and science" after he returned, but he was informed that they "did not teach it and did not intend to teach it." In 1924, after offers from Harvard and Minnesota, he accepted a faculty appointment at Cornell, where he would eventually work with Sabine, Harvey Mansfield, and other prominent political scientists and where he wrote his dissertation, which was published as a book (*The Science and Method of Politics*). This work embodied the American vision of a science of politics as well as a pluralist account of social reality, and it was by far the most philosophically informed statement of such a science of politics (based on quantitative methods, psychology, and economic models) that would be advanced in the United States during this period. Catlin's embrace of the central tenets of the emerging image of an American science of politics as well as his persistent practical political concerns made him quite at home in the company of Dewey, Merriam, Beard, Harold Lasswell, and others. After his return to England, his autobiographical assessment was that "we found political science a chaos" but "tidied it up," and along "with the Pluralists, we deposed the sovereign national state to the study of the politics of Society itself."[32]

Laski and Lindsay directly crossed paths in a symposium on Bosanquet, and their differences ultimately seemed negligible. Lindsay noted that ideas such as Bosanquet's theory of the general will had prompted L. T. Hobhouse's attack on *The Metaphysical Theory of the State* as well as R. M. MacIver's critique of the idea of the state as a person, and he suggested that confusion was involved in attempting to oppose such an idea to Austin's theory of sovereignty, since both theories were rooted in obsolete models. Austin's theory, however, did represent the juristic dimension of the state, and Bosanquet's argument, like that of Rousseau, pointed to the fact that the state reflected the "moral life of society." Lindsay suggested that Bosanquet, as well as the authors of similar nineteenth-century

---

[31] A. D. Lindsay, "Sovereignty," *Proceedings of the Aristotelian Society* 3 (1924): 235–36, 248, 252–54.

[32] George E. G. Catlin, *For God's Sake, Go!* (Gerrads Cross, UK: Colin Smythe, 1972); George E. G. Catlin, *The Science and Method of Politics* (New York: Appleton, 1927).

images of the state, had been attempting to validate democracy and popular sovereignty (e.g., Bosanquet had called Plato a democrat), but that these organic theories did not literally fit the modern state.[33] Laski largely accepted Lindsay's interpretation of Bosanquet and seemed reluctant to challenge directly the "master of Balliol," but although he did not deny that the state was "the great coordinating organ of society," he noted that it still "appears as a government issuing orders" and remained a fallible organ that did not represent any actual "common will" or "common good" but only an attempt to achieve fairness in the competition between individuals. He did not reject Lindsay's claim that there was something that could reasonably, by some functional criteria, be called the "common life" or "unity" of society, but a national society, like the international sphere, was "not a One, but a Many," which was a "collection of men and women."[34]

By the end of the decade, Lindsay's position closely approximated the theory of pluralist democracy that was being articulated in American political science. He argued that the "purpose of democratic machinery is to represent differences" and that this required "a society of democratic non-political associations." Formal politics, he suggested, was "a secondary matter" in which the role of the state was basically to care for a "common life" comprised of "voluntary non-political activities." The "essentials" of democracy were not based on some "dogma" but consisted of "toleration and recognition of differences," which allowed a forum for "innumerable voluntary associations of all kinds which exist in modern democratic society." Such opportunities, however, produced, he insisted, "a real unity of purpose out of differences," which in turn provided a kind of background consensus or "spirit of the whole" that placed limits on difference. He noted that "in actual fact politics tends to be a dirty business" involving interest and power and that the state itself was an instrument of coercion, but ultimately "the best society is that which increases spontaneity and life and variety; and that is not primarily done by the state but by all this rich complexity of voluntary associations." The role of the state was one of regulation and adjustment.[35]

Maybe the most elaborate engagement of the issues attached to the discussion of pluralism in the British literature, as well as of the role of political science, was Barker's long introduction to his translation of a portion of Gierke's massive study of the German *Genossenschaftsrecht* and the

---

[33] A. D. Lindsay and Harold J. Laski, "Symposium: Bosanquet's Theory of the General Will," *Proceedings of the Aristotelian Society,* suppl. vol., 8 (1928): 39–40, 44.

[34] Ibid., 48, 50, 54, 57.

[35] A. D. Lindsay, *The Essentials of Democracy* (Oxford: Clarendon Press, 1929), 1, 8, 34, 37, 42–43, 46–47, 70, 72–74.

natural law tradition. He appended to the volume Ernst Troeltsch's lecture "The Ideas of Natural Law and Humanity in World Politics," delivered at the Hochschule für Politik in Berlin, 1922, which juxtaposed the individualistic tradition of Western Europe to German romantic ideas, including those of Gierke, which, Barker claimed, had led to the "deification of superpersonal Groups" and especially the nineteenth-century idea of the state. Although Barker was sympathetic to many aspects of Gierke's study of "the great school of Natural Law" and groups, he was consistently critical of key elements of Gierke's basic "conception of the group" and of how Gierke forced everything into the Procrustean bed of that concept.[36] Part of Barker's sympathy with Gierke's project was related to the emphasis on law, which for Barker continued to represent a more practical and empirical study of politics than that characteristic of the curriculum in British universities. Gierke's study had been closely related to his practical endeavors (such as the formulation of the 1898 civil code that had fascinated Merriam when he studied with Gierke in Germany and wrote his dissertation on the history of the theory of sovereignty).

For Barker, society was the logically and historically prior and underlying entity, a community and a "unity" that was a natural historical fact. It was, however, also a "plurality" in that it consisted of various voluntary groups. Society constituted "the material on which there is stamped the form of the state" and thereby turned into a legal or juridical organization with a constitution that possessed and exercised the function of sovereignty. For both Gierke and Barker, the basic role of the state was the regulation of groups, but Barker took issue with Gierke's "theory of the real personality of groups" and particularly his assumption that the "whole" was more real than the parts and with the ethic that flowed from this assumption.[37] While it was one thing to "plead the cause of liberty of association," it was another thing to "plead that associations are beings or minds or real persons." For Barker, the "individual personality is the one intrinsic value of human life" and should not be attributed to other than individual persons. This, he claimed, was a basic difference between the German and British traditions. Although Barker did not subscribe to any literal rendering of contract theory or assume that there was a primordial presocial situation, he believed that there was "a case to be made for the view that the State, as distinct from Society, is a legal association which fundamentally rests on the presuppositions of contract." The state, for Barker, was a legal person as were the groups that composed it, but the nature of this thing that was both unity and multiplicity was difficult

[36] Gierke, *Natural Law*, xi–xii.
[37] Ibid., xxiii, xxiv, xxxiii.

to articulate.[38] In his view, society was a historical and cultural "community" and the state was an "association" of individuals joined by legal relations for the purpose of regulation, a stage on which actors took on a certain role as "juridical creations, or artifices, or fictions." "It is not the natural Ego which enters a court of law, which appears before the law," and "legal personality is a mental construct." Groups as legal persons were real in their status as artifacts but not natural, and which groups were to be afforded legal status depended on "a principle of selection, determined by the very nature of the state," which was designed "to secure a minimum of friction, and the maximum of development, among all the moral personalities which are members of the association." Groups were not "organisms" but "organizations" and although ontologically distinct from individuals, they moved and interacted as agents in the same universe of law and politics. From Barker's perspective, the practical problem with Gierke's doctrine was that it tended, as did the formulations of Maitland, Duguit, and Figgis, to be drawn in the direction of syndicalism and to "eliminate the state in favor of groups," but this, he noted, was not even compatible with Gierke's elevation of the state and the national community to a special status. But then there was, he argued, also the opposite and centripetal tendency of the doctrine to be employed in the service of consolidation such as in Fascist Italy and in what appeared to be emerging case in modern Germany.[39]

In both England and the United States, it was difficult to let go of an image of unity that supported the idea of popular sovereignty, but by the end of the 1930s, this reduced to the attenuated liberal consensus to which Sabine and others such as C. H. McIlwain would seek to give a historical dimension.[40] The "democratic dogma" was replaced by an empirical and normative theory of pluralist democracy and a vision of political science that had been significantly informed and reinforced by the British literature that would in turn prepare the way for the emigration of the American science of politics after World War II. Social reality was configured as fundamentally a collection of various types of voluntary associations, and the "state" was increasingly a synonym for "government" as an instrument of control and adjustment among groups in a complex society. The image of society as an organic unity was being replaced by an idea of an underlying consensus based partly on common values but partly on a pragmatic acceptance of the rules of the game in the interaction among groups and between groups and public policy, and the concept of groups

[38] Ibid. xlix, lvi, lx.

[39] Ibid., lxx, lxxi, lxxvi, lxxxii.

[40] Charles Howard McIlwain, *The Growth of Political Thought in the West* (New York: Macmillan, 1932).

as organic entities was fading toward an image of groups as individuals bound together by common interests. The methods and research programs of political science were being adapted to the study of groups, and the normative vision of the discipline was being revised to demonstrate how the world of politics so described and explained constituted democracy and representative government. Finally, the history of political thought was devoted to valorizing this image of democratic politics and the discipline of studying it.

Although the influence of the British literature in the United States was not as pervasive as that which had been exercised by German philosophy during the nineteenth century, it played a significant role in the controversy about pluralism and in the formation of a tradition of pluralist democracy. By the early 1930s, direct engagement with texts from abroad had receded, but by the end of the decade another wave of German philosophy began a new conquest of American political science as émigré scholars set out to challenge the theory of pluralism, and attending methods of study, and the historical imagery that had come to define the American vision of democracy and what, in the discourse of the discipline as well as in political discourse, was by then called liberalism.[41]

---

[41] For a fuller discussion of these developments, see Gunnell, *Descent of Political Theory* and *Imagining the American Polity*; and chapter 10 by Adcock and Bevir in this volume.

Eight

Birth of a Discipline: Interpreting British Political Studies in the 1950s and 1960s

MICHAEL KENNY

THERE ARE A NUMBER of signs in recent scholarship that practitioners of political studies in Britain are developing a more reflexive and curious sensibility toward the historical development of their discipline.[1] The appearance in 1999 of a volume, published under the auspices of the British Academy, devoted to a reexamination of the discipline and its various subfields, is one indication of a possible trend.[2] The majority of these essays focus upon specific subfields within the discipline. Those that consider its overall development tend to fall back upon a familiar image of the 1950s and 1960s, presenting it as an infancy, a period of "muddling through" prior to the maturation and flourishing that occurred after the late 1960s.[3] This interpretation plays an important role in shaping contemporary practitioners' understanding of the distinctive character and trajectory of British political studies. It is one that needs reappraisal, I will suggest, because of its unnuanced representation of a period in which

---

[1] I am grateful to the editors of this volume and the anonymous referees for their various comments on an earlier draft of this chapter.

[2] Jack Hayward, "British Approaches to Politics: The Dawn of a Self-Deprecating Discipline," in *The British Study of Politics in the Twentieth Century*, ed. Jack Hayward, Brian Barry, and Archie Brown (Oxford: Oxford University Press, 1999); Mark Bevir, "Prisoners of Professionalism: On the Construction and Responsibility of Political Studies; A Review Article," *Public Administration* 79, no. 2 (2001): 469–509; Robert Adcock and Mark Bevir, "The History of Political Science," *Political Studies Review* 3 (2005): 1–16; Dennis Kavanagh and Richard Rose, "British Politics since 1945: The Changing Field of Study," in *New Trends in British Politics: Issues for Research*, ed. Dennis Kavanagh and Richard Rose (London: Sage, 1977); Michael Kenny, "The Case for Disciplinary History: British Political Studies in the 1950s and 1960s," *British Journal of Politics and International Relations* 6 (2004): 565–83.

[3] Jack Hayward, "The Political Science of Muddling Through: The *de facto* Paradigm?" in *The Political Science of British Politics*, ed. Jack Hayward and Philip Norton (Brighton, UK: Harvester Wheatsheaf, 1986); Hayward, "British Approaches"; Brian Barry, "The Study of Politics as a Vocation," in *The British Study of Politics in the Twentieth Century*, ed. Jack Hayward, Brian Barry, and Archie Brown (Oxford: Oxford University Press, 1999).

some crucial alterations to the overall character and identity of the discipline took place.

A natural accompaniment to this conventional view of these years is the notion that the scholarly output associated with it can be simply characterized as intellectually insular, theoretically naïve, and complacent about the merits of British institutions and parliamentary government. It is certainly the case, I will suggest, that the study of the indigenous polity was shaped and informed by some of the normative assumptions associated with scholarly output from the interwar period, and also true that these ideas and assumptions made some of the work of this era complacent, insular, and teleological to contemporary tastes. Yet I will argue that in important respects this period is not simply the amateurish antithesis to the output of the professionalized era characterized by greater knowledge, theoretical sophistication, and methodological awareness. In fact, some of the enduring characteristics of the British discipline were laid down in these years, some significant and valuable scholarship was produced, and the Whiggish orthodoxies of the early century were challenged from within this intellectual community. None of these developments are readily comprehensible from within the antihistorical mindset of many contemporary practitioners of political science.

This is the version of "discipline history" that appears to prevail among the majority of British political scientists. It hinges upon the idea that winning disciplinary autonomy and, in particular, throwing off the influence of history, law, and philosophy, were prerequisites for the achievement of a modern academic discipline. This is one reason why anything smacking of the historicism of the late nineteenth and early twentieth centuries is still highly suspect to some political scientists, hence the suspicion in some quarters to the various species of evolutionary and institutionalist thinking. This hostility is underpinned by a largely unreflective embrace of the merits of professionalism. This generates the view that the development of a mature and independent discipline was delayed at this time because of a prevailing amateurism among scholars working in the field of political studies, a condition linked by some to the undue influence of the "holy trinity" of institutions—Oxford, Cambridge, and the London School of Economics.[4] According to some current advocates of a professionalized political science, it was only when the patronage and influence of scholars from these institutions was challenged through the rise of institutional alternatives and rival departments that an independent

---

[4] Barry, "Study of Politics as a Vocation"; Robert Wokler, "The Professoriate of Political Thought in England since 1914: A Tale of Three Chairs," in *The History of Political Thought in National Context*, ed. Dario Castiglione and Iain Hampsher-Monk (Cambridge: Cambridge University Press, 2001).

discipline could emerge.[5] Professionalization, in the judgment of Brian Barry, gave the academic study of politics a degree of intellectual detachment, a specialized focus, and its own methods of inquiry. The limitations of such a perspective upon the disciplinary past are however increasingly apparent. Some of Barry's fellow contributors in the British Academy volume suggest the need for a more complex narrative of how the disciplinary field as a whole, and particular subfields within it, have developed, and place considerable value upon the task of reengaging with earlier periods in its historical development.[6]

In this chapter I seek to bolster and exemplify this latter position. I suggest, in particular, the merits of a more careful appraisal of the evolution of, and alterations to, the Whig tradition that characterized the discipline in the 1950s and 1960s and the different approaches to the study of British politics that these spawned. Some important differences arose between practitioners who were all broadly influenced by the Whig tradition, yet who developed contrary views about the subject as a whole. On the one hand were those such as Michael Oakeshott, who argued the case for the intrinsic singularity of British political development and the appropriate modes of understanding its character, and the efforts of others, for instance W.J.M. Mackenzie, to develop an indigenous political science that involved a subtle blending of older ideas and novel perspectives in the discipline after 1970. Moreover, there also emerged in this period some important dissident ideas that presaged the importation of non-British theoretical perspectives. A sharper understanding of this period arises from an appreciation of the interplay between some of these positions. At the same time, as various historians have suggested, a sense of the contingent and contested character of the intellectual development of a discipline is limited if we confine ourselves to an "internalist" account of its major intellectual trends.[7] A deeper understanding requires attention to the wider social and intellectual environment to which its practitioners were responding and by which they were in part shaped. I also therefore weigh some of the contingent political factors that spawned powerful dilemmas for practitioners in these years and that helped loosen the grip of hitherto unquestioned Whiggish orthodoxies. I draw attention as well to the impact and importance of the changing relationship between the state and the university sector as a whole and the social sciences in particular.

    [5] Hayward, "The Political Science of Muddling Through"; Jack Hayward, "Political Science in Britain," *European Journal of Political Research* 20, no. 2 (1991): 301–22.

    [6] Hayward, "British Approaches."

    [7] Stefan Collini, "'Disciplinary History' and 'Intellectual History': Reflections on the Historiography of the Social Sciences in Britain and France," *Revue de synthese* 3, no. 4 (1988): 389; though also see John G. Gunnell, *The Descent of Political Theory* (Chicago: University of Chicago Press, 1993), 9.

The Institutional Birth of Political Studies

The period from 1945 to the late 1960s was a vital one in the establishment of political studies as an independent and autonomous discipline.
During these years, politics emerged as an independent subject for the
first time within the university system. Until then, it had generally been
taught either on individual papers within other degrees or was confined
to specialist programs, such as the Bachelor of Arts in public administration at Manchester University. By the end of the 1960s, departments devoted to the teaching of politics existed at most universities. The forces
behind this rapid growth were most obviously exogenous ones. The rapid
expansion of higher education coincided with a rise in the prestige of the
social sciences in British universities. The formation of the polytechnics
in the 1960s, in which the social sciences were well represented, was an
equally important development.[8] These trends, as well as a growing interest in the subject in the wake of renewed ideological debate and political
crisis, generated an impetus toward the development of self-standing degree programs and clusters of scholars in newly formed departments.

There were other signs too of the emergence of an independent discipline. In 1950 the Political Studies Association (PSA) was formed, a body
that represented teachers and scholars of the subject. No regular opportunities then existed for specialists in politics to come together to discuss
their research or to take stock of the discipline as a whole. One of the
most important functions of the fledgling PSA, which continues to this
day, involved the organization of an annual conference. In 1953, the association was able to fulfill one of its earliest ambitions: it announced the
formation of a major new journal, *Political Studies*.[9]

Both the PSA and *Political Studies* had at best a small influence on the
development of politics as a university subject in the subsequent decade.
As the higher education sector expanded, most universities began to hire
at least a couple of teachers in public administration, government, or political theory. Starting with 100 members in 1950, PSA's membership
grew steadily, if not spectacularly, to 170 by 1960. Neither PSA nor *Political Studies* attempted to institute a particular intellectual approach or to
lay down prescriptive norms for the discipline, though both reflected the
prevailing Whiggish understanding of British political development and
the values associated with it. There were, until the early 1960s, few dedi-

---

[8] Joni Lovenduski, "The Profession of Political Science in Britain," *Studies in Public Policy* 64, Centre for the Study of Public Policy, University of Strathclyde, Glasgow, 1981.

[9] For an account of the formation of PSA and *Political Studies* see Kenny, "The Case for
Disciplinary History."

cated textbooks on British government. Courses on UK politics or constitutional history revealingly drew upon staple texts infused with nineteenth-century liberalism, such as: Bagehot's *English Constitution* (1867);
J. S. Mill's *Considerations on Representative Government* (1861); Lowell's *Government of England* (1908); H. E. Dale's *The Higher Civil Service of Great Britain* (1861); and *The Haldane Report on the Machinery
of Government* (1918).[10] The formation of PSA was an important moment in terms of the constitution of a fledgling community of researchers
within the field of political studies, but was not necessarily a staging post
toward the conscious formation of a new discipline. British political studies was constituted as a pluralistic community, rather than a unified discipline, an understanding reflected in W. J. Mackenzie's observation: "I see
the 'discipline' as a group of people rather than as a set of principles, as
a continuing debate rather than as an \enquiry in the style of natural science, as an enterprise which is an integral part of real politics."[11]

Whig Interpretations of British Politics

The leading tradition shaping scholarly political inquiry during this period remained an indigenous blend of Whig historicism and English liberalism that betrayed the continuing influence of some of the major figures
in the discipline writing between the wars.[12] This broad perspective was
closely associated with the articulation of the ideal of "the Westminster
model" of British parliamentary government outlined in Dennis Kavanagh's chapter in this volume. Studies of the constituent parts of the British polity were redolent with the assumption that political change ought
to be evolutionary and gradual and should be undertaken in accordance
with the underlying ethos of the Constitution. The polity had emerged
from centuries of continuity and slow adaptation ever since the Glorious
Revolution of 1688. Its durable and flexible political institutions ac-
counted for British success in maintaining economic strength, its status
as an imperial power, and the achievement of continuous political stability. These were all consequences of the balance achieved between "the
supremacy of Parliament, the flexibility and foresight of the governing
class and the resulting responsiveness of British institutions to new de-

---

[10] Norman Chester, "Political Studies in Britain: Recollections and Comments," *Political
Studies*, 23, nos. 2–3 (1975): 151–64.

[11] W.J.M. Mackenzie, "Political Theory and Political Education," in *Explorations in
Government: Collected Papers, 1951–1968* (London: Macmillan, 1975), ix; and on Mac-
kenzie's vision of the discipline in this period more generally see Kenny, "The Case for
Disciplinary History."

[12] Kavanagh and Rose, "British Politics since 1945."

mands and pressures."[13] This account was informed by the normative assertion that British historical development was shaped by the imperative of the liberty of the individual, and its political system rested upon institutions that fostered compromise and mutual toleration and ensured limited but accountable government.[14] The Westminster "model" of parliamentary government that arose from this perspective offered a distinctive and pervasive framework.

Within this understanding, considerable scope was given to the role and influence of ideas. A powerful strand within the British study of politics presented the relationship that had unfolded between domestic political thought and political practice as unique to the indigenous polity.[15] Andrew Gamble has unpacked the most salient, recurrent elements of this approach to the United Kingdom's political institutions in the postwar decades.[16] He identifies behind it a constitutional doctrine, derived from Dicey, in which sovereignty was afforded to a system of parliamentary government that operated within limits that had evolved over time. In this paradigm, all other branches of the state were subordinated to parliamentary authority. The cabinet, the prime minister, and the civil service together constituted an executive that was subjected to the rigor of parliamentary scrutiny. Not surprisingly, there barely existed within political studies of the 1950s and 1960s independent usage of the state as a concept-idea, as opposed to the term *government*.

Much of the scholarship inspired by this model focused upon the totality of the system of parliamentary government and the balance effected between its component parts. The 1960s witnessed the publication of about a dozen new works on British politics that were to become standard texts for students. These included: Birch, *The British System of Government* (1967); Mackintosh, *The Government and Politics of Britain* (1970); Moodie, *The Government of Great Britain* (1962); Punnett, *British Government and Politics* (1968); Rose, *Politics in England* (1965); and Stacey, *The Government of Modern Britain* (1968).[17] Despite the

[13] Andrew Gamble, "Theories of British Politics," *Political Studies* 38, no. 3 (1990): 407.

[14] Ibid., 408.

[15] Michael Kenny, "Ideas, Ideologies and the British Tradition," in *Fundamentals in British Politics*, ed. Ian Holliday, Andrew Gamble, and Geraint Parry (Basingstoke, UK: Macmillan, 1999).

[16] Gamble, "Theories of British Politics."

[17] Anthony Harold Birch, *The British System of Government* (New York: Praeger, 1967); John P. Mackintosh, *The Government and Politics of Britain* (London: Hutchinson, 1970); Graeme C. Moodie, *The Government of Great Britain* (New York: Crowell, 1962); R. M. Punnett, *British Government and Politics* (New York: Norton, 1968); Richard Rose, *Politics in England* (Boston: Little, Brown, 1964); Frank A. Stacey, *The Government of Modern Britain* (Oxford: Clarendon Press, 1968).

growing sense of unease about Britain's relative economic position in these years, these authors generally felt able, as Trevor Smith puts it:

> to dilate about the emergence and endurance of the postwar consensus based on the policies of Keynes and Beveridge, point to the political stability and prosperity of the 1950s, and conclude with an optimistic flourish noting how Britain, first under Harold Macmillan and then under Harold Wilson, was modernizing itself with the adoption of French-style economic planning, Swedish-style Ombudsmen, an Italian-style Industrial Reorganization Corporation, an American-style revamping of parliamentary committees and so on.[18]

The normative themes underwriting this approach—that the British system had evolved in accordance with the imperatives of individual liberty and social progress—owed much to Victorian liberalism; the historicized conception of the British Constitution to Dicey; and the evolutionary perspective on British democracy to various nineteenth-century thinkers, John Stuart Mill most obviously.

The broadly liberal framework established in relation to domestic political institutions had its functional complement within the realm of political theory in the 1950s; both within scholarship pertaining to the most influential indigenous political thinkers, especially Hobbes, Smith, Locke, and Mill, but also within analytic philosophy. Liberalism remained the prevailing frame of reference within these latter fields. In addition, however, several important defenses of the liberal polity were offered from an unusual source: a trio of émigré intellectuals, none of whom were formally engaged in the teaching of politics—Friedrich von Hayek, Karl Popper, and Isaiah Berlin. Their distinctive, but overlapping, efforts to construct a broadly liberal alternative to the totalitarian political model, and especially the Soviet model of socialism, were highly influential in these years.[19] One contextual feature of their work which has been largely ignored by more recent scholarship[20] arises from a consideration of the impact of the Cold War of the late 1940s and early 1950s upon political thinking in Britain, and indeed upon the fledgling discipline.[21] One way of reading these figures' work is in terms of the development of a more robust alternative to the historicist and idealist traditions of indigenous

---

[18] Trevor Smith, "Political Science and Modern British Society," *Government and Opposition*, 21, no. 4 (1986): 435.

[19] Perry Anderson, "Components of the National Culture," in *English Questions* (London: Verso, 1992; originally published in 1968), 48–104; "A Culture in Contraflow," in *English Questions* (London: Verso, 1992; originally published in 1990), 193–301.

[20] An important exception here is N. O'Sullivan, "Visions of Freedom: The Response to Totalitarianism," in Hayward, Barry, and Brown, *British Study of Politics*

[21] Anthony Arblaster, *The Rise and Decline of Western Liberalism* (Oxford: Basil Blackwell, 1984).

liberalism. Each suggested a normative justification of liberalism that reflected a sense of political threat, associated particularly with the communist and fascist experiences. They also developed a sharper sense of the dichotomy between liberalism and the traditions of socialism (a distinction that was rather more blurred in Britain than elsewhere) and an important critique of the implications of aspects of the state's development in the twentieth century, such as the increasing prevalence of planning, for core liberal values such as individual liberty. Together with other émigré figures, like Lewis Namier, they contributed importantly to a reshaping of the intellectual culture of Britain in the 1950s, as Perry Anderson has observed.[22]

Berlin and Popper exercised some degree of influence upon the fledgling discipline, though neither regarded himself as a member of it. Popper's critique of the normative foundations of the kinds of "evolutionary positivism" that underlay the thinking of some of the major political intellectuals writing in the early years of the century,[23] influenced a subsequent generation of practitioners and helped place questions of methodology and epistemology on the intellectual agendas and educational curriculums of the discipline from the late 1960s. These indirect contributions to the evolution of political studies have in general been overlooked, in part because of the lingering convention that these were the years in which political philosophy was on its deathbed, awaiting salvation from Rawls. As Robert Adcock and Mark Bevir also suggest in this volume, this was in fact an important and fertile period in the development and refinement of academically based political theory.

The Evolution of Whiggish Ideas

This period also witnessed a significant alteration within the Whig-liberal tradition established during the first part of the century and traced in the chapters by den Otter and Kavanagh. Whiggish ideas still constituted much of the intellectual horizon of practitioners of political studies but were increasingly open to contrasting interpretations, allowing room for some measure of disagreement about the character and purpose of this fledgling academic discipline. The appearance of two distinct positions on these questions can be discerned during these years. Both sponsored contrasting accounts of the purpose and methods of political analysis.

[22] Anderson, "Components of the National Culture."

[23] Popper himself used the label "historicism" to capture the various theoretical positions that he sought to attack. See, for example, Karl Popper, *The Poverty of Historicism* (Boston: Beacon Press, 1957).

Oakeshottian Idealism

The first of these positions stemmed from the continuation of the "idealist" tradition of study of indigenous institutions and ideas. This tradition
influenced various efforts to elaborate the ethical spirit that informed the
development of the particular institutions and overall system of parliamentary government. An important exemplar of such an approach was
the philosopher Michael Oakeshott. He offered a liberal-conservative
variant of the Whig interpretation of British parliamentary government,
a position that exercised considerable influence over a group of scholars
of political ideas in subsequent years. Idealist philosophical themes were
central to his thought, not least in his powerful normative account of the
merits of a political tradition. Clearly influenced by Whig-liberal ideas
about the development and character of political institutions, Oakeshott
offered a rather different elaboration of "the British tradition," one that
drew heavily upon his appropriation of Hobbes's model of civil association.[24] He lamented the shift toward state planning and collectivist provision in the 1940s as a dangerous break from the wisdom resident within
Britain's leading traditions, and saw these as developments that might
lead to the loss of liberty and imperil limited government.[25]

Oakeshott's arguments harked back to a lineage that incorporated
Richard Hooker and Edmund Burke ("Old Toryism" in Samuel Beer's
terminology).[26] Oakeshott offered a rigorous justification for a native
antirationalist and tradition-based notion of political understanding.
While his articulation of an antiperfectionist conception of the purpose
of politics was anathema to many other political thinkers, he provided an
influential depiction of a uniquely British mode of political understanding
through his attack upon the alien character of abstract reason and ideological thought in general.[27] He, and those he influenced, tended to focus
their energies within the fields of philosophy and political thought, motivated, somewhat paradoxically, by the project of justifying the atheoretical character of British politics. Several of Oakeshott's students went on
to propound the idea of political understanding as necessarily historical
in kind, questioning the idea that political judgment could be founded

---

[24] Michael Oakeshott, *Hobbes on Civil Association* (Berkeley and Los Angeles: University of California Press, 1975).

[25] Michael Oakeshott, *The Social and Political Doctrines of Contemporary Europe*
(Cambridge: Cambridge University Press, 1939).

[26] Samuel H. Beer, *Modern British Politics: A Study of Parties and Pressure Groups* (London: Faber, 1965).

[27] Michael Oakeshott, *Rationalism in Politics and Other Essays* (London: Methuen,
1962).

on either pure factual knowledge or detached reason.[28] Political analysis, Oakeshott argued in his inaugural lecture at the LSE, should be conceived as "an ecological study of a tradition of behaviour, not an anatomical study of mechanical devices or the investigation of an ideology."[29] The historical mode of understanding that he advocated was of a particular kind, designed to divine the central intimations of a given tradition and to convert these into a guide for political practice.

Toward a British Political Science

The powerful political critique that Oakeshott provided of the social liberalism guiding government in the mid-twentieth century was one of his most important intellectual legacies in subsequent years. In this earlier period, his thinking about British political development and the character of the study of politics was developed in direct opposition to the increasingly powerful modernist project of founding an independent, yet still distinctively British, empirical science of politics. The latter position was associated with a number of figures, including W.J.M. Mackenzie, Samuel Beer, and Samuel Finer, all of whom were arguing that the British tradition required updating and that indigenous intellectual virtues should be blended with some of the theoretical models associated with American political science.[30] One indication of this fissure was the disagreement about the nature of early-century and postwar collectivism between Oakeshott and his followers and the equally Whiggish argument offered, in 1965, by Samuel Beer. The latter interpreted the challenge posed by the growth in state capacity and the expansion of the scope of the public sector in the years after 1945 in a very different manner to Oakeshott, yet deployed a framework that was redolent of many of the same historicist assumptions. Contra Oakeshott's idealization of the limited, or constitutional, state of the nineteenth century, Beer, in his influential study *Modern British Politics* (1965), celebrated the capacity of the British system to incorporate the new collectivism without abandoning its guiding ethos.

Beer was in fact one of a number of leading figures in the fledgling discipline who promoted the idea of a fusion of indigenous British approaches and some of the methodologies and theories emanating from the United States. The notion of a British science of politics was by no means a new one. The late-nineteenth-century idea of political science as

---

[28] W. H. Greenleaf, *The British Political Tradition*, vol. 1, *The Rise of Collectivism* (London: Methuen, 1983).

[29] Michael Oakeshott, "Political Education," in *Rationalism in Politics*, 121.

[30] Beer, *Modern British Politics*; Mackenzie, "Political Theory and Political Education"; Kenny, "Case for Disciplinary History."

a distinctive vocation, itself a recycling of Aristotelian conceptions of the unique significance of a science of politics, was deliberately revived by such figures as William Robson and W.J.M. Mackenzie in these years. Robson, who had argued for the sobriquet "Political Science" (as opposed to "Studies") at the inaugural meeting of the PSA in 1950, was a keen proponent of the development of a professionalized, autonomous discipline, one that would take the lead of counterparts in United States and France. Mackenzie too, in his widely read *Politics and Social Science* (1967), drew a stark contrast between the professionalization and consolidation of political science in these contexts and British eclecticism and indifference to theory.

Yet Mackenzie's thoughts on the nature of political science in Britain also reflect his continuing adherence to elder understandings of the polity's distinct character, culture, and historical traditions. His ideas were nearer to the sentiments of the bulk of his colleagues in the subject than Robson's. Mackenzie argued for a more serious and independent study of empirical data and an increased awareness of methodological and theoretical options among British practitioners.[31] Importantly, however, early-century Whiggery still constituted many of the intellectual horizons within which these figures operated.[32] In a thoughtful discussion of the implications of modeling the social sciences upon their natural scientific equivalents, Mackenzie proposed a distinction between a political science that aspired to replicate the laws and methods of chemistry or physics and that which might reconnect with the evolutionary and organicist frameworks developed within the biological sciences.

Increasingly the Whiggish conception of politics as a field that was best approached through the gateways of history, philosophy, or constitutional law was in tension with the notion of a much narrower, more specialized, and autonomous discipline. Arguments for the latter drew strength from examples of professional specialism that had been developed by other social sciences, notably economics, and by an increasingly pervasive modernist, technocratic mood in the political culture at large. Mackenzie, and other leading figures, sought to fuse these different conceptions, rather than simply choosing the latter over the former. In so doing, they advanced a powerful normative conception of the distinctive nature of British political science, a perspective that molded much of the distinctive intellectual character and culture of the discipline over the following decades.

One practical instance of this kind of fusion was the collaboration between David Butler and Donald Stokes that resulted in the production

---

[31] W.J.M. Mackenzie, *Politics and Social Science* (Baltimore: Penguin, 1967); Mackenzie, "Political Theory and Political Education."

[32] Kenny, "Case for Disciplinary History," 573–76.

of the highly influential volume *Political Change in Britain.*[33] Butler had become the principal figure within the Nuffield elections studies that first appeared after 1945.[34] The introductions to the studies, penned by Butler in the 1950s and 1960s, reveal his adoption of an "insider's" approach to Westminster and informed judgments about the tactics and personalities of leading political figures. His collaboration with Donald Stokes marked a striking shift of emphasis within the Nuffield studies. The authors argued the merits of a more systematic assessment of the variables shaping voting behavior and weighted the significance of various causal factors using the formal modeling techniques associated with the Michigan school.[35] This analysis was interspersed with the more familiar assessment of the tactics and strategies deployed in the electoral campaigns of the major parties. Butler and Stokes presented their study as both a departure from ("our work is not narrowly British") and a partial continuation of "(t)he distinctively British contribution to election studies . . . pioneered by R. B. MacCallum."[36] Given these studies' centrality to the study of elections and political behavior in Britain, this represented a significant inroad into British politics by a leading exponent of political science. While this was a distinctive and, in some respects, contingent collaboration, it is also more widely revealing. Although Oxford University is often cited in the profession as a major institutional obstacle to the maturation of an indigenous political science, it actually performed a more ambivalent role in these years.[37] Its role as an international center of English-speaking scholarship, and specifically as an attractive location for stop-overs by leading American and European scholars, meant that it also provided an important gateway through which some non-British theories and approaches could gain a foothold.

Those advocating a British political science were also influenced to varying degrees by the behavioralist literature emanating from the United States. This paradigm was highly influential upon particular individuals and had a wider intellectual impact, through David Easton's analytical emphasis upon elements—social processes, structure, and system—that rarely figured within mainstream work on the British polity. One manifestation of this development was the growth of a small subfield of political

---

[33] David Butler and Donald Stokes, *Political Change in Britain: Forces Shaping Electoral Choice* (New York: St. Martin's Press, 1969). I am indebted to Andrew Gamble for suggesting the importance of this collaboration to me.

[34] Ronald B. McCallum and Alison Readman. *The British General Election of 1945* (London: Oxford University Press, 1947).

[35] Butler and Stokes, *Political Change in Britain*, 16.

[36] Ibid., 11, 15.

[37] Chester, "Political Studies in Britain."

sociology.[38] Another was the emergence of a developed body of research devoted to the empirical study of mass political behavior.[39]

Some important tensions emerged between proponents of historicist studies and those advocating the application of greater methodological rigor and theoretical insight. Yet figures like Mackenzie were largely successful in brokering these contending impulses in a conception of a distinctively British political science. This involved a respect for some of the insights associated with historical and philosophical modes of analysis as well as a limited engagement with some parts of American political science and a recommendation of the importance of data gathering, classification, and research methodologies. One indication of the success of this reformation of the Whig tradition was the general absence of self-conscious dispute over methods and theories within the discipline during these years. The obvious exception that helps prove this rule was Bernard Crick's *The American Science of Politics* (1959), an extensive critical engagement with the work of the intellectual figureheads of behavioralism, especially Harold Lasswell and Charles Merriam. Crick was highly unusual in seeking critical engagement with the luminaries of political science, and in many respects his argument reflected and influenced debates within American political science rather than the thinking of his British colleagues. Such a spirit continued to inform the development of the British community in the years after 1970 as well. As Crick has observed, apart from the departments at Essex and Strathclyde (where behavioralism became a major presence in the 1970s and 1980s), "most of the other new departments hedged their bets and lazily or wisely added a behaviourist or so to political ideas and institutions men."[40]

This abiding ethos within British political studies toward compromise and the partial appropriation of American approaches is reflected in the description of the role and mission of *Political Studies* subsequently offered by its first editor, Wilfrid Harrison.[41] He was acutely aware of the methodological challenge laid down in the United States by such figures as Harold Laswell and David Easton, yet intuitively kept the journal at arm's length from their theories. Under his guidance, the journal constructed a largely homegrown audience and reflected a range of familiar tastes. In its first decade, *Political Studies* showed the continuing influence of the ideas and institutions discourse that was the hallmark of early-

[38] Robert Edward Dowse, "The Recourse to Political Sociology," in *The Political Science of British Politics*, ed. Jack Hayward and Philip Norton (Brighton, UK: Wheatsheaf Books, 1986).

[39] An early instance of which is provided in Jean Blondel, *Voters, Parties and Leaders: The Social Fabric of British Politics* (Harmondsworth, UK: Penguin, 1965).

[40] Bernard Crick, "The British Way," *Government and Opposition* 15, nos. 3–4 (1980): 297–307, 300.

[41] See also Chester, "Political Studies in Britain."

century thinking about politics in Britain.[42] Space was occasionally given to pieces that reflected the dictates of American political science, but the methodological and theoretical differences underpinning these and other submissions were not raised or debated in the fledgling discipline. The journal's issues were more likely to include philosophical treatments of ethical problems and examinations of the textual meanings of some of the major texts and authors within the canon of political thought. While such a position generated a degree of tension between institutionalists and philosophers within the fledgling PSA,[43] many practitioners found themselves teaching both aspects of the curriculum and saw their related discourses as closely intertwined.

Yet the Whiggish tradition in British political science that Mackenzie and others brokered itself came under pressure toward the end of the 1960s and beyond. This is apparent, for instance, from the tone and implications of a burgeoning literature devoted to the inadequacies of parliamentary government, specifically some of the antiquated procedures and rules in Parliament. Some of these studies, like Stuart Walkland's *The Legislative Process in Great Britain* (1968), sought to put the study of Parliament in a wider social context.[44] Others detached Westminster from other state institutions and began to apply some of the techniques and methods, notably quantitative analysis, associated with political science: for instance, Robert Jackson's *Rebels and Whips* (1968) and Hugh Berrington's study *Backbench Opinion in the House of Commons* (1973).[45] The general ethos of these studies was modernizing and reformist, arguing for adjustments to the workings of Parliament so that its functions could be discharged in modern circumstances. The exemplar here was Bernard Crick's *The Reform of Parliament* (1964),[46] a study that emerged from the discussions of the influential group of researchers and civil servants who formed the Study of Parliament Group.

New Political Challenges

Academic disciplines and their constitutive identities develop in relation to a tangle of political, institutional, and intellectual dilemmas. Within the world of political studies in the 1960s, a growing chorus of dissident

[42] Wilfred Harrison, "A British Journal of Political Studies: An Editorial Note," *Political Studies* 1, no. 1 (1953): 1–5.

[43] S. E. Finer, "Political Science: An Idiosyncratic Retrospect," *Government and Opposition* 15, nos. 3–4 (1980): 363–64.

[44] S. A. Walkland, *The Legislative Process in Great Britain* (New York: Praeger, 1968).

[45] Robert J. Jackson, *Rebels and Whips* (London: Macmillan, 1968); Hugh B. Berrington, *Backbench Opinion in the House of Commons, 1945–1955* (Oxford: Pergamon, 1973).

[46] Bernard Crick, *The Reform of Parliament* (London: Weidenfeld and Nicolson, 1964).

voices coincided with a rising tide of conflict and controversy in political life. The latter was sparked by domestic economic crisis and the more conflictual international environment shaped by the polarities associated with the Cold War. The effects of the Cold War were paradoxical for political science in the United Kingdom. To a degree, the emergence of the Soviet "threat" helped the "Americanization" favored by members of the social scientific community in the United Kingdom. This trend was reflected both in the increasing interest shown by younger scholars in American techniques and theories and by the success of figures like Isaiah Berlin in closing the gap between the "Cold War" liberalism of 1950s America and the outlook of British political philosophy. Yet the experience and consequences of the war in Vietnam created the opposite effect from the mid-to-late 1960s onward. For the generations of students and younger scholars finding posts in the expanding discipline from this period, opposition to American foreign policy was one of the catalysts for greater openness toward nonliberal ideological positions and different kinds of critical theory.

Various cultural changes, including the erosion of some of the collective identities that had ordered political allegiance in previous decades, as well as the impact of modernist cultural currents, percolated into political life from the mid-1950s and were the sources of opposition to prevailing understandings about the study of British politics.[47] In a political atmosphere where the themes of economic and political modernization were increasingly familiar, powerful dilemmas arose for a conception of political life that regarded continuity and antiquity as virtues and that was still legitimated by Victorian notions of character and progress. Bevir observes the pressures that these ideals encountered through the impact of modernism in the first half of the century.[48] Within the study of politics, the latter is more clearly discernible from the early-to-mid-1960s as the foundational assumptions of the Westminster model and Whig versions of history began to wane. Familiar understandings of the Westminster model were increasingly questioned by the 1960s, and by the following decade this conception began to lose its hegemonic status. Public debate about the worrying plight of the British economy and its comparative lack of competitiveness combined in the early 1960s with the painful realization that Britain might not be as influential and independent a player within international affairs as was the case before 1939. Different experiences shaped the second of these dilemmas, not least attempts to manage decolonization and the Suez crisis of 1956.

---

[47] Michael Kenny, *The First New Left: British Intellectuals after Stalin* (London: Lawrence and Wishart, 1995).

[48] Bevir, "Prisoners of Professionalism."

The dualistic framework established by the Cold War at the international level intertwined with domestic political developments. As the Conservatives adapted to the welfare state developed by the post-1945 Labour administration, and accepted the new boundary between public and private sectors established during this period, many proclaimed that a major turning point in British party politics had been reached. Instead of the issues and concepts central to early-century elite discourse—constitution, citizenship, and nationhood—new themes dominated domestic political life—macroeconomic growth, affluence, and security. The political writings of this period typically reflected the belief that the major parties were no longer pursuing divergent ideological goals. Now they were apparently involved in squabbling over minor differences, often over methods rather than ends.[49] This idea gained further ground when the Macmillan administration introduced the machinery for national economic planning in the early 1960s.

One further contextual consideration needs analysis if the transitional character of political studies in these years is to be adequately grasped. This point concerns the shifting attitude struck by state actors toward the social sciences and the impact of these changes upon the fledgling discipline of political studies. Prior to the Second World War, the state's relationship with the academy was, in the most general terms, organized through two overarching imperatives. One involved the functional need to train future cohorts of administrators and public servants. The second concerned the perpetuation of an intellectual stratum that would offer guidance and wisdom to the political elite and constitute a public culture that would disseminate authoritative notions of the nation's history and character.[50] These imperatives also played an important role in shaping the self-understandings of some of the foundational figures within the study of politics in Britain in the first half of the twentieth century.[51]

From 1945, such notions were gradually displaced by changing state imperatives, affecting the social sciences in particular and intellectual practice more generally. During the Second World War, social scientists played an important role within a number of departments in Whitehall, not least in preparing the ground for the welfare reforms of the postwar period.[52] The idea of an instrumental relationship between social studies

[49] Anthony Crosland, *The Future of Socialism* (London: Cape, 1956).

[50] Julia Stapleton, *Englishness and the Study of Politics: The Social and Political Thought of Ernest Barker* (Cambridge: Cambridge University Press, 1994).

[51] Stefan Collini, Donald Winch and John Burrow, *That Noble Science of Politics: A Study in Nineteenth-Century Intellectual History* (Cambridge: Cambridge University Press, 1983); Julia Stapleton, *Political Intellectuals and Public Identities in Britain since 1850* (Manchester: Manchester University Press, 2001).

[52] Hayward, "Political Science in Britain."

and government policy emerged as an important rival paradigm affecting the relationship of salaried academics to the state in the 1960s. Even more important was the effect of the rapid expansion of higher education that resulted in the construction of new universities and increased funding of the whole sector. A particular emphasis was placed upon the development of the social sciences, disciplines that could be more easily associated with the new modernism sweeping through British social life.[53] It made increasing institutional and intellectual sense, as a result, to position political studies in closer proximity to the social sciences. This setting proved increasingly fertile for the growth of empiricist and science-based approaches to political analysis that were explicitly hostile to idealist and historicist paradigms.

A second shift in the relations between the state and the academy arose from a changing sense of the function and purpose of intellectuals in general. As the state expanded its scope and functions enormously during the 1940s, it increasingly sought to deploy expertise and specialists in relation to specific policy areas, such as housing, education, or welfare. As this mode of intellectual practice was rewarded and favored, the model of the Victorian moralist receded from public view. This is not to suggest that the state simply conjured up one type of intellectual to replace another. But a change in the balance of influence between rival notions of intellectual practice was, to some degree, orchestrated by the postwar state. The emergence of a self-standing discipline of politics, within which it made sense to conceive the discipline as detachable from its traditional roots, can be better understood in this context.

Partial Challengers to the Westminster Consensus

A further explanation of the erosion of Whiggish understandings of British politics was the appearance of various dissenting approaches, drawing upon non-Whiggish traditions of political thought, at the shoulder of "mainstream" analyses of politics in this period. Such has been the popularity of the idea that British intellectual culture in general and political studies in particular were captured either by Whig ideology, a native empiricism, or a pervasive intellectual conservatism, that dissident voices have sometimes been overlooked in its historiography. Perry Anderson's characterization of the intellectual landscape at this time has done much to establish this perspective: "The predominant outlook of the English intelligentsia in the post-war settlement, once the Cold War set in, was parochial and quietist: adhering to the established political consensus

---

[53] Lovenduski, "The Profession of Political Science in Britain."

without exercising itself greatly to construct or defend it."[54] The contributions of two traditions are missing from Anderson's picture, however, but are worth emphasizing during this period. Both represented "partial challengers" to the prevailing Whig-liberal view of British political development. Within this period at least, the hegemony of the Whig narrative of British development was such that each of them was compelled to put down some roots in its intellectual soil. Only after 1968, when the political understanding associated with this narrative began to lose legitimacy, did these views become the sources of independent schools of interpretation and the allies of wider ideological developments.

Civic Humanism

The first of these challengers exerted some influence in these years within the study of political ideas. This was a residual strain of civic humanism. The origins of this tradition have come more clearly into view in the wake of recent scholarship devoted to rescuing a potent republican tradition in modern political discourse. In this period, this heritage was deployed by several scholars committed to the distinctiveness of politics as an intrinsically valuable activity and the promotion of the ideals of public service and active citizenship. This lineage was suspicious of the ethical and political implications of liberal individualism in general and utilitarian models of political behavior in particular. Its adherents also celebrated the importance of historical understanding, though history was here stripped of the moral or teleological sense of purpose associated with the developmental historicism of the nineteenth century.

During these years Bernard Crick's arguments for and J.G.A. Pocock's retrieval of a republican conception of politics,[55] as well as the emerging work of younger scholars like Quentin Skinner, were central to reviving civic humanism in contemporary politics. Crick's best-selling *In Defense of Politics* (1962) provided a potent appropriation of the Aristotelian conception of political virtue combined with an embrace of the modern problematic of group pluralism. Politics was the process whereby groups and individual citizens came together in an atmosphere of restraint and toleration to determine the common good. With his determination to delegitimate "antipolitical" philosophies like Marxism and his hostility to Oakeshottian conservatism, Crick offered an important justification of a leftward inflection of the dominant liberal paradigm.

---

[54] Anderson, "A Culture in Contraflow," 194.
[55] J.G.A. Pocock, *The Ancient Constitution and the Feudal Law: A Study of English Historical Thought in the Seventeenth Century* (Cambridge: Cambridge University Press, 1957).

Anglo-Marxism

A different challenger that began to exert some influence upon interpretations of politics in this period is that which Crick and others regarded as a dubious presence within the tent of political studies—Marxism. While this lineage was politically and intellectually marginalized in Britain following the advent of the first Cold War in the late 1940s, an indigenous Marxist tradition had survived. This tradition represented one part of a broad strand of writing committed to providing a Labour-inclined version of the Whig consensus. Anglo-Marxism had its roots in late-nineteenth-century abridgments of Marxist themes by British radicals and various attempts to "domesticate" Marx's ideas for a domestic audience.[56] One by-product of this position was a revival in the 1940s of a libertarian socialism that was hostile both to the Soviet Union and the growing power of the modern state. Through the writings of J. B. Priestley and George Orwell in the 1940s and the historian Edward Thompson in the 1950s, this peculiarly English tradition was an active presence within the public sphere in these years.[57]

The Marxist element of the socialist heritage was sustained after 1945, notably within the talented historians' group of the Communist Party of Great Britain (including Christopher Hill, Victor Kiernan, Eric Hobsbawm, John Saville, A. L. Morton, Raphael Samuel, and Edward Thompson).[58] These figures sought to challenge contemporary political understanding, pointing to the richness of a tradition of subaltern popular activism stretching from the Chartists to the postwar labour movement, and through their endeavours to rekindle memories of the breadth and creativity of the British socialist tradition. This vision was carried forward into the fledgling New Left milieu of the late 1950s, once many of these figures left the Communist Party in disgust at the Soviet repression of the Hungarian uprising. The New Left attracted an array of talent within the academy, and its combination of intellectual seriousness and adventure proved attractive to many able graduates and young academics.[59] It also provided a base for nondoctrinaire Marxists to exercise their talents as political critics and analysts, and undoubtedly shaped the expectations of

[56] Bevir, "Prisoners of Professionalism," 479; John Cowley, *The Victorian Encounter with Marx: A Study of E. Belfort Bax* (London: British Academic Press, 1992).

[57] Michael Kenny, "Reputations: Edward Palmer Thompson," *Political Quarterly* 70, no. 30 (1999): 319–29.

[58] Eric J. Hobsbawm, "The Historians Group of the Communist Party," in *Rebels and Their Causes: Essays in Honour of A. L. Morton*, ed. Maurice Cornforth (London: Lawrence and Wishart, 1978).

[59] Chun Lin, *The British New Left* (Edinburgh: Edinburgh University Press, 1993); Kenny, *The First New Left*.

some of the next generation of students of the discipline of politics. Though these critics were not part of the world of political studies in the 1950s, it is significant that even prior to the importation of Continental Marxist thinking in the 1970s, veterans of the New Left—Ralph Miliband being one important example—offered influential critiques of British parliamentary government and the limits of the Labour party in particular.[60]

Even Anglo-Marxism, however, offered only a partial challenge to Whig-liberal constructions of the history and character of the British polity. Its adherents developed their sense of the legitimate objects of political inquiry in relation to conventional demarcations and emphases. Thus, Miliband accepted the Whig sense of the stability and continuity that characterized the British political culture and hence regarded the prospects for an elected socialist government with pessimism.[61] Equally, the influential critique of the aristocratic hegemony over, and cultural parochialism of, British society offered by Anderson and Tom Nairn in the 1960s relied upon an acceptance of much of the self-understanding of the British political elite.[62] Critics of the British system, who were certainly more vocal and numerous in the 1960s still tended to focus upon those subjects central to the Westminster model—the unitary state, institutional continuity, class compromise, bureaucratic neutrality, and ministerial responsibility.

Professionalization and Political Scholarship in the United Kingdom

Marxists in particular, but socialists and other radicals generally, struggled to gain a hearing within the evolving world of academic political studies during this period. Yet this was less true of political debate and thought outside the walls of the academy, a situation that soon affected this fledgling discipline as well. A variety of ideological and intellectual voices came to public prominence from the 1940s onward, primarily through print journalism, radio, and, from the late 1950s, television, with liberalism generally the center of gravity of public political discourse. One of the consequences of the new winds of professionalism, however, was to delegitimate the confident sense of connection with the life of the public culture, and indeed with political parties, enjoyed by earlier generations

---

[60] Ralph Miliband, *Parliamentary Socialism: A Study in the Politics of Labour* (London: Allen and Unwin, 1961); Michael Newman, *Ralph Miliband and the Politics of the New Left* (London: Merlin, 2002).

[61] Miliband, *Parliamentary Socialism*.

[62] Perry Anderson and Tom Nairn, "Origins of the Present Crisis," in Anderson, *English Questions* (London: Verso, 1992; first published in 1964), 15–47.

of scholarly interpreters of the political—Ernest Barker, G.D.H. Cole, and Harold Laski for instance in the first half of the century.

The model of the political scientist that gained credence in the 1960s involved an emphasis upon specialization, particularly in terms of methodological and theoretical knowledge, the adoption of a technical language, and greater value upon the ideal of disinterested, impartial analysis. Though these were not the only causes of a growing gap between the proliferating media of public debate and the academic study of politics, the very rapid advent of a hegemonic discourse of professionalization helped disseminate some important new ideas about the status and habitus of the political academic. Some individual scholars continued to enjoy access to media outlets, especially those whose expertise lay in the fields of electoral behavior. Scholars whose work has spanned the worlds of public debate and the academy increasingly found themselves working against the grain of current academic life since this era. While there have been undoubted benefits from the professionalization of political studies in Britain (the rise of more objective criteria for determining career development and transparency in appointment procedures for example), it is worth reflecting upon what has been lost with the demise of the Whig-liberal political intellectual. The sense of close connection to public discourse that political academics continued to enjoy into the 1950s and the accompanying nonspecialist intellectual identity that many practitioners then possessed have all but passed away in academic life. While much of the amateurishness associated with these roles need not be the subject of regret, the discipline has, in other respects, lost its primary sense of normative purpose and involvement with the political world. What exactly has replaced these commitments in its more professionalized incarnation remains a key question for the discipline in the early twenty-first century.

More generally, the contemporary assumption that the discipline stultified and produced little of longer-term merit in this period requires revision. Some important intellectual tensions were apparent during these years, and the identity of political studies over the next two decades took shape. In this sense, the question posed by Crick in a retrospective essay published in 1980 remains pertinent: is there a "British way" of studying and understanding politics?[63] The interpretation of this period that I propose supports the contention of those who suggest that a proper answer to this inquiry requires something other than generalizations about the empirical or conservative bent of British, or English, intellectual culture. What Crick presents as "the British way" was a pattern of thinking that was in key respects developed by figures like Mackenzie and Beer in this

---

[63] Crick, "The British Way."

particular period—a skillful fusion of traditional and novel ideas about the study of the political. This perspective involved the successful blending of aspects of the traditions laid down in the late nineteenth and early twentieth centuries with a new sense of politics as a modern, independent discipline that had its home within the social sciences.

Contemporary caricatures of the early years of the discipline stem from a simplistic and teleological contrast between its "prehistory" and later maturation. Such a stance has served to deflect attention from the plurality of approaches to the study of politics that were brought together within this scholarly community. Whiggish ideas about the history, values, and character of the British polity were intermingled with newer emphases upon empirical verification and a degree of methodological rigor as various figures sought to establish a distinctively British variant of the international political science community.[64] The best way to legitimate this intellectual mixture was to hold to the idea that this discipline was characterized, in Britain, by its methodological pluralism. This allowed the primary division of labor between political philosophy and the historicist study of institutions to be extended to include empiricists and political scientists, as well as liberal philosophers, Oakeshottian conservatives, and civic humanists.

Toward the end of this period, the first signs of the erosion of this paradigm became apparent, and the way was prepared for the adoption of theories that were overtly hostile to the Whiggish orthodoxy. As political studies gained newer and younger adherents and a presence in more universities, it became correspondingly harder to socialize practitioners in accordance with accepted traditions, and the terms of this settlement came under greater strain. An increasing friction was apparent between the now-receding developmental historicism that had characterized the early decades of the century and the modernist empiricism that began to influence younger members of the profession. But within the small, newly institutionalized academic discipline in the United Kingdom, the sparks generated by the coexistence of these rival paradigms did not tend to ignite public disagreements over methods or epistemology. To a considerable degree, this was an outcome of the particular characterization of British political science that emerged in the work of figures like Mackenzie and Beer in the 1960s.

---

[64] William Alexander Robson, *The University Teaching of Social Sciences: Political Science* (Paris: UNESCO, 1954).

Nine

Interpreting Behavioralism

ROBERT ADCOCK

THE BEHAVIORAL MOVEMENT of the 1950s and 1960s is central to the way most contemporary American political scientists envision their discipline's past.[1] While far from agreeing on a single interpretation of the movement's character or merit, political scientists share a common belief that it wrought intellectual transformation on a large scale. Indeed, the sense of scale is such as to make periodization into prebehavioral, behavioral, and postbehavioral eras the common framework within which political scientists envision their predecessors. For radical historicists, however, any such framework—even, perhaps especially, one so prevalent as to constitute disciplinary common sense—is a selective perspective whose genealogy they might uncover and whose evolving and contestable content they might endeavor to reshape. My interpretation here will pursue a moderate revisionism. I seek to temper, but not to reject, the belief that behavioralism was revolutionary in its character and impact. I seek, in doing so, to refine our aggregate portrait of the specific changes associated with it, rejecting some images—such as that of behavioralism turning the discipline away from history—but reinforcing others, such as the image of the movement as a crusade to make the discipline more "systematic" and "scientific."

The vision of behavioralism as a transformative movement was first crafted not to capture an already accomplished intellectual shift, but as a rallying cry to promote change. This image took shape in the early 1950s, at the outset of what came to be known as the "behavioral revolution." Its most memorable formulation was probably that found in David Easton's 1953 *The Political System: An Inquiry into the State of Political Science*.[2] This book gave distinctive expression to a call for a more "systematic" and "scientific" study of politics that had been gaining adherents since the late 1940s. This movement began life as an insurgent minority, and it retained that self-identity for some time. In the late 1950s, at least some

[1] The author would like to thank Mark Bevir, Daniel Geary, Nils Gilman, Martin Jay, Alison Kaufman, Eric Schickler, Richard Snyder, and Shannon Stimson for their comments on earlier versions of this material.
[2] David Easton, *The Political System* (New York: Knopf, 1953).

behavioralists still felt sufficiently marginalized to debate breaking away from the discipline and forming a new professional association.[3] Though disciplinary recognition did come to behavioralists soon thereafter—including, in the 1960s, presidency of the American Political Science Association (APSA) for David Truman, Gabriel Almond, Robert Dahl, and David Easton, and editorship of the association's journal, the *American Political Science Review (APSR)*, for Austin Ranney—behavioralism never achieved quite the degree of hegemony with which it is commonly credited or accused. Indeed, for at least some scholars who subscribed to it, the movement would appear in retrospect to have fallen short, leaving a political science that in the 1970s still seemed largely "prebehavioral."[4]

Doubts about the success of the behavioral movement were not, however, shared by those hostile to it. By the late 1960s, opponents had turned the vision of a transformed political science against behavioralism. They used it to fashion a rallying call of their own, depicting themselves as the noble and embattled resistance to a hegemonic wave of scientism.[5] In its first twenty years the image of a behavioral revolution thus evolved from a rallying cry of young behavioralists looking confidently to the future, into the feared other of antibehavioral scholars bemoaning the present. By the early 1980s use of the image would shift again: no longer conjuring up either future promise or contemporary combat, it settled down as the received way to envision the recent past. In the chapter by Adcock, Bevir, and Stimson we see how new institutionalist scholars have ascribed novelty to their own agendas by portraying them as departures from this envisioned past. In doing so they portray behavioralism as having downplayed institutions, challenged the autonomy of the state, and turned away from the use of history. While these retrospective charges have been challenged—both by elder statesmen of behavioralism,[6] and more recently, by some new institutionalists distancing themselves from views they held in the 1980s[7]—a notion of "ahistorical behavioralism" has

[3] See the interview with David Easton in *Political Science in America*, ed. Michael A. Baer, Malcolm E. Jewell, and Lee Sigelman (Lexington: University Press of Kentucky, 1991), 208.

[4] See for example the 1978 APSA Presidential Address of John C. Wahlke, "Pre-behavioralism in Political Science," *American Political Science Review* 73, no. 1 (1979): 9–31.

[5] See, for example, Sheldon S. Wolin, "Political Theory as a Vocation," *American Political Science Review* 63, no. 4 (1969): 1062–82. For more on Wolin and his stance, see chapter 10 in this volume.

[6] Gabriel A. Almond, "The Return to the State," *American Political Science Review* 82, no. 3 (1988): 853–74.

[7] Karen Orren and Stephen Skowronek, "Order and Time in Institutional Study," in *Political Science in History: Research Programs and Political Traditions*, ed. James Farr, John S. Dryzek, and Stephen T. Leonard (New York: Cambridge University Press, 1995); Ira Katznelson, *Desolation and Enlightenment* (New York: Columbia University Press, 2003).

proven peculiarly hardy, persisting to the current day as a pivotal point of reference in disciplinary debate.[8]

Against this backdrop of evolving interpretations, I pursue two main lines of argument.[9] First I respond to the prevalent image of behavioralism as a revolutionary intellectual movement. Rather than taking this image for granted, I seek to specify to what extent and in what ways the behavioral scholarship of the 1950s and 1960s did and did not depart from prior trends. My second line of argument responds more fully to one specific belief: the claim that behavioralism turned the discipline away from history. This belief supports the persistence, up to the current day, of the rhetorically powerful image of behavioralism as ahistorical. I hope by challenging the belief to undermine that image. Both of my lines of argument entail making judgments comparing the behavioral movement to prior tendencies in political science. I hence begin by identifying some major trends in the discipline before 1950. I then turn to the rise of behavioralism and offer an initial synthetic portrait of the movement. Such a broad brush-stroke portrait must, however, pass too rapidly over important matters of detail. To round out my account, I hence explore, in the last half of the chapter, the dynamics of behavioral era developments in two subfields in particular: American and comparative politics, respectively.

Before Behavioralism

In the early 1940s, the APSA sought to organize a series of working groups, each of which would bring together leading figures in an area of research to discuss the current state and future agenda of work in that area. Over the next few years ten such panels, covering a wide spectrum of the discipline, took shape. The endeavor led to an edited volume, *Research in Political Science*, which contained reports from each panel, and summary reflections from its editor, Ernest Griffith. What does the volume suggest was on the minds of prominent political scientists in the early to mid-1940s? In his summary, Griffith singles out "the concept of 'political

---

[8] See, for example, Rogers Smith's recent use of the concept. Rogers M. Smith, "Identities, Interests, and the Future of Political Science," *Perspectives on Politics* 2, no. 2 (2004): 301–12.

[9] Using these two lines of inquiry to focus my account produces a decidedly internalist account. To supplement my account, readers might consult some of the following works, which all take a more externalist approach: Terence Ball, "American Political Science in Its Postwar Political Context," in *Discipline and History: Political Science in the United States*, ed. James Farr and Raymond Seidelmann (Ann Arbor: University of Michigan Press, 1993); Ido Oren, *Our Enemies and US* (Ithaca, NY: Cornell University Press, 2003), esp. chap. 4; Nils Gilman, *Mandarins of the Future* (Baltimore: Johns Hopkins University Press, 2003), esp. chap. 4.

behavior' " as being pervasive in "panel after panel." Indeed, he goes so
far to assert: "political behavior has largely replaced legal structures as
the cardinal point of emphasis among political scientists."[10] While his
claim may overstate the case, it suggests, at the very minimum, that the
study of political behavior was widely seen as a prominent and promising
agenda by American political scientists *before* the onset of the movement
of the 1950s and 1960s that has passed into disciplinary memory as the
"behavioral revolution."

Calls for political scientists to look beyond the formal structures of
government and study the behavior of political actors, associations, and
public opinion are, in fact, as old, indeed older, than the discipline in
America.[11] Efforts to put this call into practice in studying the American
polity were made even before the First World War, most prominently in
books by James Bryce and A. L. Lowell.[12] During the interwar decades,
the attention to public opinion and political parties found in Bryce and
Lowell was supplemented by a new current of research focusing on the
role of pressure groups in America. This research gained notice and prestige alongside the debates around pluralism and democracy explored in
this volume by John Gunnell. A string of APSA presidents—Peter Odegard, Pendleton Herring, and E. E. Schattschneider—built their careers
on studies of pressure groups.[13] By the 1940s there was thus a substantial
body of political science research on public opinion, parties, and pressure
groups in America. The use of "political behavior" as a label for such
topics of research was, moreover, also well established.

The growing prominence of such research among scholars of American
politics was accompanied by a decline in the prestige of research based on
work with historical documents. While hints of this shift can be found
earlier, it became particularly evident during the interwar decades. The
decline was, however, not fueled by a rejection of primary historical re-

---

[10] Ernest S. Griffith, ed., *Research in Political Science* (Chapel Hill: University of North
Carolina Press, 1948), 224. See also the survey by former APSA president William Anderson, "Political Science North and South," *Journal of Politics* 11, no. 2 (1949): 298–317.

[11] For an early example, see Woodrow Wilson, "Of the Study of Politics," *New Princeton
Review*, 62nd year (1887): 188–99. The call is made again in A. L. Lowell's 1909 Presidential Address to the APSA, which reads at multiple points like the rallying cries that behavioralists would offer half a century later. A. L. Lowell, "The Physiology of Politics," *American
Political Science Review* 4, no. 1 (1910): 1–15.

[12] James Bryce, *The American Commonwealth*, 2 vols. (New York: Macmillan, 1893);
A. L. Lowell, *Public Opinion and Popular Government* (New York: Longmans Green,
1913).

[13] Peter H. Odegard, *Pressure Politics: The Story of the Anti-saloon League* (New York:
Columbia University Press, 1928); Pendleton Herring, *Group Representation before Con-
gress* (Baltimore: Johns Hopkins University Press, 1929); E. E. Schattschneider, *Politics,
Pressures, and the Tariff* (New York: Prentice-Hall, 1935).

search as unscientific, but by the positive draw of other research techniques, which seemed novel, exciting, and better suited to the study of political behavior. This shift in techniques was paralleled by decline in the attention and prestige given to synthetic narratives of American political history. Charles Beard's provocative grand narratives did more to highlight by contrast the shifts taking place in political science than they did to stem that change. With the rise of behavior studies, the character of practices and concerns distinguishing "political scientists" from "historians" in the study of American politics became steadily clearer. By the 1940s, Beard had come to appear more a historian than a political scientist.

Studies of American political behavior in the interwar decades were marked by two distinctive tendencies. First, these studies were largely qualitative in character, with field interviews and case studies playing a major role.[14] Thus, when we recover the fact that the disciplinary establishment was, by the mid-1940s, already warmly receptive to the study of behavior, we should also recall that it was common among this establishment to see Charles Merriam's 1920s push for quantification and statistical analysis as, at best, a distraction that had had mercifully little impact.[15] The second noteworthy tendency in interwar studies of American political behavior was the prevalence of a reformist conception of social science. Under this loosely pragmatist conception social science was approached as centered on identifying political and social problems, studying them, and proposing reform measures. A final flourish—or perhaps debacle—of this sensibility among scholars of American political behavior was found in the proposal "Toward a More Responsible Two-Party System," developed in the 1940s under the auspices of the APSA.[16] As we shall see, this qualitative, discursive, and programmatic document provides a specific point of contrast against which to grasp what exactly behavioralists sought to break with in the study of American politics. It thereby helps us understand the dynamic of the subfield's development far better than the diffuse and dubious image of an "old institutionalism" uninterested in behavior.

While the study of American politics up through 1950 is marked by a steady upward trajectory of behavior studies, such a trend was less pronounced and less uniform elsewhere in the discipline. The image of an

[14] A lonely exception is found in the studies of Harold Gosnell of the University of Chicago, but these fell outside the interwar mainstream. See, for example, Harold F. Gosnell, *Machine Politics* (Chicago: University of Chicago Press, 1937), with its foreword by the neopositivist sociologist William Ogburn.

[15] Griffith, *Research in Political Science*, 213.

[16] "Toward a More Responsible Two-Party System," *American Political Science Review* 44, suppl. (1950).

old institutionalism focusing on formal government structures does, in particular, have some truth in regard to comparative studies. Largely lacking the funding that would support overseas research in later decades, a significant part of interwar comparative political science was wedded to surveying formal institutions via published materials. Alongside such studies there were, however, notable exceptions that qualify any overly monolithic image. The elder figures in the study of public opinion and parties, Bryce and Lowell, had never been concerned solely with American politics, and in the early 1920s both published new comparative studies displaying their trademark attention to these behavior topics.[17] Their example may suggest that comparative study of behavior was, at this time, most possible for scholars who were personally well traveled and well connected. An alternative to the gentleman-of-the-world inquiry of Bryce and Lowell was, however, pioneered in the late 1920s by the ever-enterprising Charles Merriam. Drawing on Rockefeller funding—as he had when helping establish the Social Science Research Council (SSRC) earlier in the decade—Merriam organized a multiinvestigator comparative study of citizen socialization. Each investigator was to study only one country, but to do so in relation to a shared set of concerns so that broad comparative findings might emerge.[18] The collaborative approach pioneered here as well as the specific research topic studied would both find prominent echoes in the 1950s and 1960s in the projects of Merriam's student and leading behavioralist, Gabriel Almond.

Those echoes jump, however, over the shifts in comparative political science during the 1930s and 1940s, when a wave of European scholars brought to the subfield new perspectives and concerns. A first shift was evident in the 1930s in influential new treatments of comparative government by Herman Finer (a Graham Wallas student who would later join the Chicago faculty) and Carl Friedrich (an Alfred Weber student who had joined the Harvard faculty).[19] Finer and Friedrich deployed a modernist stance that synthesized comparative material around analytical frameworks rather than nation-by-nation accounts. These efforts to frame and

[17] James Bryce, *Modern Democracies*, 2 vols. (London: Macmillan, 1921); A. L. Lowell, *Public Opinion in War and Peace* (Cambridge: Harvard University Press, 1923).

[18] This collective endeavor resulted in a multiple-volume series of books, with each investigator publishing a sole-authored country study, while Merriam wrote a capstone comparative study. Charles E. Merriam, *The Making of Citizens* (Chicago: University of Chicago Press, 1931).

[19] Herman Finer, *Theory and Practice of Modern Government*, 2 vols. (London: Methuen, 1932); Carl J. Friedrich, *Constitutional Government and Politics* (New York: Harper, 1937). Running through reprints, new editions, and substantial revisions (and, for Friedrich's work, a title change to *Constitutional Government and Democracy*), these books dominated education in comparative government well into the 1950s.

deploy systematic analytical schemes reflected trends in modernist social science in interwar Europe that were also taken up—at a higher level of abstraction—by the sociologist Talcott Parsons. But we should credit Finer and Friedrich with bringing this effort to comparative political science some two decades before Parsons's theorizing became a major influence upon the subfield.

A second shift was the flourishing of new concerns following from the rise of fascism in Europe. The frightening developments as Europe moved from crisis to crisis, and ultimately into World War II, reinvigorated interest among American political scientists in contemporary Europe. It also provided the comparative subfield with an inflow of émigrés—such as Karl Loewenstein, Sigmund Neumann, and Franz Neumann—equipped to address that interest. By the 1940s the character of the Nazi regime and the category of "totalitarian" regimes had become central subjects of attention and discussion among comparative political scientists.[20]

How did historical research fare amid these various developments? The strand of the comparative subfield that may be plausibly labeled "old institutionalist" and the more behavior-oriented work of Bryce and Lowell were both descended from the comparative historical tradition discussed by James Farr in chapter 4. But both strands testify to a subordination of the historical concerns central to that tradition in its nineteenth-century heyday. By the end of the 1920s new research in both strands was more focused on keeping contemporary accounts up-to-date than on conducting new historical work. Given the rate, scale, and significance of ongoing political changes—as well as a reformist stance that saw a main payoff of comparative work in the practical advice that might be gleaned for America from studying other countries—this focus had a clear positive attraction. As in the study of American politics, it was the positive draw of research focused on the present day that crystallized distinctions between the work of political scientists and that of historians.

The contemporary focus of the comparative subfield already evident by the late 1920s was not substantially altered during the 1930s and 1940s. A limited reenergizing of the subfield's historical dimension might be noted in the way that existing historical findings were reworked to provide background material in line with new perspectives and concerns. But

---

[20] Karl Loewenstein, *Hitler's Germany: The Nazi Background to War* (New York: Macmillan, 1939); Sigmund Neumann, *Permanent Revolution: The Total State in a World at War* (New York: Harper and Brothers, 1942); Franz Neumann, *Behemoth: The Structure and Practice of National Socialism* (New York: Oxford University Press, 1942). Friedrich's work on totalitarianism did not appear in print until the 1950s, but he was already working on it in the late 1930s. Carl J. Friedrich and Zbigniew K. Brzezinski, *Totalitarian Dictatorship and Autocracy* (Cambridge: Harvard University Press, 1956).

such endeavors should not obscure the fact that few comparative political scientists were doing new historical research. When, in 1941, Friedrich asserted that it was "impossible to be a scientist in politics without a thorough training in the critical methods of modern historical research,"[21] he voiced a view that was the exception, rather than the norm. Within American political science as a whole, this once-dominant view retained its former sway only in a second subfield—political theory—in which Friedrich also played a leading role. When summing up the APSA panels of the 1940s, the editor of *Research in Political Science* emphasized the "complete omission from the discussions of any real emphasis on the historical approach," but paused to note the panel on political theory as the main exception to this generalization.[22]

I would thus contend, as does Gunnell in chapter 7, that a shift of political science away from historical work was already entrenched by the end of the interwar decades and that this shift was rooted in the draw of other forms of research, not in any active dismissal of history as unscientific. Up into the 1940s most political scientists were uninterested in, or even actively hostile to, neopositivist crusades seeking to tighten the standards of social science. They thought of themselves as scientists, and they did so with little anxiety or, for that matter, self-reflection. A low-key notion of science as fact gathering and objective reporting prevailed. This gave little reason to prefer quantitative over qualitative research or to query the scientific standing of historical work. While fewer and fewer political scientists outside of political theory did such work, their shift of approach was not accompanied by any belief that colleagues who did so were exceptions from, or hindrances to, a scientific discipline.

Disciplinary Self-Criticism and the Rise of Behavioralism

The blending of low-key empiricism with reformist sensibilities that characterized much of interwar American political science would come under challenge in the 1940s. Perhaps the most penetrating criticisms came from German émigrés who had recently entered the discipline, such as Hans Morgenthau.[23] But complaints were also on the rise among homegrown scholars. An early critique, offered in 1940 by Benjamin Lippincott,

[21] Carl J. Friedrich, *Constitutional Government and Democracy* (Boston: Little, Brown, 1941), 577.

[22] See Griffith, *Research in Political Science*, 211–12. For more on the developmental historicism of interwar political theory and the subfield's development after World War II, see the following chapter by Adcock and Bevir.

[23] Hans J. Morgenthau, *Scientific Man vs. Power Politics* (Chicago: University of Chicago Press, 1946). See also the discussion of Leo Strauss in chapter 10 in this volume.

charged the discipline with being mired in atheoretical description.[24] A decade later, when Lippincott reiterated this charge in UNESCO's world-wide review of the state of political science, his was far from a lonely voice. The same criticism echoed across most American contributions to the volume.[25] Worried that the empirical research of prior decades had failed to add up to an adequate whole, a growing number of political scientists were coming to believe that their discipline was hamstrung by atheoretical empiricism. When, in the early 1950s, David Easton portrayed American political science as mired in "hyperfactualism" and suffering from "the decline of modern political theory," he gave provocative form to sentiments that had been gaining adherents for a decade.[26]

Growing dissatisfaction with the discipline and notable overlaps in diagnoses of what ailed it did not, however, dictate a single prescription for the road ahead. The 1940s saw a widespread call for "the creative thinker, who must give meaning to the painstaking research that, while indispensable, is still not enough."[27] But by the early 1950s it was evident that there were profound disagreements regarding both the kind of theoretical endeavor needed and what other new efforts such an endeavor ought to be combined with. What we now call the "behavioral movement" took shape at this juncture as a loose grouping of scholars committed to disciplinary transformation and sharing, in broad outline, a common vision of a new political science. This vision stood in contrast, on the one hand, to an alternative vision of the way forward articulated by such émigrés as Morgenthau and Leo Strauss and, on the other hand, to the commitments of those political scientists who found the existing discipline far less unsatisfactory than it appeared to either of these divergent groups of critics.

What was the behavioralist vision of the road ahead? How did the movement propose to break with prior tendencies in the discipline? To understand behavioralism we must first recall that study of "political behavior" had been on the rise in American political science for decades. Behavioralism inherited its topical focus on subjects that are not formally part of the government structure—such as political parties, public opinion, and interest groups—and it sought to extend attention to such topics within comparative studies, where it was less developed than in the study of American politics. There was nothing grandly transformative in this effort, and

[24] Benjamin E. Lippincott, "The Bias of American Political Science," *Journal of Politics* 2, no. 2 (1940): 125–39.

[25] *Contemporary Political Science: A Survey of Methods, Research and Teaching* (Paris: UNESCO, 1950). See chapters by Lippincott, Bernstein, Cook, and Fainsod.

[26] Easton, *The Political System*; see also David Easton, "The Decline of Modern Political Theory," *Journal of Politics* 13, no. 1 (1951): 36–58.

[27] Griffith, *Research in Political Science*, 237.

an excessive emphasis on it would produce a skewed portrait of behavioralism. The movement's consolidation in the early 1950s was indeed greatly aided by the efforts of the SSRC Committee on Political Behavior (CPB) set up in late 1949, but the leading concern of the CPB was *not* promoting the study of political behavior as a substantive topic per se. If we look at the articles published in 1951 and 1952 in connection with the CPB's efforts, the core theme is a call for a more "systematic" study of politics.[28] The focus is more on how to study politics than on what to study. The truly transformative aspects of behavioralism's vision lay in the departures the movement's participants believed necessary to make their discipline systematic: behavioralists called for a new kind of theoretical work and for the use of more sophisticated empirical techniques.

The behavioralist vision of a systematic political science built on the belief that the discipline suffered from an impoverished theoretical imagination. Though this belief was itself shared by various viewpoints in the discipline, the new theoretical endeavors that behavioralism promoted had their own distinctive character. When the CPB declared "development of theory" to be one of its two core concerns,[29] it had specifically in mind the pursuit of what I discuss (with Mark Bevir) in the next chapter as "empirical theory." The search was for analytical frameworks that could give systematic order to the findings of empirical work. What was called for was, as SSRC president Pendleton Herring put it in his APSA Presidential Speech in 1953, "theory as a conceptual scheme for the analysis and ordering of empirical data on political behavior."[30] Such theory was intended both to synthesize existing research and to help direct future work. The behavioralists saw earlier political science as haphazardly directed by shifting practical problems and by reform ideals with implicit, undefended assumptions. Empirical theory would, it was hoped, direct attention to empirical questions that needed to be addressed so as to allow, in turn, for further theoretical refinement. An iterated interplay of theory and empirical research lay at the heart of the behavioralist vision:

[28] Avery Leiserson, "Systematic Research in Political Behavior," *Social Science Research Council Items* 5, no. 3 (1951): 29–32; Oliver Garceau, "Research in the Political Process," *American Political Science Review* 45, no. 1 (1951): 69–85; David B. Truman, "The Implications of Political Behavior Research," *Social Science Research Council Items* 5, no. 4 (1951): 37–39; Samuel J. Eldersveld, Alexander Heard, Samuel P. Huntington, Morris Janowitz, Avery Leiserson, Dayton D. McKean, and David B. Truman, "Research in Political Behavior," *American Political Science Review* 46, no. 4 (1952): 1003–45. For more on behavioralism's self-presentation, see James Farr, "Remembering the Revolution," in Farr, Dryzek, and Leonard, *Political Science in History*.

[29] "Committee Briefs: Political Behavior," *Social Science Research Council Items* 4, no. 2 (June 1950): 20.

[30] Pendleton Herring, "On the Study of Government," *American Political Science Review* 47, no. 4 (1953): 968.

this interplay was the means by which a systematic political science would, it was hoped, move forward along a self-directed path of cumulative scientific progress. For this to happen it was believed helpful, as Easton put it, to leave "premature policy science" behind and adopt a "pure science" conception of political science.[31]

The agenda of empirical theory received its classic elaboration in Easton's *The Political System* (1953). Easton provocatively advocated an agenda that was, however, already under way. The behavioralist pursuit of empirical theory had begun slightly earlier with Harold Lasswell's *Power and Society* (1950) (coauthored with philosopher Abraham Kaplan) and David Truman's *The Governmental Process* (1951).[32] Placing Easton's book alongside these other two works highlights the fact that the empirical theory project was, from the start, diverse. Easton's interest in a "general theory" applicable at all times and all places, pitched at a macrosocietal level and using the concepts of "systems theory," was only one endeavor. In its empirical theory efforts, the behavioral movement would encompass experimentation with a dizzying array of theoretical frameworks. No consensus would ever emerge as to the level of universality to be sought, the level of abstraction at which theory should be pitched, or the particular concepts that should play the central role in it. Indeed, the very proliferation of theoretical frameworks would, over time, undermine the prominence within the behavioral movement of the belief that novel theoretical work was key to a cumulative, systematic science.

The empirical theory project was, however, only one of two strands in the behavioralist agenda for disciplinary change. The movement's vision of a systematic political science pivoted around the ideal of a cumulative interplay of theory and empirical data, and its agenda set out to improve this interplay from both sides. Alongside its promotion of new theoretical frameworks, behavioralism thus also advocated the use of more sophisticated empirical research techniques. When the CPB declared "development of theory" as one of its guiding goals, it also declared "improvement in methods" as its second goal.[33] While the first endeavor of behavioralism ultimately proved rather disappointing—an outcome reflected in the minimal role it now plays in many political scientists' images of what the movement sought—the promotion of techniques for the systematic collection and analysis of data was far more successful. It lies, as a result, at the core of most retrospective images of behavioralism.

---

[31] Easton, *The Political System*, 78.

[32] Harold D. Lasswell and Abraham Kaplan, *Power and Society* (New Haven, CT: Yale University Press 1950); David B. Truman, *The Governmental Process* (New York: Knopf, 1951).

[33] "Committee Briefs: Political Behavior," 20.

When promoting techniques, the behavioral movement looked admiringly to other social sciences, particularly psychology and sociology. While most interwar political scientists favored a low-key empiricism with no preference for, and at times outright hostility to, quantification and statistical analysis, psychology and sociology had, in contrast, housed vibrant neopositivist currents that pioneered and applied quantitative and statistical techniques. Behavioralism aimed at, and in time succeeded in, bringing such techniques into the mainstream of political science. In doing so, behavioralism promulgated a transformed conception of what it meant to be scientific. Being systematic became the leading criterion of being scientific, and being systematic entailed self-reflection about and refinement of the methods used to gather and analyze information and, where possible, using techniques that yield quantitative data and analyze it statistically. Though a preference for quantification and statistics is not a logically necessary concomitant of a call for methodological self-consciousness, the two were intertwined in behavioralism.

The use of survey research in studies of voting behavior and public opinion has long been seen as the paradigmatic example of behavioralist success in transforming political science. As early as 1961, Robert Dahl, in an influential overview of the behavioral movement, anointed the evolution of survey research—from *The People's Choice* study of the 1940 election led by Columbia sociologist Paul Lazarsfeld, up through *The American Voter* study of the 1956 election produced by the interdisciplinary team of psychologically oriented scholars at the University of Michigan's Survey Research Center (SRC)—as the "oldest and best example of the modern scientific outlook at work."[34] The warm reception and subsequent canonization of *The American Voter* (two of its four authors, Warren Miller and Philip Converse, would later become presidents of the APSA) marks a milestone for the rise of survey research in political science. But while this rise was indeed a prominent example of behavioralist success, it should not monopolize our vision of the movement. Excessive concentration on survey research supports, at least in Dahl's article, problematic contentions about the overall character of behavioralism.

A first problematic claim of Dahl's is that behavioralism severed empirical research from theory.[35] Whether or not we think that this belief even does justice to survey research work, it is certainly a misleading image of

---

[34] Robert A. Dahl, "The Behavioral Approach in Political Science: Epitaph to a Monument to a Successful Protest," *American Political Science Review* 55, no. 4 (1961): 768; Paul F. Lazarsfeld, Bernard Berelson, and Hazel Gaudet, *The People's Choice* (New York: Knopf, 1944); Angus Campbell, Philip E. Converse, Warren E. Miller, and Donald Stokes, *The American Voter* (New York: Wiley, 1960).

[35] Dahl, "Behavioral Approach," 770–72.

the behavioral movement as a whole. As I have argued, theory held a central place in behavioralism's vision of a systematic political science, and the search for theoretical frameworks suited to a systematic discipline must be remembered as a core strand of behavioral endeavor. While we may retrospectively debate the success of the theoretical strand of behavioralism, if we do not recognize its role in the movement we cannot understand how behavioralism arose or what it aspired to.

The second problematic claim that an excessive focus on survey research can encourage is the claim that behavioralism turned political science away from the study of history. While, as I shall discuss below, early survey research was unavoidably ahistorical, there are three reasons why this point is insufficient to support an image of behavioralism as a turn away from historical work. In considering this issue we must first take into account the state of play in the discipline before the onset of behavioralism. If we judge a discipline, subfield, or movement to be historical by the extent to which it conducts and prizes original research on the past,[36] then there was little room for behavioralism to make studies of American and comparative politics substantially *more* ahistorical than they already were. Dahl's assertion that almost all studies of the behavioral movement were "a-historical in character" thus cannot be used—as he and others who quote him seek to do—to pick out a trait distinctively characteristic of behavioralism.[37]

There are, in addition, two further reasons why we should be skeptical of the image of behavioralism as a turn away from history. First, we may note that a focus on surveys underplays other quantitative and statistical techniques associated with behavioralism. For the image to hold, the ahistorical charge needs to apply, not only to survey research, but also to these other techniques. Second, we may note that Dahl's 1961 claim is, of temporal necessity, a questionable standpoint upon which to rest our overall image of a movement that was, at that point in time, only beginning to gain its full momentum. If we expand the range of techniques considered and explore the broad arc of behavioral-era developments up into the early 1970s, we see that the movement tended, if anything, to revitalize the study of the past in political science. To support this con-

---

[36] In taking this criterion as my baseline, I intentionally depart from those political scientists who have, in recent decades, intended rather more when wielding the language of "historical" versus "ahistorical." Treating study of the past as necessary, but not sufficient, to be "historical," they have sought to police boundaries between ways of conducting such study that are "historical" and others that are not. My decision to steer clear of this endeavor, in favor of a simpler view of what counts as historical work, should be seen in relation to the critical discussion of these endeavors in chapter 12, and the emphasis on the variety of ways of being historical in the introduction to this volume.

[37] Dahl, "Behavioral Approach," 771.

tention I need to add, however, more nuances to my portrait of behavioralism. Hence I will now turn to explore details in the development of the behavioral movement at the specific level of debates, respectively, in the study of American politics and of comparative politics.

Behavioralism and the Place of History in the Study of American Politics

Approached at the level of an aggregate portrait, behavioralism appears as a movement of young scholars breaking with the disciplinary mainstream. But this movement did not spring from nowhere. To come to a more nuanced understanding of its beginnings, we should consider the role of two political scientists, Pendleton Herring and V. O. Key, Jr., who had made their reputations studying American political behavior before the onset of behavioralism. Herring and Key together offered a combination of intellectual and institutional resources crucial for the consolidation of behavioralism as a movement, and in part also for its character, especially as it took shape in the study of American politics.

Herring and Key stand out as exceptions within the broad current of pre-1950 scholarship on American political behavior. Unlike many other scholars in the area, neither participated in the APSA-sponsored project, chaired by E. E. Schattschneider, that led to "Toward a More Responsible Two-Party System." Indeed, the intellectual work of each was, in its own way, at odds with the project. Herring was the leading exponent of an alternative to the project's ideal of strong, responsible parties. His *The Politics of Democracy* (1940) offered a pluralist vision in which the power of disparate interest groups in America was not a problem, but simply a fact, or perhaps even a positive good.[38] Key, on the other hand, was the discipline's leading practitioner of technically sophisticated empirical work. Trained in the "Chicago School"—the clear outlier department of interwar political science—he had learned quantitative and statistical techniques that, in the 1940s, set him apart. In 1949 he published his classic *Southern Politics*.[39] The book offered a compelling example of the exhaustive, sophisticated work that might be produced by a research team supported by a decent grant (in this case, from the Rockefeller Foundation) and using even quite basic quantitative and statistical techniques. It set a new standard for empirical work such that when "Toward a More Responsible Two-Party System" appeared in 1950, there was a reference point against which the report's qualitative portrait of the American pol-

---

[38] Pendleton Herring, *The Politics of Democracy* (New York: W. W. Norton, 1940).
[39] V.O. Key, Jr., *Southern Politics in State and Nation* (New York: Knopf, 1949).

ity could appear, especially to younger scholars, as impressionistic and uncompelling.

Herring and Key stand out, moreover, not only for the intellectual traits of their work, but also for the institutional positions they held. After a short spell working for the Carnegie Corporation, Herring was appointed president of the SSRC in 1948. By late 1949 he had paved the way for the Committee on Political Behavior and tapped Key to be its first chairman. Through Herring and Key, the CPB was, from its outset, associated both with a pluralist vision of democracy and with a high level of technical skill. This pluralist vision would take on a more refined theoretical form in *The Governmental Process*, by David Truman (an early member of the CPB, and later its chair). The promotion of technical sophistication was, however, a more complex agenda than the promotion of theory. To get political scientists to craft and employ new theoretical frameworks, such as that of Truman's book, was largely a matter of intellectual persuasion. But conduct of systematic empirical work would require skills that very few political scientists had. Promoting such work required a two-pronged strategy: training young political scientists to be able to conduct such work in the future, while also promoting more immediate results by encouraging research on political behavior by scholars from other, more technically sophisticated social sciences.

Opportunities on both these fronts were offered by the recently founded SRC at the University of Michigan. The SRC began, in 1948, to offer a summer institute of training in quantitative and statistical techniques. A summer at the institute would in time become, as it is to this day, a rite of passage for political scientists aspiring to methodological sophistication of the variety associated with the CPB's agenda. Such aspirations would not, however, come out of nowhere. They were spurred by a continuing line of new studies that, as *Southern Politics* had begun to, helped spread the belief that greater technical skills could lead to engaging results in political research. Here the SRC was again crucial. It housed an interdisciplinary set of scholars interested in studying electoral behavior using the techniques of sampling, interviewing, and data analysis that their center was refining. The group had already conducted a small-scale nationwide survey during the 1948 election season, and in the early 1950s the CPB promoted the further development of this line of research. It secured a grant from the Carnegie Corporation for a full-scale survey during the 1952 election season and used it to fund the SRC's carrying out the survey. Carnegie (this time along with the Rockefeller Foundation) again supported a national survey in 1956, this time funding the SRC directly. The data from that survey, together with the data from the other SRC surveys since 1948, provided the basis for *The American Voter*.

While Key, as the chairman of the CPB, helped to promote the SRC's work on electoral behavior, this institutional support existed alongside intellectual differences. Key's own expertise lay not in survey research, but in the gathering, summary, and analysis of aggregate data drawn from census reports and election records. The contrast between this approach and that of survey research is of interest because interplay between the two approaches was central to the dynamic of behavioral-era developments within the study of American politics, and because this interplay helped reinvigorate the pursuit of historical research in the subfield. The aggregate approach had been pioneered before survey research and its practitioners were a fair match for survey scholars with regard to technical skills. What was distinctive about survey research was that rather than relying on published data and records, it generated new data about a realm that the aggregate approach could not investigate: the psychological attitudes of individuals. Survey researchers trumpeted their novel approach as a major addition to political science. They did so both on substantive grounds—arguing that the approach made possible, for the first time, the systematic study of the role of psychological factors in mass politics—and on methodological grounds, by highlighting inferential problems with the ecological techniques used in aggregate analysis.[40]

Aggregationists, most prominently Key and later his student Walter Dean Burnham, sought in turn to establish the continuing import of their own approach. They raised doubts as to whether the questions pursued by survey researchers (who had mostly been trained in sociology or psychology) were always substantively important for political inquiry.[41] The aggregationists also identified and pursued a distinct comparative advantage of their approach. The very novelty of the data generated by surveys limited the chronological reach of survey-based analysis to the time period since the introduction of the method. Aggregate analysis could, in contrast, reach as far back as records permitted. Building on this contrast, the aggregationists sought to insert a historical dimension into the study of electoral behavior. In the 1950s Key published landmark articles on "critical elections" and "secular realignment" in which he explored over time patterns, both of sharp change followed by relative stability and

---

[40] Warren E. Miller, "Party Preference and Attitudes on Political Issues, 1948–1951," *American Political Science Review* 47, no. 1 (1953): 45–46; Campbell and others, *The American Voter*, 12–14, 36–37; Angus Campbell, "Recent Developments in Survey Studies of Political Behavior," in *Essays on the Behavioral Study of Politics*, ed. Austin Ranney (Urbana: University of Illinois Press, 1962), 31–46; Austin Ranney, "The Utility and Limitations of Aggregate Data in the Study of Electoral Behavior," in Ranney, *Essays*, 91–102.

[41] V. O. Key, Jr, "The Politically Relevant in Surveys," *Public Opinion Quarterly* 24, no. 1 (1960): 54–61.

steady change over a long period.[42] This agenda was further developed during the 1960s as Burnham set out to establish the historically bounded character of the behavioral regularities that survey researchers studied. Interpreting major characteristics of the current electorate as historical products of fairly recent vintage, Burnham held that the "political universe" of the late nineteenth century was "so sharply different from the one we all take for granted today that many of our contemporary frames of analytical reference seem irrelevant or misleading in studying it."[43]

The challenge that such historical research appeared to pose to the generalizability of the findings of survey work helped, in turn, to spur new departures among scholars associated with the SRC. Some of them began to pursue aggregate work themselves and to seek to square its results with the contemporary findings of survey research. By the early 1970s a vibrant debate had taken shape regarding the character and causes of change in the late-nineteenth- and early-twentieth-century American polity. It featured Burnham on the one side and, on the other, the prominent SRC scholar Philip Converse and the SRC trained Jerrold Rusk.[44] The dynamic of behavioral developments thus brought fresh debate about the past to the pages of the *APSR*, but the debate was conducted with tables and statistical tests that would have been unintelligible to earlier generations of political scientists. The role of SRC scholars in this debate should cast doubt on any claim that survey researchers were—at least after the initial work of establishing their approach was complete—ahistorical in temperament. Further doubts accrue when we also recognize that as time went on and surveys continued to be done, an increasing time span of data would accumulate, such that it would become more and more possible for survey researchers to directly address questions of change over time using survey data itself.

---

[42] V. O. Key, Jr., "A Theory of Critical Elections," *Journal of Politics* 17, no. 1 (1955): 3–18; V. O. Key, Jr., "Secular Realignment and the Party System," *Journal of Politics* 21, no. 2 (1959): 198–210.

[43] Walter Dean Burnham, "The Changing Shape of the American Political Universe," *American Political Science Review* 59, no. 1 (1965): 22.

[44] Jerrold G. Rusk, "The Effect of the Australian Ballot on Split-Ticket Voting," *American Political Science Review* 64, no. 4 (1970): 1220–38; Walter Dean Burnham and Jerrold G. Rusk, "Communications," *American Political Science Review* 65, no. 4 (1971): 1149–57; Philip E. Converse, "Change in the American Electorate," in *The Human Meaning of Social Change*, ed. Angus Campbell and Philip E. Converse (New York: Sage, 1972), 263–337; Walter Dean Burnham, "Theory and Voting Research: Some Reflections on Converse's 'Change in the American Electorate,'" *American Political Science Review* 68, no. 3 (1974): 1002–23; Philip E. Converse, "Comment," *American Political Science Review* 68, no. 3 (1974): 1024–27; Jerrold G. Rusk, "Comment," *American Political Science Review* 68, no. 3 (1974): 1028–49.

An upward trajectory of historical research in the study of American politics during the behavioral era is also evident beyond the confines of the exchange between survey scholars and aggregationists. While I earlier suggested that Dahl's 1961 "a-historical" claim might be seen as skewed by the limited range of techniques and time considered, we may also note that in making the claim he was, in effect, doing product differentiation for his own *Who Governs?*[45] In this 1961 behavioral classic, Dahl marshaled an array of techniques (and graduate research assistants) in a detailed study of New Haven politics that challenged views that had dominated the study of community power for decades. The book wedded the systematic empirical work associated with behavioralism to the pluralist empirical theory with which the movement had also, from the founding of the CPB, been associated. Dahl argued that a pluralist vision was the best way to capture the dynamics of power in present-day New Haven, but he did not present pluralism as a timeless verity. Instead he began *Who Governs?* with an extended historical section that saw pluralism as the most recent stage in an ongoing series of changes that had moved the city away from the oligarchy that characterized it in the late eighteenth and early nineteenth centuries. Later in the 1960s one of the research assistants on Dahl's New Haven study, Nelson Polsby, would go on to help pioneer a new literature on the historical evolution of the U.S. Congress.[46] Considered beside the arc of the interchange between aggregate and survey work, these additional examples from the study of American politics offer further support for contending that behavioralism was not antithetical to, and even served to promote, the study of the past by political scientists.

My discussion to this point has, however, skated over something of an epistemological divide. I also have not considered what boundary there might be to the range of scholarship that falls within the confines of "behavioralism." To address these questions it helps to turn again to the SRC tradition, Key, and Burnham. While agreeing that generalizations can be found that hold for limited time periods, these leading practitioners of survey and aggregate work disagreed with regard to what, if anything,

[45] Robert A. Dahl, *Who Governs?* (New Haven, CT: Yale University Press, 1961).

[46] Nelson W. Polsby, "The Institutionalization of the House of Representatives," *American Political Science Review* 62, no. 1 (1968): 142–68; Nelson W. Polsby, Miriam Gallaher, and Barry Spencer Rundquist, "The Growth of the Seniority System in the U.S. House of Representatives," *American Political Science Review* 63, no. 3 (1969): 787–807. In the 1970s this agenda in the history of Congress was forwarded by major contributions from Joseph Cooper and David Brady. See, for example, Joseph Cooper, *The Origins of the Standing Committees and Development of the Modern House* (Houston: Rice University Publications, 1970); David W. Brady and Philip Althoff, "Party Voting in the U.S. House of Representatives, 1890–1910," *Journal of Politics* 36, no. 3 (1974): 753–75.

political science could aspire to beyond this. The authors of *The American Voter* suggested that attending to the kind of factors addressed by aggregate studies could indeed produce only historically limited findings. But they hoped that survey work, by permitting scholars to probe psychological mechanisms, might reveal more "deep-seated 'laws' of social behavior"—laws that might, in turn, explain the historical changes that aggregate work had come to focus on.[47] This aspiration expressed a positivist epistemology that framed scientific achievement relative to an ideal of discovering general laws subsuming the ebb and flow of more historically delimited phenomena.

Key, in contrast, held a modernist empiricist aspiration for political science. His work updated the empiricist attitude prevalent in the political science of his youth so as to incorporate modernist preferences for quantification where possible and for empirical theory. But he did so without breaking with empiricism. When Key used his 1958 APSA Presidential Address to advocate "systematic analysis," he framed the goal of such analysis in *contrast* to the production of "grand hypotheses." Whatever beguiling "psychic satisfactions" such hypotheses might offer, they failed, Key held, to come to terms with the "incorrigibility" of political data. He argued that political science should instead seek "modest general propositions" and always remember that the "verified general proposition of one era may not hold at a later time."[48]

In the contrast between Key's address and the hope expressed in *The American Voter* we see a space of contention take shape that delimits the diversity within behavioralism. This space has marked out the mainstream in American political science ever since: it encompasses lively debate between evolving neopositivist and modernist-empiricist variants of the aspiration to a "systematic" political science forged during the consolidation and rise of behavioralism. Both of these variants can allow for, and at times even cherish, research on the past. But the space of contention is contained, and so also is the accompanying range of historical work found within the disciplinary mainstream. To study the past in a way that breaks with the beliefs underpinning the ideal of a systematic political science is to leave the mainstream.

We can get a sense for this boundary line by considering the development of Burnham's work up into the 1970s. Burnham's earliest work falls within the boundaries of behavioralism. But over time he increasingly moved beyond the limits of this endeavor. Rather than restricting his attention to the domain in which his own systematic gathering and analysis of empiri-

---

[47] Campbell and others, *The American Voter*, 36–37.

[48] V. O. Key, Jr., "The State of the Discipline," *American Political Science Review* 52, no. 4 (1958): 961.

cal data focused, Burnham took his studies as a jumping-off point for a synthetic narrative of American political history. In crafting this narrative he relied on claims about American political thought and institutions made by Louis Hartz and Samuel Huntington.[49] The narrative Burnham offered was nothing if not provocative. He envisioned the difference between nineteenth- and twentieth-century America as a tale of the triumph of capitalism at a great cost to democracy, and this in turn led him to darkly pessimistic views about the future prospects of the American polity.[50]

Behavioralism emphasized the need to go beyond reporting facts when the goal was the pursuit of empirical theory, but the debates of the early 1970s revealed a distinct lack of comfort with the synthetic pursuit on display in Burnham's historical narrative.[51] This form of synthesis requires a creative subjectivity hard to square with notions of science—whether positivist or modernist empiricist—that equate being scientific with being systematic. To compare synthetic narratives is to be reminded that when faced with the same set of facts about the past, different observers may offer competing narratives between which there may be no objective criterion on which to choose.[52] This makes synthetic historical narratives hard to square with the ideal of systematic empirical research that is fully explicit about its methods and cumulative over time. Burnham's commitment to historical synthesis moved his work beyond the boundaries of behavioralism, such that, to his critics, he increasingly seemed to be refusing to play by the rules of systematic empirical research, at least as they understood them.

Comparative Politics, History, and the Study of Political Development

While large changes occurred in the study of American politics in the 1950s and 1960s, a broader set of shifts took place among comparative

[49] The key works drawn on by Burnham are Louis Hartz, *The Liberal Tradition in America* (New York: Harcourt Brace and World, 1955) and Samuel P. Huntington, "Political Modernization: America vs. Europe," *World Politics* 18, no. 3 (1966): 378–414, reprinted in *Political Order in Changing Societies* (New Haven, CT: Yale University Press, 1968).

[50] Burnham, "Changing Shape," 22–28; Walter Deam Burnham, *Critical Elections and the Mainsprings of American Politics* (New York: Norton, 1970), esp. chap 7; Walter Dean Burnham, "Revitalization and Decay," *Journal of Politics* 38, no. 3 (1976): 146–72.

[51] See the exchanges between Burnham, Converse, and Rusk cited in n. 44.

[52] The role of subjectivity in shaping synthetic narratives was made evident when Huntington came to offer his own synthesis, which—while drawing his earlier notions together with the views of Hartz and Burnham's work—differed fundamentally from Burnham's pessimistic vision. See Samuel P. Huntington, *American Politics* (Cambridge: Harvard University Press, Belknap Press, 1981).

scholars. Talk of a "behavioral revolution" is perhaps on its surest ground in connection with this intellectual break, in which the concerns and perspectives of the largely European generation prominent in the subfield in the 1930s and 1940s were rapidly supplanted by a new generation of American scholars.

The break got underway in 1952 when the CPB brought together a group of young scholars who produced a report advocating a new direction for their subfield. Published in the *APSR* in 1953, the report charged prior work with being too "descriptive," having a "formalistic" focus on governmental institutions, and a "parochial" focus on Europe. Its authors advocated a new "comparative politics" that would break with earlier scholarship (or, at least, their image of such scholarship) on all three fronts.[53] This article marked the opening of a concerted campaign. Shortly afterward, the CPB initiated formation of a second SSRC committee, the Committee on Comparative Politics (CCP), to promote the proposed transformation. In 1955 a further pair of articles, produced by two CCP subcommittees, appeared in the *APSR* spelling out visions for the future study of Western Europe and of non-Western countries.[54]

Together the three articles illuminate the full set of changes that the CCP was to promote over the next two decades. These changes drew on a variety of influences, from earlier trends in the study of American politics to recent developments in sociological theory. They were, in turn, furthered by the work of multiple scholars, many of whom were involved with only some part of the overall transformation advocated by the CCP. Hence, while the set of changes taken as a whole provides the best aggregate image of what behavioralism stood for in comparative politics, specific changes were sometimes pursued by individuals, such as Samuel Beer, who are not usually remembered as "behavioralists." We find, however, an unambiguous exemplar of the movement in Gabriel Almond, who chaired the CCP from its 1954 founding until 1964 and who directly contributed to each of the four major intellectual changes promoted by the committee.

In a first shift, comparative scholars were urged to catch up with trends in the study of American politics by devoting new research to political behavior. In its exaggerated moments, this call slighted the extent to which

[53] Roy C. Macridis and Richard Cox, "Research in Comparative Politics," *American Political Science Review* 47, no. 3 (1953): 641–75.

[54] George M. Kahin, Guy J. Pauker, and Lucian W. Pye, "Comparative Politics of Non-Western Countries," *American Political Science Review* 49, no. 4 (1955): 1022–41; Gabriel A. Almond, Taylor Cole, and Roy C. Macridis, "A Suggested Research Strategy in Western European Government and Politics," *American Political Science Review* 49, no. 4 (1955): 1042–49.

earlier comparative scholars had already pursued such research. But there was room for more attention to behavior topics, especially to pressure groups, and new research along these lines flourished in the years ahead. Two attendees of the 1952 CPB conference, Beer and Harry Eckstein, would, for example, soon undertake in Britain the kind of in-depth study of pressure groups that had developed in the United States during the interwar decades.[55]

In a second change, concentration on Europe was rejected in favor of a worldwide focus. As decolonization swept through Asia and Africa in the 1950s and 1960s and the superpowers competed for the allegiance of new political elites, young American scholars from across the social sciences turned their attention to the new nations. In political science the discussion about totalitarianism in Europe was rapidly displaced as "modernization" instead came to the center of concern. Under the guidance of the CCP this concern in turn came, during the 1960s, to center specifically on the study of "political development."[56]

In a third change, there was a theoretical effort to craft a conceptual scheme capable of encompassing the subfield's diversifying concerns in a single, universally applicable, analytical framework. Though modernist efforts to order comparative study around analytical frameworks had been pursued in the 1930s by Friedrich and Finer, the CCP generation—in accord with their aspiration to study countries from across the globe in a single framework—pursued such efforts with a new vocabulary and at a higher level of abstraction. Their conversation gravitated toward a functionalist systems theory that took the "political system" as its core unit of analysis. One key influence here was the elaboration of functional theorizing in the work of sociologists like Parsons.[57] But other influences, such as Easton's *The Political System* and work by British social anthropologists on African politics,[58] also supported the concept of the political system. At least initially, this emerging framework attracted a wider set of scholars than is often remembered today. Thus, for example, in 1958 Beer was promoting a view of the "science of politics" that took the "political system," approached in "structural-functional" terms, as the unify-

[55] Samuel H. Beer, "Pressure Groups and Parties in Britain," *American Political Science Review* 50, no. 1 (1956): 1–23; Harry Eckstein, *Pressure Group Politics* (Stanford, CA: Stanford University Press, 1960).

[56] On modernization theory in the social sciences as a whole see Gilman, *Mandarins*. For the concern with "political development," see the volumes of the CCP-sponsored *Studies in Political Development* series, starting with Lucian W. Pye, ed., *Communications and Political Development* (Princeton, NJ: Princeton University Press, 1963).

[57] Talcott Parsons, *The Social System* (Glencoe, IL: Free Press, 1951).

[58] Meyer Fortes and E. E. Evans-Pritchard, *African Political Systems* (London: Oxford University Press, 1940).

ing core of a universalizing comparative subfield.[59] It was, however, Almond's variant of this endeavor, as laid out in the opening chapter of the 1960 edited volume, *The Politics of the Developing Areas*, that left the greatest mark on disciplinary memory.[60]

A fourth and final change promoted as part of the movement for a new comparative politics—and the one that most closely parallels behavioralism in the subfield of American politics—was the rise of quantitative and statistical techniques. While Bryce and Lowell had earlier studied public opinion comparatively, this research topic would be transformed by the application of survey research methods. A major role here was again played by Almond. He had drawn on the SRC's early 1948 surveys in *The American People and Foreign Policy* (1950), and again drew on survey results in his early comparative book, *The Appeals of Communism* (1954). Then, in the late 1950s, Almond began working with Sidney Verba to organize new surveys of citizen attitudes and socialization in five different countries. Their research project led up to the behavioral classic *The Civic Culture* (1963).

As in the study of American politics, the use of new techniques was not limited to survey research. Another line of technical development centered on the collection and statistical analysis of macrolevel quantitative data about as many nations as possible. This line of work had been developing outside political science for some time, and the most influential early example of its entry into the discipline's discussions came from the sociologist (but also later APSA president), Seymour Martin Lipset. In the late 1950s he undertook, with CCP support, a cross-national study of the "social requisites of democracy." The results appeared first in a landmark *APSR* article in 1959 and then again in Lipset's 1960 *Political Man*.[61]

Amid these transformations, what happened to historical studies? Two main factors set the tone here. First, the rising tide of behavioralism was bringing comparative political scientists into close conversation with sociology just as the latter discipline was itself undergoing a revival of historical work. Secondly, there was the attitude of Almond, who was, both institutionally and intellectually, the leading figure in the behavioral movement in comparative politics. As a doctoral student at the interwar

[59] Samuel H. Beer, "The Analysis of Political Systems," in *Patterns of Government: The Major Political Systems of Europe*, ed. Samuel H. Beer and Adam B. Ulam (New York: Random House, 1958).

[60] Gabriel A. Almond, "A Functional Approach to Comparative Politics," in *The Politics of the Developing Areas*, ed. Gabriel A. Almond and James S. Coleman (Princeton, NJ: Princeton University Press, 1960).

[61] Seymour Martin Lipset, "Some Social Requisites of Democracy," *American Political Science Review* 53, no. 1 (1959): 69–105; Seymour Martin Lipset, *Political Man* (Garden City, NY: Doubleday, 1960).

University of Chicago, Almond had done a historical dissertation on the place of elites in New York City politics. He had also inherited, from his mentor Merriam, the belief that political science must embrace topical, technical, and theoretical innovations, but that this could be done in a way that would cumulatively build upon, rather than reject, the original historical thrust of the discipline.

The Civic Culture opened with a paean to Merriam and the study of citizen socialization he had organized. This opening was followed by a first chapter in which Almond and Verba situated their survey-based analysis of contemporary political cultures in relation to the history of each of the five countries for which they had gathered data. In doing so, they approached their study as an exemplar of how behavioral techniques and older historical approaches could be "supplemental and mutually supportive." If, as most historians believed, differences in historical experiences are basic to an understanding of contemporary political differences, then there must be some way in which the past lives on in the present. Almond and Verba homed in on one way that this might occur: via the historical shaping of a national political culture handed down over time. It was here that surveys came in. By revealing the attitudes of a representative sample of contemporary citizens, surveys offered a way to assess the extent to which "a country's historical experience" actually "lives on in the memories, feelings, and expectations of its population."[62]

If The Civic Culture succeeded in suggesting a way that new quantitative and statistical techniques might supplement historical inquiry, it also left open a crucial issue. The results of such techniques might be used in formulating narratives of national political history (as Burnham did for America), but they could also be used to pursue alternative epistemological ends. In particular, when combined with the kind of conceptual scheme sought by empirical theory, these techniques might be used in formulating and testing claims about recurring relationships between abstractly conceived variables. It was precisely in order to facilitate such an agenda that Almond had turned to empirical theory. His initial formulation of a functionalist theory of the political system was, however, criticized as ill suited for the study of political change. Faced with such charges, Almond set out in the early 1960s to craft a general theoretical framework better suited to this study.[63] In doing so he pursued a goal laid out in the initial APSR manifesto of 1953 and broadly shared in the

[62] Gabriel A. Almond and Sidney Verba, The Civic Culture: Political Attitudes and Democracy in Five Nations (Princeton, NJ: Princeton University Press, 1963), vii, chap. 1, 41.

[63] Gabriel A. Almond, "Political Systems and Political Change," American Behavioral Scientist 6 (1963): 3–10; Gabriel A. Almond, "A Developmental Approach to Political Systems," World Politics 17, no. 2 (1965): 183–214.

intellectual community surrounding the CCP. Indeed, alongside Almond's own effort, the CCP, under his successor as chair, Lucien Pye, also pursued its own collaborative version of this venture. Both projects culminated in edited volumes published in the 1970s.[64]

These projects shared a universalizing conception of the kind of theory that they sought. Their goal was to formulate a general framework of abstract categories that could encompass the characteristics of as many cases as possible—a goal that presupposed a positivist ideal. The hope was that as more and more examples of both historical and contemporary political change were studied within a single framework, knowledge claims about recurring relationships would take shape and be cumulatively refined. The approach to historical research engendered by this hope was suggested by the way that Almond welcomed the comparative historical studies published in the early 1960s by Lipset and his fellow sociologists, Reinhard Bendix and S. N. Eisenstadt.[65] For Almond the studies were, like research on contemporary developing nations, examples of "the impulse towards sampling more completely the universe of man's experience with politics."[66]

The theory of change that behavioral scholars advanced was centered on a typology of "crises." These were problems that all politically "developed" nations were thought to have faced at one point or another in their past and that the new nations would, in turn, have to deal with if they were to attain a similar level of "political development." Almond's theory centered on a set of four crises, while the CCP's collaborative effort came up with five: crises of identity, of legitimacy, of participation, of penetration, and of distribution. Every country's political history was, Almond explained, to be studied in terms of "the order in which they [the crises] were experienced, their magnitude and intensity, their separate or simultaneous incidence, and the ways in which elite groups in these political systems responded to these challenges." Through this process "temporal or historical episodes" would take "their final form as essentially analytic formulations in which historic time is converted into changes in the values

[64] Gabriel A. Almond, Scott C. Flanagan, and Robert J. Mundt, eds., *Crisis, Choice, and Change: Historical Studies of Political Development* (Boston: Little, Brown, 1973); Leonard Binder, James S. Coleman, Joseph LaPalombara, Lucian W. Pye, Sidney Verba, and M. Weiner, eds., *Crises and Sequences in Political Development* (Princeton, NJ: Princeton University Press, 1971); Raymond Grew, ed., *Crises of Political Development in Europe and the United States* (Princeton, NJ: Princeton University Press, 1978).

[65] S. N. Eisenstadt, *The Political Systems of Empires* (New York: Free Press, 1963); Seymour Martin Lipset, *The First New Nation* (New York: Norton, 1963); Reinhard Bendix, *Nation-Building and Citizenship* (New York: Wiley, 1964).

[66] Gabriel A. Almond and G. Bingham Powell, Jr., *Comparative Politics: A Developmental Approach* (Boston: Little, Brown, 1966), 6.

and properties of our variables."[67] This conversion process was, of course, markedly different from the approach of most historians, who, when they bring several historical episodes together, usually seek synthesis in the form of an encompassing historical narrative, rather than in the form of claims about recurring relations between abstractly defined variables.

The scholars of crisis theory saw their theoretical work as laying a basis for a systematic comparative history. Pursuit of this project would require comparative studies of European and American political history harking in certain respects back to the earliest days of the comparative government subfield. But framing comparisons of national histories in terms of a universalized set of abstract categories marked a distinctive post–World War II innovation, suggesting a shift toward a positivist epistemology. This shift accompanied the focusing of practical concerns toward advising new nations on how to set about becoming politically more like America and its European allies. The "parochial" focus of earlier comparative scholars had, by contrast, reflected both a different epistemology—one that saw the range of instructive comparison as historically and culturally bounded—and a practical focus on advising about changes and challenges arising within America and Europe.

The universalizing dimension of the CCP's agenda was, however, never without critics, and the aspiration to provide a unifying framework for a diversifying subfield was, if ever, only briefly fulfilled. Concerns were voiced at the outset by one of the leading figures of the prior generation. In a response to the initial 1953 report in the *APSR*, Friedrich held that comparative political science should focus on problems that were historically specific to certain countries at certain points in time, and worried that the subfield would lose contact with such problems if it pursued a path of "excessive abstraction."[68] By the early 1960s some members of the postwar generation were voicing similar concerns. For example, Beer at this point broke with his earlier stance and rejected the "dogma of universality" and the "utopia of a universal theory."[69] His move illustrated the growing presence in the new comparative politics of a modernist empiricism that, while more qualitatively oriented than that of Beer's Harvard colleague Key, paralleled Key's desire to stake out a position committed

[67] Gabriel A. Almond, "Approaches to Developmental Causation," in Almond, Flanagan, and Mundt, *Crisis, Choice, and Change*, 3–4, 28.

[68] Carl J. Friedrich, "Comments on the Seminar Report," *American Political Science Review* 47, no. 3 (1953): 658–61.

[69] Samuel H. Beer, "Causal Explanation and Imaginative Re-enactment," *History and Theory* 3, no. 1 (1963): 8, 13; Samuel H. Beer, "Political Science and History," in *Essays in Theory and History: An Approach to the Social Sciences*, ed. Melvin Richter (Cambridge: Harvard University Press, 1970).

to systematic inquiry, but also suspicious of specifically neopositivist interpretations of what such inquiry could and should aspire to.

Early doubts about the universalizing dimensions of behavioralism were, however, only pale precursors to the wholesale rejection of most of the literature associated with the CCP that took shape in the 1970s. The generally disappointing results of American efforts—in which social scientists were often directly involved—to promote development in the new nations and the particular failure of their work to aid the war effort in Vietnam had, by the early 1970s, made the modernization/development framework appear increasingly unsatisfactory. By the time that the edited volumes of the crisis literature finally appeared during the 1970s, their pursuit of a general theory of political development marked them as lingering survivals of an increasingly unfashionable endeavor; crisis theory would rapidly sink into caricatured oblivion alongside the broader currents of modernization theory and functionalism, out of which it had grown. While the CCP had succeeded in remaking the study of comparative politics, much of its scholarship would end up serving as a straw man rather than an inspiration for the next generation in the subfield.

Young comparative scholars who received their graduate training amid the social and political ferment of the late 1960s and early 1970s often found their intellectual inspiration outside political science. Indeed, in an ironic extension of the interdisciplinarity that behavioralism had promoted, young scholars drew on sociological literatures—such as dependency theory and world-systems theory—that had emerged from criticisms of the sociological works that scholars of the CCP had drawn on.[70] Among the range of works attracting younger scholars, perhaps the most influential were the variants of comparative historical sociology found in Bendix's *Nation-Building and Citizenship* and Barrington Moore, Jr.'s *Social Origins of Dictatorship and Democracy*. Among the diverse scholars who helped revive historical work in sociology, Bendix and Moore stood out for their shared hostility to theoretical abstraction with universalizing aims. This set them apart from other historical sociologists, such as Eisenstadt and Neil Smelser, and thereby suggested that they offered an alternative to the strands of sociology and political science that a new generation of scholars were taking up as their bête noire. Young comparativists saw Bendix and Moore, accurately or not, as pointing the way to a modernist empiricist comparative politics, analytical enough to count as systematic, but rejecting the positivist aspiration to treat all cases within a single, universal framework.

---

[70] For a discussion of the flux in the subfield at this time and the sociological works drawn on, see Peter Evans and John D. Stephens, "Studying Development since the Sixties," *Theory and Society* 17, no. 5 (1988): 713–45.

The 1970s hence saw, as had the 1950s, a generation of young scholars crafting their agendas as a rejection of their disciplinary predecessors and looking outside political science for inspiration. The lingering links to interwar political science still found in some works of the behavioral generation—especially those of Almond—were almost entirely severed by this second generation of intellectual rebellion. Detached from debts to, let alone a sympathetic engagement with, the pre-1950 discipline, the next generation of scholars would be free to reappropriate that past in an image of "old institutionalism" that would testify more eloquently to the desire for novelty than to the actual content of scholarship in the prebehavioral decades.

Conclusion

Our image of behavioralism's place in the evolution of American political science should take on varying characteristics depending on whether we attend to the topics the movement wished the discipline to research, the empirical techniques it promoted, or the kind of theory it sought to develop and bring into interplay with empirical research. As we have seen, political behavior topics such as public opinion and pressure groups were well established by the 1940s, especially among scholars of American politics. Hence, when we consider the CCP's effort to further such topics in the comparative subfield, we should envision this simply as extending a longer-term trend within political science.

When we switch to consider techniques, our image of the behavioral movement should, however, take on a different character. Here behavioralism was genuinely revolutionary and also firmly interdisciplinary. As a result of the movement's endeavors, research techniques that require considerable technical skills and first grew up outside political science—such as survey research and cross-national statistical work—became central strands in the mainstream of the discipline. They continue as such to the present day, and indeed, since the 1970s, have perhaps fared better in political science than in the disciplines in which they first developed. It is thus unsurprising that when political scientists today envision behavioralism as a turning point in the history of the discipline, they most commonly have in mind research employing quantitative and statistical techniques.

That common association is, however, problematic to the extent that it can obscure the substantial, yet more complex, and thus less memorable, impact of behavioralism's theoretical efforts. Behavioralism pursued a conception of theory as centered on the use of self-conscious abstraction to produce analytical frameworks, which were in turn believed to be useful, even essential, for scientific progress. This belief built on a vision of interactive refinement between such theory and systematic empirical research as the key to cumulative progress. Behavioralism was notably successful in propagating this conception of theory and this vision of intellectual progress; in broad outline the same conception and vision remain prevalent in much of American political science to the current day. This impact is, however, obscured by the fact that, at the level of specific theoretical frameworks, the trajectory of behavioralism's endeavors was one of high initial hopes giving way to disappointment and even disintegration. The movement thus propagated a conception of what theory should do, but the actual candidates it offered to play that role had a much shorter half-life than the conception itself.

It is against this backdrop that we might understand two longer-term shifts whose results continue to play out up to the present day. The first such shift grows out of the emergence of contention between modernist empiricist and neopositivist conceptions of systematic science as the primary ground of methodological debate in political science. The divergence between these stances is most evident in their responses to the gap between behavioralism's aspiration and its performance in the domain of theory. On the one hand, the modernist empiricist diagnoses the problem here as one of excessive abstraction and prescribes "midrange" theory that retains the conception of theory popularized by behavioralism but rejects efforts to theorize at a universal level. In contrast, the neopositivist holds the notion of scientific progress underlying the above conception of theory to be, at best, only partially furthered by midrange theory. Their response is not to reject the universalism commonly pursued in behavioralism's theoretical efforts, but to ask whether the shortcomings of these efforts might not derive from another source.

This leads into the second longer-term shift: the rise of rational-choice theory in political science. Rational-choice theory first developed during the decades of the behavioral movement but—with the exception of William Riker and the Rochester department that he led—it had little impact on political science during the heyday of the behavioral movement. Two key differences set it apart from the sociological theories prominent in behavioralism. First, its use of axiomatic reasoning gave it a formally deductive internal structure. Second, it started from microlevel assumptions about individuals, rather than macrolevel assumptions about political systems or societies. When the theoretical endeavors of behavioralism lost favor in the 1970s, rational-choice theory offered a ready alternative. It was at once similar enough in its broad conception of theory and different enough in the structure and substance of its theory to suggest a new road toward realizing a neopositivistic variant of the systematic science ideal that behavioralism had so successfully propagated.

Ten

The Remaking of Political Theory

ROBERT ADCOCK AND MARK BEVIR

POLITICAL THEORY, we are often told, lay moribund in the 1950s. Among the biggest clichés in the history of contemporary political theory are Isaiah Berlin's fears about the continuing life of political theory and Peter Laslett's famous declaration that "for the time being anyway political philosophy is dead."[1] Today these obituaries for political theory are invoked most often as a prelude to a celebration of its rebirth. We are told that almost before the ink had dried on Berlin's and Laslett's manuscripts, John Rawls, Quentin Skinner, or Sheldon Wolin had begun the intellectual labors that have since led to a golden age of theory. William Connolly implies, for example, that Wolin battled the forces of behavioralism so as to make the world safe again for political theorists.[2] Perhaps these heroic

---

[1] Isaiah Berlin, "Does Political Theory Still Exist?" in *Concepts and Categories*, ed. Henry Hardy (Oxford: Penguin, 1979); and Peter Laslett, "Introduction," in *Politics, Philosophy and Society*, 1st ser., ed. Peter Laslett (Oxford: Blackwell, 1956), viii. Similar concerns about a decline of political philosophy appeared in America, where Strauss declared it to be "in a state of decay and perhaps of putrefaction, if it has not vanished altogether," and Judith Shklar set out to study how its "disappearance" had come to pass. See Leo Strauss, "What Is Political Philosophy?" in *What Is Political Philosophy?* (Chicago: University of Chicago Press, 1959), 17; and Judith N. Shklar, *After Utopia* (Princeton, NJ: Princeton University Press, 1957), vii.

[2] William E. Connolly, "Politics and Vision," in *Democracy and Vision: Sheldon Wolin and the Vicissitudes of the Political*, ed. Areyh Botwinick and William E. Connolly (Princeton, NJ: Princeton University Press, 2001), 3–22. Also see Jason A. Frank and John Tamborino, "Introduction," in *Vocations of Political Theory*, ed. Jason A. Frank and John Tamborino, (Minneapolis: University of Minnesota Press, 2000), x–xi. On Skinner see Richard Tuck, "The Contribution of History," in *A Companion to Contemporary Political Philosophy*, ed. Robert E. Goodin and Philip Pettit (Oxford: Basil Blackwell, 1993), 72–89. Tuck's more measured argument is that Rawls revived political philosophy so that debates about fundamental values no longer were conducted through studies of past thinkers, thereby creating a space in which Skinner and others could establish a return to history. Whatever the merits of this argument, it does not appear to apply to Skinner himself, for he has said that when he set out on his research, "the idea of studying normative political theory had been made to seem old-fashioned and slightly absurd." See Petri Koikkalainen and Sami Syrjämäki, "Interview with Quentin Skinner," *Finnish Yearbook of Political Thought* 6 (2002): 37.

narratives convey a proper sense of the impact of Rawls, Skinner, or Wolin on the lives of some of their pupils and readers: the varying choice of saviors certainly can be a suggestive indicator of distinctive traditions in contemporary debates. As intellectual history, however, these heroic narratives are at best oversimplifications.

For a start, political theory—perhaps in contrast to moral philosophy—was alive and well in the 1950s. Work continued to appear within the "ideas and institutions" tradition, which had roots in developmental historicism and which had dominated the subfield of political theory since it first took shape around the turn of the century. Political theory was actually invigorated, especially in America, by the infusion of perspectives from the intellectual ferment of continental Europe, following the arrival of émigrés such as Leo Strauss. When the behavioral movement arose in America, moreover, it was no demonic scientism, and it never succeeded in sweeping aside all political theory. On the contrary, throughout the 1950s, behavioralism was a marginal heterodoxy while much of political theory remained part of the mainstream of political science. No doubt by the end of the 1960s behavioral arguments had gained significant ground across much of political science and helped to inspire, at least in America, a redefinition of the relationship of political theory to the rest of the discipline. Even then, however, behavioralism never came close either to taking over the subfield of political theory or to eliminating it. Turning, finally, to the idea of a resurgence of political theory in the 1960s, we see that it is true that distinctive approaches emerged then in the work of Wolin and Skinner, but these approaches are better characterized as responses to the intellectual ferment of the prior decade—responses informed by earlier traditions—than as a rebirth after a period of quiet or even death. Wolin and Skinner reworked the developmental historicism of the ideas and institutions tradition in two divergent directions: so as, respectively, either to merge it with émigré-influenced epic theory or to give its historicism a more radical edge.

The "Ideas and Institutions" Tradition

The problematic notion of the death of political theory arises less from the actual arguments made by Berlin and Laslett than from later interpretations of their claims. When people interpret these claims as equivalent to reports on the state of political theory in the 1950s, they mistakenly assimilate all of political theory to the specific philosophical activity to which Berlin and Laslett referred. Such philosophy was, indeed, far from constituting the dominant activity of political theorists. In Britain and America alike, political theorists characteristically spent more time studying, teaching, and writing about philosophical texts from earlier times than they did attempting to produce their own, novel philosophies. The subfield here displayed its long-standing debt to the older vision of an education in moral philosophy: young minds were to be trained to take their place in the world through the teaching of a canon of great texts. This debt was particularly strong in Britain, where faith in the moral value of the study of politics persisted more strongly than it did in America. Indeed, when Ernest Barker gave his inaugural lecture as professor of Political Science at the University of Cambridge in 1928, he described the study of politics as "a province" of "moral philosophy."[3] This debt to moral philosophy meant that political theory engaged not only topics such as the state and obligation but also those of freedom, property, and justice. Hence, Westel Willoughby—second only to William Dunning as a founder of political theory as a distinct subfield in America—expounded not only on themes such as "the individual and the state," but also on social justice and, in doing so, drew explicitly and extensively on the work of T. H. Green.[4]

Apart from moral philosophy, political theory also drew on the theory of the state and on constitutional history.[5] The theory of the state brought to the subfield a concern both with the classification of types of government and with the formal and legal analysis of institutions within the state. While scholars gave a prominent place here to Aristotle, they also paid attention to the state in its specifically modern form, as theorized in the work of Hegel, Bluntschli, and others. The formal, abstract character of the theory of state meant it overlapped with moral philosophy in addressing issues of rights and duties. Equally, its legalistic orientation produced an overlap with constitutional law and history—the other major inspiration for political theory as it took form in the late nineteenth and early twentieth centuries. At Cambridge, where the history tripos acted as a home for the study of politics, the legal historian F. W. Maitland battled against Alfred Marshall, John Seeley, and Henry Sidgwick to promote the study of legal documents, rather than abstract treatises, as a means to understand political institutions.[6] Constitutional history

---

[3] Ernest Barker, "The Study of Political Science," in *Church, State, and Study: Essays* (London: Methuen, 1930), 210.

[4] Westel W. Willoughby, "The Individual and the State," *American Political Science Review* 8, no. 1 (1914): 1–13; Westel W. Willoughby, *Social Justice: A Critical Essay* (New York: Macmillan, 1900).

[5] Barker appealed in his inaugural lecture to the similar categories of "moral philosophy," "law," and "history" while adding a fourth—"psychology"—to capture the protobehavioralism of theorists such as Wallas. See Barker, "Study of Political Science."

[6] Stefan Collini, Donald Winch and John Burrow, *That Noble Science of Politics* (Cambridge: Cambridge University Press, 1983), 341–63. Also see David Runciman, *Pluralism and the Personality of the State* (Cambridge: Cambridge University Press, 1997), 89–123.

brought to political theory a concern with law, authority, and institutions. In some hands, this involved Whiggish studies of the progressive evolution of liberty within the British or American polity. In other hands, it involved critical studies of the contingent rise of our present arrangements or attempts to recover worlds we had lost—this latter strand appears most clearly perhaps among the pluralists who followed Maitland, notably J. N. Figgis.[7] Either way, the place of constitutional history in political theory ensured that the canon included thinkers who were thought to be of crucial importance in the development of national, and at times international, institutions. In Britain, Bentham and J. S. Mill joined the canon in part because of the supposed impact of utilitarianism on nineteenth-century reforms of the state. In America, the founding fathers occupied a place in the canon largely on account of their historical importance as the creators of institutions.

Political theory could bring together moral philosophy, the theory of the state, and constitutional history with some comfort because they all embodied a diffuse idealism.[8] This diffuse idealism also helped to cement the relationship between political theorists and other students of politics. Most students of politics saw the study of political development as a guiding concern of their discipline, and they believed that this study could be pursued, at least in part, by means of an investigation of the most reflective expressions of the ideas that informed its various stages. This ideas and institutions approach emerged either from British idealism or, especially in America, from Hegel by way of German historical scholarship. It suggested that the study of politics should center on ideas, institutions, and their interplay and development. When the first chair of politics was established at Oxford in 1912, it had the title Gladstone Chair of Political Theory and Institutions. In America too, political theory complemented political science: it, first, provided students with a historical survey of political ideas framed in relation to the development of institutions and, second, introduced them to the concepts employed across the discipline. What is more, these two aspects of political theory easily blended into one another, since scholars of politics believed that their basic concepts constituted the more reflexive and successful of those that had evolved alongside the historical refinement of political institutions.

Throughout the first decades of the twentieth century, the history of political thought thus flourished on both sides of the Atlantic. It included studies of delimited periods, such as Harold Laski's *Political Thought in*

---

[7] Runciman, *Pluralism*; and David Nicholls, *The Pluralist State: The Political Ideas of J. N. Figgis and His Contemporaries* (Basingstoke, UK: Macmillan, 1975).

[8] Compare David Boucher, *Texts in Context: Revisionist Methods for Studying the History of Ideas* (Dordrecht: Martinus Nijhoff, 1985), 39–72.

England from Locke to Bentham and J. W. Allen's *A History of Political Thought in the Sixteenth Century*, as well as synthetic overviews, such as C. H. McIlwain's *Growth of Political Thought in the West* and George Sabine's *A History of Political Theory*.[9] Typically these histories of political thought were written with a sense of their having a close relationship to the historical studies of institutions then being pursued by many political scientists. Indeed, scholars often crossed back and forth over the fuzzy boundary between political theory and other aspects of the study of politics. The ideas and institutions tradition brought together scholars working primarily on ideas, those who focused on institutions, and more generalist figures who pursued diverse projects of both types. Ernest Barker and Carl Friedrich offer examples of the wide-ranging ideas-and-institutions scholar from opposite sides of the Atlantic. They produced comparative and historical institutional studies, histories of ideas, translations of canonical texts, and many other works.[10] The links between the study of ideas and the study of institutions began to attenuate only in the period after World War II. When A. D. Lindsay left Oxford to establish the new University of Keele, he took with him two of his pupils—Walter Gallie and S. E. Finer. It is in their work, rather than his, that we perhaps find the study of concepts and the study of institutions being postulated as separate activities.[11]

Behavioralism and Empirical Theory

Up until the Second World War, most political theorists continued to combine moral philosophy, the theory of the state, and constitutional history

[9] Harold J. Laski, *Political Thought in England from Locke to Bentham* (London: Williams and Northgate, 1920); J. W. Allen, *A History of Political Thought in the Sixteenth Century* (London: Meuthen, 1928); Charles Howard McIlwain, *The Growth of Political Thought in the West* (New York: Macmillan, 1932); and George H. Sabine, *A History of Political Theory* (New York: Henry Holt, 1937).

[10] See Ernest Barker, *Political Thought in England from Herbert Spencer to Present Day* (New York: Henry Holt, 1915); Ernest Barker, *The Development of Public Services in Europe, 1660–1930* (New York: Oxford University Press, 1944); Aristotle, *The Politics*, trans. Ernest Barker (Oxford: Clarendon Press, 1946); Carl J. Friedrich, *Constitutional Government and Democracy* (Boston: Little, Brown, 1941); Carl J. Friedrich, *The Age of the Baroque, 1610–1660* (New York: Harper, 1952); and Immanuel Kant, *The Philosophy of Kant*, trans. Carl J. Friedrich (New York: Modern Library, 1949).

[11] W. B. Gallie, "Essentially Contested Concepts," *Proceedings of the Aristotelian Society* 56 (1955–56): 167–98; and S. E. Finer, *Comparative Government* (London: Allen Lane, 1970). Gallie was, like Barker, a product of Oxford idealism who became professor of Political Science at Cambridge (1967–78). Finer held the Gladstone Professor of Government and Public Administration at Oxford—a post that by then had been distinguished from the Chichele Professor of Social and Political Theory—a title that rightly suggests his commitment to a modernist empiricist style of political science largely separated from political theory.

in a way that barely distinguished them from the many other students of politics who also worked within the ideas and institutions tradition. Nonetheless, the early decades of the twentieth century also witnessed the appearance of ambitions for a new and more scientific approach to the study of politics. Science here was equated with attention to the role of psychological factors and with the use of new methods for the collection and analysis of data. In Britain, Graham Wallas championed elements of such an approach, thereby prompting some of those engaged in the study of the development of ideas and institutions to define their activity against a scientific approach.[12] Barker used his inaugural lecture, for example, to say that he was "not altogether happy about the term science" and that he preferred "the name of political theory."[13] Because the proposed scientific alternative made relatively little headway in Britain, doubts about a science of politics could become a shared trope among many British students of politics, rather than a fissure line between theorists and others.

In America, Charles Merriam championed the mix of new psychological perspectives and new methodologies. Under his leadership, the Chicago department of political science became a vibrant center for novel approaches. However, while the innovative work of Chicago figures such as Harold Lasswell, Harold Gosnell, and Quincy Wright pointed toward themes that recur in the behavioral revolution, it did not provoke a split between political theorists and political scientists. For the most part American theorists and their fellow students of politics were happy to stand together under the label "political science," with this latter term being understood in a broad, noncrusading fashion. Up to the 1940s, there were few signs of the dispute that was to come.

When the dispute did come, it did not arise from an empiricist attack on theory. On the contrary, it arose precisely when American advocates of behavioralism began to emphasize the importance of theory and, in doing so, to articulate a new vision of what theory should be. Lasswell and Kaplan's *Power and Society* and David Easton's *The Political System* charged theorists with failing to provide an adequate conceptual framework for empirical research and called for a new kind of theory—"empirical theory"—that would serve this purpose better.[14] Exponents of the ideas and institutions tradition had conceived of analytic frameworks as the refinements of concepts that emerged in the evolving interplay of practice, institutions, and reflection in the history of political thought. They

---

[12] Martin J. Weiner, *Between Two Worlds: The Political Thought of Graham Wallas* (Oxford: Oxford University Press, 1971).

[13] Barker, "Study of Political Science," 194–95.

[14] Harold D. Lasswell and Abraham Kaplan, *Power and Society* (New Haven, CT: Yale University Press, 1950); David Easton, *The Political System* (New York: Knopf, 1953).

were often wary of applying these frameworks outside of the context in which they had arisen, namely, the political history of the West. In contrast, the behavioralists advocated creative theorizing that would break away from conceptual formulations rooted in particular historical contexts. They hoped instead to craft a new scientific vocabulary that would be more universally applicable and so of help in the development of general theory. Their call foreshadowed the rise of a range of new empirical vocabularies: decision theory, group theory, systems theory, structural-functional theory, and the theory of action had leapt onto the agenda of American political science by the end of the 1950s.[15]

Modernist empiricists had proposed the creative crafting of new concepts of greater scope on and off since the late nineteenth century. The behavioral vision of empirical theory went beyond these prior proposals in at least two ways. First, while earlier proponents of such conceptual efforts, like Willoughby, also pursued work in the history of political thought, the behavioralists viewed such concerns as irrelevant "historicist" preoccupations and even as active obstacles to a proper "scientific" theory.[16] Second, the behavioralists adopted positivist criteria for judging theoretical frameworks in accord with their understanding of natural science. Their leading criteria were universality, deductive structure, and instrumental utility for empirical research. They had little, if any, time for elder criteria favored within the ideas and institutions tradition, criteria such as a theory's relationship to earlier ideas or to our everyday concepts and practices. Moreover, while the postwar behavioralists were never quite clear as to just how one was to judge the utility of a theory, it was clear that the advance of substantive normative outcomes was no

---

[15] There were, of course, important differences within the range of new forms of theoretical endeavor that took shape in the decades after World War II. Most prominently, there was, as Brian Barry classically discussed, a division between endeavors with a more "sociological" cast and those with a more "economic" cast. We focus here on the sociological endeavors most prominent in political science in the 1950s and 1960s, not the economic forms of theorizing that would flourish among political scientists only somewhat later. While the pioneering political science proponent of the latter approach—William Riker—would favor the label "positive theory" to that of "empirical theory," the criteria that his vision of theory articulated are largely the same as those we discuss in relation to empirical theory. On sociological versus economic theoretical endeavors, see Brian M. Barry, *Sociologists, Economists, and Democracy* (London: Collier-Macmillan, 1970). On Riker in relation to the agenda of Easton and others, see Emily Hauptmann, "Defining 'Theory' in Postwar Political Science," in *The Politics of Method in the Human Sciences: Positivism and Its Epistemological Others*, ed. George Steinmetz (Chapel Hill, NC: Duke University Press, 2005).

[16] On modernist themes in Willoughby's work see Robert Adcock, "The Emergence of Political Science as a Discipline: History and the Study of Politics, 1875–1910," *History of Political Thought* 24 (2003): 481–508. For behavioralist attacks on historicist preoccupations, see David Easton, "The Decline of Modern Political Theory," *Journal of Politics* 13, no. 1 (1951): 36–58; and Easton, *Political System*.

longer considered an appropriate criterion. In this sense, they departed
markedly from the pragmatist leanings evident among interwar modernist empiricists, as exemplified within political theory by the work of
Charles Merriam.

Despite the novel character of empirical theory and despite its steady
growth through the 1950s and 1960s, we should not assume that it swept
all before it, even within America. On the contrary, apart from the rather
lonely figure of Easton, nearly all those who promoted empirical theory
worked mainly outside the subfield of political theory. Within the subfield
the most prominent new vision of the 1950s was that offered by Strauss.
Moreover, the ideas and institutions tradition remained strong: at Harvard, for example, generalist figures such as William Y. Elliot, Louis
Hartz, and Carl Friedrich were busy training some of the leading theorists
of the next generation, including Wolin and Judith Shklar.[17] It was, we
would suggest, precisely because empirical theory made little impact on
the subfield of political theory, while flourishing elsewhere, that the 1950s
and 1960s witnessed an increasingly important division between political
theorists and the rest of the discipline of political science in America. Contrary to the stereotype of atheoretical empiricism, few behavioralists
wanted to be caught without a theory, but they had developed their own
distinctive sense of what the character of such theory should, and should
not, be. Political scientists increasingly contrasted the empirical theory
they sought over against normative theory—an amorphous category that
encompassed pretty much every form of theorizing that they saw as irrelevant or hostile to behavioral political science. When, in the late 1960s,
those within the subfield of political theory came to embrace the notion
that they did indeed pursue a "vocation" that was qualitatively different
from that favored elsewhere in the discipline, the division between the
two camps was complete.[18]

While the differences between empirical theory and other approaches
to theory appeared in squabbles spread out across conferences, journals,
and books in America, it barely appeared in Britain. The simple explanation would be that the American behavioral movement had no impact in
Britain. However, it would be more correct to say that there was an impact, but it was selective. The behavioral movement included not only
efforts to develop a new form of theory but also attempts to develop and

[17] Easton also earned his doctorate at Harvard, but unlike Shklar or Wolin, he was profoundly disappointed with the generalist ideas and institutions education on offer. See John
G. Gunnell, *The Descent of Political Theory: The Genealogy of an American Vocation* (Chicago: University of Chicago Press, 1993), 228–29.

[18] Sheldon S. Wolin, "Political Theory as a Vocation," *American Political Science Review*
63, no. 4 (1969): 1062–82.

to apply new methods for the creation and analysis of data. Although British political scientists showed little enthusiasm for structural-functionalism or systems theory, they were receptive to new techniques such as surveys and statistical analysis. Even so, the relative weakness of empirical theory in Britain helps to explain why it did not witness the sharp division, even outright hostility, between the subfield of political theory and the rest of political science that became so notable in America.

America: Epic Political Theory

As we have seen, political theory developed in the first half of the twentieth century as a subfield largely devoted to the history of political thought understood as being tied to the development of institutions. This tradition was jolted by the impact of émigrés like Strauss and Hannah Arendt, who brought with them both their engagement with the intellectual movements of Weimar Germany and their experience of the Nazi rise to power and subsequent exile. The émigrés made Nazism and its relationship to modernity and liberalism vital topics for the history of political thought.[19] There thus emerged a powerful new concern with the diagnosis of those political and intellectual flaws at the heart of liberal modernity, which had paved the way for Nazism. Although such topics had been widespread in Weimar, in the American context they were jarring. Whereas the ideas and institutions tradition had tended to buttress liberal narratives of a progressive modernity, émigré political theorists looked to the past in order to unsettle such confidence in modern liberal ideas and institutions. When they wrote about the past, they sought to narrate how modernity went astray and to search out "lost treasure" whose juxtaposition to contemporary realities might inspire critical thinking.[20] Neither the engaged character of this work nor its taste for synthetic interpretation was entirely new to the subfield of political theory. Perhaps its most distinctive feature was, rather, the aura of urgency and importance it lent to political theory through its suggestion that creative, provocative theorizing, and perhaps only such theorizing, could tackle and hopefully dislodge those ways of thinking and acting that were dangerous, and potentially disastrous, to the health of the polity. It is this feature in particular that we have in mind in using the label "epic" theory.[21]

[19] Cf. Gunnell, *Descent of Political Theory*, 146–74.

[20] The phrase "lost treasure" comes from the title of chapter 6 ("The Revolutionary Tradition and Its Lost Treasure") of Hannah Arendt, *On Revolution* (New York: Viking Press, 1963). Also see the discussion of "pearl diving" in Arendt's introduction to Walter Benjamin, *Illuminations*, ed. Hannah Arendt (New York: Schocken Books, 1968).

[21] In adopting the label "epic" we draw on Wolin, who used this term to designate canonical thinkers whose work, in his view, sought to achieve "a great and memorable deed

The commonalities of epic theory were distinctive enough to mark out a new tradition, but also general enough to encompass a range of approaches, including those of Arendt, Strauss, and Wolin. Of these, Strauss was the clearest about the premises on which his approach rested and about the ways in which this approach broke with the ideas and institutions tradition. Earlier historians of political thought had mostly turned to the past with a perspective that presupposed either progress or, especially between the wars, relativism: Sabine's *A History of Political Theory* was probably the dominant synthetic text from its publication in 1937 until the early 1960s, and it explicitly adopted a stance of "social relativism."[22] For Strauss, in contrast, a presumption of progress made no sense when the end product of historical development appeared to be the Nazi regime, while relativism of any kind was even less acceptable, not only because it offered little ground on which to criticize the Nazis, but also because the spread of relativism had contributed, or so he believed, to the moral weakness that made the rise of Nazism possible. For Strauss, this pernicious relativism was, in turn, the outcome of dynamics that were internal to positivism and historicism. He thus advocated an approach to political theory that broke entirely with both of these leading currents of modern thought and returned instead to a classical rationalism.

During the 1940s and 1950s, Strauss developed his criticisms of modern thought while also laying the foundation for a new approach to political theory premised on the rejection of the then dominant historicism. He argued that historical knowledge should be "only preliminary and auxiliary" to the more important activity of "political philosophy," that is, to an engagement with perennial questions about the "nature of political things."[23] When Strauss appealed to a concept of "nature" that transcended historical change, he broke decisively with the ideas and institutions tradition. Whereas the exponents of the latter typically implied that the rise of a historical perspective, especially the critical method in historiography, had marked the breakthrough that laid the foundation for modern political studies, Strauss saw the modern historical approach as just the second of three stages in the dynamic of intellectual decline by which modern thought moved from an initial early-modern break with classical

---

through the medium of thought" rather than to realize narrow scholarly or scientific goals. See Sheldon S. Wolin, *Hobbes and the Epic Tradition of Political Theory* (Los Angeles: Clark Memorial Library, 1970), 4. Although Wolin was writing about "epic" figures within the canon, we believe that his characterization of this "informing intention" applies equally well, if not better, to a distinctive strand in American political theory, and in particular to his own work along with that of Strauss and Arendt. Also see the discussion in John G. Gunnell, *Political Theory: Tradition and Interpretation* (Cambridge, MA: Winthrop, 1979).

[22] Sabine, *History of Political Theory*, viii.

[23] Leo Strauss, "Political Philosophy and History," *Journal of the History of Ideas* 10, no. 1 (1949): 30.

modes of thought through to its pernicious fall into relativism and nihilism.[24] Whereas Friedrich saw Aristotle as superseded by modern thought's dynamic appreciation of historical change, Strauss saw the study of classical thinkers as "the only practicable way" to escape the "intellectual decline" involved in just such modern modes of thought.[25]

By the late 1950s Friedrich was well aware of the "profound challenge" that Strauss posed, and he sought to differentiate his own favored approach to the history of political thought from a "great books" approach that treated past works as if they offered something "akin to Biblical revelation."[26] Strauss challenged the broad spectrum of American political scientists, including ideas and institutions scholars, precisely because he attacked widespread assumptions such as the superiority of modern to classical thought. Straussian criticisms began to focus specifically on behavioralism only later, in the early 1960s, as behavioralism was graduating from being a rebellious antiorthodoxy to a new mainstream.[27] Before then, the differences between Strauss and the ideas and institutions tradition provided the setting in which Arendt published *The Human Condition* and Wolin, together with Norman Jacobson and John Schaar, began to shape a distinctive Berkeley school of political theory.[28] Indeed, the edited volume in which Friedrich tried to differentiate his approach from that of Strauss also included an essay in which Jacobson sought to defend political theory from the dual menace of scientism and moralism. Although Jacobson did not give citations to indicate whom he had in mind, the context of the late 1950s makes it probable that his targets were the new approaches to theory offered by, respectively, empirical theory and Strauss.[29]

[24] Leo Strauss, "The Three Waves of Modernity," in *An Introduction to Political Philosophy*, ed. Hilial Gildin (Detroit: Wayne State University Press, 1989).

[25] Friedrich, *Constitutional Government and Democracy*, 4–7; Leo Strauss, "On Collingwood's Philosophy of History," *Review of Metaphysics* 5 (1952): 585–86.

[26] Carl J. Friedrich, "Political Philosophy and the Science of Politics," in *Approaches to the Study of Politics*, ed. Roland Young (Evanston, IL: Northwestern University Press, 1958), 179–81 and 173. For his changing evaluation of Strauss see Carl J. Friedrich, "Thomas Hobbes: Myth Builder of the Modern World," *Journal of Social Philosophy* 3 (1938): 251–57; and Carl J. Friedrich, "Two Philosophical Interpretations of Natural Law," *Diogenes* 11 (1955): 98–112.

[27] The main Straussian critique of behavioralism was Herbert J. Storing, ed., *Essays on the Scientific Study of Politics* (New York: Holt, Rinehart and Winston, 1962).

[28] Our view of the "Berkeley School" draws on Gunnell, *Descent of Political Theory*, 259–61; and Emily Hauptmann, "A Local History of the Political," *Political Theory* 32, no. 1 (2004): 34–60.

[29] Norman Jacobson, "The Unity of Political Theory: Science, Morals, and Politics," in Young, *Approaches*, 115–24. The same two specters haunt Schaar and Wolin's bitterly critical review of the Straussian volume on behavioral political science. See John H. Schaar and Sheldon S. Wolin, "Essays on the Scientific Study of Politics: A Critique," *American Political Science Review* 57, no. 1 (1963): 125–50.

If behavioral and Straussian approaches marked out two extremes in the late 1950s, what were the alternatives? There was, of course, the option of continuing the ideas and institutions tradition, as advocated by Friedrich and Hartz.[30] However, this was not the only option on offer. By the early 1960s, Arendt and Wolin had introduced two more. Although they drew on the ideas and institutions tradition, their approaches were also infused with the epic spirit. Like Strauss, they saw political thought and the activity of politics as having gone deeply awry at some point in the modern era. Like Strauss, they championed the recovery of earlier perspectives as a means of combating the dilemmas that now beset our politically sick age.

Arendt swept onto the American stage in 1951 with the publication of *The Origins of Totalitarianism*. Her book echoed many themes from the ideas and institutions tradition, notably in its exploration of the historical roots of totalitarianism conceived as a new form of government characterized by distinctive ideological and institutional features. Indeed, ideas and institutions scholars had been struggling to understand totalitarianism in just such terms for over a decade: Friedrich had been doing so since the late 1930s, although his major work on the topic, written together with Zbigniew Brzezinski, was not published until 1956.[31] Although Arendt and Friedrich alike analyzed totalitarianism in terms of historically distinctive institutions and modes of thought, their analyses differed in one crucial respect. Whereas Arendt located totalitarianism in an epic vision of the emergent dark features of Western modernity, Friedrich chose to avoid doing so because he thought such grand narratives were "speculative and controversial."[32] When Arendt turned to questions of constitutionalism in her book *On Revolution*, she again took an established concern of ideas and institutions scholars and gave it a new epic twist by locating it against the backdrop of a grand narrative about the decline inherent in modernity. Arendt argued that the French Revolutionaries had lost sight of an older, more valuable form of politics, which had informed the American Revolution. Their doing so, she added, had had dire consequences in the nineteenth and twentieth centuries.[33]

---

[30] This option appears, for example, in Shklar's praise of Skinner as an antidote to the tropes of Strauss, Arendt, and Wolin. Skinner's work was, she wrote, "intellectual history at its best as it used to be practiced"; it did not purport to "solve a preset cross-word puzzle made up of noble, ancient philosophers and base, modern liberals," and it did not call upon the reader "to lament the loss of some lost public space." See Judith N. Shklar, "*The Foundations of Modern Political Thought*, by Quentin Skinner," *Political Theory* 7, no. 4 (1979): 549–52.

[31] Carl J. Friedrich and Zbigniew K. Brzezinski, *Totalitarian Dictatorship and Autocracy* (Cambridge: Harvard University Press, 1956).

[32] Ibid., iix.

[33] Arendt, *On Revolution*.

We can better appreciate the distinctive content of Arendt's approach if we turn to her most theoretical writings. In *The Human Condition* and several of the essays that later were included in *Between Past and Future*, she approached classic concepts of political theory, such as freedom, power, and authority, from a perspective informed by the phenomenology in which she had been trained by Heidegger and Jaspers. She described herself as performing experiments in the "critical interpretation of the past" with the "chief aim" of discovering "the real origins of traditional concepts in order to distill from them anew their original spirit which has so sadly evaporated from the very words of political language."[34] Arendt understood her political theory, in other words, to be about the recovery and analysis of the allegedly foundational experiences from which our concepts had originated. She invoked these experiences, as Strauss did "nature," to establish a quasi given with which she could fend off the relativistic implications of radical historicism while also bemoaning the decline into modernity.[35] The epic tradition's sense of loss, its worry about the present, and the heroic role it consequently ascribed to the theorist all permeate the work of Arendt just as they had that of Strauss and just as they would that of Wolin.

As a graduate student at Harvard in the late 1940s, Wolin received a generalist ideas and institutions introduction to the study of politics. He worked with Hartz and Elliott, and he wrote his dissertation on the traditional topic of the history of British constitutional theory. Wolin then spent a year pursuing postdoctoral studies at Oxford and a short time teaching at Oberlin, where he had been an undergraduate, before moving to Berkeley in 1954. His early publications were contextual studies of English thinkers such as Hooker and Hume.[36] At this time, he was working within the mainstream of a political science dominated by ideas and institutions scholars. His article on Hume and two subsequent ones on Luther and Calvin appeared in the *American Political Science Review*. All three of the articles suggested that the most important aspect of the relevant thinker resided in his attitude toward institutions.[37] It was only in

---

[34] Hannah Arendt, *Between Past and Future* (New York: Viking Press, 1968), 15.

[35] Arendt's hostility to theorizing centered on a concept of "nature" informs her attempts to differentiate her concept of the "human condition" from "human nature" and her assertion that we could never grasp the "nature" or "essence" of human things, even if such existed. Hannah Arendt, *The Human Condition* (Chicago: University of Chicago Press, 1958), 7–11.

[36] Sheldon S. Wolin, "Richard Hooker and English Conservatism," *Western Political Quarterly* 6, no. 1 (1953): 28–47; Sheldon S. Wolin, "Hume and Conservatism," *American Political Science Review* 48, no. 4 (1954): 999–1016.

[37] Sheldon S. Wolin, "Politics and Religion: Luther's Simplistic Imperative," *American Political Science Review* 50, no. 1 (1956): 24–42; and Sheldon S. Wolin, "Calvin and the Reformation: The Political Education of Protestantism," *American Political Science Review* 51, no. 2 (1957): 428–53.

the late 1950s that Wolin moved toward theorizing on a synthetic level with a greater use of abstraction and with epic themes. Two aspects of this move were foreshadowed, however, in the articles on Luther and Calvin, articles that formed the basis of two chapters in his *Politics and Vision*. First, Wolin began the essay on Luther with an attempt to define the "enterprise of political theory" in heroic terms, an attempt that he expanded upon in the first chapter of *Politics and Vision* and later extended into the idea of a distinctive "vocation." Second, Wolin began, in the essay on Calvin, to discuss institutional issues in terms of a more abstract problem of order. In *Politics and Vision*, he deployed this problem as one of several synthesizing abstractions with which to interpret the ideas of widely different thinkers, not as historically specific, but as contributions to an ongoing conversation centered on problems seen as recurring continually throughout the history of Western political thought.[38]

Wolin thus invoked recurring, abstractly framed problems as constitutive of the subject matter of a grand tradition of political theorizing in a manner that parallels Strauss's explicitly antihistoricist invocation of "nature." Yet while Strauss grounded his transhistorical canon on the notion that political philosophers engaged fundamental problems that were perennial because they arose from the very nature of things political, Wolin held that the character of politics and our ways of thinking about it were "created," not "written into the nature of things." One might ask, therefore, how could Wolin reconcile the idea of recurring problems with the kind of historicist orientation that characterized the ideas and institutions tradition? Wolin appealed here to a developmental historicism: he sought to ground the continuity he needed in the idea that the "ideas and categories . . . created by the political theorist" were handed down from generation to generation so that ways of thinking about political activities were a "legacy accruing from the historical activity of political philosophers."[39] On the one hand, he thereby suggested that his approach involved a shift in emphasis, relative to the ideas and institutions tradition, toward the creative activity of major thinkers at the expense of the history of political institutions. On the other, his practice in *Politics and Vision* did not go as far in this direction as his opening remarks suggested: it offered, instead, a slightly incongruous mix of a few chapters in which institutional history took center stage and rather more that focused on select thinkers. The ensuing decade saw Wolin moving further from the ideas to institutions tradition toward a focus on those "epic theorists" who he thought had fashioned new "paradigms" that transformed the character of subsequent

---

[38] Sheldon S. Wolin, *Politics and Vision* (Boston: Little, Brown, 1960), chap. 1.
[39] Ibid., 5.

political thought and action.[40] Wolin's attempts to distinguish his approach to political theory from that of Strauss appear here largely as minor skirmishes against a background of a shared "epic" spirit.

The theoretical endeavors of Wolin and Strauss overlapped in their appeals to recurring, abstractly framed problems, their associated emphasis on a grand conversation among canonical thinkers, and their belief that the study of these canonical thinkers can teach moral and political lessons we need to learn if we are to recognize and address the flaws of liberal modernity. When Wolin narrated the decline of the modern era, he appealed specifically to a concept of "the political" that became something of a motif of the subfield of political theory at Berkeley. He worried that politics had ceased to be a means by which collectively to formulate and pursue a common good: it had fallen to become little more than a means of aggregating and balancing private interests mediated by social and economic power. And he suggested that modern political thought, especially political science, was complicit in this fall since it had ceased to defend the integrity of the political: it had fallen, first, to a sociological science that treated political outcomes as the mere epiphenomena of social forces and, second, a liberal pluralism that conceptually and normatively bolstered the dominance of "the social" in thought and in action.[41]

Wolin's narrative of the decline of political theory was highly selective. It ignored, for example, the long lineage of antipluralist theorists of the state throughout the nineteenth and twentieth centuries. Typically these theorists understood the state to be an entity by which we might formulate and realize a common good in the modern era: they conceived of the state as ethically valuable in contrast to society, which they generally treated negatively as the site of conflict between self-interested individuals and groups. Although Wolin used the concept "the social" in a way that had much in common with these theorist's concept of society, when he invoked "the political" as its opposite, he did not intend to refer, as they had, to the state. On the contrary, he was at once both antipluralist and antistate, as, for that matter, was Arendt, who deployed a similar dichotomy between the social and the political.[42] "The political" expressed a hope, in other words, that the "common" might be located somewhere other than the

[40] Sheldon S. Wolin, "Paradigms and Political Theories," in *Politics and Experience*, ed. Preston King and B. C. Parekh (Cambridge: Cambridge University Press, 1968), 125–52; Wolin, *Hobbes and the Epic Tradition*; Wolin, "Political Theory as a Vocation."

[41] Wolin, *Politics and Vision*, chaps. 9 and 10.

[42] Compare Ernst Vollrath, "Hannah Arendt: A German-American Jewess Views the United States—and Looks Back to Germany," in *Hannah Arendt and Leo Strauss: German Émigrés and American Political Thought after World War II*, ed. Peter Graf Kielmansegg, Horst Mewes, and Elisabeth Glaser-Schmidt (Cambridge: Cambridge University Press, 1995), 45–58.

"state": it embodied memories of the classical polis and civic republicanism while also expressing a hope for forms of participatory political action that might challenge the routines of everyday politics. This suggestive, if vague, concept caught the interest of many among the subsequent generation of political theorists as they received their education in the subfield amid protest movements and campus revolts. It thereby facilitated a shift in the substantive concerns of political theorists from the state to a whole series of other topics to which the category of "the political" pointed, including social movements, civil society, and community. The blind spots of Wolin's reading of the recent past of political theory thus turned out to foreshadow the future concerns of American political theorists.

Britain: An Idealist Inheritance

A young British graduate student visited Berkeley at the very time when Wolin and Jacobson were carving out their vision of the political. Bernard Crick studied at the London School of Economics under Laski and Michael Oakeshott. When he visited Berkeley, he was immersed in a study of "the American science of politics," the topic of a doctoral thesis he submitted to the University of London in 1956 and the title of a book he published two years later, in 1958.[43] Crick, like Strauss and Wolin, was highly critical of behavioralism and its antecedents. However, while his thought mirrored theirs in many ways, it also differed from theirs in ways that reflect his debt to the fading legacy of British idealism. These differences appear even more clearly, moreover, when we turn to Skinner's response to behavioralism and the styles of political theory that arose alongside it.

Crick's attack on the American science of politics had much in common with those of Wolin and Jacobson. He too championed against it a revival of classical conceptions of politics and citizenship. More specifically, he appealed to a republican inheritance that began with Aristotle's notion of the free citizen in the polity but also found expression in Tocqueville's stress on active participation in the community and Arendt's concept of freedom as experienced in political action.[44] Crick understood "politics" as a somewhat mysterious but undeniably excellent activity in a way that mirrors Wolin's notion of "the political." He defined politics as accep-

---

[43] Bernard Crick, *The American Science of Politics* (Berkeley and Los Angeles: University of California Press, 1959).

[44] See Crick, *American Science*, 225–26; and Bernard Crick, *In Defense of Politics* (Chicago: University of Chicago Press, 1962), 16–19. These theorists remained his principal sources of inspiration. See, for example, Bernard Crick, "Hannah Arendt and the Burden of Our Times," *Political Quarterly* 68 (1997): 77–84.

tance of "the fact of the simultaneous existence of different groups, hence different interests and different traditions, within a territorial unit under a common rule."[45] So defined politics represented just one possible solution to the problem of order, a solution that contrasted with tyranny, oligarchy, kingship, despotism, and totalitarianism: whereas these other forms of order coerced or overawed people with divergent values or interests, politics involved listening to them, conciliating them, giving them a legal position, and allowing them to articulate their positions. In Crick's view, politics thus entailed freedom, although, of course, politics and freedom could be restricted to a subset of the society who fell under a common rule. The freedom that came with politics, he explained, was a republican or democratic freedom understood in terms of active participation, rather than the negative liberty beloved of liberals.

The idea of politics as freedom led Crick to defend it against what he saw as its enemies. The enemies—nationalism, technology, science, and others—depoliticized the world by eliding the key fact of the clash of values and interests. Like Wolin, Crick complained that political science ignored the political. His main argument, however, was that the science of politics was itself a peculiarly American practice: it combined a concept of science widely held by American social theorists, a concern with citizenship training that was entrenched in American political life, the generalization of the habits of American democracy, and a faith in progress or a manifest destiny for American society.[46] Crick traced these elements of the science of politics from the days of the early republic through to Merriam and Lasswell. The liberal science of politics that had thus arisen was, Crick said, similar to Marxism in that it reduced politics to power in a way that both neglected the importance of competing values and postulated correct solutions to issues of conflict so as thereby to elide the need for politics conceived as the free negotiation between competing values and interests. It thus stood accused of negating politics in a way that made it an almost totalitarian form of antitotalitarianism.

The obvious similarities between Crick's and Wolin's critiques of political science should not blind us to important differences in their thought. Crucially, whereas Wolin owed much to an émigré culture that saw a total rejection of radical historicism and positivism as the best antidotes to the tendencies that had generated fascism, Crick belonged in a postidealist culture that retained a historicist orientation and that was interacting with those strands in analytic philosophy that challenged both the distinction between analytic and synthetic propositions and also positivism more

---

[45] Crick, *Defense of Politics*, 14.
[46] Crick, *American Science*, xv.

generally. This crucial difference influenced their stances toward both political science and political theory in relation to its history.

Crick's view of the proper study of politics drew on the fading legacy of the British idealists. Even when he took up the cudgels against his teacher, Oakeshott, he did so in a way that indicated continuity. Crick accepted Oakeshott's view of politics, and so freedom, as being dependent upon tradition, where the concept of tradition served to fend off not only an empiricist scientism but also a rationalist view of politics as being capable of being predicated on first principles.[47] After World War I, the objective idealism of philosophers such as F. H. Bradley and T. H. Green had lost its sway. Nonetheless, the influence of idealism remained—as we can see in Crick as well as Oakeshott—in beliefs in the meaningful nature of human activity, the embedded nature of the individual, and a commitment to positive freedom attained in association with others. By the 1950s, the reaction against objective idealism meant that among theorists influenced by idealism these beliefs were typically accommodated within an emphasis on activity, not thought, practice, not reflection, and a related concern with pluralism, not unity. Crick thus distanced himself from Oakeshott by extending a drift away from objective idealism already apparent in Oakeshott. He argued that there are always several traditions in a complex society and that conservatives can elide plurality only by mistakenly postulating "a correct and good tradition" that expresses "the general will or the common good."[48] The fading legacy of the British idealists thus informed Crick's understanding of the proper study of politics. He went into battle against the American science of politics, for instance, under the flag of R. G. Collingwood, with his rejection of the idea "that science was the only type of knowledge."[49] Like the idealists, Crick argued that the study of politics should cover the ideals, ideas, and meanings that inspire political action, though, again following the drift away from objective idealism, he made it clear that this did not imply that "politics is the grasping for or the unfolding of the ideal."[50]

Whereas Wolin oscillated somewhat uneasily between Strauss's antihistoricism and the developmental historicism of the ideas and institutions tradition, Crick stood more squarely alongside the historicism that was passed on as part of the fading influence of British idealism. Crick sought to undermine the American science of politics on behalf of a historical political science that would take seriously the role both of ideals and the institutions they had inspired. The mentors and friends he acknowledges

---

[47] Crick, *Defense of Politics*, 112–18.
[48] Ibid., 115.
[49] Crick, *American Science*, 213.
[50] Ibid., 222.

for their help thus include not only Jacobson but also the institutionalists at Harvard—Friedrich and Hartz. Indeed, when Crick surveyed the possible alternatives to a pernicious scientism in America, he began by observing, "an infusion of émigré and refuge scholars has certainly helped to widen perspectives"—he singled our particularly Arendt but also mentioned Strauss and Eric Voegelin—only eventually to place his hopes not in these émigrés, who were defining political theory in opposition to political science, but rather in the common purpose of those "institutionalists" and "theorists" who were endeavoring "to rediscover American history."[51] For Crick, then, the defense of politics against totalitarianism required historical studies of politics, as opposed not only to the scientism of the behavioralists, but also the epic endeavors of Strauss and Wolin. Crick's belief in the historical study of politics led him, just as it had Laski and Friedrich, to study institutions and proposals for their reform as well as political ideas and their history, for he saw no clear point at which the one ended and the other begun. Thus, in the 1970s he wrote on the theory of the state and participated in the Study of Parliament Group as well as editing Machiavelli's *Discourses*.[52] In short, Crick retained the historicist orientation of the idealists and thus sympathized with much of the ideas to institutions literature.

Again, whereas Strauss and Wolin had no interest in anything indebted to positivism, Crick was open to finding inspiration in strands of analytic philosophy. He tells us, for example, that he was "sympathetic to the style of thought" of T. D. Weldon's *Vocabulary of Politics*, with its emphasis on the analysis of concepts.[53] Of course, Crick opposed any epiphenomenalism that reduced values to interests or power, as, he believed, did the American science of politics. Yet within political theory, he associated epiphenomenalism with strands of Marxism rather than analytic philosophy. He defended his account of politics, in particular, against Laski's later work.[54] Laski turned to Marxism in the 1930s, after which he began to characterize political theory as a kind of sociology of knowledge; he suggested that political theorists should explain the rise of ideologies by reference to social structures.[55] Crick argued against such a sociology of

[51] Ibid., 233.

[52] Bernard Crick, *Basic Forms of Government: A Sketch and a Model* (London: Macmillan, 1973); A. H. Hanson and Bernard Crick, eds., *The Commons in Transition* (London: Fontana, 1970); and Machiavelli, *The Discourses*, ed. Bernard Crick (Harmondsworth, UK: Penguin, 1970).

[53] Crick, *American Science*, v.

[54] Laski's hand was surely one that had fed Crick at the LSE and that Crick turned to bite in Crick, *Defense of Politics*. Crick identifies epiphenomenalism as a failing common to Marxism and the American science of politics in *American Science*, 223–24.

[55] See, for instance, Harold J. Laski, *The Rise of European Liberalism* (London: Allen and Unwin, 1936).

knowledge partly because it was self-contradictory or elitist: sociologists of knowledge, he said, confront the difficulty that they should conceive of themselves as products of circumstances that compel them to think about ideologies as they do, and the only way out of this difficulty is for them to invoke a special type of person—say, the "unattached intellectual"—who alone can transcend her circumstances. And he argued against it partly because it ignored the grandeur of humanity and the inevitability of evaluation when politics as such is challenged.

Skinner traveled from Britain to America more than a decade after Crick. From 1974 to 1979, he took a leave of absence from a fellowship at Christ's College, Cambridge in order to become a member of the Institute for Advanced Study at Princeton. Although Wolin was by that time teaching at Princeton, there are few signs that he and Skinner engaged with each other's work. By the time Skinner arrived at Princeton, he already had written several of the essays that marked him out as the methodological spokesman for what has come to be seen as a distinctive Cambridge School in the history of political thought.[56] Skinner's views, like Crick's, drew on the fading legacy of British idealism, a legacy that retained a historicist orientation and that was interacting with analytic philosophy as it was developing following the demise of logical positivism.

When Skinner was still at school, he was advised to read Collingwood's *The Idea of History*. Fascinated by it, he quickly went on to read the *Autobiography*. By the time he began his research, Collingwood was, he recalls, "the most immediate and powerful influence on the direction of my work."[57] Once again, however, what we have here is idealist motifs rather than objective idealism as such. Skinner took from Collingwood the view that the history of political theory is neither a series of responses to timeless questions nor the unfolding of an inherent logic, but rather answers to questions that themselves change fundamentally with alterations in the presuppositions that define the general intellectual context of an epoch. Texts should be seen, in this view, as action: they are attempts to solve

---

[56] The most famous and controversial of these essays was written between 1966 and 1967, though it was not published until 1969. See Quentin Skinner, "Meaning and Understanding in the History of Ideas," *History and Theory* 8, no. 1 (1969): 3–53, republished in *Meaning and Context: Quentin Skinner and His Critics*, ed. James Tully (Cambridge: Polity Press, 1988). Other essays published at that time were Quentin Skinner, "Conventions and the Understanding of Speech-Acts," *Philosophical Quarterly* 20 (1970): 118–38; and Quentin Skinner, "On Performing and Explaining Linguistic Actions," *Philosophical Quarterly* 21 (1971): 1–21.

[57] Koikkalainen and Syrjämäki, "Interview with Skinner," 45. It is also worth noting, as Skinner did, that Collingwood exercised a similar influence on other leading figures in what has been called the Cambridge School—J.G.A. Pocock and John Dunn. Quentin Skinner, "Some Problems in the Analysis of Political Thought and Action," in Tully, *Meaning and Context*, 103.

historically specific problems, not the abstractly framed, recurring problems of Strauss or Wolin. The historian of political thought tries to recover the specific problems to which texts stand as answers and thus identify what their authors were doing in writing them. Skinner filled out this position by drawing on the analytic philosophy of Wittgenstein, J. L. Austin, and Paul Grice, which emphasized that language is action—words are deeds.[58] Skinner used speech-act philosophy to argue that the history of political thought, rightly conceived, concerns the activity of authors in writing texts and that to recover this activity requires a focus on the historically specific linguistic contexts in which authors made their utterances.

Skinner deployed his contextualist philosophy against epiphenomenalism and epic theory.[59] Like Crick, he recognized several varieties of epiphenomenalism: Naimerite historians, Marxists—"in certain moods"—and behavioralists conceived of ideas as mere rationalizations that often played scarcely any role in explanations of action.[60] Of these, however, he seems to have been most concerned with Marxism. The leading exponent of the Marxist sociology of knowledge within political theory was, at that time, C. B. Macpherson. Macpherson, who was a student of Laski's, attempted to explain what he saw as similarities in the theories of Hobbes, Locke, and other seventeenth-century thinkers by suggesting that they arose as reflections of an emerging bourgeois society and market economy.[61] Skinner, in contrast, drew on speech-act theory to defend the importance of paying attention to the autonomous role of principles in politics. He insisted that when principles provided the motives for speech and action, we could not get by without invoking them: "if the agent professes to be acting for the sake of a principle, and if the principle he cites is genuinely his motive for acting, it is obvious that the principle makes a different to the action and thus needs to be cited to explain it."[62] And he argued that even when agents profess principles that they do not hold, their profession of those principles sometimes makes a difference to the

[58] Skinner has recently said—referring to Wittgenstein, Austin, and Grice—"the main influences on my own work in the theory of interpretation came directly from the mainstream of analytical philosophy." He also said that Weldon's *Vocabulary of Politics* "probably left an indelible mark" in a manner that mirrors what we know of Crick's youthful encounter with analytic philosophy. See Koikkalainen and Syrjämäki, "Interview with Skinner," 48 and 36.

[59] Skinner has constantly emphasized that the principal targets of his methodological writings are canonical and epiphenomenal approaches. See Skinner, "Meaning and Understanding"; Skinner, "Analysis of Political Thought"; and most recently, Koikkalainen and Syrjämäki, "Interview with Skinner," 39.

[60] Skinner, "Analysis of Political Thought," 109.

[61] C. B. Macpherson, *The Political Theory of Possessive Individualism* (Oxford: Clarendon Press, 1962).

[62] Skinner, "Analysis of Political Thought," 108.

way in which they then behave: when people try to legitimate their actions in moral terms, they are obliged then to behave in a way that is at least fairly compatible with the ethic they have professed, for if they do not, their ethic will appear to others as insincere, so they will fail in their attempt to legitimate their actions.

As we have seen, the epic theorists either explicitly rejected historicism or effectively did so by adopting the narrative techniques pioneered by antihistoricists. As such, they seemed to Skinner to be on a par with the antihistorical approaches to political theory that had descended from Greats, with its insistence on the timeless wisdom of canonical texts as they address our questions. Skinner insisted that these ahistorical approaches led all too often to interpretations that—even if they were plausible accounts of the words in a text—were simply incredible as historical accounts of what a text could have meant at the time it was written. These historical accounts were incredible because they entailed anachronism: they sought to make past texts address questions or convey ideas that were unknown at the time when the texts were written. Anachronism infected, for example, Strauss and Wolin's attempts to treat the history of political theory as an exercise in "the assessment of blame" for a collapse from true moral or political standards; it infected their appeals to a canon of texts that allegedly respond to one another rather than to their respective historical contexts; it infected the appeal to "abiding questions"; and it infected the use of ancient texts as a source of moral education for problems of, say, interracial and interfaith societies.[63] Skinner proposed to exclude all such unhistorical readings of texts by restricting our descriptions of a text to those that its author might have avowed. We could grasp these descriptions, he continued, if we identified the questions to which the author could have intended to provide an answer. The history of political thought thus consisted primarily of the recovery of authors' illocutionary intentions in relation to the conventions and questions of their own times.

So, whereas Strauss vehemently denounced historicism in a way that owes much to the suggestion that it leads to fascism, Skinner, like Crick, sought to defend a form of historical political science that would take seriously the role of ideas. Of course, Skinner was opposed to positivism: he was attracted to Collingwood in part because he saw him as "unquestionably the leading anti-positivist Idealist in recent English philosophy."[64] Yet to oppose positivism need not be—contrary to what Strauss and Wolin seemed at times to imply—to oppose all forms of political

---

[63] All these examples of epic theory are targets—often partly lurking in footnotes—of Skinner, "Meaning and Understanding."

[64] Skinner, "Analysis of Political Thought," 103. For the clearest example of Skinner's hostility toward positivist political science see Quentin Skinner, "The Empirical Theorists of Democracy and Their Critics," *Political Theory* 1, no. 3 (1973): 287–306.

science. On the contrary, Skinner saw his *Foundations of Modern Political Thought* in part as a contribution to the kind of human sciences then being championed as an alternative to behavioralism by analytic philosophers such as Alisdair MacIntyre, Charles Taylor, and Peter Winch, many of who had been influenced by Wittgenstein and Austin.[65] These philosophers wrote explicit criticisms of behavioralism, as did Strauss and Wolin. Yet their criticisms relied primarily on philosophical analyses of the forms of explanation appropriate to social life. In general terms, they argued that to explain social actions, political scientists have to grasp the meanings of the relevant actors, and to grasp and explain these meanings, political scientists need to locate them in the appropriate set of categories, tradition, or way of life.[66] This general form of explanation could provide, they implied, the basis for a more philosophically legitimate political science. Skinner, who was especially influenced by MacIntyre's philosophy of action, sought to contribute to such a political science by grasping the modern concept of the state and explaining how it had emerged out of various ideological traditions.[67] The *Foundations* is in part an exercise in historicist political science.

Skinner drew on recent analytic philosophy to rethink the nature of a historicist political science that studied the ideas upon which our institutions were based. In many ways, however, the form of political studies that he thus came to advocate represents a continuation of the approach to political theory that had flourished at Cambridge under figures such as Figgis and Maitland.[68] Indeed, Skinner has said that his appeals to the philosophical positions of Collingwood, Wittgenstein, and Austin were intended to give a more abstract formulation and defense of the type of history of political thought that was then being pursued by John Burrow, John Dunn, Duncan Forbes, Peter Laslett, and J.G.A. Pocock, all of whom

---

[65] Quentin Skinner, *The Foundations of Modern Political Thought*, 2 vols. (Cambridge: Cambridge University Press, 1978); and for his contribution to the philosophical debate see Quentin Skinner, "'Social Meaning' and the Explanation of Social Action," in Tully, *Meaning and Context*, 79–96.

[66] Alasdair MacIntyre, "A Mistake about Causality in Social Science," in *Philosophy, Politics, and Society*, 2nd ser., ed. Peter Laslett and W. G. Runciman (Oxford: Basil Blackwell, 1969), 48–70; Charles Taylor, *Philosophical Papers*, vol. 2, *Philosophy and the Human Sciences* (Cambridge: Cambridge University Press, 1985); Peter Winch, *The Idea of a Social Science* (London: Routledge and Kegan Paul, 1958).

[67] Skinner drew also on MacIntyre's argument that all action had to make use of a preexisting normative vocabulary for its legitimation and that these vocabularies thus influenced the forms action could take. An important influence on his *Foundations* is, in this respect, Alasdair MacIntyre, *A Short History of Ethics* (New York: Macmillan, 1966).

[68] On the overlaps between Figgis and Skinner see Mark Goldie, "J. N. Figgis and the History of Political Thought at Cambridge," in *Cambridge Minds*, ed. Richard Mason (Cambridge: Cambridge University Press, 1994), 177–92.

either were at Cambridge or else had recently finished their studies there.[69] On the one hand, these political theorists undoubtedly rebelled against some of the strands that Barker identified as having a place therein. Their sense of the parlous state of moral philosophy led them, in particular, to rebel against the idea—passed down from Greats—that there was a canon of texts embodying a timeless wisdom. Even here, however, the "traditionalism" against which they took up arms was one defined by the epic theorizing of Strauss and others as much as by the legacy of Greats. On the other hand, moreover, their rebellion against "traditionalism" was one that drew on the legacy of other strands identified by Barker, notably constitutional history but also the theory of the state. The legacy of the constitutional history appears in the close focus on specific historical documents and the stress on locating them in their historical context. And the legacy of the theory of the state appears in the choice of Hobbes, by Skinner, and of Locke, by Dunn, as the focus of research, for, as Skinner has explained, "it seemed obvious [to British scholars] that the two great founding fathers of modern political theory were Hobbes and Locke, the first being the leading exemplar of the theory of the state, the second of the theory of popular sovereignty."[70]

Conclusion

Between the wars, political theorists in Britain and America generally operated within a shared tradition of "ideas and institutions" scholarship. The remaking of political theory from the 1950s to the 1970s saw them adopt rather different approaches and emphases. To conclude, we might point toward some of these differences by tracing the fate in each country of the three strands that had gone into the tradition of ideas and institutions. Consider, first, the theory of the state. Whereas attempts to theorize the state had all but disappeared from American political theory by the late 1960s, they were merely given a more rigorous historical grounding in the work of Skinner, Dunn, and others on the development of the European and British polity. The methodological legacy of constitutional history also remained strong in Britain, where theorists still emphasized the importance of original research on historical documents. In contrast, the emphasis of American theorists on perennial issues and canonical thinkers led to a clear break with the earlier constitutional scholarship of people such as McIlwain. Little remained of such work other than a persistent

---

[69] See, for just one example, Quentin Skinner, "A Reply to my Critics," in Tully, *Meaning and Context*, 233–34.

[70] Koikkalainen and Syrjämäki, "Interview with Skinner," 41.

concern with the American founding and the meaning of its constitution.[71] Even this concern was transformed, moreover, as it became saturated with the epic motifs of the heroic theorist, moral grandeur, and moral decline.

Let us turn now to the persistence of moral philosophy as a form of political theory. In Britain, a radical historicism suggested that attempts to philosophize by making past texts speak to our concerns were almost doomed to lead to all sorts of anachronistic absurdities: the implication was, as Skinner argued so forcefully, "we must learn to do our own thinking for ourselves."[72] The American emphasis on perennial issues and canonical thinkers served, in contrast, to shelter indirect philosophizing from the import of such radical historicism. Even if new theorists entered the canon or new issues became fashionable topics, the mode of theorizing remained the distinctly conservative one of engaging the great books. These emergent differences help, finally, to explain the different ways in which Rawls was received in Britain and America. Although Rawls wrote in the context of postwar Anglo-American analytical philosophy rather than within the subfield of political theory, his work has influenced political theorists on both sides of the Atlantic since the 1970s, thereby setting up his contested role as the last of the three saviors of theory with whom we opened this chapter. In America, Rawls's dramatic impact upon ethics found few early echoes among political theorists, many of whom not only remained content to do moral philosophy through engagements with the great books but also, at least implicitly, thought of all analytic philosophy as positivistic and so pernicious. Hence, Rawls, and analytic political theory more generally, infiltrated departments of political science more slowly and somewhat later than they did departments of philosophy. In Britain, by contrast, political theorists took to Rawls remarkably quickly. They did so partly because they were generally less hostile to analytic philosophy than were many of their American counterparts. And they did so partly because he provided them—especially at Oxford where moral philosophy had always been more prominent than constitutional history—with a model of how we might do our own thinking for ourselves.

[71] Examples of this interest in the American founding include Arendt, *On Revolution*; and Norman Jacobson, "Political Science and Political Education," *American Political Science Review* 57, no. 3 (1963): 561–69. Strauss's references to the founding are brief but suggestive: see, for example, Leo Strauss, *Natural Right and History* (Chicago: University of Chicago Press, 1953), 1. The topic has been a subject of extensive concern among some of his students: Thomas G. West, "Leo Strauss and the American Founding," *Review of Politics* 53, no. 1 (1991): 157–72; Christopher Bruell, "A Return to Classical Political Philosophy and the Understanding of the American Founding," *Review of Politics* 53, no. 1 (1991): 173–86; and David Schaefer, "Leo Strauss and American Democracy," *Review of Politics* 53, no. 1 (1991): 187–99.

[72] Skinner, "Meaning and Understanding," 65.

Eleven

Traditions of Political Science in Contemporary Britain

MARK BEVIR AND R.A.W. RHODES

BRITISH POLITICAL SCIENCE has a dominant self-image based on a narrative of professionalization. This narrative tells how a Whig inheritance evolved into a more mature, largely autonomous, professional, and suitably cautious discipline. Perhaps paradoxically it also contrasts the restraint of the British discipline with the excessive scientism and professionalism of its American counterpart. It concludes with a portrait of a professional discipline producing what we might think of as modernist empiricist knowledge, that is, knowledge reached through atomization, comparison, classification, and even quantification.

Jack Hayward provides one example of the narrative of professionalization. He identifies three stages in the development of British political science since the formation of the Political Studies Association (PSA) in 1950. The first decade saw "a retrospective Whig inclination to complacent description of traditions inherited from the past," perhaps even "atheoretical empiricism." Stage two, between 1961 and 1974, was an "enthusiastic and optimistic phase of technocratic reformism" exemplified by the work of social scientists for government inquiries into the civil service and local government. Finally, since 1975, the discipline has been characterized by a "sceptical professionalism," with leading political scientists commenting on, for example, the problems of overloaded government or the costs of adversary politics.[1] For Hayward, British political science has remained insular despite, an eye-catching phrase, "homoeopathic doses of American political science."[2] Nor does he hesitate to prick American pretensions to a science of politics commenting, in another striking aphorism, that political scientists have "the capacity to offer some hindsight, a little insight, and almost no foresight." He concludes that

---

[1] Jack Hayward, "Political Science in Britain," *European Journal of Political Research* 20, no. 2 (1991): 301–22.

[2] Jack Hayward, "Cultural and Contextual Constraints upon the Development of Political Science in Great Britain," in *The Development of Political Science: A Comparative Survey*, ed. David Easton, John G. Gunnell, and Luigi Graziano (London: Routledge, 1991), 104.

British political science adapted "in a piecemeal and incremental fashion" to the "concerns of American political science but without their concomitant theoretical self-consciousness."[3]

Radical historicism might prompt a critique of the narrative of professionalization.[4] It might make us more sensitive to various traditions of political science found in Britain, and to the contingency of their historical development. So, we argue, first, there are several traditions in British political science. These include the modernist empiricism that often informs the narrative of professionalization, and idealist and socialist traditions. The narrative of professionalization seeks to write out other traditions from the history of the discipline. State policies and funding, and mainstream political scientists' pursuit of state recognition and approval, facilitate this goal. In contrast, we denaturalize the narrative of professionalization by showing it is just one among many possible stories.

We argue, second, each tradition in British political science changed in response to the dilemmas posed by changing intellectual and state agendas, but there were great differences in their responses. Changes were contingent responses to particular dilemmas. The narrative of professionalization seeks to domesticate such contingency. It suggests a smooth process of development that can be explained by reference to the internal dictates of a logic of professionalization. In contrast, we seek to denaturalize the narrative of professionalization by showing how it embodies just one possible response to various dilemmas.

Modernist Empiricism

Radical historicism encourages us to highlight several traditions of political science in Britain, by no means all of which make an appearance in the narrative of professionalization. As examples, we highlight idealism and socialism as well as the Whig and behavioral strands that have contributed so much to the dominant modernist empiricism. No survey of

---

[3] Jack Hayward, "British Approaches to Politics: The Dawn of a Self-Deprecating Discipline," in *The British Study of Politics in the Twentieth Century*, ed. Jack Hayward, Brian Barry, and Archie Brown (Oxford: Oxford University Press, 1999), 34 and 31. For an earlier discussion of this volume see Mark Bevir, "Prisoners of Professionalism: On the Construction and Responsibility of Political Studies," *Public Administration* 79, no. 2 (2001): 469–89.

[4] Almost the only historicist works that challenge the narrative of professionalization are those of Stefan Collini and Julia Stapleton. However, while their historicist approach is very different from that found in the narrative of professionalization, their Whiggism means their narratives overlap with those of modernist empiricists. For discussion see Robert Adcock and Mark Bevir, "The History of Political Science," *Political Studies Review* 3 (2005): 1–16.

British political science that focused solely on modernist empiricism can pretend to be accurate or comprehensive. Nonetheless, we might begin by recounting the fortunes of a mainstream modernist empiricism as its Whiggish inheritance encountered behavioralism and Thatcherism.

The Whig tradition is sometimes treated as a hangover from the past. There are, however, several reasons for querying this treatment. The Whig tradition persists, in particular, because it constituted the tradition against the background of which British political scientists forged mainstream modernist empiricism. The essays by Kavanagh and Kenny in this volume trace this transformation. Those essays suggest atomization, analysis, classification, comparison, and correlation gradually gained ascendancy over the contextualizing and progressive narratives of the developmental historicists discussed in the earlier essay by den Otter. Nineteenth-century theorists evoked history to postulate the beliefs, reason, or character by which they interpreted the political. When modernist empiricists, such as S. E. Finer, turned to history, they were more likely to evoke social and institutional regularities and to construct typologies than they were to interpret meanings.

Even as modernist empiricism brought novel methods and logics of inquiry to British political science, so British political scientists remained profoundly indebted to Whiggism in defining the objects of their inquiries. Whig historiography resulted in the more ahistorical idea of the Westminster model, and a vague concern with British exceptionalism remained widespread, perhaps even contributing to the complacent insularity noted by Kavanagh. Of course, there was some tension between the new modernist logics of inquiry and the older Whiggish objects of inquiry. This tension helps to explain, in turn, the gradual rise of new areas of inquiry, including electoral behaviour, policy networks, and, most recently, governance, all of which had little, if any, place in the nineteenth-century study of politics.

The persistence of Whiggism in modernist empiricism appears starkly in Vernon Bogdanor's forceful apologia. He argues the main characteristics of the Whig tradition are its aversion to "over-arching theory" and "positivism." Whiggish writers are the fundamental influences on British political science. There is Dicey, "who sought to discover what it was that distinguished the British constitution from codified constitutions." And there is Bagehot, "who . . . sought to understand political 'forms' through the analysis of political 'forces.' " British political scientists are "eclectic"; "they have rarely concentrated on just one form of analysis because it seems fashionable." At its best, British political science "has combined deep historical knowledge with breadth of perspective." American social science undoubtedly had an influence, but there is "an indigenous British approach to politics, a definite intellectual tradition, and one that is worth preserving."[5]

If British political scientists were uncomfortable with the hypothesis testing and deductive methods of behavioralism, they were at ease with the atomization, classification, and measurement of modernist empiricism. They treated institutions such as legislatures, constitutions, and policy networks as discrete objects to be compared, measured, and classified. What is more, their modernist empiricism overlapped with behavioralism at various junctures. Both adopted comparisons across time and space as a means of uncovering regularities and probabilistic explanations to be tested against neutral evidence. These overlaps provided a channel through which many British political scientists could indeed take a dose of behavioralism.

David Sanders captures the meaning of behavioralism in British political science. He associates it with, first, a particular take on empirical theory—"a set of interconnected abstract statements, consisting of assumptions, definitions and empirically testable hypotheses, which purports to describe and explain the occurrence of a given phenomenon or set of phenomena." Second, he associates it with a particular type of explanation—"the specification of the minimum non-tautological antecedent necessary and sufficient conditions required" for a phenomenon to occur.[6]

Jean Blondel was among the leading advocates of such behavioralism. His approach to comparative government was "general and analytical," considering "the general conditions which lead to the development of types of political systems."[7] So, "one is inclined to look for 'causes' and, more generally, for regularities." The use of quantification to identify such regularities is, he continues, an important ambition, since in its absence political science is "descriptive," "superficial," and indistinguishable from journalism.[8] However, even Blondel qualified his behavioralist ambitions in a way that echoed the concerns of mainstream modernist empiricists. He admitted that politics was "'messy' and somewhat unscientific," even adding, "the development of quantification in political science does depend in part on an 'act of faith.' " Blondel argued, therefore, that general or universal theories were too ambitious: " 'middle range' or 'partial systems' comparisons" are the best way of tackling "the persistent prob-

[5] Vernon Bogdanor, "Comparative Politics," in Hayward, Barry, and Brown, *British Study of Politics*, 149, 150, 175, 176–77 and 178.

[6] David Sanders, "Behavioural Analysis," in *Theory and Methods in Political Science*, 1st ed., ed. David Marsh, and Gerry Stoker (London: Macmillan, 1995), 60.

[7] Jean Blondel, *Comparative Government*, 1st ed. (London: Weidenfeld and Nicolson, 1969), ix–x. The second edition (London: Philip Allan, 1999), xvi and 4 repeats the argument.

[8] Jean Blondel, *The Discipline of Politics* (London: Butterworth, 1981), 107, 168, and 109.

lem of political institutions." Comparative government requires a general analysis of such institutions as political parties, legislatures, bureaucracies, the military, and the judiciary. Blondel focused on middle-range comparisons employing quantification whenever possible to identify and explain genuine cross-national regularities.[9]

Key words characterize Blondel's approach to comparative government: for example, "quantification," "systematic," and "regularities." They have a dual significance. They are not only the objectives of his comparative method but also criticisms of other methods, most notably case studies. They convey his behavioralist suspicions of the continuing strength within British political science of a skeptical and atheoretical Whiggism. Blondel explicitly contrasted his preferred nomothetic approach of quantitative, middle-range analysis as a source of systematic thinking and generalizations with an idiographic approach that was mainly descriptive and focused on the unique.[10] In short, Blondel, with his emphasis on facts and search for regularities, is a fine example of modernist empiricism after it has taken a dose of behavioralism.[11]

Thatcherism provided a much greater challenge to modernist empiricism in Britain than had behavioralism. It marginalized political science, and its rise challenged the old Whig nostrums of consensus, gradualism, and the capacity of British institutions to evolve and cope with crises. There were several battlegrounds. None posed a bigger challenge than the new public management (NPM). The impetus and ideas behind the Thatcher government's NPM reforms came from practitioners, economists, management consultants, and New Right think tanks. They were the source of policy innovations. They challenged many nostrums of British political science, forcing a rethink of, for example, the theory of bureaucracy. Political scientists were essentially bystanders. They did not create and promote such new ideas. Challenged by Thatcherism and NPM, students of public administration in particular were losing their institutional base in the universities. They had difficulty finding a new role and constructing a coherent intellectual identity.

---

[9] Blondel, *Discipline*, 163, 178–85, 190, and 197; Blondel, *Comparative Government*, 2nd ed., 357–59.

[10] Blondel, *Comparative Government*, 1st ed., 5; and Blondel, *Discipline*, 67.

[11] Of course Blondel is not the only example. The subfield of British election studies is dominated by this approach. Any comprehensive listing would be inordinately long but for relevant citations see Ivor Crewe and P. Norris, "In Defence of British Electoral Studies," in *British Elections and Parties Yearbook, 1991*, ed. Ivor Crewe and others (London: Harvester Wheatsheaf, 1992); and Elinor Scarborough, "The British Electorate Twenty Years On: Electoral Change and Election Surveys," *British Journal of Political Science* 17, no. 2 (1987): 219–46.

Modernist empiricists responded to the dilemmas posed by Thatcherism with a new literature on governance. This literature suggested the New Right had fallen prey to an economistic dogma, which had failed to bring the promised results. It did so by highlighting the unintended consequences of NPM, especially the perceived weaknesses of marketization.[12] Once again, British political scientists presented themselves as cautious, professional agnostics; they commented judiciously on the gap between aspirations and achievements in policy areas such as privatization, public expenditure, and civil service reform.

Governance described the pattern of public administration that had arisen unintentionally out of the reforms of the Thatcher government. It consisted of a series of networks, not pure markets. These networks were described as poorly coordinated, increasingly difficult for government to control, and perhaps worryingly unaccountable. The economists and management consultants had failed. They had pursued a formal dogmatic faith in markets when, as political scientists explained, what mattered was getting the right mix of hierarchies, markets, and networks. The governance literature also informed various attempts to atomize the rising networks from their particular contexts to construct analytic classifications. At times, these classifications purported to identify appropriate managerial strategies for the different categories of classification.

Although the literature on governance traced weaknesses in the Thatcher government reforms, it rarely suggested any rethinking of an entrenched modernist empiricism. It is important to recognize here that the impact of Thatcherism as a political movement was not matched in Britain by the impact of rational choice theory as an intellectual movement. Rational choice theory remained a minority interest among political scientists.[13] The majority dismissed it as an example of the excesses of

[12] For reviews of the literature see M. Marinetto, "Governing beyond the Centre: A Critique of the Anglo-Governance School," *Political Studies* 51, no. 3 (2003): 592–608; R.A.W. Rhodes, "Public Administration and Governance," in *Debating Governance*, ed. Jon Pierre (Oxford: Oxford University Press, 1999).

[13] Rational choice is seen as "genre" political science. Albert Weale (Essex) is the source of this appellation. At the time he made this statement, he was chair of the 2001 Research Assessment Exercise Panel (RAE), which was responsible for evaluating the research output of all British political scientists. There is little by way of an indigenous literature. We consulted colleagues specializing in rational choice. The criteria for inclusion were a book by a political scientist based in Britain and rational choice research. The resulting list was short. Excluding textbooks, the main examples include George A. Boyne, *Public Choice Theory and Local Government* (London: Macmillan, 1998); Keith Dowding and Desmond King, *Preferences, Institutions and Rational Choice* (Oxford: Oxford University Press, 1995); Patrick Dunleavy, *Democracy, Bureaucracy and Public Choice* (Hemel Hempstead, UK: Harvester Wheatsheaf, 1991); and Iain McLean, *Rational Choice and British Politics* (Oxford: Oxford University Press, 2001).

American scientism. It was considered an intellectual exercise of little relevance to the real world. Also, it was tarnished by its association with the New Right.

The absence of rational choice theory does much to explain British responses to the new institutionalism, the American origins of which will be explored in the following chapter. The first point to note is that the new institutionalism has been associated almost wholly with its sociological and historical strands, with the rational choice one being largely neglected. The other related point to note is that many British political scientists denied any novelty to the new institutionalism. In Britain, they argued, neither the behavioral revolution nor rational choice had swept the study of institutions away.[14] Hence British political scientists often took the rise of the new institutionalism in America to be a vindication of British modernist empiricism, with its skepticism toward universal theory, against the deplorable scientism characterizing American political science.

Even today, when British political scientists drape themselves in the new institutionalism, it often acts merely as a cloak of convenience. Case studies of institutions can be dressed up as a revitalized institutionalism, and British political scientists can claim they wear the latest fashionable clothes. But, in fact, they are the emperor's new clothes. If you look closely little has changed: we are in the altogether. Vivien Lowndes is one prominent example of a British political scientist who espouses the new institutionalism. She makes probably the strongest possible claim for it when she argues it is not a theory, but an organizing perspective, which provokes questions and yields fresh insights. It is not associated with any one theory and its strength lies in its multitheoretic character.[15] So understood, the new institutionalism is, at least in Britain, little more than a cloak with which Whigs and modernist empiricists can pursue the kinds of work they long have done unruffled by the pretensions of behavioralism and rational choice.

What does the research done within the mainstream of British political science look like? There is simply no space to summarize the diversity of such research, and, of course, it is dangerous to claim one author can exemplify a tradition. Nonetheless, S. E. Finer's three-volume history of government combines a Whiggish sensitivity to history with a modernist empiricist belief in comparisons across time and space, regularities, and neutral evidence. As Hayward observes, Finer is either "the last

---

[14] R.A.W. Rhodes, *Understanding Governance* (Buckingham: Open University Press, 1997), 78–79.

[15] Vivien Lowndes, "The Institutional Approach," in Marsh and Stoker, *Theory and Methods*, 2nd ed., 108.

trump reasserting an old institutionalism" or "the resounding affirmation of the potentialities of a new historical institutionalism within British political science."[16]

As early as 1954, Finer argued that although the predictions offered by political science "are short term and have a low degree of probability," it is still a science "because it can offer reasons and causes for events once those events have happened." Latterly he took the even more cautious view of political science as "interpreting a body of factual knowledge" or "making a pattern out of it," while welcoming the proliferation of professional theories and techniques that had come to constitute "a rich armoury into which we can dip to select the appropriate weapon" to study our chosen question or problem.[17]

Finer's *History* combines this modern armory with history in an attempt to explain how states came to be what they are with a specific emphasis on the creation of the modern European nation-state.[18] He searches for regularities across time and countries in an exercise in diachronic comparison. The *History* sets out to establish the distribution of the selected forms of government throughout history, analyze each according to a standard format, and assess its general character, strengths, and weaknesses according to a standardized set of criteria. It identifies similarities and differences between the forms of government using a standardized typology.[19] The typology is complex as the summary outline below shows. The book then provides, true to its title, a history of government from ancient monarchies (about 1700 BC) to AD 1875. The result may be old institutionalism or it may be new institutionalism, but, coupled with the typology, it is a fine example of an eclectic modernist empiricism at work.

Finer's Typology and Variables Summarized.[20]

1. There are four basic clusters of variables.
   (a) Territory
   (b) Type
   (c) Possession of an army and/or bureaucracy
   (d) Limitations on activities.

---

[16] Hayward, "British Approaches," 35.

[17] S. E. Finer, "Political Science: An Idiosyncratic Retrospect," *Government and Opposition* 15, nos. 3–4 (1980): 361, 363.

[18] S. E. Finer, *The History of Government from the Earliest Times*, vol. 1; *Ancient Monarchies and Empires;* vol. 2, *The Intermediate Ages;* and vol. 3, *Empires, Monarchies and the Modern State* (Oxford: Oxford University Press, 1997).

[19] Finer, *History* 1:1.

[20] Derived from Finer, *History* 1:35, 37, 60–61, 65, 72, and 78.

2. Each cluster breaks down into subvariables.
   (a) Territory breaks down into:
       (i) City
       (ii) National and
       (iii) Empire.
   (b) Type breaks down into ten combinations of:
       (i) palace
       (ii) nobility
       (iii) church and
       (iv) forum.
   (c) These types are in turn discriminated by the nature of their
       decision-making and decision-implementing personnel.
       (i) Decision-making breaks down into:
           A. Dominant personnel
           B. Characteristic political processes
           C. Legitimacy basis.
       (ii) Decision-implementing breaks down into:
           A. Bureaucracies:
              Developed
              Emergent and
              Rudimentary.
           B. Armed Forces:
              Community-in-arms
              Notables and
              Standing armies.
   (d) Constraints are:
       (i) Substantive and
       (ii) Procedural
       (iii) Horizontal (central government) and
       (iv) Vertical (center to locality).

The history of modernist empiricism in Britain fits moderately well with
the narrative of professionalization. Modernist empiricism arose against
the Whig tradition and later selectively assimilated certain elements of
various American "revolutions" from behavioralism to new institutionalism. However, we have told this narrative without reference to any supposed logic of professionalization. We have recounted instead the development of one particular tradition as its exponents responded to
intellectual challenges from abroad and elsewhere. By doing so, we have
tried to expose the contingency of what has become the mainstream of
British political science. We have also tried to open a space in which to
explore the rival claims of other, alternative traditions, which are written
out of the narrative of professionalization.

Idealism

As den Otter argued in her chapter, Whiggism and idealism overlapped in many complex ways during the late nineteenth century. The emergence of modernist empiricism and even aspects of behavioralism meant that idealism got pushed toward the margins of political science, retaining a strong presence only in the subfield of political theory. Even so, idealism was not static. Although pluralists such as Ernest Barker and A. D. Lindsay challenged the pivotal role the earlier idealists had ascribed to the state, their pluralism might be seen, as den Otter and Kavanagh have suggested, less as a rejection of idealism than as a refashioning of it following the experience of World War I. In addition, the disillusionment that followed World War I led many later theorists to reject the earlier idealists' concepts of the absolute. R. G. Collingwood, John Macmurray, Michael Oakeshott, and many others qualified or even rejected the idea of an absolute mind immanent within the world. As a result, it is perhaps questionable whether they should be described as idealists. Still, they remained profoundly indebted to many other themes associated with idealism—a vitalist analysis of human behavior, a thick concept of the person, a positive concept of freedom, and often a concern with community.[21]

In the 1960s and 1970s, idealist themes characterized two rather different approaches to the study of politics. The first approach was a conservative idealism associated primarily with Michael Oakeshott, whose importance has already been noted by Kenny. The second was a diffuse social humanism found in the work of political theorists such as Charles Taylor and, as the preceding chapter argued, Quentin Skinner.

The inheritors of idealism challenged behavioralism for its neglect of meanings, contexts, and history. Oakeshott argued political education required the "genuine historical study" of a "tradition of behaviour." He then adopted a conservative analysis of tradition as a resource to which one should typically feel allegiance. Indeed, he almost treats political traditions as "natural," as if particular polities can use them to derive unambiguously correct lessons for their current practices. He does so despite his explicit comments against such an analysis of tradition. Oakeshott thus defined the task of the political scientist as being "to understand a tradition," which is "participation in a conversation," "initiation into an inheritance," and "an exploration of its intimations."[22]

---

[21] See Mark Bevir and David O'Brien, "From Idealism to Communitarianism: The Inheritance and Legacy of John Macmurray," *History of Political Thought* 24, no. 2 (2003): 305–29.

[22] Michael Oakeshott, *Rationalism in Politics and Other Essays*, 2nd ed., expanded (Indianapolis: Liberty Press, 1991; originally published in 1962), 59–60 and 62–65.

During the 1970s and 1980s, W. H. Greenleaf and Nevil Johnson, two of Oakeshott's disciples, continued to restate the master's critique to encompass developments in British political science. Greenleaf made the point bluntly when he argued that although "the concept of a genuine social science has had its ups and downs, and it still survives, . . . we are as far from its achievement as we were when Spencer (or Bacon for that matter) first put pen to paper." Indeed, he opines, these "continuous attempts . . . serve only to demonstrate . . . the inherent futility of the enterprise."[23]

Johnson similarly wrote a book titled *The Limits of Political Science*. He found the study of politics wanting, whether in the guise of journalism or political science. Journalism was "naively descriptive and empirical, and too deeply immersed in the ebb and flow of current affairs to permit either accurate description or cool judgement." Political science was denounced for its American inspired "thoroughgoing positivism," which displayed a "remarkable naivety in the perception of the diversity of human conduct and culture, combined with a readiness to dress up uninteresting conclusions in fancy technical clothes and portentous jargon." The belief in the utility of the social sciences in general and political science in particular is "confused," "vulgar," and "mistaken."[24] Johnson argued the study of politics should allow, rather, that "a political association exists only within specific traditions." "Political association entails institutions to express its form," moreover, since "institutions serve as means of communicating and transmitting values." Institutions express human purpose.[25] The aim of the study of politics is to "gain a reflective and critical understanding of some of the varieties of human political experience." So, "explanatory work in politics is likely to refer chiefly to institutions and must rely extensively on the methods of historical research." It does not seek "to formulate statements of regularity or generalisations claiming to apply universally." History is "the source of experience," while philosophy is "the means of its critical appraisal."[26]

Social humanists such as Taylor and Skinner were equally critical of positivist approaches to political science. Taylor's doctoral thesis was a defense of a vitalist analysis of human behavior against mechanism.[27]

[23] W. H. Greenleaf, *The British Political Tradition*, Vol. 1, *The Rise of Collectivism* (London: Methuen, 1983), 286.

[24] Nevil Johnson, *The Limits of Political Science* (Oxford: Clarendon Press, 1989), 55, 81, and 104–5.

[25] Ibid., 129, 131, and 112. See also Nevil Johnson, "The Place of Institutions in the Study of Politics," *Political Studies* 23 (1975): 271–83.

[26] Johnson, *Limits*, 117 and 122–23.

[27] Charles Taylor, "Explanation by Purpose and Modern Psychological Theory" (DPhil thesis, University of Oxford, 1961). A revised version was published as Charles Taylor, *The Explanation of Behaviour* (London: Routledge, 1964).

Thereafter he wrote a series of essays explicitly challenging behavioralism and its leading tenets. He argued, in "Interpretation and the Sciences of Man," that beliefs, meanings, and language were constitutive of human actions and practices. The social sciences were unavoidably hermeneutical. His argument entailed a break with "mainstream social science" and its empiricist and positivist epistemologies. In particular, "we cannot measure such sciences against the requirements of a science of verification; we cannot judge them by their predictive capacity."[28]

In "Neutrality in Political Science," Taylor extended his argument to take direct aim at "the cult of neutrality." Behavioralists defended the superiority of their approach to that of elder ones by arguing that the latter were always permeated by value positions in a way that meant their frameworks were never scientific but rather always serving the interests of a normative or ideological theory. Behavioralists proposed instead to turn the study of politics into a technocratic "policy science," akin to engineering or medicine, which would "show us how to attain our goals." Taylor argued, however, that when behavioralists constructed theoretical frameworks to delimit the proper area of scientific inquiry, they made fundamental choices that entailed normative commitments. The work of Lasswell, Easton, and Almond secrete their norms. "We come out with a full-dress justification of democracy," Taylor said referring to Lasswell's *Power and Society*, "in a work which claims neutrality." In general, Taylor suggested that conceptual frameworks always depended on theory, and theory could not be constructed apart from values. The ties binding theoretical frameworks and values also opened up the possibility, he suggested, of seeing some values as especially meaningful responses to particular empirical contexts.[29]

Although social humanists emphasized meanings and contexts in a similar fashion to conservative idealists, they took a different view of tradition, language, and community as the relevant contexts. Social humanists placed far greater emphasis on the contingency and diversity of contexts and languages present within any given society. We have already seen how Taylor argued that political studies opened up onto the comparison of, and even judgment between, rival moral frameworks in society. Skinner likewise emphasised the plurality of languages or ideologies found in a society at any given time. At times social humanists also suggested traditions or languages were open-ended. There was no single correct way to apply them or extend them on any particular occasion.

[28] Charles Taylor, "Interpretation and the Sciences of Man," *Review of Metaphysics* 25 (1971): 51.

[29] Charles Taylor, "Neutrality in Political Science," in *Philosophy, Politics, Society*, 3rd ser., ed. Peter Laslett and W. G. Runciman (Oxford: Blackwell, 1967), 48, 27, and 46.

It was, however, the conservative analysis of tradition associated with Oakeshott that appeared in Johnson's and Greenleaf's studies of British politics. Difference, discontinuity, and dispersal were all elided. Johnson represented the British constitution as rooted in the "extraordinary and basically unbroken continuity of conventional political habits," even suggesting it "*is* these political habits and little else.*" The core notion within this inheritance is, he adds, "the complete dominance of one particular body of ideas about government, namely what we usually call the idea of parliamentary government." He even maintained there is "no alternative or competing political tradition to fall back on, no different view of the basis on which political authority might rest."[30]

Although Greenleaf declared that a tradition of behavior was "a tricky thing to get to know,"[31] he asserted; "the British political tradition as it has developed in modern times" is "constituted by a dialectic between the two opposing tendencies" of libertarianism and collectivism. In his view, there was no sharp distinction between these two strands of the British tradition; rather, they were "an impressionistic working hypothesis of an historical kind," which could be used to pull together the diverse practices and ideas of British political life. Libertarianism meant four things: an inalienable title to a realm of self-regarding action; a limited role for government; the dispersion of power; and the Rule of Law. Collectivism stood in contrast to this individuality; it was concerned with the public good, social justice, positive government, and the concentration of state power.[32] Greenleaf viewed the past century and a half as one of government growth, and so of the triumph of collectivism over individualism. Most of his four volumes is taken up with documenting this claim and answering the question of why a libertarian, individualist society sustaining a limited conception of government had been in so many ways and to such a degree replaced by a positive state pursuing explicit policies of widespread intervention in the name of social justice and the public good. Greenleaf, like Oakeshott and Johnson, implied traditions give us unambiguous answers to problems, and the British tradition tells us we should oppose state action.

It was this opposition to state action that led to Oakeshott becoming a guru in the 1980s, appealing to all shades of Conservatism.[33] His distinction between the state as a civil and an enterprise association became a mantra for those seeking to justify the minimalist state. An enterprise

---

[30] Nevil Johnson, *In Search of the Constitution* (London: Pergamon, 1977), 30.

[31] Greenleaf, *British Political Tradition* 1:13 citing Oakeshott, *Rationalism in Politics*, 61.

[32] Greenleaf, *British Political Tradition* 1:14, 15–20, and 20–23.

[33] See, for example, Ian Gilmour, *Dancing with Dogma: Britain under Thatcherism* (London: Simon and Schuster, 1992), 98; Ferdinand Mount, *The British Constitution Now: Recovery or Decline?* (London: Mandarin, 1993), 74–75; and David Willetts, *Modern Conservatism* (Harmondsworth, UK: Penguin Books, 1992), 72–73.

association is "human beings joined in pursuing some common substantive interest, in seeking the satisfaction of some common want or in promoting some common substantive interest." Persons in a civil association "are not joined in any undertaking to promote a common interest . . . but in recognition of non-instrumental rules indifferent to any interest," that is, common rules and a common government in the context of which they pursue diverse purposes. However, while Conservatives favored civil association and limited state intervention, they rarely invoked the idealist philosophy with which Oakeshott had sustained his argument.

At the time Conservatives adopted Oakeshott as a guru, social humanists were expressing strong disquiet at an aggressive liberal individualism widely associated with the New Right. They invoked ideals of fellowship, community, and citizenship as antidotes to the selfishness and social dislocation they saw in the New Right. Most obviously, Taylor, who had by then returned to Canada, developed a communitarian philosophy. He appealed to community as a necessary corrective to a society based solely on impersonal contracts and self-interest.[34] What is more, his concept of community again expressed the sort of concern with diversity and difference that characterized social humanists' accounts of context. His work on multiculturalism in Canada sought to allow for "deep diversity" by recognizing a "plurality of ways of belonging" to the community.[35]

Skinner moved cautiously away from his earlier opposition to our using past texts to resolve our problems.[36] He began to reconstruct a republican notion of liberty according to which "we must take our duties seriously, and instead of trying to evade anything more than 'the minimum demands of social life' we must seek to discharge our public obligations as wholeheartedly as possible."[37] Before long, he announced his ambition was "to question this liberal hegemony." He attempted to reenter the "intellectual world" of English republicans, such as Harrington, who had espoused a neo-roman theory of the free state and free citizens.[38]

---

[34] Charles Taylor, "Cross-Purposes: The Liberal-Communitarian Debate," in *Liberalism and the Moral Life*, ed. Nancy L. Rosenblum (Cambridge: Harvard University Press, 1989).

[35] Charles Taylor, *Reconciling the Solitudes: Essays on Canadian Federalism and Nationalism*, ed. G. Laforest (Montreal: McGill-Queen's University Press, 1993), 181–83.

[36] The first signs of this movement appeared in Quentin Skinner, "The Idea of Negative Liberty: Philosophical and Historical Perspectives," in *Philosophy in History*, ed. Richard Rorty, J. B. Schneewind, and Quentin Skinner (Cambridge: Cambridge University Press, 1984), 231–88; and Quentin Skinner, "The Republican Ideal of Political Liberty," in *Machiavelli and Republicanism*, ed. Gisela Bock, Quentin Skinner, and Maurizio Viroli (Cambridge: Cambridge University Press, 1990), 293–309. It became triumphantly clear in Quentin Skinner, *Liberty before Liberalism* (Cambridge: Cambridge University Press, 1998).

[37] Skinner, "Republican Ideal," 308.

[38] Skinner, *Liberty before Liberalism*, x. Also see Quentin Skinner, "States and Freedom of Citizens," in *States and Citizens: History, Theory, Prospects*, ed. Quentin Skinner and Bo Strath (Cambridge: Cambridge University Press, 2003).

Socialism

The long-standing, distinguished socialist tradition of political analysis in Britain has appeared in many of the earlier essays in this volume. It remains a powerful presence, with its own publishers such as Verso, Lawrence and Wishart, and Pluto; its own journals such as *New Left Review*, *Marxism Today*, and *The Socialist Register*; its own key figures, including Perry Anderson, Stuart Hall, Bob Jessop, Gareth Stedman Jones, Tom Nairn, and E. P. Thompson; and arguably its own debates such as those over labor historiography and the relation of structure to agency.

British socialists have long rejected the professional aspirations and alleged neutrality of modernist empiricism. For them, the accolade of science should be applied, if anywhere, to Marxism. Colin Leys criticizes political science because it claims to be value free, it has a pluralist conception of politics, it discusses politics in isolation from economics, it fails to think about the present historically, and it ignores the effects and social origins of ideas. Leys views politics as a struggle between the interests of labor and capital, and the political system as shaped by the needs of capital.[39] Typically British socialists responded to behavioralism, especially its aspiration to a universal scientific theory, primarily by denouncing it in just this way. Equally, socialists sometimes deployed behavioralist techniques to gather data for their alternative narratives. Ralph Miliband built much of his Marxist critique of the British state on behavioralist empirical data.[40]

Thatcherism constituted a far more significant dilemma for socialists than did behavioralism. British socialists adopted a certain historiography, arguing capitalism possessed an innate trajectory defined by its inner laws. Early opposition to capitalism was a naïve Luddism. As social critics and others came to terms with a capitalism generated independently of their beliefs, so the workers acquired greater class consciousness and began to aim at class cohesion as a means of winning political power. Their class consciousness grew in Chartism, the trade unions, the Labour Party, and the welfare state. This historiography defined a research agenda based on topics such as class, production, trades unions, the Labour Party, and the state. However, Thatcherism signaled the end to the historical

---

[39] Colin Leys, *Politics in Britain* (London: Heinemann, 1983), chap. 1.

[40] Ralph Miliband, The State in Capitalist Society (London: Weidenfeld and Nicolson, 1969); and Ralph Miliband, "The Capitalist State: Reply to Nicos Poulantzas," *New Left Review* 59 (1970): 53–60. Other examples of such use of behavioralist data can be found in the textbooks by John Dearlove and Peter Saunders, *Introduction to British Politics: Analysing a Capitalist Democracy* (Cambridge: Polity, 1984); and J. E. Kingdom, *Politics and Government in Britain* (Cambridge: Polity, 1991).

march forward of labor.[41] It cast doubt on a historiography in which labor's rise appeared as the dominant story of modernity. Socialism was on the defensive, if not vanquished.

We might distinguish two main strands in the socialist response to Thatcherism. The first is the socialist school of political economy, with its realist claim that the world exists independently of our knowledge of it and social structures have causal impact on history and politics. Typically it sought to explain Thatcherism using concepts drawn from the research agenda tied to the old historiography. The second is post-Marxism, which has been influenced by "the linguistic turn" and at times by poststructuralism. Typically it has rejected many of the concepts associated with the old historiography, turning instead to traditions, languages, and discourses as its main objects of inquiry.

Socialist political economy consists of several attempts to rethink and reapply Marxist social and economic analysis. It might seem that if there was ever a time to claim that Marxist approaches were irrelevant, it would be in today's postcommunist world, but nothing could be farther from the truth. For example, Andrew Gamble and his colleagues marshal sixteen essays to reawaken interest in "a legacy of critical social theory and social analysis which remains a key resource for today's social scientists." If historical materialism and economic determinism have been relegated to the dustbin of history, what is left? Gamble believes Marxism "continues to pose key questions about the origins, character and lines of development of the economic and social systems of the modern world."[42] David Marsh notes the varieties of Marxism but argues, first, that most modern Marxists reject economism and structuralism, preferring to emphasise contingency and accepting a key role for agents; they no longer privilege class, acknowledging the crucial role of other bases of structured inequality. Second—and this is perhaps where such work differs from post-Marxism—"almost all Marxists broadly share a realist epistemological position." He argues Marxism still offers three things to political science: explanations of the periodic crises of capitalism, an analysis of structured inequality, and a normative engagement with that inequality.[43]

---

[41] Eric J. Hobsbawm and others, *The Forward March of Labour Halted?* (London: New Left Books, 1981). On developments in Anglo-Marxist historiography since the 1970s see Mark Bevir and Frank Trentmann, "Critique within Capitalism: Historiographical Problems, Theoretical Perspectives," in *Critiques of Capital in Modern Britain and America*, ed. Mark Bevir and Frank Trentmann (Basingstoke, UK: Palgrave Macmillan, 2002), 1–25.

[42] Andrew Gamble, "Why Bother with Marxism?" in *Marxism and Social Science*, ed. Andrew Gamble, David Marsh, and Tony Tant (London: Macmillan, 1999), 7, 3, 4, and 6.

[43] David Marsh, "Resurrecting Marxism," in Gamble, Marsh and Tant, *Marxism*, 325–26, 332–33.

Realist epistemologies are often deployed by British socialists to defend a realist ontology of social structures. Once socialists assign a causal role to structures, they can argue the capitalist economy, as one such structure, constrains the development of society and the state. Socialist political economy recently has paid great attention, therefore, to the relation of structure to agency. Bob Jessop's "strategic-relational approach" is one of the most innovative attempts to conceptualize this relation. Jessop argues against all those approaches to state theory predicated on a distinction between structure and agency. He treats structure and agency only as an analytical distinction; they do not exist apart from each other. Rather, we must look at the relationship of structure to action and action to structure. So, "structures are thereby treated analytically as strategic in their form, content and operation; and actions are thereby treated analytically as structured, more or less context sensitive, and structuring." This approach involves examining both "how a given structure may privilege some actors, some identities, some strategies, . . . some actions over others" and "the ways . . . in which actors . . . take account of this differential privileging through 'strategic-context analysis.' "[44] In other words, individuals intending to realize certain objectives and outcomes make a strategic assessment of the context in which they find themselves. However, that context is not neutral. It too is strategically selective in the sense that it privileges certain strategies over others. Individuals learn from their actions and adjust their strategies. The context is changed by their actions, so individuals have to adjust to a different context. Institutions or functions no longer define the state. It is a site of strategic selectivity, a "dialectic of structures and strategies."[45]

The strategic-relational approach and critical realism have provided socialist political economy with concepts by which to explore Thatcherism and related shifts in British politics. We can explore these ideas in the debate between Hall and Jessop about the analysis of Thatcherism. Drawing on the work of Gramsci and the notion of hegemonic projects, Stuart Hall tells the story of Thatcherism replacing the existing social democratic ideology with its own vision, creating a new historic hegemonic project described as "authoritarian populism." The populism encompassed "the resonant themes of organic Toryism—nation, family, duty, authority, standards, traditionalism—with the aggressive themes of a revived neoliberalism—self-interest, competitive individualism, anti-statism." The authoritarian covered the "intensification of state control

---

[44] Bob Jessop, "Institutional Re(turns) and the Strategic-Relational Approach," *Environment and Planning A* 33, no. 7 (2001): 1213–35.

[45] Bob Jessop, *State Theory: Putting Capitalist States in Their Place* (University Park: Pennsylvania State University Press, 1990), 129.

over every sphere of economic life," "decline of the institutions of political democracy," and "curtailment of . . . 'formal' liberties." So the 1980s were characterized by centralization, the "handbagging" of intermediate institutions, the refusal to consult with interest groups, and state coercion. Thatcherism stigmatized the enemy within—for example, big unions, and big government—while creating a new historic bloc from sections of the dominant and dominated classes.[46]

Jessop and his colleagues criticize this analysis because of its one-sided focus on the ideological at the expense of its economic and political aspects. They argue for a focus on both the specific institutional forms that link state, civil society, and the economy and on the distinctive form of the state system. They use the ideas of social base, accumulation strategy, state strategy, and hegemonic project to develop their analysis of Thatcherism. So, Thatcherism involves creating a new social base through its project of popular capitalism (for example, the sale of public housing); an accumulation strategy of privatization, deregulation, and marketization; an authoritarian and centralizing state strategy; and a two-nations hegemonic project. As one might expect the analysis pays attention "not only to the social forces acting in and through the state but also to the ways in which the rules and resources of political action are altered by changes in the state itself."[47]

Post-Marxists typically pursue cultural analyses similar to that Hall provided of Thatcherism. Some follow Hall in expressing an almost humanist opposition to the structuralist legacy in poststructuralism. Gareth Stedman Jones, who has long since shed his own structuralist cloak, complained recently of "the stultifying effect of the survival, sometimes in disguised form and often barely self-aware, of a residue of reductionist and determinist assumptions dating from the 1970s."[48] He sought to move post-Marxism away from "the legacy of Foucault" toward a closer engagement with social humanists such as Skinner. No doubt, as Stedman Jones implies, many post-Marxists pursue studies of languages, discourses, and traditions, with little awareness of the underlying theoretical issues. Equally, some post-Marxists, notably Ernesto Laclau, are more

[46] See Stuart Hall, "The Great Moving Right Show," in *The Politics of Thatcherism*, ed. Stuart Hall and Martin Jacques (London: Lawrence and Wishart, 1983), 29; Stuart Hall, "Popular-Democratic versus Authoritarian Populism," in *Marxism and Democracy*, ed. Alan Hunt (London: Lawrence and Wishart, 1980), 161.

[47] Bob Jessop, K. Bonnett, S. Bromley, and T. Ling, *Thatcherism* (Cambridge: Polity, 1988).

[48] Gareth Stedman Jones, "The Determinist Fix: Some Obstacles to the Further Development of the Linguistic Approach to History in the 1990s," *History Workshop* 42 (1996): 19–35.

sympathetic toward—even openly supportive of—the structuralist legacy in poststructuralism.[49]

Laclau's version of discourse theory resembles many idealist and postidealist approaches to politics in that it understands actions, practices, and institutions as analogous to written and spoken texts: to discuss them adequately, one has to engage with the meanings they embody. It resembles the idealist inheritance too in its concern to explore such meanings by locating them in the historical context of a tradition, language, or ideology. However, Laclau draws on structural linguistics in a way few of those indebted to idealism do. Hence he often appears to conceive of the relevant context as the relations between the semantic units within the discourse, albeit that these relations are unstable, in a way that seems to allow relatively little room for human agency.

Laclau's debt to poststructuralism has undermined many of the characteristic themes of Marxist thinking. His emphasis on the role of discourses and on historical contingency leaves little room for any kind of Marxist social analysis with its basic materialism. Similarly, his rejection of the privileging of class, and so presumably of Marx's analysis of capitalism, allied to his hostility to any notion of human nature leaves little room for a Marxist ethics or politics. Why, after all, should anybody support radical struggles if these do not serve to end ills such as exploitation or to realize human potentialities? As Simon Critchley has argued, Laclau confuses recognition of the ubiquity of hegemony with an argument for democratic hegemony. What is clearly needed for the latter is an account of why we should prefer democratic hegemony to any other form of hegemony.[50]

Nonetheless, one area where Laclau does use Marxist themes is in his use, following Gramsci and Hall, of the word *hegemony*. He concentrates on the hegemonic role of discourses and the possibilities for counterhegemonic struggles. In his view, hegemonic projects set out to construct nodal points that serve partially to fix meanings and so to elide the historically contingent and politically constructed nature of a particular discourse. Yet, while hegemonic projects thus strive to fix discourses, any discursive configuration will contain social antagonisms. An antagonism is conceived here as a "blockage of identity" that occurs when the presence of an " 'Other' prevents me from being myself." To use Laclau's phrases, "the constitutive nature of antagonisms" leads to a consequent "radical

[49] Ernesto Laclau, *New Reflections on the Revolution of Our Time* (London: Verso, 1990); and Ernesto Laclau and Chantal Mouffe, *Hegemony and Socialist Strategy: Towards a Radical Democratic Politics* (London: Verso, 1985).

[50] Simon Critchley, "Ethics, Politics, and Radical Democracy—the History of a Disagreement," in *Laclau: A Critical Reader*, ed. Simon Critchley and Oliver Marchant (London: Routledge, 2005).

contingency of all objectivity," and this contingency then creates a space for counterhegemonic discourses.[51]

Most of the empirical work by post-Marxists focuses on political identities associated with gender and race. There is little work addressed to topics such as parliament, political parties, interest groups, and administrative and local politics. One exception is Griggs and Howarth's analysis of the campaign against Manchester airport's second runway.[52] They take interests and identities alike to be contingent and politically constructed. In their case study of the runway, they then ask how the local village residents and direct action protestors overcame their collective action problem. Their explanation has three elements. First, there was strong group identity in that all were affected by the environmental costs of the runaway. Second, there were a social network and political entrepreneurs. There was a strong and activist, conservationist tradition in the villages. The leaders of the several associations could call on the support of professional people and so lower the costs of the campaign. Third, new political identities were forged—"the Vegans and the Volvos." Middle-class protestors saw democratic channels as unreliable and so supported more radical forms of protest. This alliance worked because the prorunway campaign stigmatized both residents and protestors alike and used heavy-handed tactics, the media linked residents and eco-warriors as fighting a common foe, and local political entrepreneurs played policy brokering and support roles. The protestors lost. Once evicted, the eco-warriors moved on to the next protest site. Residents split over whether to mount a national-level campaign or concentrate on the public inquiry. The local authority offered an environmental mitigation package and pursued their case with "ruthless efficiency."

The Governance of Political Science

There are several traditions of political science in contemporary Britain. Each tradition has changed as its exponents have responded to various dilemmas. It is important to recognize, in addition, that the fate of the traditions is intimately bound up with the broader social and political context. In Britain, there is barely one private university, and the state is the only one major source of funds for political scientists. The develop-

---

[51] Laclau and Mouffe, *Hegemony*, 113, 115; Laclau, *New Reflections*, 26.

[52] S. Griggs and David Howarth, "New Environmental Movements and Direct Action Protests: The Campaign against Manchester Airport's Second Runway," in *Discourse Theory and Political Analysis*, ed. David Howarth, Aletta J. Norval, and Yannis Stavrakakis (Manchester: Manchester University Press, 2000).

ment of contemporary political science cannot be grasped apart from its governance. The state helped to define political science through its higher education policy, which favors some disciplines over others, by providing incentives for only certain types of research and by its own definition of significant problems, for example, through the media.

The relationship between political science and the state is, of course, symbiotic. On one hand, political scientists help to develop the ideas and techniques of governance that the state uses to try to stimulate, regulate, and control various activities within civil society, a point brought home forcefully in the final essay of this volume. On the other hand, university education and research, including political science, is one of the areas the state typically seeks to stimulate, regulate, and control using just these ideas and techniques.

Modernist empiricists typically scorned narratives of social conditions and moral character for atomistic and analytic studies of private opinions, behavior, and institutions. The resulting objectification of opinion, behavior, and institutions characteristically acted as a prelude to their governance. The state permeated new areas of civil society and private life. As it did so, it sought to tame not only its subjects but also its own policies. The state sought to monitor its own impact on education, employment, health, and housing. As the state expanded its activities, politics and administration became continuous social processes at the intersection of state and society. The changing role of the state thus overlapped with the emergence of studies of policy and implementation. Mackenzie tellingly inaugurated the study of pressure groups in Britain by arguing that party programs mattered less than the continuing process of adjusting policies.[53]

The constant extension of the state's knowledge and activity led to fears of state overload, bureaucracy, and inefficiency. These fears then provided part of the rationale for the new public management. The state increasingly struggled to objectify, monitor, and control not only its impact on society, but also its internal procedures. It began to rely on financial management and competition to secure accountability and on regulation to ensure that competition worked appropriately. When the New Right deregulated and privatized functions of the state, it often used techniques such as auditing and contract to know and to master the agencies that took the place of the state. Also, now that New Labour uses the state to enable individuals and organizations to take active responsibility for themselves, it defines appropriate forms of responsible action and monitors and responds to outcomes. In both cases, while individuals appear as agents responsible for their own position, the state still promotes a

[53] W.J.M. Mackenzie, "Pressure Groups in British Government," *British Journal of Sociology* 6 (1955): 133–48.

particular concept of responsibility by giving them skills and opportunities to find employment, to protect their health, or to provide for their future. When modernist empiricists explore these developments, they describe the emergence of new patterns of governance associated with, say, self-governing and interorganizational structures. In doing so, they objectify these structures, ascribing specific characteristics to them and encouraging the state to steer them by adopting techniques such as negotiation and an indirect style of management based on trust.[54]

So, state actors have come to believe that policy-relevant knowledge takes the form of modernist empiricist or even positivist studies. The major departments of state contract a vast amount of applied research from British universities but even pure research is state funded through the Economic and Social Research Council (ESRC). The ESRC, and its predecessor, the Social Science Research Council (SSRC), provides a clear example of the governance of political science at work. The SSRC was created in 1965 specifically to promote "policy relevant research." Their strategic plans, annual reports, and other official publications have chanted the mantra of "policy relevant research" ever since. One of its four current strategic objectives is "to increase the impact of the ESRC's research on policy and practice." It sets "thematic priorities" to guide its research funding, and all applications must indicate to which priority they will contribute.[55] It proudly proclaims, "[A]ll our decisions involve users—from public, private and voluntary sectors—as members of our Boards, and Council itself, as participants in our priority setting and programme and award selection." There is an Evidence Network, launched in 2000 with 3 million pounds worth of funding to pursue evidence-based policy and practice. There is a Connect Club—a select group of policy makers and business people who "receive regular targeted information on ESRC research in their field of concern." There are also Concordats with seven government departments for "establishing collaboration and feeding in the outputs of ESRC research." Nor is the effort to accommodate users limited to research. For postgraduate training, there is LINK, the Teaching Company Scheme, and Collaborative Research Studentships, all of which involve working with business.

Political scientists may reluctantly conspire in their own fate by playing the grantsmanship game. Even though the ESRC has been the face of

[54] Examples include E. Ferlie and A. Pettigrew, "Managing through Networks: Some Issues and Implications for the NHS," *British Journal of Management* 7 (1996): 81–99; Rhodes, *Understanding Governance*, chap. 3.

[55] In brief, they are: economic performance and development; environment and human behavior; governance and citizenship; knowledge, communication, and learning; lifecourse lifestyles and health; social stability and exclusion; and work and organizations.

government to academia for much of its existence, nonetheless many modernist empiricists and positivists agree to a significant degree with the official discourse. They can invoke the norms and regulations of the governance of political science to press their particular research agendas on to their more skeptical colleagues. For example, Keith Dowding wants "to persuade British political scientists to think seriously about the way in which they go about their business," because they need "to use . . . the social science methods they are required to teach in their departments if they want ESRC recognition for their masters and doctoral instruction."[56] Modernist empiricists and positivists have developed a symbiotic, and at times parasitic, relationship with the state. The professionalization of political science in the postwar period was a response and a contribution to the dilemmas posed by state power. Behavioralism encouraged policy-relevant research because it gave political scientists a toolkit for providing policy analysis. "Evidence-based policy making" under New Labour returns such research to center stage.

Idealists and socialists, in contrast, can be pushed aside by the state's "preference for relevance." They often reject the idea that political scientists can provide such policy-relevant knowledge. Among the idealists, Johnson notes the ESRC's "very marked shift in priorities towards practical and policy oriented research" and rails against both "the illusion of utility" and the "embarrassing" results for social research.[57] Moreover, even when socialist political economy does purport to provide scientific knowledge, it is, for obvious reasons, often a type of knowledge designed to mobilize opposition to the state rather than to enhance the effectiveness of the state. The problem for idealists and socialists is to describe their work so that it fits with the expressed priorities of government departments when these priorities have been generated by the different ideas of modernist empiricists and positivists. The ESRC's thematic priorities may not exclude their work but equally they do not signal an open door.

Conclusions

We have argued there are several traditions in British political science: for example, modernist empiricism, idealism, and socialism. We have also argued that proponents of each tradition modified it more or less drastically in response to the dilemmas posed by changing intellectual agendas,

---

[56] Keith Dowding, "There Must Be an End to Confusion: Policy Networks, Intellectual Fatigue, and the Need for Political Science Methods Courses in British Universities," *Political Studies* 49, no. 1 (2001): 90.

[57] Johnson, *Limits*, 93, 97.

such as behavioralism or neoliberalism, but there were great differences in their responses. Our narrative contrasts with the modernist empiricist one of the professionalization of British political science. The narrative of professionalization writes out other traditions from the history of the discipline and domesticates change. It presents modernist empiricist modes of knowing as inevitable, natural, or reasonable. We have sought to denaturalize modernist empiricism by recounting it as just one contingent tradition among others.

The obvious question with which to draw this chapter to a close is "whither British political science?" There are two obvious points with which to start. First, political scientists will set out against various overlapping and competing traditions, which they will modify in response to dilemmas. Political scientists will walk no single path. Second, exponents of the narrative of professionalization will seek to contain that diversity, to write out other traditions from the history of the discipline. No doubt they will be aided both by state policies and funding and by their own pursuit of state recognition and approval.

Perhaps though we might see radical change. In anthropology, as Fred Inglis points out, there has been a lethal attack on positivism and physicalism alike. He opines that the work of philosophers such as Taylor, Peter Winch, and Alasdair McIntyre means that using the methods of the natural sciences in the human sciences is "comically improper."[58] Similarly, students of international relations, at least in Britain, have begun to confront their "comically improper" shortcomings.[59] Political scientists have yet to do so. So, one possible avenue of change is for a broad interpretive or constructivist church to replace modernist empiricism. A broad interpretive church might unite many idealists and socialists. Conservative idealists, social humanists, and post-Marxists all offer historicist critiques of positivism. They debunk typologies, correlations, models, and classifications as objectifications that hide the historicity of the objects they depict and the modes by which they do so. Some socialist political economists too have begun to take seriously the role of ideas as causal and even perhaps constitutive aspects of economic policies and practices.[60]

The prospect may exist for British political scientists to take an "interpretive turn." But any such turn would collide with the entrenched modernist empiricism of the mainstream, which will hang on grimly, no doubt

[58] Fred Inglis, *Clifford Geertz: Culture, Custom and Ethics* (Oxford: Blackwell, 2000), 112.

[59] Compare Colin Hay, *Political Analysis* (Basingstoke, UK: Palgrave, 2002), chap. 6 and citations.

[60] For example, Colin Hay, "New Labour and 'Third Way Political Economy': Paving the European Road to Washington?" in Bevir and Trentmann, *Critiques of Capital*.

hoping "postmodernism"—it will be the pejorative label used to describe such a broad church—will go away. Any such turn might also collide with the state's preference for relevance. There is already a reaction to liberal ideas and a greater concern with structured inequality. But the state still continues to promote projects that purport to offer social engineering with respect to these latter themes. No doubt modernist empiricists and positivists will be more than happy to take the money and offer such advice. Arguably the prospects for "the interpretive turn" will remain bleak for as long as this symbiotic relationship persists.

Twelve

Historicizing the New Institutionalism(s)

ROBERT ADCOCK, MARK BEVIR,
AND SHANNON C. STIMSON

NEW INSTITUTIONALISM in American political science is often characterized in relation to a certain periodization of academic political studies in
the preceding century. According to this scheme, an old institutionalism
was dominant from the late nineteenth century until well into the interwar
years. In the 1950s behavioralism developed; it flourished as the disciplinary mainstream through the 1960s, only to wane in the 1970s. Emerging
from reactions against behavioralism, the new institutionalism came into
its own as a broad new paradigm underlying a range of cutting-edge research agendas during the 1980s.[1]

Such an account does capture certain elements of the discipline's past,
but its schematic character is misleading. With regard to developments
since the 1970s, it misleads in two ways. First, speaking of new institutionalism in singular terms suggests too much shared content among contemporary agendas. The diversity of the concerns and techniques that
have come to be called institutionalist in recent decades is such that we
should avoid imputing a single paradigm and instead recount a plurality
of intellectual traditions. Second, speaking of new institutionalism as *new*
and framing it against behavioralism obscures continuities between these
institutionalist traditions and behavioral-era scholarship. While each tradition departs from earlier approaches in certain respects, the character
and import of such departures differ significantly across the various new
institutionalisms. Moreover, none of these traditions has yet to move beyond the broader currents of modernist empiricism and neopositivism,
whose shared ascendancy within American political science was secured
in the decades after the Second World War.

The typology of sociological, rational choice, and historical new institutionalisms given by Peter Hall and Rosemary Taylor offers a useful entry

---

[1] The classic formulation of new institutionalism in these terms is James G. March and
Johan P. Olsen, "The New Institutionalism: Organizational Factors in Political Life," *American Political Science Review* 78, no. 3 (1984): 734–49.

point for exploring the traditions at play here.[2] Their explication of this typology in the mid-1990s is, however, a late move within the series of developments we wish to historicize. In fact, none of the three identifying labels they employ had wide currency prior to the 1990s, although the "schools of thought" to which they attach these labels are each presented as having points of origin in the late 1970s.[3] This gap raises the question of how well their three types capture the concerns and perspectives of the earlier literatures that they associate with them.

Hall and Taylor's sociological institutionalism picks out a school of thought centered in organizational studies, and their rational choice institutionalism identifies a separate school located at the intersection of economics and political science. While these types might be further disaggregated, each does map onto a lineage of scholarship marked by clear conceptual and interpersonal connections. Each corresponds to a distinct tradition that can be narrated forward from a late-1970s origin involving the conscious promotion of a distinctive approach to institutional analysis. Thus, what is now called sociological institutionalism can be narrated as developing from the work of Stanford sociologist John Meyer, with the role of foundational text assigned to his 1977 article, coauthored with Brian Rowan, "Institutionalized Organizations: Formal Structure as Myth and Ceremony."[4] Likewise, what is now called rational choice institutionalism can be narrated forward from the work of two political scientists at Washington University in St. Louis, Kenneth Shepsle and Barry Weingast.[5] The role of foundational text here is perhaps best played by

[2] Peter A. Hall and Rosemary Taylor, "Political Science and the Three Institutionalisms," *Political Studies* 44 (1996): 936–57.

[3] Ibid., 936. In locating the earliest exemplars of the "new institutionalism" in the late 1970s, Hall and Taylor's account is congruent with self-narratives offered from within each of the schools they discuss. See Paul Pierson and Theda Skocpol, "Historical Institutionalism in Contemporary Political Science," in *Political Science: The State of the Discipline*, ed. Ira Katznelson and Helen V. Miller (New York: Norton, 2002); Paul J. DiMaggio and Walter W. Powell, "Introduction," in *The New Institutionalism in Organizational Analysis*, ed. Walter W. Powell and Paul J. DiMaggio (Chicago: University of Chicago Press, 1991); Kenneth A. Shepsle, "Studying Institutions: Some Lessons from the Rational Choice Approach," in *Political Science in History: Research Programs and Political Traditions*, ed. James Farr, John S. Dryzek, and Stephen T. Leonard (New York: Cambridge University Press, 1995).

[4] John W. Meyer and Brian Rowen, "Institutionalized Organizations: Formal Structure as Myth and Ceremony," *American Journal of Sociology* 83, no. 2 (1977): 340–63.

[5] Kenneth A. Shepsle, "Institutional Arrangements and Equilibrium in Multidimensional Voting Models," *American Journal of Political Science* 23, no. 1 (1979): 27–60; Barry R. Weingast, "A Rational Choice Perspective on Congressional Norms," *American Journal of Political Science* 23, no. 2 (1979): 245–62. Shepsle and Weingast went on to write a string of articles central for the development of rational choice institutionalism, many of them coauthored. See, for example, Kenneth A. Shepsle and Barry R. Weingast, "Structure-Induced Equilibria and Legislative Choice," *Public Choice* 37 (1981): 503–19; Kenneth A. Shepsle and Barry R. Weingast, "Institutionalizing Majority Rule: A Social Choice Theory with

Shepsle's 1979 "Institutional Arrangements and Equilibrium in Multidimensional Voting Models," invoked in the following year by William Riker as the exemplar of what a "new kind of study of institutions might typically look like."[6]

The case of historical institutionalism is, however, different. More amorphous than either of their other two schools of thought, Hall and Taylor's historical institutionalism groups together works of scholarship guided by concerns and techniques so diverse that they may border on incompatibility. One can make the historical institutionalism map onto a single tradition only through a substantial retrospective reconfiguring of the character of earlier scholarship. Moreover, further reconfiguring would be needed if this agglomerative tradition were to be narrated as developing a distinct general approach to institutions that originated in the late 1970s. The claim to promote such an approach does not appear before the mid-1980s in any of the scholarship that Hall and Taylor locate under historical institutionalism. Earlier exemplars pursue agendas defined in substantive terms—as studies of revolution, of American political development, of corporatism and comparative political economy—not in terms of a new, general approach to the analysis of institutions. As late as 1985, we find the influential edited volume *Bringing the State Back In* engaging in alliance-building and agenda-setting efforts without framing its efforts in such terms.[7] Indeed, as we shall recount in this chapter, the rest of the 1980s was to pass before the notion crystallized of a distinctive school of historical institutionalism.

From the perspective of a radical historicist, this label itself also appears implausible. It may offer self-validation to one strategic grouping of scholars, but it provides little clarification of what, if anything, sets their work apart. If the label *historical* simply implies the minimal content of engaging the past, then historical studies are found in all three categories of Hall and Taylor's typology. If the label is instead meant to pick out and valorize approaches sensitive to historical context, then arguably none of

---

Policy Implications," *American Economic Review* 72, no. 2 (1982): 367–72; Kenneth A. Shepsle and Barry R. Weingast, "When Do Rules of Procedure Matter?" *Journal of Politics* 46, no. 1 (1984): 206–21; Kenneth A. Shepsle and Barry R. Weingast, "The Institutional Foundations of Committee Power," *American Political Science Review* 81, no. 1 (1987): 85–104. For Shepsle's own account of the institutional turn in rational choice, see Shepsle, "Studying Institutions." On the earlier history of rational choice theory, see S. M. Amadae, *Rationalizing Capitalist Democracy: The Cold War Origins of Rational Choice Liberalism* (Chicago: University of Chicago Press, 2003).

[6] Shepsle, "Institutional Arrangements and Equilibrium." William H. Riker, "Implications from the Disequilibrium of Majority Rule for the Study of Institutions," *American Political Science Review* 74, no. 2 (1980): 444.

[7] Peter B. Evans, Dietrich Rueschemeyer, and Theda Skocpol, eds., *Bringing the State Back In* (New York: Cambridge University Press, 1985).

their three types of new institutionalism earn this label, since all engage the past from positions imbued with the analytic gaze and hopes around which modernist empiricism and neopositivism overlap.

In the first part of this chapter we examine the decade from 1975 to 1985, tracking the rise of scholarly agendas focused on the state and on international regimes. Both of these agendas would, in the mid-to-late 1980s, be retrospectively characterized as examples of new institutionalism, and enter into conversation and contestation with the rational choice tradition that had staked its own claim to embody a new institutionalism as early as 1980. We chart these shifts in the second part of the chapter, following them through to two developments of the early 1990s. The first development is the emergence of historical institutionalism as a rallying label under which diverse political scientists in comparative and American politics located and defended their work from the challenge of rational choice. The second is the emergence among international relations scholars of a constructivism that came to engage with the tradition of sociological institutionalism. In conclusion we return to Hall and Taylor's 1996 article, to highlight the payoffs that accrue from our own radical historicizing perspective on the new institutionalisms.

Before "New Institutionalism": The Study of States and International Regimes, 1975–1985

Two conceptual shifts stand out in scholarship of late 1970s and early 1980s: an upswing in use of the concept of the state across several literatures and the development of the concept of regimes in the field of international relations. Both shifts would later be recounted as early stages of new institutionalism, but neither was understood in such terms before the mid-1980s.

Neostatism: Bringing the Concept of the State Back In

During the 1950s and 1960s, the concept of the state was unfashionable in many parts of political science and political sociology. But in the mid-to-late 1970s the pendulum swung back as a new generation of scholars, working in a range of literatures, embraced the older concept.[8] This shift

---

[8] While proponents of the state concept did draw on the earlier work of Nettl and Bendix—see J. P. Nettl, "The State as a Conceptual Variable," *World Politics* 20, no. 4 (1968): 559–92; and Reinhard Bendix and others, eds., *State and Society: A Reader in Comparative Political Sociology* (Boston: Little, Brown, 1968)—the major upswing of the concept can be dated from the appearance of several key books and articles in 1975/76: Charles Tilly, "Reflections on the History of European State-Making" and "Western State-Making and Theories of Political Transformation" in *The Formation of National States in Western Europe*, ed. Charles Tilly (Princeton, NJ: Princeton University Press, 1975), 3–83 and 601–38;

presented itself in some cases as a rather minor event—a signal of engagement with perspectives that had never quite gone out of fashion. In other cases, it presented itself as the rallying cry of young scholars resisting prevailing orthodoxies and engaged with one or more of the neo-Marxist perspectives that had flourished in the prior decade: dependency theory, world-systems theory, and structural Marxist theories of the state.[9] The wave of state-centric books and articles that appeared in 1978–79 exemplify this range of attitudes and modes of self-presentation; they include Alfred Stepan, Guillermo O'Donnell's and Peter Evans's writings on Latin America, Stephen Krasner and Peter Katzenstein's works on international and comparative political economy, and Theda Skocpol and Ellen Kay Trimberger's studies of revolution.[10]

The turn to the state in these literatures occurred largely independently, with each turn marked by its own precursors and problematics. However, there were also parallels—such as a common emphasis on the importance of international contexts for domestic politics—and efforts were soon launched to bring the various strands of scholarship together. In February of 1982, a conference was convened at Mount Kisco in New York to consider the "research implications of current theories of the state." This conference led to the formation, under the auspices of the Social Science Research Council, of a research committee, the Committee on States and Social Structures, to promote the state as an orientating concept and as a

---

Peter J. Katzenstein, "International Relations and Domestic Structures: Foreign Economic Policies of Advanced Industrial States," *International Organization* 30, no. 1 (1976): 1–45; Stephen D. Krasner, "State Power and the Structure of International Trade," *World Politics* 28, no. 3 (1976): 317–47.

[9] Andre G. Frank, *Capitalism and Underdevelopment in Latin America: Historical Studies of Chile and Brazil* (New York: Monthly Review Press, 1967); Immanuel M. Wallerstein, *The Modern World System: Capitalist Agriculture and the Origins of the European World-Economy in the Sixteenth Century* (New York: Academic, 1974); Ralph Milibrand, *The State in Capitalist Society* (New York: Basic Books, 1969); Nicos Poulantzas, *Political Power and Social Classes*, trans. Timothy O'Hagan (London: New Left Books, 1973).

[10] Alfred Stepan, *The State and Society: Peru in Comparative Perspective* (Princeton, NJ: Princeton University Press, 1978); Guillermo O'Donnell, "Reflections on Patterns of Change in the Bureaucratic Authoritarian State," *Latin American Research Review* 13, no. 1 (1978): 3–38; Peter Evans, *Dependent Development: The Alliance of Multinational, State, and Local Capital in Brazil* (Princeton, NJ: Princeton University Press, 1979); Peter J. Katzenstein, ed., *Between Power and Plenty: Foreign Economic Policies of Advanced Industrial States* (Madison: University of Wisconsin Press, 1978); Stephen D. Krasner, *Defending the National Interest: Raw Materials Investments and U.S. Foreign Policy* (Princeton, NJ: Princeton University Press, 1978); Theda Skocpol, *States and Social Revolutions: A Comparative Analysis of France, Russia, and China* (Cambridge: Cambridge University Press, 1978); Ellen Kay Trimberger, *Revolution from Above: Military Bureaucrats and Development in Japan, Turkey, Egypt and Peru* (New Brunswick, NJ: Transaction Books, 1978).

subject matter of empirical research. The committee was chaired by two conference participants, Theda Skocpol and Peter Evans, and completed by six other participants: Charles Tilly, Ira Katznelson, Stephen Krasner, Peter Katzenstein, Dietrich Rueschemeyer, and Albert Hirschman. Revised versions of papers from the conference form the bulk of the committee's first publication, *Bringing the State Back In*, which appeared in 1985 under the editorship of Evans, Rueschemeyer, and Skocpol.[11]

The title of the volume was taken from the paper that Skocpol presented at the 1982 conference and that appeared in revised form as the volume's introductory chapter. This chapter combines the broad, if somewhat vague, imagery needed to frame the various state literatures as a single movement with the rhetorical charge needed to propound a programmatic agenda. It offers the image of an ongoing "intellectual sea change," with scholars turning away from "society-centered ways of explaining politics and governmental activities" and converging "on complementary arguments and strategies of analysis" that take seriously the role of states as actors.[12] Krasner offers a similar image in a 1984 review article that frames the new statism as a transformative shift away from pluralism and the general behavioral orientation within which pluralism had flourished.[13]

Such images presuppose that political science was dominated in the 1950s and 1960s by societally reductionist theories that did not consider states to be potentially autonomous actors.[14] But this view involves major simplifications. By centering their claim to novelty upon it, the neostatists left themselves vulnerable to criticism, especially from advocates of the approaches they were claiming to transcend.[15] Gabriel Almond, for one, took advantage of the opening to launch a stinging criticism of the new agenda as little more than a mere semantic shift passed off as a substantive

[11] See Peter B. Evans, Dietrich Rueschemeyer, and Theda Skocpol, "Preface," in Evans, Rueschemeyer, and Skocpol, *Bringing the State*, vii–x.

[12] Theda Skocpol, "Bringing the State Back In: Strategies of Analysis in Current Research," in Evans, Rueschemeyer, and Skocpol, *Bringing the State*, 3–4.

[13] Stephen D. Krasner, "Approaches to the State: Alternative Conceptions and Historical Dynamics," *Comparative Politics* 16, no. 2 (1984): 223–46.

[14] Evans, Rueschemeyer, and Skocpol, "Preface," vii. Skocpol herself recognized the difficulty of making this claim in a qualifying footnote that went on to exempt many of the leading scholars of the 1960s—Samuel Huntington, Seymour Martin Lipset, Reinhard Bendix, S. N. Eisenstadt, Stein Rokkan—from the characterization offered in the main text. Skocpol, "Bringing the State," 31 n. 7.

[15] In employing "neostatism" and "neostatists" as aggregating terms we draw on language employed by Ira Katznelson, one of the members of the SSRC committee. See Ira Katznelson, "The State to the Rescue? Political Science and History Reconnect," *Social Research* 59, no. 4 (1994): 719–37.

intellectual transformation only at the cost of caricaturing the disciplinary past and thereby obscuring hard-won insights.[16]

Neither the neostatist image of paradigmatic transformation nor Almond's counterimage captures particularly well the new scholarship's relation to its predecessors. Almond was correct to reject the notion that recognizing the potential autonomy of the state was any great departure; the neostatists were right, however, that their analytic approach broke with strands of behavioralism, though the break was rather more partial than they implied. What they rejected was specifically the mode of theorizing and techniques associated with neopositivist strands of behavioralism. They rejected structural-functional theorizing and, more broadly, the whole project of crafting general, universally applicable theory. They were also wary of cross-national comparative work that took the form of large-N statistical analysis. However, they retained the goal of developing theory that was empirical (in the sense of being independent of normative commitments) and centered on generating and testing hypotheses about recurring relations between prior conditions and outcomes. What they preferred to large-N statistical analysis was a program of small-N studies hedged in by "context," but also sufficiently "analytical" to generate and test "mid-range theory." *Bringing the State Back In* thus combines disavowal of any attempt to offer a general theory of the state, with promotion of this modernist empiricist strategy of "analytical induction." Skocpol's introduction and the three editors' conclusion advocate crafting midrange theory by using analytic categories to inductively generalize from small-N comparisons and case studies.[17]

The neostatists thus remained comfortably within the parameters on which modernist empiricists and neopositivists in political science had long found common ground: the use of analytic classification, the pursuit of empirical theory, and the rejection of explicitly normative pursuits. They were far from replicating the approach of the principle-generating comparative historians of the state that we met in Farr's contribution to

[16] Gabriel A. Almond, "The Return to the State," *American Political Science Review* 82, no. 3 (1988): 853–74.

[17] Skocpol, "Bringing the State"; Peter B. Evans, Dietrich Rueschemeyer, and Theda Skocpol, "On the Road toward a More Adequate Understanding of the State," in Evans, Rueschemeyer, and Skocpol, *Bringing the State*. For further illustrations of this stance in the neostatist literature, see Peter J. Katzenstein, "Introduction," in Katzenstein, *Between Power and Plenty*; Theda Skocpol and Margaret R. Somers, "The Uses of Comparative History in Macrosocial Inquiry," *Comparative Studies in Society and History* 22, no. 2 (1980): 174–97; Ira Katznelson, "Working-Class Formation: Constructing Cases and Comparisons," in *Working-Class Formation: Nineteenth-Century Patterns in Western Europe and the United States*, ed. Ira Katznelson and Aristide R. Zolberg (Princeton, NJ: Princeton University Press, 1986).

this volume, and their conception of the state differed correspondingly. It was not nineteenth-century ethical notions of the state and social science that most neostatists adhered to, but a reading of Weber centered narrowly on his effort to define the state "in terms which abstract from the values of the present day."[18]

Neostatism and the Study of American Political Development

Neostatism first took shape in comparative and international studies, but it soon began to make major inroads among political scientists specializing in "American Political Development" (APD). Scholars in this area had long engaged with the literature of comparative politics. Indeed, the APD label for their field of specialization is a legacy of 1960s' interchanges with the political development literature produced under the aegis of the Committee on Comparative Politics and discussed in Adcock's earlier chapter. Such engagement continued in the 1970s as the CCP's search for general theory fizzled and neostatism developed.[19]

In the late 1970s and early 1980s Cornell University and the University of Chicago stand out as sites of this cross-field engagement. At Cornell, it was exemplified in the work of Martin Shefter[20] and was further developed by Stephen Skowronek in the doctoral research underpinning his *Building a New American State*.[21] When Shefter visited Chicago in 1979–80, the department's chair, Ira Katznelson, and then graduate student Amy Bridges were working on two other classic books of the early 1980s APD literature—Bridges's *A City in the Republic* and Katznelson's *City*

---

[18] Max Weber, *Economy and Society: An Outline of Interpretive Sociology*, ed. Guenther Roth and Claus Wittich (Berkeley and Los Angeles: University of California Press, 1978), 56. As we discuss below, the work of Stephen Krasner stands aside somewhat from this general characterization.

[19] As discussed in chapter 10, this shift is well captured by Charles Tilly's editorship of the penultimate CCP volume. Tilly took his editorship as an opportunity to sharply critique the committee's pursuit of a general theory of political development and to promote the "state" as the locus of a new agenda. Tilly, "Reflections" and "Western State-Making."

[20] Martin Shefter, "Party, Bureaucracy, and Political Change in the United States," in *Political Parties: Development and Decay*, ed. Louis Maisel and Joseph Cooper (Beverly Hills, CA: Sage, 1977); Martin Shefter, "Party and Patronage: Germany, England, and Italy," *Politics and Society* 7, no. 4 (1977): 403–52; Martin Shefter, "Regional Receptivity to Reform: The Legacy of the Progressive Era," *Political Science Quarterly* 98, no. 3 (1983): 459–83.

[21] Stephen Skowronek, *Building a New American State: The Expansion of National Administrative Capacities, 1877–1920* (Cambridge: Cambridge University Press, 1982). In his book's preface, Skowronek singles out two Cornell faculty for special thanks: Katzenstein for giving him his "first sense of the state" and Shefter for sharing his "insight into American political development." Skowronek, *Building*, x.

Trenches.[22] All three began to work together at this time on a comparative historical study of the working class that Katznelson was organizing with Aristide Zolberg.[23] The early 1980s also saw Theda Skocpol arrive at Chicago. While there she elaborated her own emerging concern with American political development, publishing a string of articles in the area with graduate students such as John Ikenberry, Ann Orloff, Margaret Weir, and Edwin Amenta.[24]

This network of scholars at Cornell and Chicago established the analytical approach, substantive concerns, and conceptual categories of neostatism as a cutting edge of scholarship in American political development. But their studies did not constitute the entirety of important new work in APD in the late 1970s and early 1980s. There also appeared, for example, Samuel Huntington's *American Politics: The Promise of Disharmony*, which brings the views of Louis Hartz and Walter Dean Burnham together with Huntington's earlier arguments in a synthesis of American political history centered on the interplay of ideals and institutions.[25] Lines of work

[22] Amy Bridges, *A City in the Republic: Antebellum New York and the Origins of Machine Politics* (New York: Cambridge University Press, 1984); Ira Katznelson, *City Trenches: Urban Politics and the Patterning of Class in the United States* (New York: Pantheon, 1981). Katznelson's account of the origin of America's class relations would be reframed in the distinctive neostatist form of promoting a "state-centered explanation" over "society- and economy-centered" alternatives in *Bringing the State Back In*. See Ira Katznelson, "Working-Class Formation and the State: Nineteenth-Century England in American Perspective," in Evans, Rueschemeyer, Skocpol, *Bringing the State*, 257–84.

[23] Katznelson and Zolberg, *Working-Class Formation*. When this volume appeared in 1985 Katznelson and Zolberg were still colleagues, but now at the New School for Social Research in New York, where Charles Tilly had also recently moved. While there Tilly and Katznelson were key figures in the "Proseminar on State Formation and Collective Action" in which their colleague Richard Bensel tried out many of the issues that would be explored in his American Political Development classic, *Yankee Leviathan: The Origins of Central State Authority in America, 1859–1877* (Cambridge: Cambridge University Press, 1990).

[24] Skocpol began this turn in her research focus while at Harvard. See Theda Skocpol, "Political Responses to Capitalist Crisis: Neo-Marxist Theories of the State and the Case of the New Deal," *Politics and Society* 10, no. 2 (1980): 155–201; Theda Skocpol and Kenneth Finegold, "State Capacity and Economic Intervention in the Early New Deal," *Political Science Quarterly* 97, no. 2 (1982): 255–78. For its further development at Chicago, see Theda Skocpol and G. John Ikenberry, "The Political Formation of the American Welfare State in Historical and Comparative Perspective," *Comparative Social Research* 6 (1983): 87–148; Ann Shola Orloff and Theda Skocpol, "Why Not Equal Protection? Explaining the Politics of Public Social Spending in Britain, 1900–1911, and the United States, 1880s—1920," *American Sociological Review* 49, no. 6 (1984): 726–50; Margaret Weir and Theda Skocpol, "State Structures and the Possibilities for 'Keynesian' Responses to the Great Depression in Sweden, Britain, and the United States," in Evans, Rueschemeyer, and Skocpol, *Bringing the State*, 107–63; Theda Skocpol and Edwin Amenta, "States and Social Policies," *Annual Review of Sociology* 12 (1986): 131–57.

[25] Samuel P. Huntington, *American Politics: The Promise of Disharmony* (Cambridge: Harvard University Press, Belknap Press, 1981).

rooted in behavioral scholarship of the 1960s also continued to develop. There were thus, for example, important new contributions in the study of past electoral behavior and realignments and of the history of Congress.[26] Since Huntington's book and these other lines of work build on scholarship of the decades after the Second World War, it would be a mistake to see the study of American political development as somehow starting with the rise of neostatism.[27]

Krasner, the State, and Regimes

An account of the rise and diffusion of neostatism should be qualified not only by recognizing other currents in fields that it entered, but also by recognizing that the effort to weld together a single neostatist agenda did not eliminate differences among the scholars associated with it. Differences among them existed before the Committee on States and Social Structures came together, persisted through the committee's lifespan (1983–90), and led into divergent positioning in the 1990s. While developments from the mid-1980s on are explored later in this chapter, we highlight here some earlier differences elided in the introduction and conclusion of *Bringing the State Back In*. In those chapters the volume's editors pursue alliance building and agenda setting by translating other scholars' studies into the terms of a single perspective. To illuminate some differences muted in this process, we consider the late 1970s and early 1980s work of Stephen Krasner—who sat on the committee but did not contribute to *Bringing the State Back In*—as a contrast to the perspective of the most prominent neostatist, Theda Skocpol. Attention to Krasner's developing perspective leads us in turn to the rise of the concept of "regimes" in the study of international relations—a second shift of the 1975–85 decade that, like neostatism, would later be retrospectively perceived as an early stage of new institutionalism.

The substantive engagements and concerns of Krasner's *Defending the National Interest* (1978) lie at some remove from those which Skocpol

---

[26] On electoral behavior and realignment, see: Joel H. Silbey, Allan G. Bogue, and William H. Flanigan, eds., *The History of American Electoral Behavior* (Princeton, NJ: Princeton University Press, 1978); James L. Sundquist, *Dynamics of the Party System: Alignment and Realignment of Political Parties in the United States* (Washington, DC: Brookings Institution, 1983). On congressional history, see: David W. Brady, Joseph Cooper, and Patricia Hurley, "The Decline of Party in the House of Representatives," *Legislative Studies Quarterly* 4, no. 3 (1979): 381–407; Joseph Cooper and David W. Brady, "Institutional Context and Leadership Style: The House from Cannon to Rayburn," *American Political Science Review* 75, no. 2 (1981): 411–25; Joseph Cooper and David W. Brady, "Toward a Diachronic Analysis of Congress," *American Political Science Review* 75, no. 4 (1981): 988–1006.

[27] For such a narrative, see Katznelson, "The State to the Rescue?"

pursues in *States and Social Revolutions* (1979) and which she places at
the core of neostatism in *Bringing the State Back In*. Where Skocpol's use
of the state concept is informed by her reading of Weber and Hintze,
Krasner distances himself from key aspects of Weber's approach to the
state and makes no reference to Hintze. His conception is informed instead by Meinecke's work on reason of state and Pareto's differentiation
of utility for and of the community.[28] In line with these influences, Krasner
links the state with the national interest—understood as the "international analog" of "the public interest"[29]—in a fashion more reminiscent
of those approaches Weber's definition broke with than of the Weberian
stance favored by most neostatists.

Further differences between Krasner and Skocpol emerge in their contrasting responses to structural neo-Marxism. While Skocpol dismisses
structural Marxism as failing to grasp the autonomy of the state,[30]
Krasner treats it as a serious rival to his own state-centric realism. He
acknowledges that both approaches can account for cases examined in
Defending the National Interest, such that their "relative merits are most
difficult to assess." In the end, he argues for the superiority of his approach on the ground that "the nonlogical manner in which American
leaders pursued their anticommunism is not compatible with structural
Marxism."[31] For Krasner their pursuit became nonlogical when it led to
actions at odds with the pursuit of national interest, and he attributes this
divergence to the impact of ideology. In doing so, he grants ideational
factors a significant explanatory role, albeit one constrained by their place
in a larger interest-based analytic framework. In contrast, Skopcol's
States and Social Revolutions emphatically rejects modes of explanation
centered on ideas, norms, or values.[32] It is hence unsurprising that when
surveying Krasner's book in the introduction to *Bringing the State Back
In*, Skocpol objects to its stress on "'nonrational' ideological objectives

---

[28] Krasner, *Defending the National Interest*, 42–43, 10–13.

[29] Ibid., 35–36.

[30] Skocpol, *States and Social Revolutions*, 20. Skocpol repeated the charge that recent
Marxist theorizing was inadequate in this regard in "Bringing the State," 20. This claim
provoked a sharp reaction from neo-Marxists such as Paul Cammack in "Bringing the State
Back In: A Polemic," Manchester Papers in Politics, Department of Government, University
of Manchester, 1987. Cammack published an abbreviated version of this critique: "Dependency and the Politics of Development," in *Perspectives on Development: Cross-Disciplinary Themes in Development Studies*, ed. P. F. Leeson and M. M. Minogue (Manchester:
Manchester University Press, 1988).

[31] Krasner, *Defending the National Interest*, 332–33. See also 316, 15–16, 32–34.

[32] See esp. Skocpol, *States and Social Revolutions*, chap. 1. Her chapter with Margaret
Weir in *Bringing the State Back In* does take on ideas, but does so in order to reject argu-
ments that give explanatory centrality to intellectual developments. Weir and Skocpol,
"State Structures."

of state policy," and prefers instead to look to "geopolitical 'interests' " as the best counter to structural Marxist arguments.[33]

Krasner's concern with ideational factors and with constraints on the pursuit of national interests provides the backdrop to his growing engagement, through the late 1970s and early 1980s, with the developing literature on international regimes. The concept of regimes, like that of the state, recalls the political science of an earlier era, but overall it had fared better in the behavioral era. Thus, for example, David Easton, an articulate behavioralist critic of the state concept, gives "regime" a major role in his 1965 *A Systems Analysis of Political Life*. He characterizes a regime as a set of constraints on political interaction with three elements: "values (goals and principles), norms, and structure of authority."[34] While applied to domestic rather than international politics, Easton's characterization hews closely in content to the notion of regime later favored by Krasner, as well as that of John Ruggie, who is often credited with introducing the concept to the study of international relations in the mid-1970s. Ruggie's early work in this area stresses "mutual expectations, generally agreed-to rules, regulations and plans in accordance with which organizational energies and financial commitments are allocated." Working with Ernst Haas at the University of California, Berkeley, he deployed the concept to analyze a type of "collective response" that both saw taking place in the international system in relation to technological and environmental issues.[35]

During the late 1970s the regime concept was taken up by international relations scholars working from a range of perspectives. Two conferences in the area led to a 1982 special issue of *International Organization*, which was in turn published as a volume edited by Krasner. When Krasner sets out, in the opening chapter of *International Regimes*, to group the volume's contributing scholars into schools, he places Ruggie alongside Robert Keohane, and implicitly himself, under a middle-ground stance of "modified" structural realism.[36] In doing so, he—like Skocpol and her coeditors in *Bringing the State Back In*—elides differences that would lead into divergent positioning during the subsequent rise of new institutionalism in the late 1980s and early 1990s.

[33] Skocpol, "Bringing the State," 34 n. 36.

[34] David Easton, *A Systems Analysis of Political Life* (New York: Wiley, 1965), 193.

[35] John G. Ruggie, "International Responses to Technology: Concepts and Trends," *International Organization* 29, no. 3 (1975): 569, 558, 567–68. See also Ernest B. Haas, "On Systems and International Regimes," *World Politics* 27, no. 2 (1975): 147–74.

[36] Stephen D. Krasner, "Structural Causes and Regime Consequences: Regimes as Intervening Variables," in *International Regimes*, ed. Stephen D. Krasner (Ithaca, NY: Cornell University Press, 1983), 1–21.

The divergence that would later take shape as the regimes literature evolved to become yet another institutions literature is foreshadowed in *International Regimes*, but by Ruggie's contribution rather than by Krasner's overview. Ruggie locates his approach to regimes against rather than within realism and specifically contrasts it to the approach he sees as played out in Krasner's and Kenneth Waltz's work. He suggests that Krasner and Waltz engage regimes only within the constraints of a narrow emphasis on power. He maintains, as a contrast, that the study of regimes should treat political authority as a "fusion of power with legitimate social purpose," and holds that this perspective sets his own work apart.[37] The study of regimes should, Ruggie believes, go beyond analyzing the use of power to pursue interests, to focus also on international ideational processes that he sees shaping state actors' understandings of what their interests are in the first place. The thrust of his stance had already been evident in his mid-1970s work, where he drew on Foucault's concept of episteme to argue that the development of regimes "involves not only the institutional grid of the state and of the international political order, through which behavior is acted out, but also epistemes through which political relationships are visualized."[38]

The import of the distinction made by Ruggie would become evident later in the 1980s as the concept of regime began to give way before the increasingly popular language of institutions. In an influential 1988 essay, Robert Keohane would, as we recount below, make a distinction parallel to Ruggie's, but reframe it as a contrast between two approaches to "international institutions."[39] The more thoroughgoing ideational approach, of which Ruggie's work was narrated as the prime early exemplar, would in turn, in the early 1990s, come to be labeled *constructivism*.

[37] John G. Ruggie, "International Regimes, Transactions and Change: Embedded Liberalism in the Postwar Economic Order," in Krasner, *International Regimes*, 198. Krasner's own approach to regime analysis was further fleshed out in his 1985 *Structural Conflict*, which explored north-south tensions between developing and developed nations. Krasner persisted there in a realist line of emphasis, seeing states as making decisions in pursuit of their national interest. He suggested that developing countries had consistently endorsed principles and norms that legitimate authoritative allocation based on the decisions of states rather than market allocation based on the endowments and preferences of private actors, not because they preferred "control to wealth" but because such "authoritative regimes can provide them with both, whereas market oriented ones cannot." Stephen D. Krasner, *Structural Conflict: The Third World against Global Liberalism* (Berkeley and Los Angeles: University of California Press, 1985), 5.

[38] Ruggie, "International Responses," 569.

[39] Robert O. Keohane, "International Institutions: Two Approaches," *International Studies Quarterly* 32, no. 4 (1988): 379–96.

Constructing and Contesting the "New Institutionalism(s)," 1984–1996

The discourse of a new approach to institutions has held currency among rational choice scholars in political science at least since Riker's announcement of it in 1980. Talk of such an agenda did not enter the conversation of most other political scientists, however, until after the publication of James March and Johan Olsen's "The New Institutionalism: Organizational Factors in Political Life" in the *American Political Science Review* in 1984. Within a few years, the phrase swept the discipline such that by the late 1980s, all manner of intellectual traditions were claiming to embody it in one form or another. The resulting confusion and contestation in turn spurred a series of efforts to differentiate and defend various new institutionalisms. It is our goal here to follow the dynamic of these developments, tracing the spread of new institutionalist discourse and the subsequent emergence in the early 1990s of historical institutionalism and constructivism as rallying points for scholars propounding alternatives to rational choice.

The origins of much of the confusion enveloping "the new institutionalism" lie in the article that popularized this phrase. March and Olsen there lift the new approaches to institutions within organizational sociology and rational choice out of the specific intellectual contexts in relation to which each developed and instead narrate them as exemplars of a generic paradigm shift toward a new institutionalism whose further development they wish to promote.[40] Their new institutionalism not only incorporates these two independent, divergent approaches, but also encompasses other recent agendas, such as neostatism. In constructing such a broad new institutionalism, March and Olsen rely on a caricature of the "basic vision" purported to have dominated political science since around 1950. The vision provides a straw man in contrast to which the diverse— even incompatible—character of various streams of recent scholarship is obscured. But without this caricature, the appearance of commonalities, as well as the supposed novelty of some of this scholarship, dissipates,

---

[40] March and Olsen, "The New Institutionalism." The "new" institutionalism in organizational sociology understood itself as such in contrast to the "old" approach taken by postwar sociologists, especially Talcott Parsons and Philip Selznick. The "new" institutionalism in rational choice originated as a corrective to earlier approaches to formal modeling that had not incorporated institutional structure. Contrary to the implications of March and Olsen's grand narrative, a reaction specifically against behavioralist scholarship in political science does not seem to have been an important factor in the intellectual genesis of either of these two "new institutionalisms."

leaving no grand paradigm shift to promote. Both in its agenda-setting function and in its dubious content, March and Olsen's image of the decades after the Second World War shares much with the image of a societally reductionist intellectual past offered by Skocpol in *Bringing the State Back In*. However, as we earlier noted, while that volume would later be cited as a key new institutionalist work, it did not frame itself in such terms.

The notion of promoting a general approach to institutions instead makes its appearance in the discourse of neostatism with Krasner's review article "Approaches to the State." Krasner here parallels Skocpol's imagery by contrasting statist and pluralist orientations, but his frequent recurrence to the language of institutions also makes his article far closer to March and Olsen's rhetoric of a new institutionalism.[41] Krasner's review interprets several statist works as being oriented around a common question, framed in the language of institutions: "How do institutional structures change in response to alterations in domestic and international environments and then in subsequent time periods influence these environments?"[42] This framing constructs parallels between young neostatists and the older tradition of institutional political science with a macroqualitative bent long prominent at Harvard. Thus Krasner remarks that Skowronek's *Building a New American State* "complements the work of other scholars, such as Huntington and Hartz."[43] In seeking to flesh out characteristics of a broad institutional approach under which these various scholars might be grouped, Krasner emphasizes a shared concern with the contrast "between periods of institutional creation and periods of institutional stasis." Drawing on evolutionary biology, he suggests that such historical patterns may be conceptualized in terms of "punctuated equilibrium."[44] Though his terminology is novel, the ease with which Krasner groups neostatists together with exemplars of a long established approach sits rather awkwardly alongside his claim that neostatism sets "a different agenda" for research by taking institutions seriously.[45]

[41] Krasner's intermediary position fits with the fact that, in addition to reading and commenting on the 1982 Skocpol paper that was published in revised form as the introduction to *Bringing the State Back In*, he also had provided comments on the March and Olsen article (he and James March were colleagues at Stanford).

[42] Krasner, "Approaches to the State," 224.

[43] Ibid., 238. Though Krasner does not emphasize this, there is more than chance underlying the parallels here. Indeed, by following up the chains of intellectual influence, it would be easy to suggest that much (though not all) of neostatism could be narrated as simply one offshoot of this established tradition.

[44] Ibid., 240.

[45] Ibid., 243.

An urge to conceptual novelty helped bring the state to prominence between the mid-1970s and the early 1980s, but by the mid-to-late 1980s the initial excitement associated with the concept was fading, and lines of substantive work associated with neostatism turned increasingly to the rising discourse of institutionalism. This shift was more than terminological. It reflected growing skepticism about the substantive payoff of efforts to bring the state back in. Scholars working with an analytic approach and substantive concerns typical of neostatism, such as Peter Katzenstein and Peter Gourevitch, now qualified or questioned the amount of explanatory burden that can be carried by such notions as state autonomy.[46] As the novelty of a statist agenda wore off, the relation between neostatism and other strands of scholarship opened up for reshaping. In particular, as suggested by Krasner's comments placing Skowronek in relation to Huntington and Hartz, many works pursuing the young agenda could be renarrated as partaking of a perspective that was less novel than a continuation of an older tradition especially associated with Harvard's Government Department and the works of Louis Hartz, Samuel Huntington, and Samuel Beer. While that tradition's concern with ideas alongside institutions placed it in contrast to certain variants of neostatism—such as Skocpol's structuralism—it was compatible with, and indeed had helped to generate, other variants of neostatism. The potential for combining the "ideas and institutions" thrust of the older tradition with elements of neostatism is well displayed in the mid-to-late 1980s works of Beer's student Peter Hall, who brings a distinctive concern with ideas into neostatist discussions of comparative political economy.[47]

In the face of the relative eclipse of the state as a rallying point for explanatory efforts and the potential for reshaping allegiances, the vague term "institutionalism" appealed broadly as a concept around which to reframe and promote substantive agendas and analytical perspectives. In the mid-to-late 1980s, following Krasner's turn to the discourse of institutionalism and March and Olsen's christening of her work as an example

[46] The notion plays little role in Peter J. Katzenstein, *Small States in World Markets: Industrial Policy in Europe* (Ithaca, NY: Cornell University Press, 1985); its limited explanatory payoff is argued by Peter A. Gourevitch, *Politics in Hard Times: Comparative Responses to International Economic Crises* (Ithaca, NY: Cornell University Press, 1986). For more on the rise and decline of the state autonomy agenda, see Ronald Rogowski, "Comparative Politics," in *The State of the Discipline II*, ed. Ada Finifter (Washington, DC: American Political Science Association, 1993), 439–41.

[47] In addition to Hall's career-making *Governing the Economy: The Politics of State Intervention in Britain and France* (New York: Oxford University Press, 1986), see also Peter A. Hall, "Conclusion: The Politics of Keynesian Ideas," in *The Political Power of Economic Ideas*, ed. Peter A. Hall (Princeton, NJ: Princeton University Press, 1989), 351–91.

of it, Skocpol came to identify her approach with new institutionalism.[48] The field of American political development in which her research was increasingly centered also picked up the mantle more broadly at this point. Thus, in 1986, we find Skowronek and Karen Orren, coeditors of the new journal *Studies in American Political Development*, explicitly presenting that journal's creation as part of the ongoing rise of new institutionalism.[49] By 1988, new institutionalist language was also diffusing to the field of public law and becoming increasingly prevalent within the field of international relations.[50]

The spread of new institutionalist discourse, and the remaking of intellectual identities associated with it, raised the question of how far the realignment and reshaping of traditions and agendas would go. As we have suggested, the line between neostatism and the older ideas and institutions tradition blurred in the mid-1980s to produce a shared tradition of institutionalism with a macrohistorical, qualitative bent. In the late 1980s further realignment took shape in relation to strands of historical work rooted in behavioralism.[51] The first volume of *Studies in American Political Development* includes an article by Samuel Kernell, squarely behavioralist in its use of time series and content analysis techniques.[52] The appearance of the article in the new journal suggests a concern to reach across previous fracture lines in support of a spectrum of modernist empiricist approaches to the past. This effort took on an increasingly established form in succeeding years as Amy Bridges and David Brady led an

[48] Skocpol was using the language of new institutionalism by early 1987. See the comments reporting on Skocpol's talk to the 1987 Midwest Political Science Association in Margaret Levi, "Theories of Historical and Institutional Change," *PS* 20, no. 3 (1987): 684–88, 687.

[49] Karen Orren and Steven Skowronek, "Editor's Preface," *Studies in American Political Development* 1 (1986): vii–viii.

[50] Rogers M. Smith, "Political Jurisprudence, the 'New Institutionalism,' and the Future of Public Law," *American Political Science Review* 82, no. 1 (1988): 89–108; Keohane, "International Institutions"; G. John Ikenberry, "Conclusion: An Institutional Approach to American Foreign Economic Policy," in *The State and American Foreign Policy*, ed. G. John Ikenberry, David A. Lake, and Michael Mastanduno (Ithaca, NY: Cornell University Press, 1988). This edited volume was the result of a collaborative project (encouraged by Katzenstein and Krasner) that had begun with two conferences in 1985. In addition to Ikenberry's conclusion, the chapters by Judith Goldstein and Stephen Haggard exemplify the shift from statist to institutionalist discourses ongoing as this project moved from initial conferences through to publication.

[51] On the effort to bring together the neostatist tradition with the tradition of historically oriented work growing out of behavioralism, see David Brian Robertson, "The Return to History and the New Institutionalism in American Political Science," *Social Science History* 17, no. 1 (1993): 1–36.

[52] Samuel Kernell, "The Early Nationalization of Political News in America," *Studies in American Political Development* 1 (1986): 255–78.

effort to establish a new organized APSA section—the "History and Politics" section, which formally took wing in 1990.

The new section suggests the extent to which intellectual identities, allegiances, and lines of debate had been reshaped since the heyday of neostatism. The earlier neostatist tendency to self-define by contrast to pluralism and behavioralism declined as macroqualitative studies became increasingly allied alongside historically oriented strands of behavioralism. Conversation and cooperation here was facilitated by a shared modernist empiricist concern to approach the past in an inductive manner, sufficiently analytic enough to count as social scientific and thus also well removed from the historicism typical of most historians. While historians, especially those with a proclivity to flirt with postmodern heresies, provided an extradisciplinary "other" against which to negotiate some conversations across previous fracture lines, the situation proved more charged with regard to the rising tradition of rational choice. The second volume of *Studies in American Political Development* (1987) included a pair of articles with a rational choice orientation,[53] thereby suggesting some potential for a cooperative relationship. There was, however, also ample potential for contestation, since the application of rational choice theory's neopositivist deductive logic to historical materials could be seen as posing a challenge to the macroqualitative and behavioral traditions' more inductive, modernist-empiricist approaches.

The Challenge of Rational Choice and the Crafting of "Historical Institutionalism"

Multiple strands within rational choice scholarship had converged by the late 1980s, presenting other traditions in political science with a dynamic, self-confident rival that was enriching its technical base while also expanding its substantive scope. First, there were new developments within the strand of more formalized theoretical work, whose turn to modeling political institutions in the late 1970s provides the rational choice tradition with its proprietary claim to be the first self-conscious new institutionalism to emerge within political science. In the early 1980s this strand, exemplified in the work of such figures as Barry Weingast, expanded its repertoire of concepts and tools to draw on the new economics of organization associated with such economists as Oliver Williamson.[54] Further

[53] See Terry M. Moe, "Interests, Institutions, and Positive Theory: The Politics of the NRLB," *Studies in American Political Development* 2 (1987): 236–99; J. Hansen, "Choosing Sides: The Creation of an Agricultural Policy Network in Congress, 1919–1932," *Studies in American Political Development* 2 (1987): 183–229.

[54] On the "new economics of organization" literature see the overview by Terry Moe, which closes by discussing the emerging political science applications of this approach, and in particular Weingast's employment of principal-agent models. Terry M. Moe, "The

cross-disciplinary exchange followed after leading economic historian
Douglass C. North joined Weingast and others at Washington University
in St. Louis in 1983.[55] The charge that the developing positive theory of
political institutions was only concerned with contemporary American
institutions became increasingly less plausible toward the end of the decade as Weingast, in coauthorship with North, started to work on historical material.[56]

A different road to a similar destination was taken by a second strand
in the rational choice tradition: the less formalized use of rational choice
perspectives in comparative politics that built particularly on Mancur
Olson's arguments about collective action. This perspective was pioneered in the late 1970s in Samuel Popkin's *The Rational Peasant* and
further developed in the early 1980s in Robert Bates's *Markets and States
in Tropical Africa* and *Essays on the Political Economy of Rural Africa.*[57]
Like some leading neostatists, Popkin and Bates were substantively concerned with the state, peasants, and conflict in relation to large-scale processes of political and economic change, and analytically they also sought
to navigate a course away from the structural-functionalism prominent
in comparative politics during the behavioral era. But the course they
charted diverges sharply from that taken by neostatists like Skocpol, who
retained structural-functionalism's concern to generate theory at the macrolevel while rejecting neopositivist's universalizing goal. Popkin and
Bates, in contrast, retained the goal while breaking away from the macro-

---

New Economics of Organization," *American Journal of Political Science* 28, no. 4 (1984):
739–77.

[55] In an autobiographical statement, North explains that he was drawn to Washington
University by the "exciting group of young political scientists and economists who were
attempting to develop new models of political economy." See Douglass C. North, "Autobiography, Nobel Lecture Banquet Speech," retrieved August 8, 2003, from www.nobel.se/
economics/laureates/1993/north-autobio.html. The success of the group of rational choice
scholars at Washington University is suggested by the fact that when Shepsle left there in
1986, it was for Harvard, and when Weingast left, it was for Stanford. During the 1990s,
both went on to chair their respective departments.

[56] Douglass C. North and Barry R. Weingast, "Constitutions and Commitment: The Evolution of Institutions Governing Public Choice in Seventeenth-Century England," *Journal
of Economic History* 49, no. 4 (1989): 803–32; Paul R. Milgrom, Douglass C. North, and
Barry R. Weingast, "The Role of Institutions in the Revival of Trade: The Law Merchant,
Private Judges, and the Champagne Fairs," *Economics and Politics* 2, no. 1 (1990): 1–23.

[57] Samuel L. Popkin, *The Rational Peasant: The Political Economy of Rural Society in
Vietnam* (Berkeley and Los Angeles: University of California Press, 1979); Robert H. Bates,
Markets and States in Tropical Africa: The Political Basis of Agricultural Policies (Berkeley
and Los Angeles: University of California Press, 1981). Bates's book was the first publication in the California Series on Social Choice and Political Economy, edited by Brian Barry
and Samuel Popkin. Bates singles out Popkin for special thanks in his acknowledgments.
Bates, *Markets and States*, xi.

orientation to rely instead on microlevel theory and, in particular, rational choice theory. Their "collective-choice school of political economy" quickly took up the institutionalist language already developing elsewhere in the rational choice tradition. By 1983 Bates was identifying institutions as the core concern of this school.[58] Though Popkin and Bates do engage the past, the full historical ambition of this strand of scholarship only became evident a few years later, with the 1988 publication of Margaret Levi's *Of Rule and Revenue*.[59] Levi's broad temporal scope surpasses that of any neostatist, encompassing cases from Republican Rome, Middle Age Europe, and early-modern Britain, in addition to twentieth-century Australia.

By the late 1980s, multiple strands of rational choice scholarship were thus converging on a self-consciously new institutionalist approach increasingly confident in its ability to take on the historical concerns claimed as home turf by the neostatists, who were, at the same time, busy renarrating themselves as new institutionalists. The lines of potential conflict here were evident in 1987, when the political economy section of the Midwest Political Science Association hosted a "roundtable on theories of historical and institutional change."[60] With Katznelson and Skocpol on the one side, and Bates and Levi on the other, the roundtable brought out tensions between structuralism and methodological individualism, inductive comparative case studies, and neopositivist deductive theory, which would define debates for years to come. These tensions came out more fully in Levi's "Bringing People Back into the State," published as an appendix to *Of Rule and Revenue*. Levi here criticizes neostatism for an excessive structuralism in which "individuals become little more than the embodiment of the structures they represent," while also suggesting that Skocpol's modernist empiricist strategy of "stockpiling case studies" is "not the solution." She argues that the success of a "new macro-comparative history" requires greater attention to "micro-foundations" and points to rational choice theory as the best available tool for the job.[61] From Levi's standpoint as a rational choice institutionalist, it seemed obvious that

---

[58] Robert H. Bates, *Essays on the Political Economy of Rural Africa* (Cambridge: Cambridge University Press, 1983), 134–47.

[59] Margaret Levi, *Of Rule and Revenue* (Berkeley and Los Angeles: University of California Press, 1988). Levi's book appeared in the ongoing series edited by Popkin and Barry (and now also Bates) that had begun with Bates's 1981 book. Levi dedicated the book to Douglass North, who had heavily influenced her while they were cofaculty at the University of Washington, before his move to Washington University in St. Louis.

[60] Levi, "Historical and Institutional Change," 687.

[61] Levi, *Of Rule*, 197. For more arguments along the same lines, see also Michael Taylor, "Structure, Culture and Action in the Explanation of Social Change," *Politics and Society* 17, no. 2 (1989): 115–62.

more rigorous attention to the microlevel was needed to make theoretical sense out of the kind of macrocomparative historical studies that neostatists and their emerging successors produced.

The challenge that rational choice scholars came to pose by the late 1980s seems to have provided the final thrust that led some scholars to differentiate among competing variants of new institutionalism. While earlier discussions among neostatists and their associates had spelled out attributes that would now come to be associated specifically with "historical" institutionalism, they did so without employing that label or framing their approach in contrast to rational choice. The label begins to appear only as the counterpart to conscious efforts to differentiate and defend this approach from the rational choice tradition. In January of 1990, Skocpol, Hall, Weir and a number of other scholars gathered in Boulder, Colorado, for a workshop organized to highlight "common analytic themes" in their new institutionalism.[62] The conference led to *Structuring Politics: Historical Institutionalism in Comparative Analysis*, a volume that appeared in 1992 under the editorship of three younger scholars, Sven Steinmo, Kathleen Thelen, and Frank Longstreth. While mainly framed by its editors in relation to debates in comparative politics, the volume's contributors cross subfields, repeatedly engaging American political development.[63] In their opening essay, Thelen and Steinmo narrate historical institutionalism in two ways: first, in terms of the sweeping aggregations of the stylized sequence of old institutionalism, behavioralism, and new institutionalism; and second, in terms of a contrast within new institutionalism between traditions of rational choice and historical institutionalism. The term "historical institutionalism" is credited to Skocpol, and presented as being intended "to distinguish this variant of institutionalism from the alternative, rational choice."[64]

Since, as we have seen, rational choice scholars were already confidently addressing the past, the "historical" adjective here could only serve a differentiating purpose if meant to imply more than this. The introduc-

[62] See the preface to Sven Steinmo, Kathleen Thelen, and Frank Longstreth, *Structuring Politics: Historical Institutionalism in Comparative Analysis* (New York: Cambridge University Press, 1992), ix–x.

[63] Of the volume's seven substantive chapters, three treated aspects of American political development in a paired comparison with one other country (see chapters by Colleen Dunlavy, Victoria Hattam, and Desmond King), and Margaret Weir's chapter focused on American developments alone.

[64] Kathleen Thelen and Sven Steinmo, "Historical Institutionalism in Comparative Politics," in Steinmo, Thelen, and Longstreth, *Structuring Politics*, 1–32. The specific attribution of the "historical institutionalism" term to Skocpol comes in fn. 4, p. 28. Notably, the emphasis on this term seems to have developed only at or after the conference, which was itself entitled "The New Institutionalism: State, Society, and Economy in Advanced Industrial Societies."

tion of the term appears as a preemptive attempt to claim for one group of scholars the right to judge what it means to be historical and, in particular, to draw the boundary of the historical so as to exclude rational choice with its universalizing microtheory. Key to this boundary-drawing endeavor is the belief that a historical approach treats people's motives and actions as dependent on particular institutional settings.[65] This emphasis on the role played by social and institutional contexts in structuring individuals' preferences and choices can, however, be taken only so far, before calling into question the practices of abstraction and comparison necessitated by the goal of using analytical induction to generate and test midrange empirical theory. In its allegiance to a modernist empiricist *tertium quid* in which context and comparison can both be appealed to,[66] but neither taken so far as to bring out its potential contradiction with the other, the emerging school of historical institutionalism inherited the analytical stance and theoretical aporias of earlier neostatism. While a distinctive rational choice institutionalism can be identified by its use of specific forms of microtheory, the self-proclaimed historical institutionalism follows neostatism in evading, or being opportunistically pluralistic, about theoretical issues. This is one of several interpersonal and conceptual connections between neostatism and historical institutionalism—exemplified in the central role played by Skocpol and macrohistorical small-N analysis in both groupings. Such connections explain why, when historical institutionalists claim *Bringing the State Back In* as a founding document, they are largely correct to do so, even though there is something curiously anachronistic about giving that status to an edited volume in which the discourse of new institutionalism is itself absent.

Historical institutionalism, however, also differs from neostatism in ways that reflect the other strands on which it draws. Thus, while much of neostatism tends to a form of structuralism that gives little weight to ideas, norms, or values as independent explanatory variables, historical institutionalism takes a different approach that makes Hall's work, rather than Skocpol's, perhaps its best exemplar. Thelen and Steinmo, in their introductory essay, identify "ideational innovation," albeit within "institutional constraints," as a previously neglected area that offers a new "frontier" for historical institutionalists.[67] By the time that Hall himself,

[65] See for the example the emphasis that Thelen and Steinmo place on the role of "institutional context" in shaping individuals goals and preferences in their effort to spell out points of divergence between historical and rational choice institutionalists. Ibid., 7–10.

[66] See for example, Thelen's later articulation, along with coauthor Richard Locke, of the notion of "contextualized comparisons." Richard M. Locke and Kathleen Thelen, "Apples and Oranges Revisited: Contextualized Comparisons and the Study of Comparative Labor Politics," *Politics and Society* 23, no. 3 (1995): 337–67.

[67] Thelen and Steinmo, "Historical Institutionalism," 22–26.

together with Taylor, came, a few years later, to offer his own presentation of historical institutionalism, we find attention to the role of ideas being incorporated as a key feature meant to differentiate this school from other new institutionalisms.[68] Another distinctive change, central to the very emergence of historical institutionalism as a self-conscious grouping, is the shifting of the outside "other" in contrast to which the identity of the group is contrasted and negotiated. The role once played by historically questionable images of the behavioral-era past comes to be played by unnuanced aggregate images of rational choice scholarship.

Alternative Trajectories

The move to a self-identified historical institutionalism was not, however, the only path forward from neostatism. While discussions in both comparative politics and American political development in the early 1990s tended to follow this path, some scholars rejected the invitation to approach rational choice as a new other against which to reframe and rearticulate their identity and allegiances. Thus, for example, when Martin Shefter republished several of his articles as a book in 1994, he identified with a "state-centered approach" and the "new institutionalism" as broadly presented by March and Olsen, but rejected a notion of competing new institutionalisms in favor of a cooperative framing of the relation between attention to "strategic choices" and to "macro-historical context."[69]

Alternative trajectories in the early 1990s were particularly prominent in the field of international relations. Here historical institutionalism failed to catch on as a self-identification even for scholars who had served alongside Skocpol on the SSRC Committee on States and Social Structures. Thus while Krasner's early discussions of path dependence and punctuated equilibrium proved popular with budding historical institutionalists, his own later work does not frame itself in historical institutionalist terms. Particularly interesting here is the path taken by a further committee member, Peter Katzenstein, whose work up through the mid-1980s is usually invoked alongside Hall's and Skocpol's as foundational for historical institutionalism.[70] He has played at most a minor role in

---

[68] Hall and Taylor, "Three Institutionalisms," 942.

[69] Martin Shefter, *Political Parties and the State: The American Historical Experience* (Princeton, NJ: Princeton University Press, 1994), 3.

[70] Steinmo, Thelen and Longstreth, "Preface," *Structuring Politics*, ix. At the outset of this volume, Katzenstein's work is folded in with that of Hall and Skocpol as representing the historical institutionalist side of the "new" institutionalism. See p. 1. While not a contributor to the volume, Katzenstein did attend the Colorado conference in 1990 out of which it grew.

articulating and defending this new grouping. In part this may be attributed to the fact that, by the late 1980s, his substantive engagements had moved largely into the field of international relations, where this self-identification carried little weight. It should also be seen, however, in relation to Katzenstein's moves within international relations debates, where he came down on the side of Ruggie.[71]

The set of intellectual conversations and alignments that Katzenstein took up hew closely to the tradition of scholarship in international relations that follows from Ruggie's version of the regime concept. As discussed earlier, by the mid-1980s, Ruggie was seeking to differentiate his approach to regimes from that of Krasner and others who came to the concept later. In a 1986 article, coauthored with Frederic Kratochwil, Ruggie further articulates his stance, emphasizing the social construction of the identities and interests of states making up an international regime, and the corresponding normative and "inescapable intersubjective quality" of such a regime.[72] Contrasting his stance to that of realists—who he holds approach international organizations in terms of a static structure of regulative rules—Ruggie presents the conduct of states as governed by an identity based system of potentially transformative constitutive as well as regulative rules. In so doing, he frames his stance as an "interpretive" challenge to the "positivist" focus within international organizations theory, which he fears had come to dominate regime analysis.[73]

Critical efforts to engage Ruggie's variant of regime analysis in the late 1980s overlapped with the diffusion of institutionalism discourse into the study of international relations, such that in the course of these efforts, the debate was reframed in the terms of contrasting approaches to international institutions. It is in such terms that Robert Keohane, in 1988, presents Ruggie's work as exemplifying one of two approaches in IR literature on institutions. He characterizes it as a "reflective" approach and, while holding out hope for eventual synthesis, juxtaposes it to an alternative "rationalistic" approach, which he characterizes as intertwined with the developing tradition of rational choice and as displayed in his own

---

[71] Peter J. Katzenstein, "Die neue Institutionalismus und internationale Regime: Amerika, Japan und Westdeutschland in der internationalen Politik" in *Macht und Ohnmacht politischer Institutionen*, ed. Hans-Hermann Hartwich (Opladen: Westdeutscher Verlag, 1989). The intellectual exchange here goes back several years with pointers of the path Katzenstein was to take already evident in his 1985 book. In the book's preface he noted his participation in colloquiums organized by Ruggie; while in the text he praised Ruggie's contribution to the Krasner volume on regimes and made "ideology" one of three components of his own key concept of "democratic corporatism." Katzenstein, *Small States*, 13, 78, 87–89.

[72] Friedrich Kratochwil and John G. Ruggie, "International Organization: A State of the Art on an Art of the State," *International Organization* 40, no. 4 (1986): 764.

[73] Ibid., 765–66.

work, along with that of Douglass North and Krasner. According to Keohane, in either approach the concept of institution might be critiqued for its "fuzziness."[74] But despite such concerns, the institution concept was clearly on the ascendant at this time, and in the 1990s, it largely supplants that of regime.[75]

While the discourse of institutionalism used by Keohane thus embodied a larger trend, his particular label for Ruggie's approach did not persist. It was soon supplanted by the alternative term *constructivism*, as promoted by Alexander Wendt in an influential 1992 article. Wendt uses the term to label a "cognitive, intersubjective" tradition associated with Ruggie's work, which he also contrasts with a competing "rationalist-behavioralist" tradition.[76] In doing so he presents and propounds a constructivist approach to institutions as "fundamentally cognitive entities" and to "institutionalization" as "a process of internalizing new identities and interests."[77] While Wendt draws largely on older sociological work, especially by G. H. Mead, the perspective on institutions that he articulates is also suggestive of that developed since the late 1970s within organizational sociology. In the mid-1990s this incipient connection was fleshed out, bringing a third new institutionalism—sociological institutionalism—into play in political science.

In the mid-1990s, Peter Katzenstein teamed up with Wendt and several other younger scholars to produce the edited volume *The Culture of National Security*. Katzenstein, in his introduction to this volume, spells out disagreements with the path dependency approach of Krasner's punctuated equilibrium and also invokes sociological institutionalism as a key, third angle to the institutionalism debates in political science. He showcases the perspectives on culture and identity associated with sociological

[74] Keohane, "International Institutions," 379, 382.

[75] In the recent *Handbook of International Relations* Beth Simmons and Lisa Martin criticize the regime literature as having given rise to "such definitional confusion that scholars in the 1990s have sought a simpler conception as well as a new label" and claim that "[t]he word 'institution' has now largely replaced 'regime' in the scholarly IR literature." Beth A. Simmons and Lisa Martin, "International Organizations and Institutions," in *Handbook of International Relations*, ed. Walter Carlnaes, Thomas Risse, and Beth A. Simmons (London: Sage, 2002), 6. There does not, however, seem to be anything more confusing about the definition of regimes than that of institutions, though identifying it in terms of a set of principles, norms, rules, or procedures has proved problematic. See Stephan Haggard and Beth A. Simmons, "Theories of International Regimes," *International Organization* 41, no. 3 (1987): 494–95.

[76] Alexander Wendt, "Anarchy Is What States Make of It: The Social Construction of Power Politics," *International Organization* 46, no. 2 (1992): 393–94. While Wendt's article was key to popularizing the term "constructivism," he credited it to the earlier work of Nicholas Onuf.

[77] Ibid., 399.

institutionalism as crucial for understanding the causal processes that define interests and "constitute the actors that shape national security politics and global insecurities."[78] One of the contributors to this volume, Martha Finnemore, has not only solidified the use of frameworks and terminology drawn from sociologists, but also contends that the sociological institutionalists' use of the term "institution" is "very different" from that of rational choice and historical institutionalists. For her, "incommensurable definitions mean that despite similarities in labelling, these approaches—all called institutionalist—have little in common."[79] Sociological institutionalism, with its treatment of cultural norms and rules as institutions, is welcomed by Finnemore as more than just a parallel to political science's homegrown constructivism. It is, she holds, compatible with that tradition and yet different enough to offer new resources to improve it. In particular, Finnemore suggests that sociological institutionalism offers "a much richer and more detailed theoretical framework than has constructivism."[80]

Finnemore here displays a concern characteristic of constructivists who seek to engage context without departing from modernist empiricism. In displaying concern about theoretical clarity relative to a longer standing approach—whether that be sociological or rational choice institutionalism—constructivists committed to this stance parallel their similarly committed counterparts in historical institutionalism. Even while these constructivists conceptualize context and institutions in somewhat different ways than do historical institutionalists, their shared concern is emblematic of a broad, but problematic, endeavor of modernist empiricist scholars. They want to emphasize context, but nevertheless remain committed to analytic generalization and, in particular, to the notion that empirical theory is key to achieving this goal.

Conclusion

With the mid-1990s entry of sociological institutionalism into political science's evolving conversations, our account reaches the point in time at which Hall and Taylor crafted their 1996 overview of three new institutionalisms. By highlighting differences between our account and theirs, both in terms of method and results, we seek in this conclusion to

---

[78] Peter J. Katzenstein, ed. *The Culture of National Security: Norms and Identity in World Politics* (New York: Columbia University Press, 1996), 16.

[79] Martha Finnemore, "Norms, Culture, and World Politics: Insights from Sociology's Institutionalism," *International Organization* 50, no. 2 (1996): 326.

[80] Ibid., 327.

illuminate distinctive features of the radical historicizing approach we have taken. We want to suggest that the image of the recent past generated by this approach is more historically satisfying and that it better prepares us to engage with the ongoing stream of intellectual shifts within political science.

The difference in method here centers on a contrast between typological and tradition-centered ways of summarizing intellectual debates—a contrast that is emblematic of the general differences between modernist empiricism and radical historicism. Hall and Taylor's typological effort recounts the various new institutionalisms by identifying features meant to pick out each of them as an aggregate type. Our goal in this chapter has not been to propose an alternative set of types—there are perhaps enough typologies already in the literature—but rather to explore what the payoffs are of focusing on traditions instead of types. Aggregation here centers on the intellectual, professional, and conceptual links among individuals found within the shifting patterns of conversation and contestation in any arena of ongoing debate. Typologies cut into these patterns at one point in time, and we can be led astray when a one-off typology is projected backward or forward in time. Such projection makes lines of conversation and disagreement appear static, thereby obscuring shifts in self-understandings, allegiances, and hostilities that have occurred in the past and that are likely to persist in the future. In contrast, it is just such shifts that capture attention in our tradition-centered approach, which tracks scholars remaking their intellectual projects as they renegotiate their engagement and confrontation with others.

A main substantive payoff to this approach lies in its sensitivity to the sequencing of past developments and its attentiveness to processes of shifting interaction and debate. We have approached the typology of rational choice, historical, and sociological institutionalism not as a static grid applicable at anytime since the late 1970s, but as the articulation of a distinctive mid-1990s perspective offered from within political science's ongoing conversations. Before the mid-1990s sociological institutionalism was not invoked as a player in those conversations. It only became so when political scientists like Katzenstein and Finnemore began to look outside their discipline for alternatives to the perspectives then dominating its discussion of institutions. The framing of that discussion as a rivalry between historical and rational choice institutionalism had itself only crystallized a few years earlier in the early 1990s, and it remained unpersuasive to some. The concern with defensively differentiating between variants of new institutionalism that underlay this framing had in turn developed only after the spread of institutionalist discourse in the mid-to-late 1980s. During this period, the neostatist and the regime literatures of the late 1970s and early 1980s were recast as examples of institutionalism. But prior to the mid-1980s, the notion of a new institutionalism had, among political scientists, been found only among rational choice scholars. None of these points about sequencing finds their way into Hall and Taylor's typological account, but they are essential components of any historicized account of the new institutionalisms in political science.

In addition to overlooking details of sequencing, a typological perspective on the new institutionalisms also downplays interactions between contending approaches and changes within them over time. Our account suggests that we cannot understand the articulation of a self-proclaimed historical institutionalism outside of the process of interaction in the late 1980s through which some scholars came to believe that their intellectual agenda needed to be rearticulated to better engage the perceived threat of rational choice. The failure of this new articulation to win universal acclaim, even among those who might have been expected to coalesce around it, reminds us, moreover, that scholars in a tradition need not react uniformly to interaction with other traditions, but rather that each reacts to her own interpretation of any such interaction. With regard to change over time, an assertion that historical institutionalism is peculiarly sensitive to the role of ideas makes sense only if one also refuses to retrospectively project this term too far into the past. Hall and Taylor's static approach leaves their reader potentially unaware that attentiveness to ideas marks a significant departure from the structuralist tendencies of much of the late 1970s and early 1980s neostatist literature in which they locate the early exemplars of historical institutionalism. By noting this change, a radical historicist stance helps us to recognize a point of tension differentiating those historical institutionalists who favor this attentiveness, such as Hall, from those whose intellectual positions remain marked by the legacies of an earlier structuralism, such as Skocpol.

A review of the contrasts between rational choice and historical institutionalism explored in this chapter can in turn suggest how our radical historicizing perspective goes beyond the goal of better remembering the past to also orient us in relation to developments ongoing today. The rational choice institutionalism revolves around a well-articulated and developing body of microtheory. This theory makes it possible to identify rational choice institutionalism as a distinctive neopositivist approach that is, for better or worse, clearly novel with regard to political science's longer-standing approaches to institutions. There are several notable contrasts here with historical institutionalism. In the absence of a coherent shared theoretical core, it is difficult to conclude that the "historical" label identifies one distinctive approach, rather than simply jumbling up an eclectic range of modernist empiricist efforts, some of which are perhaps incompatible. Moreover, under either interpretation, it is harder to identify here the kind of novelty that the label "new institutionalism" stakes a claim to than it is to do so for rational choice institutionalism.

Recent developments suggest that these contrasts have continuing legacies. Rational choice theory's highlighting of questions about the motor of change in macrohistorical studies challenges the conceptual vagueness of punctuated equilibrium, critical junctures, and path dependence. Increasingly aware that their approach lacks the microlevel grit demanded in the wake of rational choice theory, some historical institutionalists recently have sought to unpack such concepts on the microlevel. In doing so they draw on older economic theories and end up rediscovering perspectives that rational choice scholars have worked with for years.[81] Such moves further problematize efforts to identify historical institutionalism as a distinct approach. As with the earlier neostatism, efforts to define and promote historical institutionalism continue to rely largely on reactive, rhetorical forms of self-identification. For example, in their chapter in the recent *Political Science: State of the Discipline* volume, Skocpol and Pierson define historical institutionalism in contrast to rational choice and to survey-based behavioral work, asserting three features meant to pick out historical institutionalists: (1) they are concerned with "big, substantive questions"; (2) they "take time seriously"; and (3) they pay "attention to contexts and configurations."[82] These assertions are made in the absence of criteria for their application, arguments in defense of such criteria, or much evidence that other scholars are in fact very different from historical institutionalists in these regards. Attention to context here again functions as a rhetorically essential but vague middle ground staked out by the conjunction of a hostility to universalizing theoretical efforts and a fear of "getting mired in thick description,"[83] but lacking an account of what "context" is and how attention to it squares with a belief in analytic abstraction as essential to explanation and generalization.

[81] Paul Pierson, "Increasing Returns, Path Dependence, and the Study of Politics," *American Political Science Review* 94, no. 2 (2000): 251–67; James Mahoney, "Path Dependence in Historical Sociology," *Theory and Society* 29, no. 4 (2000): 507–48.

[82] Pierson and Skocpol, "Historical Institutionalism," 695–96. Compare with Mark Blyth, "Institutions and Ideas," in *Theory and Methods in Political Science*, ed. David Marsh and Gerry Stoker, 2nd ed. (Basingstoke, UK: Palgrave, 2002), 292–310.

[83] Pierson and Skocpol, "Historical Institutionalism," 710–11. Hostility to universal theory sometimes takes the specific form of noting apparent similarities between rational choice theory and behavioral era structural-functionalism, with the assumption evidently being that pointing out such a similarity somehow constitutes a critique of rational choice theory. Hence Skocpol emphasizes apparently similar beliefs in "One True and Unified Theory," and even, at times, suggests that the structural-functionalists were "forebears" of rational choice theory and rational choice theorists, their "successors." Theda Skocpol, "Theory Tackles History," *Social Science History* 24, no. 4 (2000): 675–76.

As the ambiguities of historical institutionalism have persisted unabated, doubts about the value of the defensive distinction that the category was initially intended to embody have also persisted, or even spread. For example, when Kathleen Thelen recently returned to the task of considering historical institutionalism alongside rational choice, she raised doubts about aspects of her and Steinmo's earlier characterizations and placed new emphasis on the potential compatibility of rational choice with macroqualitative work.[84] If the contrast between historical and rational choice institutionalisms is thus perhaps in decline as a way of narrating approaches, other previously underplayed differences may be becoming the focuses of new lines of intellectual contestation and identity. One particular candidate for such a role is the difference within historical institutionalism between more structuralist and more ideational approaches. In light of the continuing vibrancy of constructivism in international relations, and the attention to the sociological institutionalism associated with it, there are plenty of discussion partners to provide the basis for the articulation of an ideational institutionalism in comparative politics, American political development, and international relations.[85]

While we would welcome the articulation of just such an ideational institutionalism, we would like to close by expressing our reservations about the proclamations of novelty and progress all too likely to accompany it. As several chapters in this volume attest, a focus on the interplay of ideas and institutions is the longest-standing approach within American political science. Given such a background, prospective proponents of an ideational institutionalism might be better advised to narrate themselves as inheriting a long-standing tradition, and thereby avoid the disciplinary forgetting and pseudonovel reinventions all too pervasive in political science. The trumpeting of novelty in the name of progress has been, however, one of the most pervasive features of political science since the 1950s, and the emergence of a self-narrative that does not trumpet such novelty would probably presuppose a break with the beliefs about how and why we do social science around which modernist empiricism and neopositivism have cohabited for half a century.

---

[84] Kathleen Thelen, "Historical Institutionalism in Comparative Politics," *Annual Review of Political Science* 2 (1999): 369–404.

[85] For some examples of what this conversation might look like, see Sheri E. Berman, "Ideas, Norms and Culture in Political Analysis," *Comparative Politics* 33, no. 2 (January 2001): 231–50; Robert C. Lieberman, "Ideas, Institutions, and Political Order: Explaining Political Change," *American Political Science Review* 96, no. 4 (2002): 697–712; and Martha Finnemore and Kathryn Sikkink, "Taking Stock: The Constructivist Research Program in International Relations and Comparative Politics," *Annual Review of Political Science* 4 (2001): 391–416.

The odds against such a break are suggested by developments within the constructivist tradition with which the more ideationally inclined scholars of comparative politics and American political development may enter into conversation. Constructivism in the 1990s has been marked by increasing divergence regarding allegiance or hostility to such beliefs. Already articulated as a distinction between "modernist" and "postmodernist" variants of constructivism in Wendt's classic 1992 article, this differentiation has recently been rearticulated by the elder statesman Ruggie in his *Constructing the World Polity*. Ruggie here presents the strand of constructivism in which he locates his own work—and that of Haas, Kratochwil, Finnemore, and the later Katzenstein—as maintaining "a commitment to the idea of social science," as remaining "rooted in the classical tradition of Durkheim and Weber," and as exhibiting an "epistemological affinity" to pragmatism, speech-act theory, and the work of Searle. He contrasts this strand to an alternative postmodernist constructivism—associated with Foucault and Derrida—in which "little hope is held out for legitimate social science."[86] Such distinctions by necessity elide the parallels between pragmatism and postmodernism argued for by contemporary scholars like Richard Bernstein and Richard Rorty. Bypassing such arguments serves to reinforce modernist empiricism by evading the anxieties that an open-minded engagement with postmodernism might induce. Engagement of this sort might be one route by which an emergent ideational institutionalism could come to adopt the radical historicism that is noticeably absent from any of the new institutionalisms to date. But such a novel new institutionalism is perhaps far less likely an outcome than another rearticulation of the old, rhetorically wrapped up as yet another break from a misremembered past into the ever hopeful light of progress.

---

[86] John G. Ruggie, *Constructing the World Polity: Essays on International Institutionalization* (London: Routledge, 1998), 35–36.

Thirteen

Institutionalism and the Third Way

MARK BEVIR

HOW SHOULD WE EXPLAIN New Labour's attempts to reform the British state?[1] Broadly speaking, we might say that New Labour's Third Way arose as a response to a perceived crisis in an overloaded state characterized by centralization and vertical integration. The perception of a crisis in the hierarchic state inspired a search by political actors for more flexible, dynamic, and responsive patterns of organization. However, because there were various analyses of the crisis, this broad explanation of the Third Way leaves open the question of why New Labour conceived of the crisis in the particular way it did. In what follows, I want to explore the possibility that New Labour's construction of the crisis of the state draws on the new institutionalism in American political science, albeit indirectly by way of British social scientists and British think tanks.[2] When political science thus influences public policy, the history of political science acts as a study of modes of governance; it becomes an exploration of the beliefs and practices by which we are governed.

What follows maps the narratives told by political scientists onto public policy. One such mapping is widely recognized: public choice theory promoted marketization and the new public management as adopted by the New Right. Another mapping seems to have gone unnoticed: the new institutionalism promoted networks and joined-up governance as adopted by New Labour. To avoid misunderstanding, however, I should immediately say that these mappings represent broad conjunctures, not invariant ones. Some public choice theorists do not advocate marketization and the new public management, and some institutionalists do not advocate networks and joined-up governance. The New Right drew on conservative authoritarian ideas as well as introducing neoliberal reforms in the public sector, and New Labour is notably eclectic,

---

[1] For an attempt to provide a more detailed answer to this question see Mark Bevir, *New Labour: A Critique* (London: Routledge, 2005).

[2] On the impact of American political science on American governance see Richard J. Stillman, "21st Century United States Governance: Statecraft as Reformcraft," *Public Administration* 81, no. 1 (2003): 19–40.

taking ideas from neoliberals and others even as it introduces institutionalist reforms to the public sector. Nonetheless, just as we acknowledge
such qualifications while recognizing the reasonableness of the broad
conjuncture often drawn between neoliberalism and the New Right, so
we might do so while accepting the interaction between institutionalism
and New Labour.

We conjoin public choice theory with marketization and the New
Right partly because of the conceptual links between their ideas and
partly because of temporal links found in the lives of key actors. In pointing to a similar conjunction between institutionalism, network theory,
and New Labour, I will concentrate on drawing out the conceptual links,
arguing, for example, that institutionalism often inspires a focus on networks, that New Labour draws on institutionalist themes in its rebuttal
of the New Right, and that New Labour's vision of joined-up governance
overlaps with network theory. Although these conceptual links sometimes point to temporal ones in the lives of key actors, I will rarely pause
to make the latter explicit. Instead I now will briefly highlight some of
the key actors.

The leading actors in my history are a diffuse, intersecting group of
social scientists, policy advisers, and politicians. Together they effectively
combine the Third Way, network theory, and institutionalism into a recognizable package. The main proponents of network theory are self-proclaimed institutionalists. They include American social scientists like
Mark Granovetter, Paul DiMaggio, and Walter Powell as well as British
ones such as Rod Rhodes and Gerry Stoker.[3] Some leading British advocates of network theory, including Stoker, provide policy advice to New
Labour. More indirectly, New Labour politicians, such as the prime minister, Tony Blair, the chancellor of the exchequer, Gordon Brown, and Peter
Mandelson often appeal to ideas that are tied to institutionalism, including stakeholder economics, communitarianism, and social capital theory.[4]

[3] Mark Granovetter, "The Strength of Weak Ties," *American Journal of Sociology* 78,
no. 6 (1973): 1360–80; Mark Granovetter, "Economic Action and Social Structure: The
Problem of Embeddedness," *American Journal of Sociology* 91, no. 3 (1985): 481–510;
Paul J. DiMaggio and Walter W. Powell, "The Iron Cage Revisited: Institutional Isomor-
phism and Collective Rationality in Organizational Fields," in *The New Institutionalism in
Organizational Analysis*, ed. Walter W. Powell and Paul J. DiMaggio (Chicago: Chicago
University Press, 1991); Walter W. Powell, "Neither Market nor Hierarchy: Network Forms
of Organization," *Research in Organizational Behaviour* 12 (1990): 295–336; R.A.W.
Rhodes, *Understanding Governance: Policy Networks, Governance, Reflexivity, and Accountability* (Buckingham: Open University Press, 1997), chaps. 2 and 4; and Gerry Stoker,
"Urban Political Science and the Challenge of Urban Governance," in *Debating Governance*, ed. Jon Pierre (Oxford: Oxford University Press, 2000), 93.

[4] See respectively Tony Blair, "A Stakeholder Society," *Fabian Review* 103 (1996): 1–4;
Tony Blair, *New Britain: My Vision of a Young Country* (London: Fourth Estate, 1996),
290–321. For the links between institutionalism and stakeholder economics see J. A. Kay,

The most important actors in my history are, however, the researchers in center-left think tanks, such as Demos, the Foreign Policy Centre, and the Institute for Public Policy Research.[5] These think tanks constitute a conveyor belt that relays ideas and concerns back and forth between institutionalists and the government in much the same way as did the Adam Smith Institute and the Centre for Policy Studies between neoliberals and the New Right.[6] Geoff Mulgan was the cofounder and first director of Demos, and he is still chairman of its Advisory Council. Before founding Demos in 1993, he worked from 1990 to 1992 as a senior policy adviser to Brown. Today he works in the prime minister's policy unit. Demos's current director, Tom Bentley, took up the post after working, from 1998 to 1999, as a special adviser to David Blunkett, the secretary of state for Education and Employment. Its deputy director, Beth Egan, has been on secondment to assist Brown during his time as chancellor of the exchequer. Several of the researchers at Demos also have been employed within New Labour. Charles Leadbeater, for example, authored a white paper entitled *Our Competitive Future*.[7] Perri 6 is a Demos researcher who straddles both the academy, where he defends neo-Durkheimian institutionalism, and government, where he provides New Labour with regular policy advice on holistic government. He has also collaborated with Stoker on various occasions. Similar connections within people's lives tie Demos to other center-left think tanks and then these think tanks to New Labour. Daniel Stedman Jones, a Demos researcher, has worked in the prime minister's Policy Unit and also at the Institute for Public Policy. Mark Leonard became the director of the Foreign Policy Centre after having been a senior researcher for Demos. He also advises New Labour as a member of the Foreign and Commonwealth Office Panel.

Foundations of Corporate Success: How Business Strategies Add Value (Oxford: Oxford University Press, 1993). For those between institutionalism and communitarianism see Philip Selznick, *The Moral Commonwealth: Social Theory and the Promise of Community* (Berkeley and Los Angeles: University of California Press, 1992). For those between institutionalism, social capital, and the Third Way see Simon Szreter, *A New Political Economy for New Labour: The Importance of Social Capital*, Policy Paper no. 15, Political Economy Research Centre, University of Sheffield, 1998.

[5] The reports of these think tanks often draw on institutionalism and network theory from both Britain and the United States. In addition, the think tanks have links with British political scientists: Stoker has published work with Demos. Finally, several of the researchers within the think tanks have held Harkness Fellowships and the like with which to study in America: Mulgan went to MIT.

[6] On the New Right see Richard Cockett, *Thinking the Unthinkable: Think-Tanks and the Economic Counter-revolution* (London: HarperCollins, 1994).

[7] *Our Competitive Future: Building the Knowledge Driven Economy*, Cm. 4176 (1998).

The New Institutionalism

The conceptual links from institutionalism to New Labour are not always straightforward. The last chapter suggested the new institutionalism arose in part as a response from within political science to rational choice theory. New Labour, in contrast, represents a social democratic response to the New Right. However, the overlap between rational choice theory and the New Right means that New Labour has comfortably deployed aspects of the new institutionalism in its attempt to revive social democracy. The conceptual links thus become clearest against the background of rational choice theory.

Rational choice theorists treat social practices as the products of the actions of utility-maximizing individuals.[8] Doing so typically enables them to postulate the market as an inherently efficient form of social organization. They explain the perceived crisis in the bureaucratic state, therefore, by reference to its inherent inefficiency, lack of flexibility, and inadequate responsiveness when compared to markets. According to neoliberals, the inefficiencies of bureaucracy, especially in the context of a global economy, force states to become more efficient by adopting marketization, contracting out, new management techniques, staff cuts, and stricter budgeting.[9]

The spread of rational choice theory within political science challenged a widespread commitment to a midlevel analysis that concentrated on describing broad institutional and behavioral patterns and producing typologies and correlations between social categories. The previous chapter suggested that new institutionalism consists of a diverse cluster of attempts to preserve midlevel analysis by emphasising our social embeddedness and thereby the role of institutional structures and cultural norms as determinants of social life. The institutionalists reject the use of neoclassical economic theory to explain political practices, turning instead to midlevel analyses of the rules and structures that, in their view, largely settle what happens at the microlevel. Institutions, they tell us, are "collections of standard operating procedures and structures that define and defend interest" or "formal rules, compliance procedures and standard op-

---

[8] The history of rational choice theory currently remains the preserve of uncritical disciplinary studies—a search for illustrious ancestors—as opposed to critical, contextual studies. One notable exception is S. M. Amadae, *Rationalizing Capitalist Democracy: The Cold War Origins of Rational Choice Liberalism* (Chicago: University of Chicago Press, 2003).

[9] David Osborne and Ted Baebler, *Reinventing Government: How the Entrepreneurial Spirit Is Transforming the Public Sector* (Reading, MA: Addison-Wesley, 1992).

erating practices that structure relationships between individuals in various units of the polity and the economy."[10]

Significantly, the new institutionalism inspired an account of the crisis of the state very different from the neoliberal one that we associate with rational choice theory. Whereas rational choice theorists often deploy assumptions about utility-maximizing agents to postulate the market as the form of organization, circumstances permitting, that best expresses rationality, institutionalists typically argue that agents are embedded in institutions and that networks are the organizations best suited to our embedded nature. On one hand, institutionalists use the concept of a "network" to describe the inevitable nature of all organizations given our social embeddedness—hierarchies and markets are networks. Because the concepts of "embeddedness" and "network" suggest human action is always already structured by social relationships, they provide institutionalists, such as Granovetter and Powell and DiMaggio, with a rebuttal of rational choice theory.[11] On the other hand, institutionalists suggest that "networks" are better suited to many tasks than hierarchies or markets. The concepts of "embeddedness" and "network" provide institutionalists with a rebuttal of the neoliberal policies of the New Right, since they imply the state should turn to networks, not markets, trust, not competition, and diplomacy, not the new public management.[12] Typically institutionalists, such as Perri 6, combine these two ways of conceiving of networks by suggesting that although all organizations take the form of embedded networks, those that best resemble the ideal-type of a network reap the benefits of so doing.[13]

Institutionalists accept the rational choice suggestion that hierarchies are inflexible and unresponsive, but instead of promoting markets, they appeal to networks as a suitably flexible and responsive alternative, one that recognizes social actors operate in structured relationships. Institutionalists argue that economic efficiency and success derive from stable

[10] James G. March and Johan P. Olsen, "The New Institutionalism: Organizational Factors in Political Life," *American Political Science Review* 78, no. 3 (1984): 738; and Peter A. Hall, *Governing the Economy: The Politics of State Intervention in Britain and France* (Cambridge: Polity Press, 1986), 20.

[11] Granovetter, "Economic Action"; and Powell and DiMaggio, *New Institutionalism.*

[12] Mark Granovetter, "Business Groups," in *Handbook of Economic Sociology,* ed. Neil J. Smelser and Richard Swedberg (Princeton, NJ: Princeton University Press, 1994), 453–75; Powell, "Neither Market nor Hierarchy.".

[13] Institutionalists often elide good in the sense of promoting community with good in terms of a quasi-Darwinian notion of success. Perri 6, for example, says, "a 'good' institution . . . is a more viable one than others that might, in a given social setting, emerge. . . . [It] is one that promotes organic rather than mechanical solidarities." Perri 6, "Neo-Durkheimian Institutional Theory," Paper presented to Conference on Institutional Theory in Political Science, Loch Lomond, 1999.

relationships characterized by trust, social participation, voluntary associations, and friendship, at least as much as from markets and competition.
Although hierarchies can provide a setting for trust and stability, institutionalists often suggest the time for hierarchies has passed: hierarchies
were useful for the routinized patterns of behavior that dominated Fordist
economies, but they are ill-suited to delivering the innovation and entrepreneurship that states now have to foster if they are to compete effectively in the new knowledge-driven global economy.[14] The new economy
requires networks in which trust and participation are combined with
flexibility, responsiveness, and innovation. Network theory appealed here
to its apparent ability to account for what appeared to be economic successes that were difficult for rational choice theorists to explain by reference to competition—Japanese alliance capitalism and the high-tech sectors in Silicon Valley and north-central Italy.[15] What once seemed to be
the cutting-edge, most prosperous parts of the new economy apparently
thrived precisely because they were organized as networks.

Institutionalism suggests that we need to understand the effects of the
policies of the New Right not through abstract models built on assumptions about utility-maximizing agents but in terms of their impact on a
socially embedded set of actors. Institutionalists such as Rhodes and
Stoker argue that marketization and the new public management had various unintended consequences as a result of entrenched institutional patterns and norms.[16] Neoliberal reforms fragmented service delivery,
thereby weakening central control without establishing proper markets.
They created networks, as opposed to either the old hierarchies or the
neoliberal vision of markets. Recent institutionalist studies of central and
local government in Britain thus suggest that the neoliberal reforms of
the 1980s undermined the capacity of the state to act by itself without
establishing the neoliberal vision. According to institutionalists, the state
now acts as one of several organizations that come together in diverse
networks to deliver services. The state is characterized by power-depen-
dent organizations that form semiautonomous, self-governing networks.

[14] For the link between networks and innovation see Walter W. Powell, Kenneth W.
Koput, and Laurel Smith-Doerr, "Interorganizational Collaboration and the Locus of Innovation: Networks of Learning in Biotechnology," *Administrative Science Quarterly* 41, no.
1 (1996): 116–45; and Chris DeBresson and Fernand Amesse, eds., *Networks of Innovators*,
Special Issue of *Research Policy* 20, no. 5 (1991).

[15] Granovetter, "Business Groups"; Robert D. Putnam, *Making Democracy Work: Civic
Traditions in Modern Italy* (Princeton, NJ: Princeton University Press, 1993), 160

[16] Rhodes, *Understanding Governance*, particularly chaps. 1 and 3; R.A.W. Rhodes, "It's
the Mix that Matters: From Marketisation to Diplomacy," *Australian Journal of Public
Administration* 56 (1997): 40–53; and Gerry Stoker, "Introduction: The Unintended Costs
and Benefits of New Management Reform for British Local Governance," in *The New Management of British Local Governance*, ed. Gerry Stoker (London: Macmillan, 1999), 1–21.

The Third Way

In interpreting New Labour, we will find, first, that it constructs dilemmas such as state overload in ways subtly different from the New Right, since it does so against the background of a social democratic tradition. We will find, second, that it responds to these dilemmas in ways that reflect both this tradition and its particular construction of the dilemmas. As I have already suggested, moreover, New Labour here conceives of the dilemmas, and responds to them, in ways that are entwined with institutionalism and network theory. Of course, neither institutionalism nor network theory is inherently social democratic. Rather, they can sustain various political positions, including Christian democracy and paternalist authoritarianism.[17] In practice, however, institutionalism and network theory have found a home in New Labour due to personal ties, overlaps in their responses to the New Right and neoliberalism, and a shared, if often unrecognized, debt to a tradition of Christian idealism.[18] We will find this to be so not only of New Labour's rhetoric but also of many of its public sector policies.[19]

The Dilemmas

We might locate New Labour at the juncture where a social democratic tradition struggles to come to terms with dilemmas initially highlighted by the New Right. Of course, the social democratic tradition contains several competing strands, so when we invoke it, or for that matter New

[17] Because network theorists use their theory to explain the successes of Asian economies, New Labour politicians at times have found themselves asking what British social democracy might learn from authoritarian states such as Singapore. See Tony Blair, Speech to the Singapore Business Community, January 8, 1996.

[18] While here is not the place to document the temporal and conceptual links that fix the tradition of Christian idealism, we might note that Karl Polanyi, one of the godfathers of institutionalism, was a member of the Christian left inspired by John Macmurray, the idealist philosopher who inspired Blair's conversion to socialism: Mark Bevir and David O'Brien, "From Idealism to Communitarianism: The Inheritance and Legacy of John Macmurray," *History of Political Thought* 24, no. 2 (2003): 305–29. We also might note how Reinhard Bendix, another godfather of institutionalism, interpreted Max Weber so as to ignore his debt to Nietzsche in favor of a more straightforward, almost Hegelian reading: Wilhelm Hennis, *Max Weber: Essays in Reconstruction,* trans. Keith Tribe (London: Allen and Unwin, 1988); Friedrich H. Tenbruck, "The Problem of Thematic Unity in the Work of Max Weber," *British Journal of Sociology* 31, no. 3 (1980): 316–51.

[19] Of course, New Labour's eclecticism means its policies also reflect other webs of belief: welfare to work, for example, not only gets the unemployed to network, it also cuts welfare bills and uses coercion to lower wage levels in a way neoliberals might recognize as their own.

Labour, Old Labour, or the New Right, we simplify complex patterns of belief. Broadly speaking, however, we can identify a social democratic tradition for which the individual exists and attains the good only in the context of community. Blair often expresses this belief, insisting, for example, that we are "citizens of a community," not "separate economic actors competing in the marketplace of life."[20] Social democrats join institutionalists in arguing that sociality and solidarity are integral features of human life.[21] We make sense of the world, including our own interests, in the context of social institutions that constrain us, enable our creativity, and bind us to one another in community.

Social democrats used a belief in our socially embedded nature to help justify commitments to social justice, citizenship, and fellowship. For much of the postwar period, social democrats saw the Keynesian welfare state as a means of realizing these commitments. The state would promote equality by demand management, welfare provision, and progressive taxation. Our social nature and our responsibilities to our fellow citizens were unpacked in terms of universal social rights to a minimal standard of living, including adequate food, clothing, and housing, as well as protection from ill health and unemployment. The welfare state also embodied a command model of public service provision that had become popular with social democrats between the two world wars.

During the 1970s and 1980s, a number of dilemmas confronted social democrats: worries about the underclass challenged the welfare state, worries about state overload posed questions of the command model of public-service provision, and worries about inflation undermined the Keynesian macroeconomic framework. Typically these dilemmas were highlighted by the New Right, which thus established a hegemony over discussion of them, a hegemony apparent in New Labour's adoption of positions similar to those of the New Right.

One similarity between New Labour and the New Right appears in that New Labour, at least implicitly, conceives of the global economy as a competitive setting that renders economic efficiency and success absolute prerequisites for, and even the leading criteria of, almost everything else. When institutionalists invoke costs of learning to explain the persistence of otherwise inefficient institutions, and when New Labour represents flexible labor markets and welfare reform as economic imperatives of the global economy, they tacitly accept the neoliberal idea of an unavoidable, universal, and tyrannical economic rationality—a rationality that operates at the microlevel but creates structural constraints to which we have

[20] Blair, *New Britain*, 300.
[21] Compare Granovetter, "Economic Action"; Perri 6, "Neo-Durkheimian"; Blair, *New Britain*.

no option but to bow.[22] When New Labour bows to unavoidable economic rationality, it adopts themes that spread out to alter other parts of
its heritage. The social democratic ideal, for example, becomes less one
of social cooperation aimed at securing the good life for all than one of
economic partnership in which robust competition, with everyone having
a chance to compete, secures prosperity for all.

Another significant similarity between New Labour and the New Right
lies in their overlapping rejections of the bureaucratic hierarchies associated with Old Labour. New Labour accepts that the state suffered a crisis
because hierarchies were inefficient in the new global economy. In this
respect, New Labour again transforms the social democratic tradition to
mirror the New Right. Mandelson and Liddle, for example, explicitly
reject the "municipal socialism" and "centralised nationalism" of Labour's past when they insist that New Labour "does not seek to provide
centralised 'statist' solutions to every social and economic problem."[23]

Despite the similarities between New Labour and the New Right, we
should be wary of interpreting the former as a capitulation to the latter.[24]
If we did so, we would risk neglecting the constructed and contingent
nature of social life in a way that would leave us few resources by which
to explain their differences. Although New Labour and the New Right
have conceived the dilemmas in broadly similar terms, they have done so
against the background of different traditions, the continuing influence
of which explains the differences in their thinking and their policies. While
New Labour represents a response to the New Right, social democrats
have constructed the dilemmas facing the welfare state, public services,
and economy against the background of their social democratic tradition,
and so in a way different from the New Right.

In the case of the welfare state, social democrats sometimes express
worries about the underclass, but they generally portray this class as
trapped on welfare not because of psychological dependency but because
of institutional factors such as the way welfare payments get reduced once
claimants start to earn even modest wages. Some of New Labour's policy
advisers even suggest that the welfare state traps people in poverty because it fails to conceive of poverty as social exclusion or "network poverty." Dependency gets conceptualized by New Labour in terms of insufficient or inappropriate social embeddedness. According to Perri 6, for
example, the most common way of getting a job is through informal net-

---

[22] Colin Hay, *The Political Economy of New Labour: Labouring under False Pretences*
(Manchester: Manchester University Press, 1999).
[23] Peter Mandelson and Roger Liddle, *The Blair Revolution: Can New Labour Deliver?*
(London: Faber and Faber, 1996), 27.
[24] Contrast Hay, *Political Economy*.

works of friends, former colleagues, and acquaintances.[25] The welfare state traps people in unemployment by lumping them together, thereby undermining their ability to enter the social networks where jobs are found. If unemployed people volunteer, they are treated as being unavailable for work, and yet, Perri 6 continues, volunteering is an important way of entering the networks and making the contacts that result in employment. Likewise, training schemes for the unemployed are provided by specialist bodies that deal with them alone, instead of by companies that connect them to the employed.

In the case of public services, when social democrats deplore the inefficiency and rigidity of the provision of goods by a hierarchic bureaucracy, they rarely describe such inefficiency and rigidity as inherent consequences of public ownership, as does the New Right. On the contrary, New Labour's Third Way embodies a rebuttal of the New Right since it implies the New Right's faith in markets ignored our social embeddedness. Advocates of the Third Way argue that public services should reflect our sociality in that they should encourage an ethic of mutual cooperation, even if, when appropriate, they rely on market mechanisms to increase choice and promote responsibility. David Clark, then the minister for public services, explained, for example, that policies such as market testing "will not be pursued blindly as an article of faith," although they "will continue where they offer best value for money."[26] Although New Labour accepts that markets can be an appropriate means of delivering public services, it insists that markets are not always the most efficient way to deliver services, since they can go against the public interest, reinforce inequalities, and entrench privilege, all of which damages economic performance. For New Labour, the problem with public services is one of adapting them to new times, not rolling back the state to promote market competition.

In the case of the economy, social democrats have often rejected Keynesian macroeconomics but only rarely adopted the monetarist doctrines associated with the New Right. New Labour follows the New Right in taking macroeconomic stability, especially low inflation, to be the leading prerequisite of growth and high, long-term levels of employment—"government's first job is to ensure a stable macroeconomic environment."[27]

[25] Perri 6, *Escaping Poverty: From Safety Nets to Networks of Opportunity* (London: Demos, 1997). Compare Mark Granovetter, *Getting a Job: A Study of Contracts and Careers* (Cambridge: Harvard University Press, 1974); Mark Granovetter, "The Sociological and Economic Approaches to Labor Market Analysis: A Social Structural View," in *Industries, Firms and Jobs: Sociological and Economic Approaches*, ed. George Farkas and Paula England (New York: Plenum Press, 1988).

[26] David Clark, "The Civil Service and the New Government," speech, London, June 17, 1997.

[27] *Our Competitive Future*, 12.

New Labour also follows the New Right, therefore, in concentrating on supply-side reforms rather than demand management. Nonetheless, New Labour's supply-side vision reflects an institutionalist narrative—and the heritage of Wilsonian socialism—as opposed to neoliberalism.[28] New Labour follows the institutionalists in suggesting the problem is not one of removing barriers to competition but of coming to terms with the new economy. Leadbeater writes of a thin-air economy in which knowledge is all important and in which the vital ingredients for success are flexibility and innovation.[29] Mulgan similarly evokes a new "connexity" that has arisen from a revolution in communications and technology and has brought a shift from liberal individualism and old-style social democracy to new forms of interdependence.[30] For New Labour, the problems facing Britain's economy derive from a short-term outlook that neglects investment in the supply-side as much as from inflation. By constructing the dilemma facing the economy differently from neoliberals, New Labour opens up another space in which to denounce the New Right. This denunciation, like the institutionalist response to neoliberalism, highlights the dangers of neglecting social embeddedness and fetishizing the market. An appeal to social embeddedness appears, for example, in New Labour's flirtation with stakeholder economics, itself a part of the institutional economics from which the institutionalist narrative takes much of its inspiration.[31] According to New Labour, because the New Right failed to recognize that firms are social organizations, its policies encouraged an excessive individualism that privileged short-term concerns, created unnecessary economic volatility, and increased divisions within society.[32] The Third Way begins with our social nature and the importance of a community

[28] Wilson's reputation has improved noticeably alongside the Labour Party's rejection of demand management in favor of intervening in the supply-side to promote knowledge and technology. See Richard Coopey, Steve Fielding, and Nick Tiratsoo, eds., *The Wilson Governments, 1964–1970* (London: Pinter, 1993); Ben Pimlott, *Harold Wilson* (London: HarperCollins, 1992).

[29] Charles Leadbeater, *Living on Thin Air: The New Economy* (Harmondsworth, UK: Penguin, 1999).

[30] Geoff Mulgan, *Connexity: How to Live in a Connected World* (London: Jonathon Cape, 1997).

[31] For the link between sociological institutionalism and institutional economics see especially Mark Granovetter and Richard Swedberg, eds., *The Sociology of Economic Life* (Boulder, CO: Westview Press, 1992).

[32] Blair, "A Stakeholder Society"; and also Tony Blair, "The Stakeholder Economy," speech, Derby, January 18, 1996; Tony Blair, "Faith in the City—Ten Years On," speech, London, January 29, 1996; Tony Blair, "John Smith Memorial Lecture," speech, London, February 7, 1996.

composed of mutual rights and obligations and then suggests these considerations show social cohesion to be integral to economic prosperity.[33]

The Response

New Labour has trumpeted several big ideas—stakeholder society, social
capital, communitarianism, and the Third Way—to convey its distinctive
response to the crisis of the state. Whatever the brand label, New Labour
advocates a society of stakeholders enabled by a state that forms with
them partnerships and networks based on trust. New Labour's response
to the perceived crisis of the state overlaps with, and draws on, institutionalism and network theory. Having accepted aspects of the New
Right's challenge to the Keynesian welfare state while rejecting its turn to
markets and monetarism as inappropriate given our social embeddedness,
New Labour advocates instead networks of institutions and individuals
acting in partnership and held together by relations of trust. New Labour
does not exclude bureaucratic hierarchy or quasi market competition;
rather, it advocates a mix of hierarchies, markets, and networks, with the
choice among them depending on the nature of the service: "services
should be provided through the sector best placed to provide those services most effectively," where "this can be the public, private or voluntary
sector, or partnerships between these sectors."[34] New Labour thus uses
institutionalism and network theory to create an alternative to both Old
Labour and the New Right.

In the case of the welfare state, a belief in our social embeddedness encourages New Labour to envisage a world of citizens linked together by
reciprocal duties and responsibilities. These citizens join the state in a cooperative enterprise aimed at producing an economically and socially vibrant
nation. The state acts not as a safety net but as an enabler: it provides
citizens with opportunities for advancement, but it is up to the citizens
to take advantage of these opportunities. New Labour seeks to promote
individual responsibility through cooperation. Frank Field, former minister for Welfare Reform, wrote, for example, of an "age of mutuality" during which "self-interest . . . will also promote the common good," before
emphasizing the importance of locating responsibility for self-improve-

---

[33] Tony Blair, *The Third Way: New Politics for the New Century*, Fabian Pamphlet no.
588 (London: Fabian Society, 1998); and also Tony Blair, "Facing the Modern Challenge:
The Third Way in Britain and South Africa," speech, Cape Town, January 8, 1999; Tony
Blair, "To the IPPR," speech, London, January 14, 1999; Tony Blair, "Third Way, Phase
Two," *Prospect*, March 10–14, 2001.

[34] *Modern Public Services for Britain: Investing in Reform*, Cm. 4011 (1998).

ment with individuals.[35] Blair too has said, "[T]he modern welfare state is not founded on a paternalistic government giving out more benefits but on an enabling government that through work and education helps people to help themselves."[36] The enabling state represents an allegedly new type of partnership—"a new contract between citizen and sate."[37]

One clear aim of this new partnership is to overcome social exclusion and network poverty. New Labour's New Deal for the Unemployed aims "to make work pay" by eradicating the institutional disincentives to employment created by the rules governing taxation and benefits: a Working Families Tax Credit, for example, will supplement earnings from paid employment with cash benefits so that every family containing a full-time worker will have a guaranteed minimum income of a 190 pounds a week.[38] The New Deal also aims to connect the unemployed to the employed. The young unemployed are given four options, including volunteering as well as paid work, training, and participation in an environmental task force.[39] The government also offers a subsidy to employers lasting six months for each worker they recruit from among the long-term unemployed. New Labour appears already to be acting on Perri 6's advice that welfare-to-work schemes should maximize the opportunities for the unemployed to make contacts with those in work.

In the case of public services, the Labour government conceives of networks as peculiarly appropriate to its ideals of partnership and an enabling state. The Service First program, in particular, promotes Quality Networks composed of locally organized groups of people, from all areas and levels of the public sector, who work together in partnerships based on trust. The purposes of these networks include the development of principles of best practice, the sharing of troubleshooting skills, and the building of partnerships between relevant organizations. They aim to encourage "public services to work together . . . to ensure that services are . . . effective and co-ordinated."[40] Although the idea of Quality Networks applies primarily to public sector organizations, the government has extended the underlying principles to voluntary and private sector organizations. A Cabinet Office publication announces, "[W]e will work in partnership with the private sector, extending the circle of those involved in public service."[41]

---

[35] Frank Field, *Reforming Welfare* (London: Social Markets Foundation, 1997), 78–80.

[36] Blair, *New Britain*, 302.

[37] *New Ambitions for Our Country: A New Contract for Welfare*, Cm. 3805 (1998), v.

[38] *Steering a Course for Lasting Prosperity*, Cm. 4076 (1998), 61.

[39] *New Ambitions*, 25.

[40] Cabinet Office, *Service First*, at http://www.servicefirst.gov.uk/sfirst/bk12toc.html (accessed October 1, 1998).

[41] United Kingdom, Cabinet Office, *Better Quality Services*, http://www.open.gov.uk/co/quality/qualmenu.html (accessed October 1, 1998).

Although New Labour's emphasis on individual involvement overlaps with themes found in the New Right, its model of service delivery does not follow that of the New Right. On the contrary, New Labour argues that many features of the new public management, such as quasi markets and contracting out, maintained an unhealthy dichotomy between the public and private sectors: public bodies did not connect properly with private companies but merely contracted services out to them—this argument is used to justify abolishing the internal market in the National Health Service (NHS). In contrast, the Third Way is supposed to develop networks that enable public and private organizations properly to collaborate. In more concrete terms, the government has revived Private Finance Initiatives in an attempt to create mechanisms by which public and private organizations can form partnerships and networks to finance and undertake projects. Typically these projects constitute an investment in the supply-side through, say, the construction and repair of schools or the transport infrastructure.

New Labour's networks for public service delivery are supposed to be based on trust. Blair describes trust as "the recognition of a mutual purpose for which we work together and in which we all benefit."[42] Trust matters, New Labour tells us, because we are interdependent social beings who achieve more by working together than by competing; effective and high quality public services are best achieved through cooperative relations based on trust. Blair talks of building relationships of trust between all actors in society: trust is promoted between organizations by means of the Quality Networks program; it is promoted inside organizations through "management within boundaries"; and it is promoted between organizations and individuals by means of the Service First program.

In the case of the economy, New Labour tells us that the state should become an enabling institution organized around self-organizing networks. The state will promote a culture of collaboration and investment in infrastructure, research, and training, all of which are integral to a competitive supply-side. "The Government has a key role in acting as a catalyst, investor, and regulator to strengthen the supply-side of the economy."[43] It can best fulfill this role, moreover, by entering into partnerships and networks with individuals, voluntary bodies, and private companies. Hence, New Labour now champions Individual Learning Accounts, with the state and employers giving individuals a grant toward training provided the individuals provide a small initial sum. Hence also, the government has formed a partnership with the Wellcome Trust to

[42] Blair, New Britain, 292.
[43] Our Competitive Future, 7.

spend nigh-on 1.5 billion pounds improving the technological base of British industry.

New Labour clearly regards networks as good institutions in two senses. Networks are ethical in that they reflect our social embeddedness within a community that gives us rights and responsibilities. And networks are good in that they promote competitiveness. The prosperity, as much as social revival, of community depends on clusters of self-governing institutions, such as schools, housing associations, and local councils, working together in networks. The models here are the economic success stories beloved of institutionalists—the Asian Tigers, Silicon Valley, and north-central Italy. Leadbeater draws out, for example, the lessons to be learned from California.[44] He argues economic competitiveness depends on entrepreneurship and knowledge, especially of software, the Internet, and biotechnology. California promotes a culture of creative individualism that fosters the openness and experimentalism essential to such entrepreneurship and knowledge. The high-tech companies of Silicon Valley form networks in which they share information and collaborate on projects. The networks of high-tech firms are, moreover, models of stakeholding, being embedded in the moral community: they have extensive schemes of employee ownership, they focus on building loyalty among employees and customers, and they set high standards of corporate responsibility. If Britain builds networks of social entrepreneurs and civic leaders, Leadbeater implies, it will share the flexibility, responsiveness, and prosperity of California.

Investment in the supply-side and the creation of networks are the solution, for New Labour, to Britain's economic ills. The new, knowledge-driven global economy offers opportunities and constraints. It allows, and requires, us to create innovative ideas and to turn them into jobs and economic growth. Britain, New Labour explains, has to become an outward-looking, flexible, and creative center. To do so, as the institutionalists suggest, we have to develop networks, connexity, and social capital. Hence why Blair, following governmental advisers such as Leonard, wants to rebrand Great Britain as "cool Britannia"—a people and society characterized by "know-how, creativity, risk-taking, and, most of all, originality."[45]

New Labour's stance toward the state overlaps with and draws on institutionalism and network theory. Of course, there are disagreements and debates among the politicians and policy advisers of New Labour: Lead-

---

[44] Leadbeater, *Living on Thin Air*; Charles Leadbeater, *Britain: The California of Europe?* (London: Demos, 1999); and for the extension of his vision to the European Union, Charles Leadbeater, *Europe's New Economy* (London: Centre for European Reform, 1999).

[45] Cited in J. Heastfield, "Brand New Britain," *LM Magazine*, November 1997. Also see Mark Leonard, *Britain: Renewing Our Identity* (London: Demos, 1997).

beater and Mulgan have suggested that the idea of stakeholding proposed by Will Hutton and John Kay is too cumbersome to meet the demands of the entrepreneurial, knowledge-driven economy of today, while Stoker has pointed to some of the tensions within New Labour's projects.[46] Nonetheless, these disagreements generally occur within a broad, shared framework: Leadbeater and Mulgan allow that stakeholding remains a viable idea, while Stoker suggests that politics is all about dealing with such tensions. The elite of New Labour rely on an overlapping consensus common to institutionalism and the new social democracy. They speak a language of social embeddedness, sociality, community, social capital, networks, and partnership.

Joined-Up Governance

New Labour's response to the perceived crisis of the state overlaps with and draws on institutionalism. Against the background of a social democratic tradition, New Labour has constructed the dilemmas facing the state in a way that points to rejection of Old Labour and the New Right and affirmation of social embeddedness, partnership, networks, and trust. Blair glosses this vision as "joined-up problems need joined-up solutions."[47] Joined-up governance is the slogan New Labour uses to invoke its vision of a state reformed in accord with its Third Way. The idea of joined-up governance thus belongs at the juncture where New Labour and institutionalism provide an alternative narrative of recent changes in the state to the neoliberal one of the New Right. Indeed, joined-up governance invokes networks as a way to resolve not only the perceived crisis of the old-fashioned bureaucratic state but also the additional damage that New Labour and institutionalists suggest has been wrought on the state by the reforms introduced by the New Right. It stands, that is to say, as New Labour's response to dilemmas of fragmentation, steering, and managerialism.

The Dilemmas

As we have seen, the Third Way deploys institutionalism to challenge the neoliberal narrative. The New Right, it implies, failed to recognize our sociality and community, and consequently fetishized markets in a way

[46] Charles Leadbeater and Geoff Mulgan, *Mistakeholding: Whatever Happened to Labour's Big Idea?* (London: Demos, 1996); Gerry Stoker, "The Three Projects of New Labour," *Renewal* 8 (2000): 7–15.
[47] *Observer*, May 31, 1998.

that damaged the efficiency, flexibility, and responsiveness of the public sector and economy. This challenge to the New Right suggests that its misguided policies have created additional dilemmas for the state—coordination, control, and ethics. Joined-up governance attempts to resolve these concerns.

A lack of coordination is one of the most widely invoked consequences of the public sector reforms of the New Right. Services are delivered by a combination of government, special-purpose bodies, and the voluntary and private sectors. There are 5,521 special-purpose bodies that spend over 39 billion pounds and to which ministers make about 70,000 patronage appointments. Marketization has resulted, critics say, in excessive fragmentation.

According to institutionalists, the fragmentation associated with the New Right merely exacerbates a lack of coordination also characteristic of hierarchies. Perri 6, for example, argues that the organization of government into separate departments with their own budgets undermines attempts to deal with "wicked problems" that cut across departmental cages.[48] The reforms of the New Right, he implies, made it even harder to deal adequately with these wicked problems since they created a plethora of agencies that are only too willing to pass problems on to others in order to ensure they meet the quasi market criteria of success under which they operate. So, for instance, schools exclude difficult children who then turn to crime; and the mentally ill are returned to the community, where they are liable to become a law-and-order problem. Government, he concludes, needs to be holistic.

While the New Right has exasperated the problem of coordination, it is, institutionalists and New Labour suggest, the external fact of globalization that has made this problem a pressing one. The Foreign Policy Centre declares, for example, that the problems of today "have exploded across the boundaries of nations and departments of state" so that we now live in a "shrinking and fast-moving world"—"a globalized world" in which factories in Cardiff shut down because of troubles in the economy of South Korea.[49] As a result of globalization, we need to move away from traditional bureaucratic modes of coordination toward networks formed around particular issues: "the Foreign Policy Centre will abandon the idea of desk officers monitoring geographical areas or government departments, and organise its thinking around the cross-cutting issues to come up with joined-up solutions."[50]

[48] Perri 6, *Holistic Government* (London: Demos, 1997); Perri 6, Diana Leat, Kimberly Seltzer, and Gerry Stoker, *Governing in the Round: Strategies for Holistic Government* (London: Demos, 1999).

[49] Foreign Policy Centre, *Mission Centre*, at http://www/fpc.org.uk/mission.

[50] Ibid.

The Labour government indicates its sensitivity to issues of coordination in *Modernising Government*. This white paper illustrates the problem by pointing to the large number of organizations involved in providing long-term domiciliary care.[51] It also follows Perri 6 in its analysis of the rigidity and limits of central departments. It too calls for holistic, joined-up governance.

A lack of control is another problem associated with the reforms of the New Right. Institutionalists, such as Stoker, suggest that fragmentation has led to an increasingly diverse range of institutions being involved in the process of governance so that there is an increasingly pressing need for the central core to provide suitable leadership.[52] The New Right exasperated this problem by getting rid of functions through privatization and regulation. The unintended consequence of its doing so, institutionalists such as Rhodes tell us, was a loss of control—a hollowing out of the state.[53] The New Right created numerous special-purpose agencies that are difficult for the state to steer. There is even a suspicion that some privatized companies have captured their regulatory bodies. New Labour often echoes the institutionalists' account of the issue of control. It has tried to increase the strategic capacity of central government by turning toward a corporate approach, by strengthening horizontal policy making, and by increasing the role of the Cabinet Office.[54]

Excessive managerialism is yet another problem often linked to the reforms of the New Right. Although views differ on the extent to which the senior civil service has acquired more than a veneer of the new managerialism, social democrats and institutionalists fear that managerialism will erode public-service ethics. The apparent spread of patronage under the New Right, in particular, provoked worries about standards of public conduct. In addition, the new public management was seen as undermining the sense of public duty associated with the generalist tradition of the civil service.

The Response

Institutionalists and social democrats have drawn on their traditions to ascribe problems of coordination, control, and public ethics to the public sector reforms of the New Right. They also draw on the same traditions

---

[51] *Modernising Government*, Cm 4310 (1999), 24.

[52] Jon Pierre and Gerry Stoker, "Towards Multi-level Governance," in *Developments in British Politics 6*, ed. Patrick Dunleavy, Andrew Gamble, Ian Holliday, and Gillian Peele (Basingstoke, UK: Macmillan, 2000).

[53] Rhodes, *Understanding Governance*, 17–19.

[54] The many attempts to strengthen No. 10 are discussed by Peter Hennessey, "The Blair Style of Government," *Government and Opposition* 33 (1998): 3–20.

to prescribe solutions to these problems. New Labour's vision of joined-up governance tackles these problems using the tools championed by institutionalists and network theorists. These tools, New Labour suggests, can create a public sector that is flexible, responsive, entrepreneurial, and efficient, a public sector in tune with the new knowledge-based, global economy.

In response to fragmentation, institutionalists appeal to networks as offering flexible yet effective coordination. New Labour, similarly, claims that the delivery of services depends, as never before, upon our linking organizations: we need responsive connections between organizations that coexist within a relatively unstructured framework. Networks allegedly can coordinate departments in a way that will not produce a new system of cages, since networks are decentralized and characterized by an indirect and diplomatic style of management.

New Labour describes one of the main challenges facing the civil service as "improving collaborative working across organisational boundaries."[55] It hopes to meet the challenge by "ensuring that policy making is more joined-up and strategic."[56] New Labour has thus created a Social Exclusion Unit to "develop integrated and sustainable approaches to the problems of the worst housing estates, including crime, drugs, unemployment, community breakdown, and bad schools."[57] The unit has established employment, education, and health zones operating under a single regeneration budget. These Action Zones are meant to enable the state to operate across departmental cages when dealing with wicked problems. New Labour has also turned to networks in search of coordination within the areas of employment, education, and health. In the case of employment, the government has established Action Teams that focus on network poverty conceived as "a cycle of decline" in which "children from workless or low income households are much less likely to stay at school, which in turn has a significant impact on their chances of work."[58] In the case of health, it initiated "a new statutory duty for NHS Trusts to work in partnership with other NHS organisations," so that the various bodies that deliver services work together to develop integrated systems of care.[59] In the case of education, it created zones composed of about twenty schools, covering all age ranges and operating under an action forum

[55] *Modernising Government*, 56.

[56] Ibid., 6.

[57] *Bringing Britain Together: A National Strategy for Neighbourhood Renewal*, Cm. 4045 (1998).

[58] Department for Education and Employment, *Action Teams*, at http://www.dfee. gov.uk/actionteams/what.cfm, accessed January 6, 2001.

[59] *The New National Health Service: Modern, Dependable*, Cm. 3807 (1997), 45.

composed of the local education authority in partnership with businesses, parents, and community groups.

Because institutionalists often champion networks as a superior form of organization, they have paid considerable attention to the question of how best to control them.[60] Typically they concentrate on presenting the styles of management they believe fit different types of network, where each type is defined by reference to allegedly objective social facts such as the structure of the relations within it. Almost all of the popular management styles seek to provide scope for central government to steer networks while also promoting a culture of trust through greater diplomacy and negotiation. Stoker, for example, lists techniques for steering urban governance that clearly strive to avoid hierarchy: they include indirect management through cultural persuasion, communication, and monitoring, as well as more direct steering through financial subsidies.[61]

New Labour similarly promotes a culture of trust while attempting to deploy a range of techniques to ensure central control. In the case of local government, for example, Mulgan and Perri 6 argue that local authorities have to show they can be trusted, but that as and when they do, central government should devolve greater powers and services to them.[62] In practice, New Labour's Local Government Act (2000) considerably increases the powers of local government at the same time as the central government is intervening through persuasion and "naming and shaming" in an attempt to ensure councils respond to its agenda in the way it thinks appropriate.[63] Elsewhere too New Labour combines a decentralization that gives greater scope to other bodies with attempts to specify in great detail what these bodies should do, to persuade them to do what is specified, and to regulate them in relation to the specifications. In the case of employment, the government describes the Action Teams as "a flexible programme, based on local initiative," but it relies on direct financial control to hold them to the three criteria it prescribes for judging them— a rise in the proportion of people in work, an improvement in the employment rates of disadvantaged groups, and the number of people employed

[60] For an overview see Walter J. M. Kickert, Erik-Hans Klijn, and Joop. F. M. Koppenjan, "Managing Networks in the Public Sector: Findings and Reflections," in *Managing Complex Networks: Strategies for the Public Sector*, ed. Walter J. M. Kickert, Erik-Hans Klijn, and Joop F. M. Koppenjan (London: Sage, 1998).

[61] Stoker, "Urban Political Science," 98–104.

[62] Geoff Mulgan and Perri 6, "The Local Is Coming Home: Decentralisation by Degrees," *Demos Quarterly* 9 (1996): 3–7.

[63] Vivien Lowndes, "Rebuilding Trust in Central/Local Relations: Policy or Passion?" in *Renewing Local Democracy: The Modernisation Agenda in British Local Government*, ed. Lawrence Pratchett (London: Frank Cass, 2000).

through the "direct efforts of the Team."[64] In the case of health, it suggests that local variations in standards of care can be overcome by organizations sharing principles of best practice, but it specifies national standards and preferred models for specific types of service.[65] In the case of education, even as schools have acquired more powers, so the center has defined measures of literacy and numeracy.

The government generally adopts an instrumental approach to network management. New Labour assumes the center can devise and impose tools that will foster integration within networks and thereby realize the objectives of the central government. Measures such as the creation of Action Zones have a centralizing thrust. They seek to coordinate departments and local authorities by imposing a new style of management on other agencies, and they are to operate and be evaluated by criteria defined at the center. Indeed, the government openly says that while it does "not want to run local services from the centre," it "is not afraid to take action where standards slip."[66] The center owns zones, and local agendas are recognized only if they conform to that of the center.

Fears about the erosion of the traditional public service ethos quickly inspired interest in a code of ethics. The Treasury and Civil Service Committee proposed such a code complete with an independent appeal to the Civil Service Commissioners.[67] New Labour intends to give this code statutory force.[68] The *Ministerial Code* states that ministers have "a duty to uphold the political impartiality of the Civil Service" and "to ensure that influence over appointments is not abused for partisan purposes."[69] The *Modernising Government* white paper also asserts New Labour's commitment to public services and public servants, declaring, "[W]e will value public service, not denigrate it."[70]

Networks, New Labour implies, can resolve the problems of coordination and control and so, in conjunction with a suitable ethical code, establish a responsible, efficient, and effective public sector. The government and its advisers equate networks with a flexibility and responsiveness they

---

[64] United Kingdom, Department of Education and Employment, *Action Teams*.

[65] United Kingdom, Department of Health, *The New NHS, Modern and Dependable: A National Framework for Assessing Performance* (1998); United Kingdom, Department of Health, *A First Class Service: Quality in the New NHS* (1999).

[66] *Modernising Government*, 55.

[67] United Kingdom, Cabinet Office, *Civil Service Management Code* (1994), paras. 101–12 and pp. cxxvi–cxxvii.

[68] United Kingdom, Parliament, *The Civil Service: Taking Forward Continuity and Change*, Cm. 2748 (1995), 5–6.

[69] United Kingdom, Cabinet Office, *Ministerial Code: A Code of Conduct and Guidance on Procedures for Ministers* (1997), 21 para. 56.

[70] Ibid., 13.

think peculiarly important for the new economy. For Perri 6, the flexibility of networks means joined-up governance will be able to identify and tackle problems before they become acute.[71] It also means that governmental bodies will be able to work in partnership with private sector ones to generate additional finance and expertise. The alleged responsiveness of networks implies that joined-up governance will tackle issues in the round instead of through numerous separate agencies. It also implies that the state will focus on changing cultural habits through information and persuasion instead of changing behavior through coercion and control. More generally, networks appear as organizations peculiarly conducive to the growth, in Leadbeater's words, of a "civic enterprise culture."[72] The flexibility and responsiveness of joined-up governance allegedly encourages an innovative, people-focused culture that attracts civic entrepreneurs—visionary individuals whose skills lie in building networks and establishing trust. We are thus taken from a world of risk-averse static organizations staffed by bureaucrats to one of complex networks within which social entrepreneurs create synergies and virtuous cycles.

New Labour's concept of joined-up governance overlaps with, and draws on, institutionalism and network theory. Of course, here too there are disagreements and debates among the politicians and policy advisers of New Labour: Perri 6 and other Demos researchers call on the government to learn from its early mistakes and to devolve more.[73] Yet the disagreements occur in a shared framework: Perri 6 elides his concept of holistic government with joined-up governance while appealing to Action Zones and Single Regeneration Budgets as concrete examples of his vision.[74] The elite of New Labour rely on an overlapping consensus common to institutionalism and the new social democracy. They speak the language of networks, zones, steering, partnership, trust, and civic entrepreneurship.

Conclusion

I have suggested that we can clump together New Labour, joined-up governance, and institutionalism in much the same way as we already do the New Right, the new public management, and rational choice theory. We would thus provide a historical account of some of the beliefs by which we are now governed. Hence, we also would raise questions about the

[71] Compare Perri 6, *Holistic Government*.

[72] Compare Charles Leadbeater, *The Rise of the Social Entrepreneur* (London: Demos, 1997); Charles Leadbeater and Sue Goss, *Civic Entrepreneurship* (London: Demos, 1998).

[73] Perri 6 and others, *Governing in the Round*.

[74] Perri 6, *Holistic Government*.

relationship between, first, the radical historicism that has inspired this account of the Third Way and, second, the historical component of the new institutionalism that this account has suggested informs the Third Way itself.

Radical historicism overlaps considerably with institutionalism. It too entails belief in social embeddedness, and it too points to the importance of institutions—though these might better be conceived as traditions or practices—as the contexts in which agents respond to the world. Radical historicism even encourages a belief in networks as a ubiquitous form of social organization: all social life is about interdependent actors engaging in interactions predicated on interpretations of one another. Nonetheless, radical historicism modifies or undercuts two interlinked tendencies often apparent in institutionalism and also New Labour. First, radical historicism challenges the tendency to marginalize questions about the diverse actions and beliefs of agents in any particular institutional setting.[75] Institutions should be seen as practices that are constantly being re-created and modified through the actions of the agents within them, actions that usually create and also embody a conflict over meanings. Second, radical historicism challenges the assumption of predictability and so the possibility of control. Social life arises from the bottom up, beginning with the contingent actions of innumerable individuals rather than fixed rules or norms.

Insofar as institutionalists tend to marginalize microlevel studies of contingent beliefs and desires, they suggest there is just the one story to tell—a story of objective facts about social pressures, entrenched institutions, and policy outcomes. In contrast, radical historicism emphasizes that different people construct the pressures, institutions, and outcomes differently depending in part on the tradition against the background of which they do so. It relates narratives of the many different stories that motivate relevant actors and so have historical significance. From the perspective of a radical historicist, the institutionalist story of New Labour is not the only one: it is not a pure and neutral account of a given history, but rather a historical event with its own problematic genealogy. To denaturalize institutionalism and New Labour in this way is to ask, who is telling this story and why? What alternative stories might be told? Which stories do we want to be governed by?

---

[75] The marginalization of meanings, contingency, and agency surely derives from the institutionalists often avowed commitment to "structural" analysis as opposed to historical narratives. See Granovetter, "Sociological and Economic Approaches"; Paul J. DiMaggio, "Structural Analysis of Organizational Fields," in *Research in Organizational Behavior*, vol. 8, ed. Barry M. Staw and L. L. Cummings, (Greenwich, CT: JAI Press, 1986).

Bibliography ──────────────────────────

Adams, Herbert B. "The Germanic Origins of New England Towns." *Johns Hopkins University Studies in Historical and Political Science* 2 (1882): 5–38.

———. "Special Methods of Historical Study." In G. S. Hall, *Methods of Teaching History*.

———. "Is History Past Politics?" *Johns Hopkins University Studies in Historical and Political Science* 13 (1895): 67–81.

Adcock, Robert. "The Emergence of Political Science as a Discipline: History and the Study of Politics in America, 1875–1910." *History of Political Thought* 24 (2003): 481–508.

Adcock, Robert, and Mark Bevir. "The History of Political Science." *Political Studies Review* 3 (2005): 1–16.

Allen, J. W. *A History of Political Thought in the Sixteenth Century.* London: Methuen, 1928.

Almond, Gabriel A. *The American People and Foreign Policy.* New York: Harcourt Brace, 1950.

———. *The Appeals of Communism.* Princeton, NJ: Princeton University Press, 1954.

———. "A Functional Approach to Comparative Politics." In *The Politics of the Developing Areas*, edited by Gabriel A. Almond and James S. Coleman. Princeton, NJ: Princeton University Press, 1960.

———. "Political Systems and Political Change." *American Behavioral Scientist* 6 (1963): 3–10.

———. "A Developmental Approach to Political Systems." *World Politics* 17, no. 2 (1965): 183–214.

———. "Approaches to Developmental Causation." In Almond, Flanagan, and Mundt, *Crisis, Choice, and Change*.

———. "The Return to the State." *American Political Science Review* 82, no. 3 (1988): 853–74.

———. *A Discipline Divided.* London: Sage, 1990.

———. "Political Science: The History of the Discipline." In *A New Handbook of Political Science*, edited by Robert E. Goodin and Hans-Dieter Klingemann, 50–96. Oxford: Oxford University Press, 1995.

Almond, Gabriel A., Taylor Cole, and Roy C. Macridis. "A Suggested Research Strategy in Western European Government and Politics." *American Political Science Review* 49, no. 4 (1955): 1042–49.

Almond, Gabriel A., Scott C. Flanagan, and Robert J. Mundt, eds. *Crisis, Choice, and Change: Historical Studies of Political Development.* Boston: Little, Brown, 1973.

Almond, Gabriel A., and G. Bingham Powell, Jr. *Comparative Politics: A Developmental Approach.* Boston: Little, Brown, 1966.

Almond, Gabriel A., and Sidney Verba. *The Civic Culture: Political Attitudes and Democracy in Five Nations*. Princeton, NJ: Princeton University Press, 1963.

Amadae, S. M. *Rationalizing Capitalist Democracy: The Cold War Origins of Rational Choice Liberalism*. Chicago: University of Chicago Press, 2003.

American Historical Commission on the Social Studies. *Conclusions and Recommendations of the Commission*. New York: Scribner's Sons, 1934.

Anderson, Perry. "Components of the National Culture." In Anderson, *English Questions*, 48–104. First published in 1968.

———. "A Culture in Contraflow." In Anderson, *English Questions*, 193–301. First published in 1990.

———. *English Questions*. London: Verso, 1992.

Anderson, Perry, and Tom Nairn. "Origins of the Present Crisis." In Anderson, *English Questions*, 15–47. First published in 1964.

Anderson, William. "Political Science Enters the Twentieth Century." In Anna Haddow, *Political Science in American Colleges and Universities, 1636–1900*, 257–66. New York: Appleton-Century, 1939.

———. "Political Science North and South." *Journal of Politics* 11, no. 2 (1949): 298–317.

Arblaster, Anthony. *The Rise and Decline of Western Liberalism*. Oxford: Basil Blackwell, 1984.

Arendt, Hannah. *The Human Condition*. Chicago: University of Chicago Press, 1958.

———. *On Revolution*. New York: Viking, 1963.

———. *Between Past and Future*. New York: Viking, 1968.

Aristotle. *The Politics*. Translated by Ernest Barker. Oxford: Clarendon Press, 1946.

Armitage, David, Jane Ohlmeyer, Ned C. Landsman, Eliga H. Gould, and J.G.A. Pocock. "*AHR* Forum: The New British History in Atlantic Perspective." *American Historical Review* 104 (1999): 426–500.

Ashley, W. J. "On the Study of Economic History." In *Surveys, Historic and Economic*. New York: Longmans Green, 1900.

Baer, Michael A., Malcolm E. Jewell, and Lee Sigelman, eds. *Political Science in America: Oral Histories of a Discipline*. Lexington: University of Kentucky Press, 1991.

Ball, Terence. "An Ambivalent Alliance: Political Science and American Democracy." In Farr, Dryzek, and Leonard, *Political Science in History*.

———. "American Political Science in Its Postwar Political Context." In Farr and Seidelmann, *Discipline and History*.

Bann, Stephen. *The Clothing of Clio: A Study of the Representation of History in Nineteenth Century Britain and France*. Cambridge: Cambridge University Press, 1984.

Bannister, Robert C. *Sociology and Scientism: The American Quest for Objectivity, 1880–1940*. Chapel Hill: University of North Carolina Press, 1987.

Barker, Ernest. *The Political Thought of Plato and Aristotle*. New York: G. P. Putnam's, 1906.

———. "The 'Rule of Law.' " *Political Quarterly* 1 (May 1914): 117–27.

———. "The Discredited State." *Political Quarterly* 2 (February 1915): 101–21.

———. *Political Thought in England from Herbert Spencer to the Present Day.* New York: Henry Holt, 1915.

———. *Greek Political Theory: Plato and His Predecessors.* London: Methuen, 1925.

———. "The Study of Political Science." In *Church, State, and Study: Essays.* London: Methuen, 1930.

———. *Reflections on Government.* Oxford: Oxford University Press, 1942.

———. *The Development of Public Services in Europe, 1660–1930.* New York: Oxford University Press, 1944.

———. *Essays on Government.* Oxford: Oxford University Press, 1945.

———. *The Character of England.* Oxford: Clarendon Press, 1947.

———. *Age and Youth.* Oxford: Oxford University Press, 1955.

Barrow, Clyde W. *More Than a Historian: The Political and Economic Thought of Charles A. Beard.* New Brunswick, NJ: Transaction Publishers, 2000.

Barry, Andrew, Thomas Osborne, and Nicholas Rose, eds. *Foucault and Political Reason.* London: UCL Press, 1996.

Barry, Brian. *Sociologists, Economists, and Democracy.* London: Collier-Macmillan, 1970.

———. "The Study of Politics as a Vocation." In Hayward, Barry, Brown, *British Study of Politics.*

Bartelson, Jens. *The Critique of the State.* Cambridge: Cambridge University Press, 2001.

Bassett, R. *The Essentials of Parliamentary Democracy.* London: Macmillan, 1935.

Bates, Robert H. *Markets and States in Tropical Africa: The Political Basis of Agricultural Policies.* Berkeley and Los Angeles: University of California Press, 1981.

———. *Essays on the Political Economy of Rural Africa.* Cambridge: Cambridge University Press, 1983.

Beard, Charles A. "Politics." In *Columbia University Lectures on Science, Philosophy and Arts, 1907–1908.* New York: Columbia University Press, 1908.

———. *American Government and Politics.* New York, Macmillan, 1910.

———. *An Economic Interpretation of the Constitution of the United States.* New York: Macmillan, 1913.

———. "Methods of Training for Public Service." *School and Society* 2 (December 25, 1915).

———. "Time, Technology and the Creative Spirit in Political Science." *American Political Science Review* 21, no. 1 (1927): 1–11.

———. "Political Science." In *Research in the Social Sciences: Its Fundamental Methods and Objectives,* edited by Wilson Gee. New York: Macmillan, 1929.

———. *A Charter for the Social Sciences in the Schools.* New York: Scribner's Sons, 1932.

———. "Written History as an Act of Faith." *American Historical Review* 39, no. 2 (1934): 219–31.

———. "Peace for America: Solving Domestic Crises by War." *New Republic* 86, March 11, 1936.

———. *The Republic.* New York: Viking, 1944.

Beard, Charles A. "Who's to Write the History of the War?" *Saturday Evening Post* 220, October 4, 1947.

———. *President Roosevelt and the Coming of the War, 1941: A Study in Appearances and Realities*. New Haven, CT: Yale University Press, 1948.

Beard, Charles A., and Mary Beard. Collection. DePauw University.

Beard, Charles A., and Alfred Vagts. "Currents of Thought in Historiography." *American Historical Review* 42, no. 3 (1937): 460–83.

Beer, Samuel H. "Pressure Groups and Parties in Britain." *American Political Science Review* 50, no. 1 (1956): 1–23.

———. "The Analysis of Political Systems." In *Patterns of Government: The Major Political Systems of Europe*, edited by Samuel H. Beer and Adam B. Ulam. New York: Random House, 1958.

———. "Causal Explanation and Imaginative Re-enactment." *History and Theory* 3, no. 1 (1963): 6–29.

———. *Modern British Politics: A Study of Parties and Pressure Groups*. London: Faber, 1965.

———. "Political Science and History." In *Essays in Theory and History: An Approach to the Social Sciences*, edited by Melvin Richter. Cambridge: Harvard University Press, 1970.

Bendix, Reinhard. *Nation-Building and Citizenship*. New York: Wiley, 1964.

Bendix, Reinhard, and others, eds. *State and Society: A Reader in Comparative Political Sociology*. Boston: Little, Brown, 1968.

Benjamin, Walter. *Illuminations*. Edited by Hannah Arendt. New York: Schocken Books, 1968.

Bensel, Richard. *Yankee Leviathan: The Origins of Central State Authority in America, 1859–1877*. Cambridge: Cambridge University Press, 1990.

Bentley, Arthur. *The Process of Government: A Study of Social Pressures*. Chicago: University of Chicago Press, 1908.

Berlin, Isaiah. "Does Political Theory Still Exist?" In *Concepts and Categories*, edited by Henry Hardy. Oxford: Penguin, 1979.

Berman, Sheri E. "Ideas, Norms and Culture in Political Analysis." *Comparative Politics* 33, no. 2 (January 2001): 231–50.

Berrington, Hugh B. *Backbench Opinion in the House of Commons, 1945–1955*. Oxford: Pergamon, 1973.

Bevir, Mark. "Are There Perennial Problems in Political Theory?" *Political Studies* 42 (1994): 662–75.

———. "Graham Wallas Today." *Political Quarterly* 68 (1997): 284–92.

———. *The Logic of the History of Ideas*. Cambridge: Cambridge University Press, 1999.

———. "Prisoners of Professionalism: On the Construction and Responsibility of Political Studies; A Review Article" *Public Administration* 79, no. 2 (2001): 469–89.

———. "Sidney Webb: Utilitarianism, Positivism and Social Democracy." *Journal of Modern History* 74 (2002): 217–52.

———. *New Labour: A Critique*. London: Routledge, 2005.

Bevir, Mark, and David O'Brien. "From Idealism to Communitarianism: The Inheritance and Legacy of John Macmurray." *History of Political Thought* 24,
no. 2 (2003): 305–29.

Bevir, Mark and Frank Trentmann. "Critique within Capitalism: Historiographical Problems, Theoretical Perspectives." In Bevir and Trentmann, *Critiques of
Capital*, 1–25.

———. eds. *Critiques of Capital in Modern Britain and America: Transatlantic
Exchanges, 1800 to the Present Day.* Basingstoke, UK: Palgrave Macmillan,
2002.

Binder, Leonard, James S. Coleman, Joseph LaPalombara, Lucian W. Pye, Sidney
Verba, and M. Weiner, eds. *Crises and Sequences in Political Development.*
Princeton, NJ: Princeton University Press, 1971.

Birch, Anthony Harold. *The British System of Government.* New York: Praeger,
1967.

Blaas, P.B.M. *Continuity and Anachronism: Parliamentary and Constitutional
Development in Whig Historiography and the Anti-Whig Reaction between
1890 and 1930.* The Hague: Martinus Nijhoff, 1978.

Blackmar, Frank W., and John Lewis Gillin. *Outlines of Sociology.* New York:
Macmillan, 1915.

Blair, Tony. "A Stakeholder Society." *Fabian Review* 103 (1996): 1–4.

———. *New Britain: My Vision of a Young Country.* London: Fourth Estate, 1996.

———. Speech to the Singapore Business Community. January 8, 1996.

———. "The Stakeholder Economy." Speech, Derby. January 18, 1996.

———. "Faith in the City—Ten Years On." Speech, London. January 29, 1996.

———. "John Smith Memorial Lecture." Speech, London. February 7, 1996.

———. *The Third Way: New Politics for the New Century.* Fabian Pamphlet no.
588. London: Fabian Society, 1998.

———. "Facing the Modern Challenge: The Third Way in Britain and South Africa." Speech, Cape Town. January 8, 1999.

———. "To the IPPR." Speech, London. January 14, 1999.

———. "Third Way, Phase Two." *Prospect*, March 10–14, 2001.

Blondel, Jean. *Voters, Parties and Leaders: The Social Fabric of British Politics.*
Harmondsworth, UK: Penguin, 1965.

———. *Comparative Government.* 1st ed., London: Weidenfeld and Nicolson,
1969; 2nd ed., London: Philip Allan, 1999.

———. *The Discipline of Politics.* London: Butterworth, 1981.

Blyth, Mark. "Institutions and Ideas." In Marsh and Stoker, *Theory and Methods*,
2nd ed.

Bogdanor, Vernon. "Comparative Politics." In Hayward, Barry, and Brown, *British Study of Politics.*

Bosanquet, Bernard. *Philosophical Theory of the State.* London: Macmillan,
1899.

———. Letter to the Editor. *Times*, September 20, 1920.

Boucher, David. "The Creation of the Past: British Idealism and Michael Oakeshott's Philosophy of History." *History and Theory* 23, no. 2 (1984): 193–214.

———. *Texts in Context: Revisionist Methods for Studying the History of Ideas.*
Dordrecht: Martinus Nijhoff, 1985.

Bowler, Peter J. *The Invention of Progress: The Victorians and the Past*. Oxford: Basil Blackwell, 1989.

Boyne, George A. *Public Choice Theory and Local Government*. London: Macmillan, 1998.

Braybrooke, David, and Charles E. Lindblom. *A Strategy of Decision: Policy Evaluation as a Social Process*. New York: Free Press, 1963.

Bradley, F. H. *Ethical Studies*. Oxford: Clarendon Press, 1876.

———. "The Pre-suppositions of a Critical History." In *Collected Essays*. 2 vols., 1:1–70. Oxford: Clarendon Press, 1935.

Brady, David W., and Philip Althoff. "Party Voting in the U.S. House of Representatives, 1890–1910." *Journal of Politics* 36, no. 3 (1974): 753–75.

Brady, David W., Joseph Cooper, and Patricia Hurley. "The Decline of Party in the House of Representatives." *Legislative Studies Quarterly* 4, no. 3 (1979): 381–407.

Bridges, Amy. *A City in the Republic: Antebellum New York and the Origins of Machine Politics*. New York: Cambridge University Press, 1984.

British Humanist League, London. West London Ethical Society. Minutes of General Meetings, December 4, 1902.

Bruell, Christopher. "A Return to Classical Political Philosophy and the Understanding of the American Founding." *Review of Politics* 53, no. 1 (1991): 173–86.

Bryce, James. "The Historical Aspect of Democracy." In *Essays in Reform*, 239–78. London: Macmillan, 1867.

———. *The American Commonwealth*. 2 vols. New York: Macmillan, 1893. First published in 1888.

———. *The Relations of the Advanced and Backward Races*. Oxford: Clarendon Press, 1903.

———. *Studies in Contemporary Biography*. New York: Macmillan, 1903.

———. "The Relations of Political Science to History and to Practice." *American Political Science Review* 3 (1909): 1–19.

———. *Modern Democracies*. 2 vols. London: Macmillan, 1921.

Budd, Susan. *Varieties of Unbelief: Atheists and Agnostics in English Society, 1850–1960*. London: Heinemann Education Books, 1978.

Burchell, Graham, Colin Gordon, and Peter Miller, eds. *The Foucault Effect: Studies in Governmentality*. London: Harvester Wheatsheaf, 1991.

Burgess, John W. "On Methods of Historical Study and Research in Columbia University." In G. S. Hall, *Methods of Teaching History*.

———. *Political Science and Comparative Constitutional Law*. 2 vols. Boston: Ginn, 1890.

———. "The Ideal of the American Commonwealth." *Political Science Quarterly* 10 (1895): 404–25.

———. "Political Science and History." *Annual Report of the American Historical Association for 1896*, 203–11. Washington, DC: Government Printing Office, 1897.

———. "Chief Questions of Present American Politics." *Political Science Quarterly* 23 (1908): 385–409.

———. *The Foundations of Political Science*. New York: Columbia University Press, 1933.

Burnham, Walter Dean. "The Changing Shape of the American Political Universe." *American Political Science Review* 59, no. 1 (1965): 7–28.

———. *Critical Elections and the Mainsprings of American Politics*. New York: Norton, 1970.

———. "Theory and Voting Research: Some Reflections on Converse's 'Change in the American Electorate.' " *American Political Science Review* 68, no. 3 (1974): 1002–23.

———. "Revitalization and Decay." *Journal of Politics* 38, no. 3 (1976): 146–72.

Burnham, Walter Dean, and Jerrold G. Rusk. "Communications." *American Political Science Review* 65, no. 4 (1971): 1149–57.

Burns, C. Delisle, B. Russell, and G.D.H. Cole. "Symposium: The Nature of the State in View of Its External Relations." *Proceedings of the Aristotelian Society* 16 (1915–16): 290–325.

Burrow, John W. *Evolution and Society: A Study in Victorian Social Theory*. Cambridge: Cambridge University Press, 1966.

———. *A Liberal Descent: Victorian Historians and the English Past*. Cambridge: Cambridge University Press, 1981.

———. *Whigs and Liberals: Continuity and Change in English Political Thought*. Oxford: Clarendon, 1988.

Butler, David, and Donald Stokes. *Political Change in Britain: Forces Shaping Electoral Choice*. New York: St. Martin's Press, 1969.

Butler, Leslie. "The Mugwump Dilemma: Democracy and Cultural Authority in Victorian America." PhD diss., Yale University, 1997.

Cameron, James Reese. *Frederick William Maitland and the History of English Law*. Norman: University of Oklahoma Press, 1961.

Cammack, Paul. "Bringing the State Back In: A Polemic." Manchester Papers in Politics, Department of Government, University of Manchester, 1987.

———. "Dependency and the Politics of Development." In *Perspectives on Development: Cross-Disciplinary Themes in Development Studies*, edited by P. F. Leeson and M. M. Minogue. Manchester: Manchester University Press, 1988.

Campbell, Angus. "Recent Developments in Survey Studies of Political Behavior." In *Essays on the Behavioral Study of Politics*, edited by Austin Ranney, 31–46. Urbana: University of Illinois Press, 1962.

Campbell, Angus, Philip E. Converse, Warren E. Miller, and Donald Stokes. *The American Voter*. New York: Wiley, 1960.

Carrington, Paul D. "William Gardiner Hammond and the Lieber Revival." *Cardozo Law Review* 16 (1995): 2135–52.

Castiglione, Dario, and Iain Hampsher-Monk. "Introduction: The History of Political Thought and the National Discourses of Politics." In Castiglione and Hampsher-Monk, *Political Thought in National Context*.

———. *The History of Political Thought in National Context*. Cambridge: Cambridge University Press, 2001.

Catlin, George E. G. *The Science and Method of Politics*. New York: Appleton, 1927.

———. *For God's Sake, Go!* Gerrads Cross, UK: Colin Smythe, 1972.

Chester, Norman. "Political Studies in Britain: Recollections and Comments." *Political Studies* 23, nos. 2–3 (1975): 151–64.

———. *Economics, Politics, and Social Studies in Oxford, 1900–1985.* Basingstoke, UK: Macmillan, 1986.

Clark, David. "The Civil Service and the New Government." Speech, London. June 17, 1997.

Cockett, Richard. *Thinking the Unthinkable: Think-Tanks and the Economic Counter-revolution.* London: HarperCollins, 1994.

Cole, G.D.H. *Guild Socialism Re-stated.* London: Parsons, 1920.

———. *Social Theory.* London: Methuen, 1920.

Collingwood, R. G. *An Autobiography.* Oxford: Oxford University Press, 1939.

Collini, Stefan. "'Disciplinary History' and 'Intellectual History': Reflections on the Historiography of the Social Sciences in Britain and France." *Revue de synthese* 3, no. 4 (1988): 387–99.

———. *Public Moralists: Political Thought and Intellectual Life in Britain, 1850–1930.* Oxford: Clarendon Press, 1991.

———. "Postscript: Disciplines, Canons, and Publics; The History of 'The History of Political Thought' in Comparative Perspective." In Castiglione and Hampsher-Monk, *Political Thought in National Context.*

Collini, Stefan, Donald Winch, and John Burrow. *That Noble Science of Politics: A Study in Nineteenth-Century Intellectual History.* Cambridge: Cambridge University Press, 1983.

"Committee Briefs: Political Behavior." *Social Science Research Council Items* 4, no. 2 (1950): 20.

Connolly, William E. "Politics and Vision." In *Democracy and Vision: Sheldon Wolin and the Vicissitudes of the Political,* edited by Areyh Botwinick and William E. Connolly. Princeton, NJ: Princeton University Press, 2001.

Contemporary Political Science: A Survey of Methods, Research and Teaching. Paris: UNESCO, 1950.

Converse, Philip E. "Change in the American Electorate." In *The Human Meaning of Social Change,* edited by Angus Campbell and Philip E. Converse, 263–337. New York: Sage, 1972.

———. "Comment." *American Political Science Review* 68, no. 3 (1974): 1024–27.

Cooper, Joseph. *The Origins of the Standing Committees and Development of the Modern House.* Houston: Rice University Publications, 1970.

Cooper, Joseph, and David W. Brady. "Institutional Context and Leadership Style: The House from Cannon to Rayburn." *American Political Science Review* 75, no. 2 (1981): 411–25.

———. "Toward a Diachronic Analysis of Congress." *American Political Science Review* 75, no. 4 (1981): 988–1006.

Coopey, Richard, Steve Fielding, and Nick Tiratsoo, eds. *The Wilson Governments, 1964–1970.* London: Pinter, 1993.

Cosgrove, Richard A. *Our Lady the Common Law: The Anglo-American Legal Community, 1870–1930.* New York: New York University Press, 1987.

Counts, George S. "Charles Beard, the Public Man." In *Charles A. Beard: An Appraisal*, edited by Howard K. Beale. Lexington: University Press of Kentucky, 1954.

———. Collection. University of Southern Illinois.

Cowley, John. *The Victorian Encounter with Marx: A Study of E. Belfort Bax*. London: British Academic Press, 1992.

Cowley, Malcolm, and Bernard Smith. *Books That Changed Our Mind*. New York: Kelmscott Editions, 1939.

Creighton, Louise, W. R. Sorley, J. S. Mackenzie, A. D. Lindsay, H. Rashdall, and Hilda D. Oakeley. *The International Crisis: The Theory of the State*. London: Oxford University Press, 1916.

Crewe, Ivor, and P. Norris. "In Defence of British Electoral Studies." In *British Elections and Parties Yearbook, 1991*, edited by Ivor Crewe and others. London: Harvester Wheatsheaf, 1992.

Crick, Bernard. *The American Science of Politics: Its Origins and Conditions*. Berkeley and Los Angeles: University of California Press, 1959.

———. *In Defense of Politics*. Chicago: University of Chicago Press, 1962.

———. *The Reform of Parliament*. London: Weidenfeld and Nicolson, 1964.

———. "The Tendencies in Political Studies." *New Society*, November 3, 1966.

———. *Basic Forms of Government: A Sketch and a Model*. London: Macmillan, 1973.

———. "The British Way." *Government and Opposition* 15, nos. 3–4 (1980): 297–307.

———. "Hannah Arendt and the Burden of Our Times." *Political Quarterly* 68 (1997): 77–84.

Critchley, Simon. "Ethics, Politics, and Radical Democracy—the History of a Disagreement." In *Laclau: A Critical Reader*, edited by Simon Critchley and Oliver Marchant. London: Routledge, 2005.

Crosland, Anthony. *The Future of Socialism*. London: Cape, 1956.

Crunden, Robert M. *Ministers of Reform: The Progressives' Achievement in American Civilization*. New York: Basic Books, 1982.

Dahl, Robert A. "The Behavioral Approach in Political Science: Epitaph to a Monument to a Successful Protest." *American Political Science Review* 55, no. 4 (1961): 763–72.

———. *Who Governs?* New Haven, CT: Yale University Press, 1961.

Dahrendorf, Ralf. *A History of the London School of Economics and Political Science, 1895–1995*. New York: Oxford University Press, 1995.

Dearlove, John, and Peter Saunders. *Introduction to British Politics: Analysing a Capitalist Democracy*. Cambridge: Polity, 1984.

DeBresson, Chris, and Fernand Amesse, eds. *Networks of Innovators*. Special Issue of *Research Policy* 20, no. 5 (1991).

Dewey, John. "Interpretation of the Savage Mind." *Psychological Review* 9 (1902): 217–30.

———. *The Public and Its Problems*. New York: Henry Holt, 1927.

———. "Philosophy." In *Research in the Social Sciences: Its Fundamental Methods and Objectives*, edited by Wilson Gee. New York: Macmillan, 1929.

———. "Social Science and Social Control." *New Republic* 76, July 29, 1931.

Dewey, John. *Liberalism and Social Action*. New York: G. P. Putnam, 1935. Reprinted New York: Capricorn Books, 1963.

Dewey, John, and Arthur Bentley. *Knowing and the Known*. Boston: Beacon Press, 1949.

Dicey, Albert Venn. *Introduction to the Study of the Law of the Constitution*. London: Macmillan, 1889.

———. *Lectures on the Relation between Law and Public Opinion in England during the Nineteenth Century*. London: Macmillan, 1905.

Dickinson, John. "Democratic Realities and the Democratic Dogma." *American Political Science Review* 24, no. 2 (1930): 283–309.

DiMaggio, Paul J. "Structural Analysis of Organizational Fields." In *Research in Organizational Behavior*, vol. 8, edited by Barry M. Staw and L. L. Cummings. Greenwich, CT: JAI, 1986.

DiMaggio, Paul J., and Walter W. Powell. "Introduction" and "The Iron Cage Revisited: Institutional Isomorphism and Collective Rationality in Organizational Fields." In *The New Institutionalism in Organizational Analysis*, edited by Walter W. Powell and Paul J. DiMaggio. Chicago: University of Chicago Press, 1991.

Dowding, Keith. "There Must Be an End to Confusion: Policy Networks, Intellectual Fatigue, and the Need for Political Science Methods Courses in British Universities." *Political Studies* 49, no. 1 (2001): 89–105.

Dowding, Keith, and Desmond King. *Preferences, Institutions and Rational Choice*. Oxford: Oxford University Press, 1995.

Dowse, Robert Edward. "The Recourse to Political Sociology." In Hayward and Norton, *The Political Science of British Politics*.

Dryzek, John S., and Stephen T. Leonard. "History and Discipline in Political Science." *American Political Science Review* 82, no. 4 (1988): 1245–60.

Duguit, Leon. *Law in the Modern State*. Translated by Frida Laski and Harold Laski. New York: R. W. Huebsch, 1919.

Dunleavy, Patrick. *Democracy, Bureaucracy and Public Choice*. Hemel Hempstead, UK: Harvester Wheatsheaf, 1991.

Dunning, William A. "Review of Hannis Taylor, *The Origin and Growth of the English Constitution*." *Political Science Quarterly* 5 (1890): 188–90.

———. "Remarks." *Annual Report of the American Historical Association for 1896*, 211–14. Washington, DC: Government Printing Office, 1897.

———. *Truth in History and Other Essays*. Edited by J. G. de Roulhac Hamilton. New York: Columbia University Press, 1937.

Easton, David. "The Decline of Modern Political Theory." *Journal of Politics* 13, no. 1 (1951): 36–58.

———. *The Political System*. New York: Knopf, 1953.

———. *A Systems Analysis of Political Life*. New York: Wiley, 1965.

Eckstein, Harry. *Pressure Group Politics*. Stanford, CA: Stanford University Press, 1960.

Eisenstadt, S. N. *The Political Systems of Empires*. New York: Free Press, 1963.

Eldersveld, Samuel J., Alexander Heard, Samuel P. Huntington, Morris Janowitz, Avery Leiserson, Dayton D. McKean, and David B. Truman. "Research in Political Behavior." *American Political Science Review* 46, no. 4 (1952): 1003–45.

Elliott, William Yandell. *The Pragmatic Revolt in Politics: Syndicalism, Fascism, and the Constitutional State*. New York: Macmillan, 1928.

English, Richard, and Michael Kenny. "Public Intellectuals and the Question of British Decline." *British Journal of Politics and International Relations* 3 (2001): 259–83.

Evans, Peter. *Dependent Development: The Alliance of Multinational, State, and Local Capital in Brazil*. Princeton, NJ: Princeton University Press, 1979.

Evans, Peter, Dietrich Rueschemeyer, and Theda Skocpol. "On the Road toward a More Adequate Understanding of the State." In Evans, Rueschemeyer, and Skocpol, *Bringing the State*, 347–66.

———, eds. *Bringing the State Back In*. New York: Cambridge University Press, 1985.

Evans, Peter, and John D. Stephens. "Studying Development since the Sixties." *Theory and Society* 17, no. 5 (1988): 713–45.

Falby, Alison. "Gerald Heard (1889–1971) and British Intellectual Culture between the Wars." DPhil thesis, Oxford University, 2000.

Farr, James. "Francis Lieber and the Interpretation of American Political Science." *Journal of Politics* 52, no. 4 (1990): 1027–49.

———. "From Modern Republic to Administrative State." In *Regime and Discipline: Democracy and the Development of Political Science*, edited by David Easton, John G. Gunnell, and Michael B. Stein, 131–67. Ann Arbor: University of Michigan Press, 1995.

———. "Remembering the Revolution." In Farr, Dryzek, and Leonard, *Political Science in History*.

———. "John Dewey and American Political Science." *American Journal of Political Science* 43 (April 1999): 520–41.

———. "Political Science." In Porter and Ross, *The Modern Social Sciences*.

Farr, James, John S. Dryzek, and Stephen T. Leonard, eds. *Political Science in History: Research Programs and Political Traditions*. New York: Cambridge University Press, 1995.

Farr, James, and Raymond Seidelman, eds. *Discipline and History: Political Science in the United States*. Ann Arbor: University of Michigan Press, 1993.

Ferlie, E., and A. Pettigrew. "Managing through Networks: Some Issues and Implications for the NHS." *British Journal of Management* 7 (1996): 81–99.

Field, Frank. *Reforming Welfare*. London: Social Markets Foundation, 1997.

Figgis, J. N. *The Divine Right of Kings*. Cambridge: Cambridge University Press, 1896; 2nd ed., 1914.

Finer, Herman. *Theory and Practice of Modern Government*. 2 vols. London: Methuen, 1932.

Finer, S. E. *Comparative Government*. London: Penguin, 1970.

———. "Political Science: An Idiosyncratic Retrospect." *Government and Opposition* 15, nos. 3–4 (1980).

———. *The History of Government from the Earliest Times*. Vol. 1, *Ancient Monarchies and Empires;* vol. 2: *The Intermediate Ages;* and vol. 3; *Empires, Monarchies and the Modern State*. Oxford: Oxford University Press, 1997.

Finnemore, Martha. "Norms, Culture, and World Politics: Insights from Sociology's Institutionalism." *International Organization* 50, no. 2 (1996): 325–47.

Finnemore, Martha, and Kathryn Sikkink. "Taking Stock: The Constructivist Research Program in International Relations and Comparative Politics." *Annual Review of Political Science* 4 (2001): 391–416.

Fiske, John. "The Laws of History." *North American Review* 109 (1869): 197–230.

———. *American Political Ideas, Viewed from the Standpoint of Universal History.* New York: Harper and Brothers, 1885.

———. "The Germs of National Sovereignty in the United States." *Atlantic Monthly* 58 (1886): 648–66.

———. *The Beginnings of New England.* Boston: Houghton Mifflin, 1889.

Ford, Henry Jones. *The Rise and Growth of American Politics: A Sketch of Constitutional Development.* New York: Macmillan, 1898.

———. "The Scope of Political Science." *Proceedings of the APSA, 1905* (1906): 203–16.

Fortes, Meyer, and E. E. Evans-Pritchard. *African Political Systems.* London: Oxford University Press, 1940.

Foucault, Michel. *The Archaeology of Knowledge.* London: Tavistock, 1972.

———. *Discipline and Punish: The Birth of the Prison.* Harmondsworth, UK: Penguin, 1977.

Frank, Andre G. *Capitalism and Underdevelopment in Latin America: Historical Studies of Chile and Brazil.* New York: Monthly Review, 1967.

Frank, Jason A., and John Tamborino. "Introduction." In *Vocations of Political Theory*, edited by Jason A. Frank and John Tamborino. Minneapolis: University of Minnesota Press, 2000.

Freeden, Michael. "J. A. Hobson as a New Liberal Theorist." *Journal of History of Ideas* 34, no. 3 (1973): 421–43.

———. *Liberalism Divided: A Study of British Political Thought, 1914–1939.* Oxford: Oxford University Press, 1986.

Freeman, Edward A. "The Unity of History." In *Comparative Politics.* London: Macmillan, 1873.

———. *Greater Greece and Greater Britain.* London: Macmillan, 1886.

Freidel, Frank. *Francis Lieber: Nineteenth Century Liberal.* Baton Rouge: Louisiana State University Press, 1947.

Friedrich, Carl J. *Constitutional Government and Politics.* New York: Harper, 1937.

———. "Thomas Hobbes: Myth Builder of the Modern World." *Journal of Social Philosophy* 3 (1938): 251–57.

———. *Constitutional Government and Democracy.* Boston: Little, Brown, 1941.

———. *The Age of the Baroque, 1610–1660.* New York: Harper, 1952.

———. "Comments on the Seminar Report." *American Political Science Review* 47, no. 3 (1953): 658–61.

———. "Two Philosophical Interpretations of Natural Law." *Diogenes* 11 (1955): 98–112.

———. "Political Philosophy and the Science of Politics." In *Approaches to the Study of Politics*, edited by Roland Young. Evanston, IL: Northwestern University Press, 1958.

Friedrich, Carl J., and Zbigniew K. Brzezinski. *Totalitarian Dictatorship and Autocracy*. Cambridge: Harvard University Press, 1956.

Gallie, W. B. "Essentially Contested Concepts." *Proceedings of the Aristotelian Society* 56 (1955–56): 167–98.

Gamble, Andrew. "Theories of British Politics." *Political Studies* 38, no. 3 (1990): 404–20.

———. "Why Bother with Marxism?" In *Marxism and Social Science*, edited by Andrew Gamble, David Marsh, and Tony Tant. London: Macmillan, 1999.

Garceau, Oliver. "Research in the Political Process." *American Political Science Review* 45, no. 1 (1951): 69–85.

Garner, James W. *Introduction to Political Science: A Treatise on the Origin, Nature, Functions, and Organization of the State*. New York: American Book, 1910.

———. *The German War Code*. Urbana: University of Illinois Press under the direction of the War Committee, 1918.

George, Henry. *Progress and Poverty*. New York: Appleton, 1880.

Gierke, Otto. *Natural Law and the Theory of Society, 1500–1800*. Translated by Ernest Barker. 2 vols. Cambridge: Cambridge University Press, 1934.

Gilman, Nils. *Mandarins of the Future: Modernization Theory in Cold War America*. Baltimore: Johns Hopkins University Press, 2003.

Gilmour, Ian. *Dancing with Dogma: Britain under Thatcherism*. London: Simon and Schuster, 1992.

Goldie, Mark. "J. N. Figgis and the History of Political Thought at Cambridge." In *Cambridge Minds*, edited by Richard Mason. Cambridge: Cambridge University Press, 1994.

Goldman, Lawrence. *Science, Reform and Politics in Victorian Britain: The Social Science Association, 1857–1886*. Cambridge: Cambridge University Press, 2002.

Goodnow, Frank J. *Politics and Administration: A Study in Government*. New York: Macmillan, 1900.

Gosnell, Harold F. *Machine Politics*. Chicago: University of Chicago Press, 1937.

Gourevitch, Peter A. *Politics in Hard Times: Comparative Responses to International Economic Crises*. Ithaca, NY: Cornell University Press, 1986.

Gracia, Jorge. "The Logic of the History of Ideas or the Sociology of the History of Beliefs?" *Philosophical Books* 42 (2001): 177–86.

Granovetter, Mark. "The Strength of Weak Ties." *American Journal of Sociology* 78, no. 6 (1973): 1360–80.

———. *Getting a Job: A Study of Contracts and Careers*. Cambridge: Harvard University Press, 1974.

———. "Economic Action and Social Structure: The Problem of Embeddedness." *American Journal of Sociology* 91, no. 3 (1985): 481–510.

———. "The Sociological and Economic Approaches to Labor Market Analysis: A Social Structural View." In *Industries, Firms and Jobs: Sociological and Economic Approaches*, edited by George Farkas and Paula England. New York: Plenum Press, 1988.

———. "Business Groups." In *Handbook of Economic Sociology*, edited by Neil J. Smelser and Richard Swedberg. Princeton, NJ: Princeton University Press, 1994.

Granovetter, Mark, and Richard Swedberg, eds. *The Sociology of Economic Life.* Boulder, CO: Westview Press, 1992.

Green, E. H. H. *The Crisis of Conservatism: The Politics, Ideology and Economics of the British Conservative Party, 1880–1914.* London: Routledge, 1995.

Green, John Richard. *The Making of England.* London: Macmillan, 1882.

———. *The Conquest of England.* London: Macmillan, 1883.

———. *A Short History of the English People.* London: Macmillan, 1884.

Green, Thomas Hill. *Prolegomena to Ethics.* Oxford: Clarendon Press, 1883.

———. "Introduction to Hume's Treatise on Human Nature." In *Works*, vol. 1.

———. "On the Different Senses of Freedom." In *Works*, vol. 2.

———. *Works of Thomas Hill Green.* 3 vols. Edited by R. L. Nettleship. London: Longmans, Green, 1893–1906.

Greenleaf, W. H. *The British Political Tradition.* Vol. 1, *The Rise of Collectivism.* London: Methuen, 1983.

Grew, Raymond, ed. *Crises of Political Development in Europe and the United States.* Princeton, NJ: Princeton University Press, 1978.

Griffith, Ernest S., ed. *Research in Political Science.* Chapel Hill: University of North Carolina Press, 1948.

Griggs, S., and David Howarth. "New Environmental Movements and Direct Action Protests: The Campaign against Manchester Airport's Second Runway." In *Discourse Theory and Political Analysis*, edited by David Howarth, Aletta J. Norval, and Yannis Stavrakakis. Manchester: Manchester University Press, 2000.

Gruber, Carol S. *Mars and Minerva: World War I and the Uses of the Higher Learning in America.* Baton Rouge: Louisiana State University Press, 1975.

Gunnell, John G. *Political Theory: Tradition and Interpretation.* Cambridge, MA: Winthrop, 1979.

———. "Continuity and Innovation in the History of Political Science: The Case of Charles Merriam." *Journal of the History of the Behavioral Sciences* 28 (April 1992): 133–42.

———. *The Descent of Political Theory: The Genealogy of an American Vocation.* Chicago: University of Chicago Press, 1993.

———. "The Declination of the 'State' and the Origins of American Pluralism." In Farr, Dryzek, and Leonard, *Political Science in History*, 19–40.

———. "The Archaeology of American Liberalism." *Journal of Political Ideologies* 6, no. 2 (2001): 125–45.

———. *Imagining the American Polity: Political Science and the Discourse of Democracy.* University Park: Pennsylvania State University Press, 2004.

———. "The Real Revolution in Political Science." *PS* 37, no. 1 (2004): 47–50.

Haas, Ernest B. "On Systems and International Regimes." *World Politics* 27, no. 2 (1975): 147–74.

Haber, Samuel. *Efficiency and Uplift: Scientific Management in the Progressive Era.* Chicago: University of Chicago Press, 1964.

Haggard, Stephen, and Beth A. Simmons. "Theories of International Regimes." *International Organization* 41, no. 3 (1987): 491–517.

Hall, David D. "The Victorian Connection." *American Quarterly* 27 (December 1975): 561–74.

Hall, G. Stanley, ed. *Methods of Teaching History.* Boston: D. C. Heath, 1883.

Hall, Peter A. *Governing the Economy: The Politics of State Intervention in Britain and France*. New York: Oxford University Press, 1986.

———. "Conclusion: The Politics of Keynesian Ideas." In *The Political Power of Economic Ideas*, edited by Peter A. Hall, 351–91. Princeton, NJ: Princeton University Press, 1989.

Hall, Peter A., and Rosemary Taylor. "Political Science and the Three Institutionalisms." *Political Studies* 44 (1996): 936–57.

Hall, Stuart. "Popular-Democratic versus Authoritarian Populism." In *Marxism and Democracy*, edited by Alan Hunt. London: Lawrence and Wishart, 1980.

———. "The Great Moving Right Show." In *The Politics of Thatcherism*, edited by Stuart Hall and Martin Jacques. London: Lawrence and Wishart, 1983.

Hammond, J. L., and Barbara Hammond. *The Village Labourer, 1760–1832*. London: Longmans Green, 1911.

———. *The Town Labourer, 1872–1949*. London: Longmans Green, 1917.

———. *The Skilled Labourer, 1760–1832*. London: Longmans Green, 1919.

Hansen, J. "Choosing Sides: The Creation of an Agricultural Policy Network in Congress, 1919–1932." *Studies in American Political Development* 2 (1987): 183–229.

Hanson, A. H., and Bernard Crick, eds. *The Commons in Transition*. London: Fontana, 1970.

Harris, José. "Platonism, Positivism, and Progressivism: Aspects of British Sociological Thought in the Early Twentieth Century." In *Citizenship and Community: Liberals, Radicals, and Collective Identities in the British Isles, 1865–1931*, edited by Eugenio F. Biagini. Cambridge: Cambridge University Press, 1996.

Harrison, Frederic. *The Meaning of History*. London: Macmillan, 1894.

———. "The Historical Method of Professor Freeman." *Nineteenth Century* 44 (1898): 192–806.

Harrison, Wilfred. "A British Journal of Political Studies: An Editorial Note." *Political Studies* 1, no. 1 (1953): 1–5.

Hart, Albert B. "Methods of Teaching American History." In Hall, *Methods of Teaching History*.

———. *Actual Government, As Applied under American Conditions*. New York: Longmans Green, 1903,

Hartz, Louis. *The Liberal Tradition in America: An Interpretation of American Political Thought since the Revolution*. New York: Harcourt Brace and World, 1955.

Haskell, Thomas L. *The Emergence of Professional Social Science: The American Social Science Association and the Crisis of Authority*. Urbana: University of Illinois Press, 1977.

Hauptmann, Emily. "A Local History of the Political." *Political Theory* 32, no. 1 (2004): 34–60.

———. "Defining 'Theory' in Postwar Political Science." In *The Politics of Method in the Human Sciences: Positivism and Its Epistemological Others*, edited by George Steinmetz. Chapel Hill, NC: Duke University Press, 2005.

Hay, Colin. *The Political Economy of New Labour: Labouring under False Pretences*. Manchester: Manchester University Press, 1999.

Hay, Colin. "New Labour and 'Third Way Political Economy': Paving the European Road to Washington?" In Bevir and Trentmann, *Critiques of Capital*.

————. *Political Analysis*. Basingstoke, UK: Palgrave, 2002.

Hays, Samuel P. *Conservation and the Gospel of Efficiency: The Progressive Conservation Movement, 1890–1920*. Cambridge: Harvard University Press, 1959.

Hayward, Jack. "The Political Science of Muddling Through: The *de facto* Paradigm?" In Hayward and Norton, *Political Science of British Politics*.

————. "Cultural and Contextual Constraints upon the Development of Political Science in Great Britain." In *The Development of Political Science: A Comparative Survey*, edited by David Easton, John G. Gunnell, and Luigi Graziano. London: Routledge, 1991.

————. "Political Science in Britain." *European Journal of Political Research* 20, no. 2 (1991): 301–22.

————. "British Approaches to Politics: The Dawn of a Self-Deprecating Discipline." In Hayward, Barry, and Brown, *British Study of Politics*.

Hayward, Jack, Brian Barry, and Archie Brown, eds. *The British Study of Politics in the Twentieth Century*. Oxford: Oxford University Press, 1999.

Hayward, Jack, and Philip Norton, eds. *The Political Science of British Politics*. Brighton, UK: Harvester Wheatsheaf, 1986.

Heastfield, J. "Brand New Britain." *LM Magazine*, November 1997.

Hennessey, Peter. "The Blair Style of Government." *Government and Opposition* 33 (1998): 3–20.

Hennis, Wilhelm. *Max Weber: Essays in Reconstruction*. Translated by Keith Tribe. London: Allen and Unwin, 1988.

Herring, Hubert. "Charles A. Beard: Freelance among the Historians." *Harper's* 178, March 1939.

Herring, Pendleton. *Group Representation before Congress*. Baltimore: Johns Hopkins University Press, 1929.

————. *The Politics of Democracy*. New York: Norton, 1940.

————. "On the Study of Government." *American Political Science Review* 47, no. 4 (1953): 961–74.

Hewart, Gordon. *The New Despotism*. New York: Cosmopolitan, 1929.

Hirst, Paul, Q. ed. *The Pluralist Theory of the State: Selected Writings of G.D.H. Cole, J. N. Figgis and H. J. Laski*. London: Routledge, 1989.

Hobhouse, L. T. *Social Evolution and Political Theory*. New York: Columbia University Press, 1911.

————. *The Metaphysical Theory of the State*. London: Allen and Unwin, 1918.

Hobsbawm, Eric J. "The Historians Group of the Communist Party." In *Rebels and Their Causes: Essays in Honour of A. L. Morton*, edited by Maurice Cornforth. London: Lawrence and Wishart, 1978.

Hobsbawm, Eric J., and others, *The Forward March of Labour Halted?* London: New Left Books, 1981.

Hobson, J. A. *The Social Problem*. London: Nisbet, 1901.

————. *Work and Wealth*. London: Macmillan, 1914.

Horsman, Reginald. "Origins of Racial Anglo-Saxonism in Great Britain before 1850." *Journal of the History of Ideas* 27 (1976): 387–410.

Huntington, Samuel P. "Political Modernization: America vs. Europe." *World Politics* 18, no. 3 (1966): 378–414. Reprinted in *Political Order in Changing Societies*. New Haven, CT: Yale University Press, 1968.

———. *American Politics: The Promise of Disharmony*. Cambridge: Harvard University Press, Belknap Press 1981.

Huxley, T. H. "Natural Rights and Political Rights." In *Collected Essays*. 9 vols., vol. 1. London: Macmillan, 1894.

Ikenberry, G. John. "Conclusion: An Institutional Approach to American Foreign Economic Policy." In *The State and American Foreign Policy*, edited by G. John Ikenberry, David A. Lake, and Michael Mastanduno. Ithaca, NY: Cornell University Press, 1988.

Inglis, Fred. *Clifford Geertz: Culture, Custom and Ethics*. Oxford: Basil Blackwell, 2000.

Jackson, Robert J. *Rebels and Whips*. London: Macmillan, 1968.

Jacobson, Norman. "The Unity of Political Theory: Science, Morals, and Politics." In *Approaches to the Study of Politics*, edited by Roland Young. Evanston, IL: Northwestern University Press, 1958.

———. "Political Science and Political Education." *American Political Science Review* 57, no. 3 (1963): 561–69.

Jann, Rosemary. *The Art and Science of Victorian History*. Columbus: Ohio State University Press, 1985.

Jellinek, Georg. *The Declaration of the Rights of Man and of Citizen*. Translated by Max Farrand. New York: Henry Holt, 1901.

Jenkyns, Richard. *The Victorians and Ancient Greece*. Oxford: Basil Blackwell, 1980.

Jennings, Ivor. *Law and the Constitution*. London: University of London Press, 1933.

———. *Cabinet Government*. Cambridge: Cambridge University Press, 1936.

———. *Constitutional Laws of the British Empire*. Oxford: Clarendon Press, 1938.

———. *Parliament*. Cambridge: Cambridge University Press, 1939.

———. *A Federation for Western Europe*. Cambridge: Cambridge University Press, 1940.

Jensen, Richard. "History and the Political Scientist." In *Politics and the Social Sciences*, edited by Seymour Martin Lipset, 1–28. New York: Doubleday, 1969.

Jessop, Bob. *State Theory: Putting Capitalist States in their Place*. University Park: Pennsylvania State University Press, 1990.

———. "Institutional Re(turns) and the Strategic-Relational Approach." *Environment and Planning A* 33, no. 7 (2001): 1213–35.

Jessop, Bob, K. Bonnett, S. Bromley, and T. Ling, *Thatcherism*. Cambridge: Polity, 1988.

Johnson, Nevil. "The Place of Institutions in the Study of Politics." *Political Studies* 23 (1975): 271–83.

———. *In Search of the Constitution*. London: Pergamon, 1977.

———. *The Limits of Political Science*. Oxford: Clarendon, 1989.

Jones, Gareth Stedman. "The Determinist Fix: Some Obstacles to the Further Development of the Linguistic Approach to History in the 1990s." *History Workshop* 42 (1996): 19–35.
Jowett, Benjamin, trans. *"The Politics" of Aristotle*. Oxford: Clarendon Press,
1885.
Kadish, Alon, and Keith Tribe. *The Market for Political Economy: The Advent
of Economics in British University Culture, 1850–1905*. London: Routledge,
1993.
Kahin, George M., Guy J. Pauker, and Lucian W. Pye. "Comparative Politics of
Non-Western Countries." *American Political Science Review* 49, no. 4 (1955):
1022–41.
Kant, Immanuel. *The Philosophy of Kant*. Translated by Carl J. Friedrich. New
York: Modern Library, 1949.
Karl, Barry D. *Executive Reorganization and Reform in the New Deal: Genesis
of Administrative Management*. Cambridge: Harvard University Press, 1963.
———. *Charles Merriam and the Study of Politics*. Chicago: University of Chi-
cago Press, 1974.
Katzenstein, Peter J. "International Relations and Domestic Structures: Foreign
Economic Policies of Advanced Industrial States." *International Organization*
30, no. 1 (1976): 1–45.
———, ed. *Between Power and Plenty: Foreign Economic Policies of Advanced
Industrial States*. Madison: University of Wisconsin Press, 1978.
———. *Small States in World Markets: Industrial Policy in Europe*. Ithaca, NY:
Cornell University Press, 1985.
———. "Die neue Institutionalismus und internationale Regime: Amerika, Japan
und Westdeutschland in der internationalen Politik." In *Macht und Ohnmacht
politischer Institutionen*, edited by Hans-Hermann Hartwich. Opladen: West-
deutscher Verlag, 1989.
———, ed. *The Culture of National Security: Norms and Identity in World Poli-
tics*. New York: Columbia University Press, 1996.
Katznelson, Ira. *City Trenches: Urban Politics and the Patterning of Class in the
United States*. New York: Pantheon, 1981.
———. "Working-Class Formation and the State: Nineteenth-Century England
in American Perspective." In Evans, Rueschemeyer, Skocpol, *Bringing the State*.
———. "Working-Class Formation: Constructing Cases and Comparisons." In
Katznelson and Zolberg, *Working-Class Formation*.
———. "The State to the Rescue? Political Science and History Reconnect." *So-
cial Research* 59, no. 4 (1994): 719–37.
———. *Desolation and Enlightenment: Political Knowledge after Total War, To-
talitarianism, and the Holocaust*. New York: Columbia University Press, 2003.
Katznelson, Ira, and Aristide R. Zolberg, eds. *Working-Class Formation: Nine-
teenth-Century Patterns in Western Europe and the United States*. Princeton,
NJ: Princeton University Press, 1986.
Kaufman-Osborn, Timothy V. *Politics/Sense/Experience: A Pragmatic Inquiry
into the Promise of Democracy*. Ithaca, NY: Cornell University Press, 1991.
Kavanagh, Dennis. "The American Science of British Politics." *Political Studies*
22, no. 3 (1974): 251–70.

Kavanagh, Dennis, and Richard Rose. "British Politics since 1945: The Changing Field of Study." In *New Trends in British Politics: Issues for Research*, edited by Dennis Kavanagh and Richard Rose. London: Sage, 1977.

Kay, J. A. *Foundations of Corporate Success: How Business Strategies Add Value.* Oxford: Oxford University Press, 1993.

Kenny, Michael. *The First New Left: British Intellectuals after Stalin.* London: Lawrence and Wishart, 1995.

———. "Ideas, Ideologies and the British Tradition." In *Fundamentals in British Politics*, edited by Ian Holliday, Andrew Gamble, and Geraint Parry. Basingstoke, UK: Macmillan, 1999.

———. "Reputations: Edward Palmer Thompson." *Political Quarterly* 70, no. 30 (1999): 319–29.

———. "The Case for Disciplinary History: British Political Studies in the 1950s and 1960s." *British Journal of Politics and International Relations* 6 (2004): 565–83.

Keohane, Robert O. "International Institutions: Two Approaches." *International Studies Quarterly* 32, no. 4 (1988): 379–96.

Kernell, Samuel. "The Early Nationalization of Political News in America." *Studies in American Political Development* 1 (1986): 255–78.

Key, V. O., Jr. *Southern Politics in State and Nation.* New York: Knopf, 1949.

———. "A Theory of Critical Elections." *Journal of Politics* 17, no. 1 (1955): 3–18.

———. "The State of the Discipline." *American Political Science Review* 52, no. 4 (1958): 961–71.

———. "Secular Realignment and the Party System." *Journal of Politics* 21, no. 2 (1959): 198–210.

———. "The Politically Relevant in Surveys." *Public Opinion Quarterly* 24, no. 1 (1960): 54–61.

Kickert, Walter J. M., Erik-Hans Klijn, and Joop F. M. Koppenjan. "Managing Networks in the Public Sector: Findings and Reflections." In *Managing Complex Networks: Strategies for the Public Sector*, edited by Walter J. M. Kickert, Erik-Hans Klijn, and Joop F. M. Koppenjan. London: Sage, 1998.

King, Preston. *The Study of Politics: A Collection of Inaugural Addresses.* London: Cass, 1977.

Kingdom, J. E. *Politics and Government in Britain.* Cambridge: Polity, 1991.

Kloppenberg, James T. *Uncertain Victory: Social Democracy and Progressivism in European and American Thought, 1870–1920.* New York: Oxford University Press, 1986.

Koikkalainen, Petri, and Sami Syrjämäki. "Interview with Quentin Skinner." *Finnish Yearbook of Political Thought* 6 (2002): 32–63.

Koot, Gerard M. *English Historical Economics, 1870–1926: The Rise of Economic History and Neomercantilism.* Cambridge: Cambridge University Press, 1987.

Kramnick, Isaac, and Barry Sheerman. *Harold Laski: A Life on the Left.* London: Hamish Hamilton, 1993.

Krasner, Stephen D. "State Power and the Structure of International Trade." *World Politics* 28, no. 3 (1976): 317–47.

Krasner, Stephen D. *Defending the National Interest: Raw Materials Investments and U.S. Foreign Policy*. Princeton, NJ: Princeton University Press, 1978.

———. "Approaches to the State: Alternative Conceptions and Historical Dynamics." *Comparative Politics* 16, no. 2 (1984): 223–46.

———, ed. *International Regimes*. Ithaca, NY: Cornell University Press, 1983.

———. "Structural Causes and Regime Consequences: Regimes as Intervening Variables." In Krasner, *International Regimes*, 1–21.

———. *Structural Conflict: The Third World against Global Liberalism*. Berkeley and Los Angeles: University of California Press, 1985.

Kratochwil, Friedrich, and John G. Ruggie. "International Organization: A State of the Art on an Art of the State." *International Organization* 40, no. 4 (1986): 753–75.

Laborde, Cécile. *Pluralist Thought and the State in Britain and France, 1900–1925*. New York: St. Martin's Press, 2000.

Laclau, Ernesto. *New Reflections on the Revolution of Our Time*. London: Verso, 1990.

Laclau, Ernesto, and Chantal Mouffe. *Hegemony and Socialist Strategy: Towards a Radical Democratic Politics*. London: Verso, 1985.

Lakatos, Imre. "History of Science and Its Rational Reconstructions." In *Philosophical Writings*. Vol. 1, *The Methodology of Scientific Research Programmes*, 102–38. Cambridge: Cambridge University Press, 1978.

Lane, Melissa. "Why History of Ideas at All?" *History of European Ideas* 28 (2002): 33–41.

Langlois, Charles Victor, and Charles Seignobos. *Introduction aux études historiques*. Paris: Hachette, 1898.

Laski, Harold J. *Studies in the Problem of Sovereignty*. New Haven, CT: Yale University Press, 1917.

———. *Authority in the Modern State*. New Haven, CT: Yale University Press, 1919.

———. *Political Thought in England from Locke to Bentham*. London: Williams and Northgate, 1920.

———. *The Foundations of Sovereignty and Other Essays*. New York: Harcourt Brace, 1921.

———. *A Grammar of Politics*. London: Allen and Unwin, 1925.

———. *The Rise of European Liberalism*. London: Allen and Unwin, 1936.

———. *Democracy in Crisis*. London: Allen and Unwin, 1938.

———. *Parliamentary Government in England*. London: Allen and Unwin, 1938.

———. *Reflections on the Constitution*. Manchester: Manchester University Press, 1951.

Laslett, Peter. "Introduction." In *Politics, Philosophy and Society*, 1st ser., edited by Peter Laslett. Oxford: Blackwell, 1956.

Lasswell, Harold D., and Abraham Kaplan. *Power and Society*. New Haven, CT: Yale University Press, 1950.

Lazarsfeld, Paul F., Bernard Berelson, and Hazel Gaudet. *The People's Choice*. New York: Knopf, 1944.

Leadbeater, Charles. *The Rise of the Social Entrepreneur*. London: Demos, 1997.

———. *Britain: The California of Europe?* London: Demos, 1999.

————. *Europe's New Economy*. London: Centre for European Reform, 1999.

————. *Living on Thin Air: The New Economy*. Harmondsworth, UK: Penguin, 1999.

Leadbeater, Charles, and Sue Goss. *Civic Entrepreneurship*. London: Demos, 1998.

Leadbeater, Charles, and Geoff Mulgan. *Mistakeholding: Whatever Happened to Labour's Big Idea?* London: Demos, 1996.

Lecky, William E. H. *The Political Value of History*. London: Arnold, 1892.

Leiserson, Avery. "Systematic Research in Political Behavior." *Social Science Research Council Items* 5 (1951): 29–32.

Leonard, Mark. *Britain: Renewing Our Identity*. London: Demos, 1997.

Leslie, Margaret. "In Defense of Anachronism." *Political Studies* 18 (1970): 433–47.

Leslie, T. E. Cliffe. *Essays in Political and Moral Philosophy*. Dublin: Hodges Figgis, 1879.

Levi, Margaret. "Theories of Historical and Institutional Change." *PS* 20, no. 3 (1987): 684–88.

————. *Of Rule and Revenue*. Berkeley and Los Angeles: University of California Press, 1988.

Levine, Philippa. *The Amateur and the Professional: Antiquarians, Historians and Archaeologists in Victorian Britain, 1838–1886*. Cambridge: Cambridge University Press, 1986.

Leys, Colin. *Politics in Britain*. London: Heinemann, 1983.

Liberal Industrial Inquiry. *Britian's Industrial Future*. London: Benn, 1928.

Lieber, Francis, ed. *Encyclopedia Americana*, s.v. "Politics." 13 vols. Philadelphia: Carey, Lea, and Blanchard, 1857. First published in 1829–32.

————. *Manual of Political Ethics*. Edited by Theodore D. Woolsey. 2 vols. Philadelphia: J. B. Lippincott, 1911. First published in 1838.

————. *Civil Liberty and Self-Government*. Edited by Theodore D. Woolsey. 4th ed., 2 vols. Philadelphia: J. B. Lippincott, 1901. First published in 1853.

————. *Miscellaneous Writings*. 2 vols. Philadelphia: J. B. Lippincott, 1881.

Lieberman, Robert C. "Ideas, Institutions, and Political Order: Explaining Political Change." *American Political Science Review* 96, no. 4 (2002): 697–712.

Lin, Chun. *The British New Left*. Edinburgh: Edinburgh University Press, 1993.

Lindsay, A. D. "The State in Recent Political Theory." *Political Quarterly* 1 (May 1914): 128–45.

————. "Sovereignty." *Proceedings of the Aristotelian Society* 3 (1924): 235–54.

————. *The Essentials of Democracy*. Oxford: Clarendon Press, 1929.

Lindsay, A. D., and Harold J. Laski. "Symposium: Bosanquet's Theory of the General Will." *Proceedings of the Aristotelian Society*, suppl. vol., 8 (1928): 31–61.

Lippincott, Benjamin E. "The Bias of American Political Science." *Journal of Politics* 2, no. 2 (1940): 125–39.

Lippmann, Walter. *Public Opinion*. New York: Macmillan, 1922.

————. *The Phantom Public*. New York: Harcourt, Brace, 1925.

Lipset, Seymour Martin. "Some Social Requisites of Democracy." *American Political Science Review* 53, no. 1 (1959): 69–105.

————. *Political Man*. Garden City, NY: Doubleday, 1960.

Lipset, Seymour Martin. *The First New Nation.* New York: Norton, 1963.

Locke, Richard M., and Kathleen Thelen. "Apples and Oranges Revisited: Con-textualized Comparisons and the Study of Comparative Labor Politics." *Politics and Society* 23, no. 3 (1995): 337–67.

Loewenstein, Karl. *Hitler's Germany: The Nazi Background to War.* New York: Macmillan, 1939.

London School of Economics and Politics. Calendar. 1902.

Loughlin, Martin. *Public Law and Political Theory.* Oxford: Oxford University Press, 1992.

Lovenduski, Joni. "The Profession of Political Science in Britain." *Studies in Public Policy* 64, Centre for the Study of Public Policy, University of Strathclyde, Glasgow, 1981.

Low, Sidney. *The Governance of England.* London: Fisher Unwin, 1904.

Lowell, A. L. *The Government of England.* New York: Macmillan, 1908.

———. "The Physiology of Politics." *American Political Science Review* 4, no. 1 (1910): 1–15.

———. *Public Opinion and Popular Government.* New York: Longmans Green, 1913.

———. *Public Opinion in War and Peace.* Cambridge: Harvard University Press, 1923.

Lowndes, Vivien. "Rebuilding Trust in Central/Local Relations: Policy or Passion?" In *Renewing Local Democracy: The Modernisation Agenda in British Local Government,* edited by Lawrence Pratchett. London: Frank Cass, 2000.

———. "The Institutional Approach." In Marsh and Stoker, *Theory and Methods,* 2nd ed.

Macfarlane, Alan. *The Making of the Modern World: Visions from the West and East.* London: Palgrave, 2002.

Machiavelli, Niccolò. *The Discourses.* Edited by Bernard Crick. Harmondsworth, UK: Penguin, 1970.

MacIntyre, Alasdair. *A Short History of Ethics.* New York: Macmillan, 1966.

———. "A Mistake about Causality in Social Science." In *Philosophy, Politics, and Society,* 2nd ser, edited by Peter Laslett and W. G. Runciman. Oxford: Basil Blackwell, 1969.

Mackenzie, W.J.M. "Pressure Groups in British Government." *British Journal of Sociology* 6 (1955): 133–48.

———. *Politics and Social Science.* Baltimore: Penguin, 1967.

———. *Explorations in Government: Collected Papers, 1951–1968.* London: Macmillan, 1975.

———. "Political Theory and Political Education." In *Explorations in Government.*

Mackillop, Ian Duncan. *The British Ethical Societies.* Cambridge: Cambridge University Press, 1986.

Mackintosh, John P. *The Government and Politics of Britain.* London: Hutchinson, 1970.

Macpherson, C. B. *The Political Theory of Possessive Individualism.* Oxford: Clarendon Press, 1962.

Macridis, Roy C., and Richard Cox. "Research in Comparative Politics." *American Political Science Review* 47, no. 3 (1953): 641–75.

Macy, Jesse. "The Relation of History to Politics." *Annual Report of the American Historical Association for 1893*, 179–88. Washington, DC: Government Printing Office, 1895.

Mahoney, James. "Path Dependence in Historical Sociology." *Theory and Society* 29, no. 4 (2000): 507–48.

Maine, Henry. *Ancient Law: Its Connection with the Early History of Society, and Its Relation to Modern Ideas*. London: Murray, 1861.

———. *The Collected Papers of Frederick William Maitland*. 3 vols. Edited by H.A.L. Fisher. Cambridge: Cambridge University Press, 1911.

———. "Old English Law." In *Collected Papers of Maitland*, vol. 3.

———. "The Surnames of English Villages." In *Collected Papers of Maitland*, vol. 2.

———. *The Constitutional History of England*. Cambridge: Cambridge University Press, 1911.

———. *The Domesday Book and Beyond: Three Essays in the Early History of England*. Cambridge: Cambridge University Press, 1897.

Maitland, Frederic William, and Frederick Pollock. *The History of English Law before the Time of Edward I*. 2 vols. Cambridge: Cambridge University Press, 1968. First published in 1895.

Mandelson, Peter, and Roger Liddle. *The Blair Revolution: Can New Labour Deliver?* London: Faber and Faber, 1996.

Mandler, Peter. *Aristocratic Government in the Age of Reform: Whigs and Liberals, 1830–1852*. Oxford: Oxford University Press, 1990.

———. *History and National Life*. London: Profile Books, 2002.

March, James G., and Johan P. Olsen. "The New Institutionalism: Organizational Factors in Political Life." *American Political Science Review* 78, no. 3 (1984): 734–49.

Marinetto, M. "Governing beyond the Centre: A Critique of the Anglo-Governance School." *Political Studies* 51, no. 3 (2003): 592–608.

Marsh, David. "Resurrecting Marxism." In *Marxism and Social Science*, edited by Andrew Gamble, David Marsh, and Tony Tant. London: Macmillan, 1999.

Marsh, David, and Gerry Stoker, eds. *Theory and Methods in Political Science*. 1st ed. London: Macmillan, 1995. 2nd ed., Basingstoke: Palgrave, 2002.

Marx, Karl. "Introduction to Contribution to the Critique of Hegel's *Philosophy of Law*." In *Marx-Engels Collected Works*, vol. 3. New York: International, 1975. First published in 1844.

Matthews, Fred H. *Quest for an American Sociology: Robert E. Park and the Chicago School*. Montreal: McGill-Queen's University Press, 1977.

McCallum, Ronald B., and Alison Readman. *The British General Election of 1945*. London: Oxford University Press, 1947.

McIlwain, Charles Howard. *The Growth of Political Thought in the West*. New York: Macmillan, 1932.

McLean, Iain. *Rational Choice and British Politics*. Oxford: Oxford University Press, 2001.

Menand, Louis. *The Metaphysical Club*. New York: Farrar, Strauss, and Giroux, 2001.

Merriam, Charles E. *History of the Theory of Sovereignty since Rousseau*. New York: Columbia University Press, 1900.

Merriam, Charles E. *A History of American Political Theories*. New York: Macmillan, 1903.

———. *American Political Ideas: Studies in the Development of American Political Thought, 1865–1917*. New York: Macmillan, 1920.

———. *New Aspects of Politics*. Chicago: University of Chicago Press, 1970. First published in 1925.

———. "Progress in Political Research." *American Political Science Review* 20, no. 1 (1926): 1–13.

———. "William Archibald Dunning." In *American Masters of Social Science*, edited by Howard W. Odum. New York: Henry Holt, 1927.

———. *The Making of Citizens: A Comparative Study of Methods of Civic Training*. Chicago: University of Chicago Press, 1931.

———. *Civic Education in the United States*. New York: Scribner's Sons, 1934.

———. "The Education of Charles Merriam." In *The Future of Government in the United States: Essays in Honor of Charles E. Merriam*, edited by Leonard D. White. Chicago: University of Chicago Press, 1942.

———. *Systematic Politics*. Chicago: University of Chicago Press, 1945.

———. "Physics and Politics." *American Political Science Review* 40, no. 3 (1946): 445–57.

———. Papers. University of Chicago Library.

Meyer, John W., and Brian Rowen. "Institutionalized Organizations: Formal Structure as Myth and Ceremony." *American Journal of Sociology* 83, no. 2 (1977): 340–63.

Milgrom, Paul R., Douglass C. North, and Barry R. Weingast. "The Role of Institutions in the Revival of Trade: The Law Merchant, Private Judges, and the Champagne Fairs." *Economics and Politics* 2, no. 1 (1990): 1–23.

Miliband, Ralph. *Parliamentary Socialism: A Study in the Politics of Labour*. London: Allen and Unwin, 1961.

———. *The State in Capitalist Society*. London: Weidenfeld and Nicolson, 1969.

———. "The Capitalist State: Reply to Nicos Poulantzas." *New Left Review* 59 (1970): 53–60.

Mill, John Stuart. *Auguste Comte and Positivism*. London: Truebner, 1865.

Mills, Frederick C., chair. "Quantification—the Quest for Precision—a Round Table Discussion." In *Eleven Twenty-Six: A Decade of Social Science Research*, edited by Louis Wirth. Chicago: University of Chicago Press, 1940.

Miller, Warren E. "Party Preference and Attitudes on Political Issues, 1948–1951." *American Political Science Review* 47, no. 1 (1953): 45–60.

Mitchell, Rosemary. *Picturing the Past: English History in Text and Image, 1830–1870*. Oxford: Oxford University Press, 2000.

Moe, Terry M. "The New Economics of Organization." *American Journal of Political Science* 28, no. 4 (1984): 739–77.

———. "Interests, Institutions, and Positive Theory: The Politics of the NRLB." *Studies in American Political Development* 2 (1987): 236–99.

Montesquieu, Charles Louis. *The Spirit of the Laws*. Edited by Anne Cohler, Basia Miler, and Harold Stone. Cambridge: Cambridge University Press, 1989. First published in 1748.

Moodie, Graeme C. *The Government of Great Britain*. New York: Crowell, 1962.

Morgenthau, Hans J. *Scientific Man vs. Power Politics*. Chicago: University of Chicago Press, 1946.

Moses, Bernard. "Outline of Lectures on the Constitutional History of England and Scandinavia." *Daily Evening Tribune*. Oakland, CA, 1878.

———. "Social Science and Its Method." *Berkeley Journal of Social Science* 1 (1880): 1–14.

———. "A Brief Survey of the Field of Political Inquiry." *Berkeleyan*, September 15, 1884, 27–30.

Mount, Ferdinand. *The British Constitution Now: Recovery or Decline?* London: Mandarin, 1993.

Muir, Ramsay. *How Britain Is Governed: A Critical Analysis of Modern Developments in the British System of Government*. London: Constable, 1930.

Mulford, Elisha. *The Nation: Foundations of Civil Order and Political Life in the United States*. New York: Hurd and Houghton, 1870.

Mulgan, Geoff. *Connexity: How to Live in a Connected World*. London: Jonathon Cape, 1997.

Mulgan, Geoff, and Perri 6. "The Local Is Coming Home: Decentralisation by Degrees." *Demos Quarterly* 9 (1996): 3–7.

Nettl, J. P. "The State as a Conceptual Variable." *World Politics* 20, no. 4 (1968): 559–92.

Neumann, Franz. *Behemoth: The Structure and Practice of National Socialism*. New York: Oxford University Press, 1942.

Neumann, Sigmund. *Permanent Revolution: The Total State in a World at War*. New York: Harper and Brothers, 1942.

Newman, Michael. *Harold Laski: A Political Biography*. London: Macmillan, 1993.

———. *Ralph Miliband and the Politics of the New Left*. London: Merlin, 2002.

Nicholls, David. *The Pluralist State: The Political Ideas of J. N. Figgis and His Contemporaries*. Basingstoke, UK: Macmillan, 1975.

Nore, Ellen. *Charles A. Beard: An Intellectual Biography*. Carbondale: Southern Illinois University Press, 1983.

North, Douglass C. "Autobiography, Nobel Lecture Banquet Speech." Retrieved August 8, 2003, from www.nobel.se/economics/laureates/1993/north-autobio.html.

North, Douglass C., and Barry R. Weingast. "Constitutions and Commitment: The Evolution of Institutions Governing Public Choice in Seventeenth-Century England." *Journal of Economic History* 49, no. 4 (1989): 803–32.

Novick, Peter. *That Noble Dream: The "Objectivity Question" and the American Historical Profession*. Cambridge: Cambridge University Press, 1988.

Oakeshott, Michael. *The Social and Political Doctrines of Contemporary Europe*. Cambridge: Cambridge University Press, 1939.

———. *Hobbes on Civil Association*. Berkeley and Los Angeles: University of California Press, 1975.

Oakeshott, Michael. *Rationalism in Politics and Other Essays*. 1st edition, London: Methuen, 1962; 2nd, ed. expanded. Indianapolis: Liberty Fund, 1991.

O'Brien, D. "Edwin Cannan: Economic Theory and the History of Economic Thought." *Research in the History of Economic Thought and Methodology* 17 (1999): 1–21.

Odegard, Peter H. *Pressure Politics: The Story of the Anti-Saloon League*. New York: Columbia University Press, 1928.

O'Donnell, Guillermo. "Reflections on Patterns of Change in the Bureaucratic Authoritarian State." *Latin American Research Review* 13, no. 1 (1978): 3–38.

Oren, Ido. *Our Enemies and US: America's Rivalries and the Making of Political Science*. Ithaca, NY: Cornell University Press, 2003.

Orloff, Ann Shola, and Theda Skocpol. "Why Not Equal Protection? Explaining the Politics of Public Social Spending in Britain, 1900–1911, and the United States, 1880s–1920." *American Sociological Review* 49, no. 6 (1984): 726–50.

Orren, Karen, and Stephen Skowronek. "Editor's Preface." *Studies in American Political Development* 1 (1986): vii–viii.

———. "Order and Time in Institutional Study." In Farr, Dryzek, and Leonard, *Political Science in History*.

Osborne, David, and Ted Baebler. *Reinventing Government: How the Entrepreneurial Spirit Is Transforming the Public Sector*. Reading, MA: Addison-Wesley, 1992.

O'Sullivan, N. "Visions of Freedom: The Response to Totalitarianism." In Hayward, Barry, and Brown, *British Study of Politics*.

Otter, Sandra den. *The British Idealists and Social Explanation*. Oxford: Oxford University Press, 1996.

Parker, Christopher. *The English Historical Tradition since 1850*. Edinburgh: John Donald, 1990.

Parsons, Talcott. *The Social System*. Glencoe, IL: Free Press, 1951.

Phillips, Mark. *Society and Sentiment: Genres of Historical Writing in Britain, 1740–1820*. Princeton, NJ: Princeton University Press, 2000.

Pierre, Jon, ed. *Debating Governance*. Oxford: Oxford University Press, 1999.

Pierre, Jon, and Gerry Stoker. "Towards Multi-Level Governance." In *Developments in British Politics* 6, edited by Patrick Dunleavy, Andrew Gamble, Ian Holliday, and Gillian Peele. Basingstoke, UK: Macmillan, 2000.

Pierson, Paul. "Increasing Returns, Path Dependence, and the Study of Politics." *American Political Science Review* 94, no. 2 (2000): 251–67.

Pierson, Paul, and Theda Skocpol. "Historical Institutionalism in Contemporary Political Science." In *Political Science: The State of the Discipline*, edited by Ira Katznelson and Helen V. Miller. New York: Norton, 2002.

Pimlott, Ben. *Harold Wilson*. London: HarperCollins, 1992.

Pocock, J.G.A. *The Ancient Constitution and the Feudal Law: A Study of English Historical Thought in the Seventeenth Century*. Cambridge: Cambridge University Press, 1957.

———. "British History: A Plea for a New Subject." *Journal of Modern History* 47 (1975): 601–28.

Pollock, Frederick. *An Introduction to the History of the Science of Politics*. London: Macmillan, 1890.

Polsby, Nelson W. "The Institutionalization of the House of Representatives." *American Political Science Review* 62, no. 1 (1968): 142–68.

Polsby, Nelson W., Miriam Gallaher, and Barry Spencer Rundquist. "The Growth of the Seniority System in the U.S. House of Representatives." *American Political Science Review* 63, no. 3 (1969): 787–807.

Popkin, Samuel L. *The Rational Peasant: The Political Economy of Rural Society in Vietnam.* Berkeley and Los Angeles: University of California Press, 1979.

Popper, Karl. *The Poverty of Historicism.* Boston: Beacon, 1957.

Porter, Theodore M. *Trust in Numbers: The Pursuit of Objectivity in Science and Public Life.* Princeton, NJ: Princeton University Press, 1995.

Porter, Theodore M., and Dorothy Ross. *The Modern Social Sciences.* Vol. 7 in *The Cambridge History of Science.* Cambridge: Cambridge University Press, 2003.

Poulantzas, Nicos. *Political Power and Social Classes.* Translated by Timothy O'Hagan. London: New Left Books, 1973.

Powell, Walter W. "Neither Market nor Hierarchy: Network Forms of Organization." *Research in Organizational Behaviour* 12 (1990): 295–336.

Powell, Walter W., Kenneth W. Koput, and Laurel Smith-Doerr. "Interorganizational Collaboration and the Locus of Innovation: Networks of Learning in Biotechnology." *Administrative Science Quarterly* 41, no. 1 (1996): 116–45.

Punnett, R. M. *British Government and Politics.* New York: Norton, 1968.

Putnam, Robert D. *Making Democracy Work: Civic Traditions in Modern Italy.* Princeton, NJ: Princeton University Press, 1993.

Pye, Lucian W., ed. *Communications and Political Development.* Princeton, NJ: Princeton University Press, 1963.

Qualter, Terence H. *Graham Wallas and the Great Society.* New York: St. Martin's Press, 1979.

Ranney, Austin. "The Utility and Limitations of Aggregate Data in the Study of Electoral Behavior." In *Essays on the Behavioral Study of Politics,* edited by Austin Ranney, 91–102. Urbana: University of Illinois Press, 1962.

Reinsch, Paul S. "The American Political Science Association." *Iowa Journal of History and Politics* 2 (1904): 155–61.

Rhodes, R.A.W. "It's the Mix that Matters: From Marketisation to Diplomacy." *Australian Journal of Public Administration* 56 (1997): 40–53.

———. *Understanding Governance: Policy Networks, Governance, Reflexivity, and Accountability.* Buckingham: Open University Press, 1997.

———. "Public Administration and Governance." In Pierre, *Debating Governance.*

Ricci, David. *The Tragedy of Political Science: Politics, Scholarship, and Democracy.* New Haven, CT: Yale University Press, 1984.

Riker, William H. "Implications from the Disequilibrium of Majority Rule for the Study of Institutions." *American Political Science Review* 74, no. 2 (1980): 432–46.

———. "The Two-Party System and Duverger's Law: An Essay on the History of Political Science." *American Political Science Review* 76 (1982): 753–66.

Ritchie, David George. *Darwin and Hegel, with other Philosophical Studies.* London: Sonnenschein, 1893.

———. *Darwinism and Politics.* 3rd edition. London: Sonnenschein, 1895.

Ritchie, David George. *Principles of State Interference: Four Essays on the Political Philosophy of Mr. Herbert Spencer, J. S. Mill, and T. H. Green.* London: Sonnenschein, 1896.

———. "Social Evolution." *International Journal of Ethics* 6 (1896): 165–81.

Robertson, David Brian. "The Return to History and the New Institutionalism in American Political Science." *Social Science History* 17, no. 1 (1993): 1–36.

Robinson, James Harvey. *The New History: Essays Illustrating the Modern Historical Outlook.* New York: Macmillan, 1912.

Robson, William Alexander. *The University Teaching of Social Sciences: Political Science.* Paris: UNESCO, 1954.

Rogers, Daniel T. *Atlantic Crossings: Social Politics in a Progressive Age.* Cambridge: Harvard University Press, 1998.

Rogowski, Ronald. "Comparative Politics." In *The State of the Discipline II*, edited by Ada Finifter. Washington, DC: American Political Science Association, 1993.

Rose, Richard. *Politics in England.* Boston: Little, Brown, 1964.

———. "Institutionalizing Professional Political Science in Europe: A Dynamic Model." *European Journal of Political Research* 18 (1990): 581–604.

Ross, Dorothy. "Historical Consciousness in Nineteenth-Century America." *American Historical Review* 89 (1984): 909–28.

———. "On the Misunderstanding of Ranke and the Origins of the Historical Profession in America." In *Leopold von Ranke and the Shaping of the Historical Discipline*, edited by Georg G. Iggers and James M. Powell, 154–213. Syracuse, NY: Syracuse University Press, 1990.

———. *The Origins of American Social Science.* Cambridge: Cambridge University Press, 1991.

———. "The Development of the Social Sciences." In Farr and Seidelman, *Discipline and History*, 81–104.

———. "Changing Contours of the Social Science Disciplines." In Porter and Ross, *The Modern Social Sciences.*

Ruggie, John G. "International Responses to Technology: Concepts and Trends." *International Organization* 29, no. 3 (1975): 557–83.

———. "International Regimes, Transactions and Change: Embedded Liberalism in the Postwar Economic Order." In Krasner, *International Regimes.*

———. *Constructing the World Polity: Essays on International Institutionalization.* London: Routledge, 1998.

Runciman, David. *Pluralism and the Personality of the State.* Cambridge: Cambridge University Press, 1997.

Rusk, Jerrold G. "The Effect of the Australian Ballot on Split-Ticket Voting." *American Political Science Review* 64, no. 4 (1970): 1220–38.

———. "Comment." *American Political Science Review* 68, no. 3 (1974): 1028–49.

Russell, Bertrand. *Principles of Social Reconstruction.* London: Allen and Unwin, 1916.

Sabine, George H. *A History of Political Theory.* New York: Henry Holt, 1937.

Sanborn, Franklin B. "The Social Sciences: Their Growth and Future." *Journal of Social Science* 21 (September 1886): 1–12.

Sanders, David. "Behavioural Analysis." In Marsh and Stoker, *Theory and Methods*, 1st ed.

Scarborough, Elinor. "The British Electorate Twenty Years On: Electoral Change and Election Surveys." *British Journal of Political Science* 17, no. 2 (1987): 219–46.

Schaar, John H., and Sheldon S. Wolin. "Essays on the Scientific Study of Politics: A Critique." *American Political Science Review* 57, no. 1 (1963): 125–50.

Schaefer, David. "Leo Strauss and American Democracy." *Review of Politics* 53, no. 1 (1991): 187–99.

Schattschneider, E. E. *Politics, Pressures, and the Tariff*. New York: Prentice-Hall, 1935.

Schmidt, Brian. *The Political Discourse of Anarchy: A Disciplinary History of International Relations*. Albany State University of New York Press, 1998.

Scott, Peter. *The Crisis of the University*. London: Croom Helm, 1984.

Seeley, John R. *Expansion of England*. New York: Macmillan, 1888.

———. *Introduction to Political Science*. London: Macmillan, 1896. Reprinted, 1926.

———. "Ethics and Religion." In *Ethics and Religion*. London: Swan Sonnenschein, 1900.

Seidelman, Raymond, with the assistance of Edward J. Harpham. *Disenchanted Realists: Political Science and the American Crisis, 1884–1984*. Albany: State University of New York Press, 1984.

Seidman, Steven. "Beyond Presentism and Historicism: Understanding the History of Social Science." *Sociological Inquiry* 53 (1983): 79–94.

Selznick, Philip. *The Moral Commonwealth: Social Theory and the Promise of Community*. Berkeley and Los Angeles: University of California Press, 1992.

Shefter, Martin. "Party and Patronage: Germany, England, and Italy." *Politics and Society* 7, no. 4 (1977): 403–52.

———. "Party, Bureaucracy, and Political Change in the United States." In *Political Parties: Development and Decay*, edited by Louis Maisel and Joseph Cooper. Beverly Hills, CA: Sage, 1977.

———. "Regional Receptivity to Reform: The Legacy of the Progressive Era." *Political Science Quarterly* 98, no. 3 (1983): 459–83.

———. *Political Parties and the State: The American Historical Experience*. Princeton, NJ: Princeton University Press, 1994.

Shepard, Walter J. "Democracy in Transition." *American Political Science Review* 29, no. 1 (1935): 1–20.

Shepsle, Kenneth A. "Institutional Arrangements and Equilibrium in Multidimensional Voting Models." *American Journal of Political Science* 23, no. 1 (1979): 27–60.

———. "Studying Institutions: Some Lessons from the Rational Choice Approach." In Farr, Dryzek, and Leonard, *Political Science in History*.

Sheplse, Kenneth A., and Barry R. Weingast. "Structure-Induced Equilibria and Legislative Choice." *Public Choice* 37 (1981): 503–19.

———. "Institutionalizing Majority Rule: A Social Choice Theory with Policy Implications." *American Economic Review* 72, no. 2 (1982): 367–72.

Sheplse, Kenneth A., and Barry R. Weingast. "When Do Rules of Procedure Matter?" *Journal of Politics* 46, no. 1 (1984): 206–21.

————. "The Institutional Foundations of Committee Power." *American Political Science Review* 81, no. 1 (1987): 85–104.

Shklar, Judith N. *After Utopia*. Princeton, NJ: Princeton University Press, 1957.

————. "*The Foundations of Modern Political Thought*, by Quentin Skinner." *Political Theory* 7, no. 4 (1979): 549–52.

Sidgwick, Arthur. *Henry Sidgwick: A Memoir*. London: Macmillan, 1906.

Sidgwick, Henry. "The Historical Method." *Mind* 11, no. 42 (1886): 203–19.

Silbey, Joel H., Allan G. Bogue, and William H. Flanigan, eds. *The History of American Electoral Behavior*. Princeton, NJ: Princeton University Press, 1978.

Simmons, Beth A., and Lisa Martin, "International Organizations and Institutions." In *Handbook of International Relations*, edited by Walter Carlnaes, Thomas Risse, and Beth A. Simmons. London: Sage, 2002.

6, Perri. *Escaping Poverty: From Safety Nets to Networks of Opportunity*. London: Demos, 1997.

————. *Holistic Government*. London: Demos, 1997.

————. "Neo-Durkheimian Institutional Theory." Paper presented to Conference on Institutional Theory in Political Science, Loch Lomond, 1999.

6, Perri, Diana Leat, Kimberly Seltzer, and Gerry Stoker, *Governing in the Round: Strategies for Holistic Government*. London: Demos, 1999.

Skinner, Quentin. "Meaning and Understanding in the History of Ideas." *History and Theory* 8, no. 1 (1969): 3–53. Republished in Tully, *Meaning and Context*.

————. "Conventions and the Understanding of Speech-Acts." *Philosophical Quarterly* 20 (1970): 118–38.

————. "On Performing and Explaining Linguistic Actions." *Philosophical Quarterly* 21 (1971): 1–21.

————. "The Empirical Theorists of Democracy and Their Critics." *Political Theory* 1, no. 3 (1973): 287–306.

————. *The Foundations of Modern Political Thought*. 2 vols. Cambridge: Cambridge University Press, 1978.

————. "The Idea of Negative Liberty: Philosophical and Historical Perspectives." In *Philosophy in History*, edited by Richard Rorty, J. B. Schneewind, and Quentin Skinner, 231–88. Cambridge: Cambridge University Press, 1984.

————. " 'Social Meaning' and the Explanation of Social Action," "Some Problems in the Analysis of Political Thought and Action," and "A Reply to my Critics." In Tully, *Meaning and Context*.

————. "The Republican Ideal of Political Liberty." In *Machiavelli and Republicanism*, edited by Gisela Bock, Quentin Skinner, and Maurizio Viroli, 293–309. Cambridge: Cambridge University Press, 1990.

————. *Liberty Before Liberalism*. Cambridge: Cambridge University Press, 1998.

————. "States and Freedom of Citizens." In *States and Citizens: History, Theory, Prospects*, edited by Quentin Skinner and Bo Strath. Cambridge: Cambridge University Press, 2003.

Skocpol, Theda. *States and Social Revolutions: A Comparative Analysis of France, Russia, and China*. Cambridge: Cambridge University Press, 1978.

———. "Political Responses to Capitalist Crisis: Neo-Marxist Theories of the State and the Case of the New Deal." *Politics and Society* 10, no. 2 (1980): 155–201.

———. "Bringing the State Back In: Strategies of Analysis in Current Research." In Evans, Rueschemeyer, and Skocpol, *Bringing the State*, 3–37.

———. "Theory Tackles History." *Social Science History* 24, no. 4 (2000): 669–76.

Skocpol, Theda, and Edwin Amenta. "States and Social Policies." *Annual Review of Sociology* 12 (1986): 131–57.

Skocpol, Theda, and Kenneth Finegold. "State Capacity and Economic Intervention in the Early New Deal." *Political Science Quarterly* 97, no. 2 (1982): 255–78.

Skocpol, Theda, and G. John Ikenberry. "The Political Formation of the American Welfare State in Historical and Comparative Perspective." *Comparative Social Research* 6 (1983): 87–148.

Skocpol, Theda, and Margaret R. Somers. "The Uses of Comparative History in Macrosocial Inquiry." *Comparative Studies in Society and History* 22, no. 2 (1980): 174–97.

Skowronek, Stephen. *Building a New American State: The Expansion of National Administrative Capacities, 1877–1920*. Cambridge: Cambridge University Press, 1982.

Slee, Peter R. H. *Learning and Liberal Education: The Study of Modern History in the Universities of Oxford, Cambridge, and Manchester, 1800–1914*. Manchester: Manchester University Press, 1986.

Sloane, William M. "History and Democracy." *American Historical Review* 1 (1895): 1–23.

———. "The Science of History in the Nineteenth Century." In *Congress of Arts and Sciences, Universal Exposition, St. Louis, 1904*, edited by Howard J. Rogers, 2 vols. Boston: Houghton Mifflin, 1906.

Smith, Arthur L. *Frederic William Maitland: Two Lectures and a Bibliography*. New York: Burt Franklin, 1908.

Smith, Mark C. *Social Science in the Crucible: The American Debate over Objectivity and Purpose, 1918–1941*. Durham, NC: Duke University Press, 1994.

Smith, Rogers M. "Political Jurisprudence, the 'New Institutionalism,' and the Future of Public Law." *American Political Science Review* 82, no. 1 (1988): 89–108.

———. "Identities, Interests, and the Future of Political Science." *Perspectives on Politics* 2, no. 2 (2004): 301–12.

Smith, Trevor. "Political Science and Modern British Society." *Government and Opposition* 21, no. 4 (1986): 420–36.

Soffer, Reba N. *Discipline and Power: The University, History and the Making of an English Elite, 1870–1930*. Stanford, CA: Stanford University Press, 1994.

Somit, Albert, and Joseph Tanenhaus. *The Development of Political Science: From Burgess to Behavioralism*. Boston: Allyn and Bacon, 1967.

Stacey, Frank A. *The Government of Modern Britain*. Oxford: Clarendon Press, 1968.

Stapleton, Julia. *Englishness and the Study of Politics: The Social and Political Thought of Ernest Barker*. Cambridge: Cambridge University Press, 1994.

Stapleton, Julia. *Political Intellectuals and Public Identities in Britain since 1850*. Manchester: Manchester University Press, 2001.

Steinmo, Sven, Kathleen Thelen, and Frank Longstreth. *Structuring Politics: Historical Institutionalism in Comparative Analysis*. New York: Cambridge University Press, 1992.

Stepan, Alfred. *The State and Society: Peru in Comparative Perspective*. Princeton, NJ: Princeton University Press, 1978.

Stephen, Leslie. "Obituary of Henry Sidgwick." *Mind*, n.s., 11, no. 37 (1901): 1–17.

Stephens, H. Morse. "Remarks upon Professor Burgess's Paper." *Annual Report of the American Historical Association for 1896*, 211–15. Washington, DC: Government Printing Office, 1897.

Stillman, Richard J. "21st Century United States Governance: Statecraft as Reformcraft." *Public Administration* 81, no. 1 (2003): 19–40.

Stocking, George W., Jr. "On the Limits of 'Presentism' and 'Historicism' in the Historiography of the Behavioral Sciences." *Journal of the History of the Behavioral Sciences* 1 (1965): 211–17.

Stoker, Gerry. "Introduction: The Unintended Costs and Benefits of New Management Reform for British Local Governance." In *The New Management of British Local Governance*, edited by Gerry Stoker. London: Macmillan, 1999.

———. "Urban Political Science and the Challenge of Urban Governance." In Pierre, *Debating Governance*.

———. "The Three Projects of New Labour." *Renewal* 8 (2000): 7–15.

Storing, Herbert J., ed. *Essays on the Scientific Study of Politics*. New York: Holt, Rinehart and Winston, 1962.

Strauss, Leo. "Political Philosophy and History," *Journal of the History of Ideas* 10, no. 1 (1949): 30–50.

———. "On Collingwood's Philosophy of History." *Review of Metaphysics* 5 (1952): 585–86.

———. *Natural Right and History*. Chicago: University of Chicago Press, 1953.

———. "What Is Political Philosophy?" In *What Is Political Philosophy?* Chicago: University of Chicago Press, 1959.

———. "The Three Waves of Modernity." In *An Introduction to Political Philosophy*, edited by Hilial Gildin. Detroit, MI: Wayne State University Press, 1989.

Stubbs, William. *The Constitutional History of England in Its Origin and Development*, 3 vols. Oxford: Clarendon, 1874–78.

———. "On the Purposes and Methods of Historical Study." In *Seventeen Lectures on the Study of Medieval and Modern History*. Oxford: Clarendon, 1886.

———. *The Letters of William Stubbs, Bishop of Oxford, 1825–1901*. Edited by William Holden Hutton. London: Constable, 1904.

Sundquist, James L. *Dynamics of the Party System: Alignment and Realignment of Political Parties in the United States*. Washington, DC: Brookings Institution, 1983.

Szreter, Simon. *A New Political Economy for New Labour: The Importance of Social Capital*. Policy Paper no. 15, Political Economy Research Centre, University of Sheffield, 1998.

Tarlton, Charles D. "Historicity, Meaning and Revisionism in the Study of Political Thought." *History and Theory* 12 (1973): 307–28.

Taylor, Charles. "Explanation by Purpose and Modern Psychological Theory." DPhil thesis, University of Oxford, 1961.

———. *The Explanation of Behaviour.* London: Routledge, 1964.

———. "Neutrality in Political Science." In *Philosophy, Politics, Society*, 3rd ser. edited by Peter Laslett and W. G. Runciman. Oxford: Blackwell, 1967.

———. "Interpretation and the Sciences of Man." *Review of Metaphysics* 25 (1971).

———. *Philosophical Papers.* Vol. 2, *Philosophy and the Human Sciences.* Cambridge: Cambridge University Press, 1985.

———. "Cross-Purposes: The Liberal-Communitarian Debate." In *Liberalism and the Moral Life*, edited by Nancy L. Rosenblum. Cambridge: Harvard University Press, 1989.

———. *Reconciling the Solitudes: Essays on Canadian Federalism and Nationalism.* Edited by G. Laforest. Montreal: McGill-Queen's University Press, 1993.

Taylor, Michael. "Structure, Culture and Action in the Explanation of Social Change." *Politics and Society* 17, no. 2 (1989): 115–62.

Tenbruck, Friedrich H. "The Problem of Thematic Unity in the Work of Max Weber." *British Journal of Sociology* 31, no. 3 (1980): 316–51.

Thelen, Kathleen. "Historical Institutionalism in Comparative Politics." *Annual Review of Political Science* 2 (1999): 369–404.

Thelen, Kathleen, and Sven Steinmo. "Historical Institutionalism in Comparative Politics." In Steinmo, Thelen, and Longstreth, *Structuring Politics.*

Tilly, Charles. "Reflections on the History of European State-Making" and "Western State-Making and Theories of Political Transformation." In *The Formation of National States in Western Europe*, edited by Charles Tilly, 3–83 and 601–38. Princeton, NJ: Princeton University Press, 1975.

"Toward a More Responsible Two-Party System." *American Political Science Review* 44, suppl. (1950).

Toynbee, Arnold. *Lectures on the Industrial Revolution in England.* Edited by Benjamin Jowett. London: Rivingtons, 1884.

Tribe, Keith. "The Historicization of Political Economy?" In *British and German Historiography, 1750–1950*, edited by Benedikt Stuchtey and Peter Wende, 211–28. Oxford: Oxford University Press, 1998.

Trimberger, Ellen Kay. *Revolution from Above: Military Bureaucrats and Development in Japan, Turkey, Egypt and Peru.* New Brunswick, NJ: Transaction Books, 1978.

Truman, David B. *The Governmental Process.* New York: Knopf, 1951.

———. "The Implications of Political Behavior Research." *Social Science Research Council Items* 5 (1951): 37–39.

Tuck, Richard. "The Contribution of History." In *A Companion to Contemporary Political Philosophy*, edited by Robert E. Goodin and Philip Pettit, 72–89. Oxford: Basil Blackwell, 1993.

Tulloch, Hugh. *James Bryce's "American Commonwealth."* Woodbridge, UK: Bydell Press, 1988.

Tully, James, ed. *Meaning and Context: Quentin Skinner and His Critics*. Cambridge: Polity Press, 1988.

Turner, Frank M. *The Greek Heritage in Victorian Britain*. New Haven, CT: Yale University Press, 1981.

———. *Contesting Cultural Authority: Essays in Victorian Intellectual Life*. Cambridge: Cambridge University Press, 1993.

Tyrrell, Ian. *The Absent Marx: Class Analysis and Liberal History in Twentieth-Century America*. New York: Greenwood Press, 1986.

United Kingdom. Cabinet Office. *Civil Service Management Code*. 1994.

———. Cabinet Office. *Ministerial Code: A Code of Conduct and Guidance on Procedures for Ministers*. 1997.

———. Cabinet Office, *Better Quality Services*. http://www.open.gov.uk/co/quality/qualmenu.html. October 1, 1998.

———. Cabinet Office. *Service First*. http://www.servicefirst.gov.uk/sfirst/bk12toc.html. October 1, 1998.

———. Department for Education and Employment. *Action Teams*. http://www.dfee.gov.uk/actionteams/what.cfm. January 6, 2001.

———. Department of Health. *The New NHS, Modern and Dependable: A National Framework for Assessing Performance*. 1998.

———. Department of Health. *A First Class Service: Quality in the New NHS*. 1999.

———. Parliament. *The Civil Service: Taking Forward Continuity and Change*. Cm. 2748. 1995.

———. Parliament. *The New National Health Service: Modern, Dependable*. Cm. 3807. 1997.

———. Parliament. *New Ambitions for Our Country: A New Contract for Welfare*. Cm. 3805. 1998.

———. Parliament. *Modern Public Services for Britain: Investing in Reform*. Cm. 4011. 1998.

———. Parliament. *Bringing Britain Together: A National Strategy for Neighbourhood Renewal*. Cm. 4045. 1998.

———. Parliament. *Steering a Course for Lasting Prosperity*. Cm. 4076. 1998.

———. Parliament. *Our Competitive Future: Building the Knowledge Driven Economy*. Cm. 4176. 1998.

———. Parliament. *Modernising Government*. Cm 4310. 1999.

Vinogradoff, P. "Frederick William Maitland." *English Historical Review* 22, no. 86 (1907): 280–89.

Vollrath, Ernst. "Hannah Arendt: A German-American Jewess Views the United States—and Looks Back to Germany." In *Hannah Arendt and Leo Strauss: German Émigrés and American Political Thought after World War II*, edited by Peter Graf Kielmansegg, Horst Mewes, and Elisabeth Glaser-Schmidt. Cambridge: Cambridge University Press, 1995.

Vout, Malcolm. *Oxford and the Emergence of Political Science in England, 1945–1960*. Strathclyde: Centre for the Study of Public Policy, 1990.

Wahlke, John C. "Pre-behavioralism in Political Science." *American Political Science Review* 73, no. 1 (1979): 9–31.

Walkland, S. A. *The Legislative Process in Great Britain*. New York: Praeger, 1968.

Wallas, Graham. *Human Nature in Politics*. London: Constable, 1908.

———. *The Great Society: A Psychological Analysis*. London: Macmillan, 1914.

———. *Our Social Heritage*. London: Allen and Unwin, 1921.

Wallerstein, Immanuel M. *The Modern World System: Capitalist Agriculture and the Origins of the European World-Economy in the Sixteenth Century*. New York: Academic, 1974.

Webb, Sidney. "Twentieth Century Politics." In *The Basis and Policy of Socialism*. London: Fifield, 1908.

Webb, Sidney, and Beatrice Webb. *English Local Government from the Revolution to the Municipal Corporation Act: The Parish and the County*. London: Longman, Green and Co., 1906.

Weber, Max. *Economy and Society: An Outline of Interpretive Sociology*. Edited by Guenther Roth and Claus Wittich. Berkeley and Los Angeles: University of California Press, 1978.

Weiner, Martin J. *Between Two Worlds: The Political Thought of Graham Wallas*. Oxford: Clarendon Press, 1971.

Weingast, Barry R. "A Rational Choice Perspective on Congressional Norms." *American Journal of Political Science* 23, no. 2 (1979): 245–62.

Weir, Margaret, and Theda Skocpol. "State Structures and the Possibilities for 'Keynesian' Responses to the Great Depression in Sweden, Britain, and the United States." In Evans, Rueschemeyer, and Skocpol, *Bringing the State*, 107–63.

Weldon, T. D. *The Vocabulary of Politics*. Harmondsworth, UK: Penguin Books, 1953.

Wendt, Alexander. "Anarchy Is What States Make of It: The Social Construction of Power Politics." *International Organization* 46, no. 2 (1992): 391–425.

West, Thomas G. "Leo Strauss and the American Founding." *Review of Politics* 53, no. 1 (1991): 157–72.

White, Leonard D. "The Local Community Research Committee and the Social Science Research Building." In *Chicago: An Experiment in Social Science Research*, edited by Leonard D. White. Chicago: University of Chicago Press, 1929.

———. "Introduction." In *The Future of Government in the United States: Essays in Honor of Charles E. Merriam*, edited by Leonard D. White. Chicago: University of Chicago Press, 1942.

White, Morton G. *Social Thought in America: The Revolt against Formalism*. New York: Viking, 1949.

Wiebe, Robert H. *The Search for Order, 1877–1920*. New York: Hill and Wang, 1967.

Wilkins, Burleigh Taylor. "Frederick York Powell and Charles A. Beard: A Study in Anglo-American Historiography." *American Quarterly* 11, no. 1 (1959): 21–39.

Willetts, David. *Modern Conservatism*. Harmondsworth, UK: Penguin, 1992.

Willoughby, Westel W. *The Nature of the State*. New York: Macmillan, 1896.

———. *The Rights and Duties of American Citizenship*. New York: American Book, 1898.

———. *Social Justice: A Critical Essay*. New York: Macmillan, 1900.

———. "The American Political Science Association." *Political Science Quarterly* 19, no. 1 (1904): 107–11.

Willoughby, Westel W. "The Political Theories of Professor John W. Burgess." *Yale Review* 17 (1908): 58–84.

———. "The Individual and the State." *American Political Science Review* 8, no. 1 (1914): 1–13.

———. *Prussian Political Philosophy.* New York: Appleton, 1918.

Wilson, Woodrow. *Congressional Government.* Boston: Houghton Mifflin, 1885.

———. "Of the Study of Politics." *New Princeton Review,* 62nd year (1887): 188–99.

———. *The State: Elements of Historical and Practical Politics.* Boston: D. C. Heath, 1889.

———. "Bryce's *American Commonwealth.*" *Political Science Quarterly* 4, no. 1 (1889): 153–69. Reprinted in Robert C. Brooks, *Bryce's "American Commonwealth": 50th Anniversary,* 169–88. New York: Macmillan, 1939.

Winch, Peter. *The Idea of a Social Science.* London: Routledge and Kegan Paul, 1958.

Wokler, Robert. "The Professoriate of Political Thought in England since 1914: A Tale of Three Chairs." In Castiglione and Hampsher-Monk, *Political Thought in National Context.*

Wolin, Sheldon S. "Richard Hooker and English Conservatism." *Western Political Quarterly* 6, no. 1 (1953): 28–47.

———. "Hume and Conservatism." *American Political Science Review* 48, no. 4 (1954): 999–1016.

———. "Politics and Religion: Luther's Simplistic Imperative." *American Political Science Review* 50, no. 1 (1956): 24–42.

———. "Calvin and the Reformation: The Political Education of Protestantism." *American Political Science Review* 51, no. 2 (1957): 428–53.

———. *Politics and Vision.* Boston: Little, Brown, 1960.

———. "Paradigms and Political Theories." In *Politics and Experience,* edited by Preston King and B. C. Parekh. Cambridge: Cambridge University Press, 1968.

———. "Political Theory as a Vocation." *American Political Science Review* 63, no. 4 (1969): 1062–82.

———. *Hobbes and the Epic Tradition of Political Theory.* Los Angeles: Clark Memorial Library, 1970.

Woolsey, Theodore D. *Political Science, or The State, Theoretically and Practically Considered.* 2 vols. New York: Scribner, 1878.

Wormell, Deborah. *Sir John Seeley and the Uses of History.* Cambridge: Cambridge University Press, 1980.

Wright, A. W. *G.D.H. Cole and Socialist Democracy.* Oxford: Oxford University, 1979.

Wright, T. R. *The Religion of Humanity: The Impact of Comtean Positivism on Victorian Britain.* Cambridge: Cambridge University Press, 1986.

Zylstra, Bernard. *From Pluralism to Collectivism: The Development of Harold Laski's Political Thought.* Assen, The Netherlands: Koninklijke Van Gorcum, 1968.

Index